Eighth Edition

PROFESSIONAL COUNSELING

A PROCESS GUIDE TO HELPING

Harold L. Hackney
Syracuse University

Janine M. Bernard
Syracuse University

PEARSON

Boston   Columbus   Indianapolis   New York   San Francisco
Amsterdam   Cape Town   Dubai   London   Madrid   Milan   Munich   Paris   Montreal   Toronto
Delhi   Mexico City   São Paulo   Sydney   Hong Kong   Seoul   Singapore   Taipei   Tokyo

Vice President and Editorial Director: Jeffery W. Johnston
Vice President and Publisher: Kevin M. Davis
Editorial Assistant: Marisia Styles
Executive Field Marketing Manager: Krista Clark
Senior Product Marketing Manager: Christopher Barry
Project Manager: Lauren Carlson
Program Manager: Janelle Criner
Operations Specialist: Deidra Skahill
Cover Design Director: Diane Ernsberger
Cover Photo: Shutterstock, © Photo Love
Full-Service Project Management: Garima Khosla, iEnergizer Aptara®, Inc.
Composition: iEnergizer Aptara®, Inc.
Printer/Binder: Edwards Brothers Malloy
Cover Printer: Phoenix Color/Hagerstown
Text Font: 10/12 Times

Library of Congress Cataloging-in-Publication Data

Hackney, Harold
  Professional counseling : a process guide to helping / Harold L. Hackney, Syracuse University
Janine M. Bernard, Syracuse University. — Eighth edition.
    pages cm
  Revision of: The professional counselor / Harold L. Hackney, Sherry Cormier. 2013. 7th ed.
  Includes bibliographical references and index.
  ISBN 978-0-13-416577-6 — ISBN 0-13-416577-2
  1. Mental health counseling. 2. Counseling. I. Bernard, Janine M. II. Title.
  RC466.C67 2017
  616.89—dc23   2015021938

10 9 8 7 6 5 4 3 2 1

ISBN 10:   0-13-416577-2
ISBN 13: 978-0-13-416577-6

PREFACE

NEW TO THIS EDITION

The eighth edition of *Professional Counseling* introduces a slightly new title and a new coauthor. Our new title (from *The Professional Counselor*) stresses the *process* of counseling as the crux of the text, which, of course, is what it has always been. With this edition, Dr. Janine M. Bernard brings her expertise in the supervision of counselors as an important lens through which to look at the fundamentals of how the counseling process is explained to counselors-in-training. As with other new editions, we set out to enhance and broaden the concepts inherent in the process of helping others. Professional counseling is a vibrant and evolving entity. It grows through the practice of skilled counselors, explorations of researchers, and musings of thoughtful scholars. This text, therefore, continues to evolve to reflect the current nuances we see in our beloved profession. Those nuances also reflect our experiences with our students as we observe their challenges, hear their questions, and see what seems to resonate with them. There is no question that our students, most of whom now represent the Millennial Generation, inform us about the counseling process, sometimes in ways we didn't see coming! Therefore, with the helpful suggestions of independent reviewers, dedicated students and colleagues, new areas for improvement emerge. New to this edition are the following:

- A revision of the 5-stage model of counseling to a 4-stage model that carries working relationship skills across all stages
- Adding new case examples and revising older ones to illustrate how skills and competencies are applied to clients more likely seen in mental health agencies and those who present in educational settings
- Updating how culture is infused into the counseling process
- More than 40 new end-of-chapter web-based video samples that illustrate skills and procedures discussed in each chapter
- A new section on how to evaluate your counseling
- Many new sections within chapters, including the introduction of "second-order" interventions
- A new section in each intervention chapter concerning how interventions are used in Dialectical Behavior Therapy and, where appropriate, Motivational Interviewing
- The addition of new forms in Appendix B

FEATURES OF THIS BOOK

This edition maintains a number of features that have long set this book apart from most other introductory counseling textbooks and include the following:

- A four-stage model that provides students with a roadmap for assessing client progress, helps students plan for interventions, and encourages students to view counseling as an intentional process with an end in sight.
- Clear guidelines for assessing cases using four orientations—affective, cognitive, behavioral, and systemic—that help students apply what they have learned in counseling theory courses to the actual practice of counseling.
- The application of the four orientations for interventions to two popular therapy approaches, Dialectical Behavior Therapy and Motivational Interviewing.

- Cultural dimensions of counseling viewed as positionality versus an emphasis on demographics, as well as a more nuanced treatment of culture throughout the text. Examples include the addition of what might be considered "lesser" cultural identities (e.g., urban culture, military culture) but may play significant roles in the development of problems (Chapter 1); the use of assessment tools, such as the genogram to track cultural dimensions for individuals and families (Chapter 6); references to culture throughout all interventions chapters so as to remind the reader of the role of cultural identities and realities in counseling, but in a manner that does not reinforce stereotypes (Chapters 8 through 11).
- Sections throughout the text that apply chapter content to working with children.
- Identification of "meaning" as a counseling issue and how it is addressed for both spiritual and nonspiritual clients.
- Sections in each chapter that discuss how clients react to the stages of counseling and to different intervention orientations.
- Separate chapters on client assessment (Chapter 5) and treatment planning (Chapter 7) that help students incorporate specific counseling interventions as they are learning them.
- Discussion of treatment planning that reflects the influence of third-party payors and the necessity of knowing how to plan treatments that meet third-party criteria.
- Helpful boxed material throughout the chapters that summarizes and illustrates skills.
- A series of forms and guides (Appendix B) that illustrate the management of counseling cases.
- A chart that identifies those Council for the Accreditation of Counseling and Related Educational Programs Standards (CACREP, 2016) that are addressed in each of the chapters.

HOW THE BOOK IS ORGANIZED

Beginning with Chapter 1, *Conceptualizing Professional Counseling,* we provide a context for counseling, including how to think about the profession and the process. We discuss the counseling relationship, conditions that facilitate positive relationships, considerations of what successful counseling is like, characteristics of effective counselors, and a case illustration for how to measure counseling outcomes.

In Chapter 2, we explore the *Language of Counseling*. What is it that counselors say that sets them apart from other caregivers? What special ways do counselors use language? What is their purpose in using this language? How does this language affect the client? And how does the counselor's language change, depending on a client's goals? We address this professional communication through basic nonverbal and verbal helping skills, as well as advanced verbal skills.

Chapter 3, *The Essential Structure of Counseling,* sets the format for the remainder of the book by discussing the counseling process as a passage through four stages of development. We give students a way to conceptualize the process, beginning with establishing the relationship while simultaneously assessing (understanding) the client's presenting problem, helping the client recognize what can be achieved (goals), structuring the sessions (using a variety of interventions) with the problem definition and goals firmly in mind, and helping the client complete the counseling relationship successfully.

Chapter 4, *Initiating and Maintaining a Working Relationship,* highlights the importance of the counseling relationship in all of counseling. We do not consider establishing a working relationship with a client as a "stage" of counseling because it permeates *all* stages. This chapter gives the reader a "place to go" regardless of what stage of counseling he or she is in to review the essential ingredients of a positive working relationship.

Chapters 5 through 7 are best viewed as a unit. Chapter 5, *Assessing Client Problems*, centers on how clients present their issues and how the counselor can facilitate this process. Topics such as intake interviews and genograms are included as these help structure what the counselor is hearing. Although the focus at this point is how the client understands his or her problem and how this problem is experienced, the counselor is beginning to conceptualize what is presented by utilizing theory-based filters. These are presented briefly in Chapter 5 as components of the problem: feelings, cognitions, behaviors, and interpersonal relationships. These components become more dominant later in the book and drive the full discussion of interventions in Chapters 8 through 11.

Chapter 6, *Developing Counseling Goals*, grounds the reader in the important topic of goal setting. Goals derive from the careful assessment that has been completed in the prior stage although the very act of setting goals can open up new areas for assessment as well. It is at this stage that many counselors begin to appreciate how fluid is the process of counseling.

Chapter 7, *Defining Strategies and Selecting Interventions,* serves as a transition chapter from what has come before and the intervention chapters that follow. The chapter focuses on treatment planning that uses the information gleaned from assessment and goal setting. What were described as components of the problem in Chapter 5 are now framed in a way that will lead to the selection of interventions: problems as complicated by feeling states, problems as errors in thought processes, problems as behavior patterns, and problems as interpersonal or systemic conditions.

Up to this point in the text, we have been talking about skills and stages that are generic to all counseling. They could be called core skills and processes. Some authors refer to them as common factors. In Chapters 8 through 11, we move into areas that are more specific to working from a particular orientation or domain. Although we believe that good counselors have some level of expertise in all of the interventions that are presented in these chapters, we also accept that each counselor will veer more toward some clusters of interventions than others.

The change to the word *intervention* at this point in the text is deliberate and it should be defined as different from *skill* or *technique*. As noted earlier, we view skills as core to all counseling. Regardless of one's orientation, asking good open-ended questions, reflecting well, summarizing what the client has said, and so forth, are all endemic to the counseling process. A technique comes closer to an intervention and some authors may even use the two terms interchangeably. Still, techniques can be used for a very specific process goal and not be tied to outcome goals. For example, a counselor might use a relaxation exercise at the beginning of each counseling session because the client tends to arrive to sessions anxious. This is an excellent use of a technique, but does not fit our definition of an intervention.

By contrast, interventions are chosen only after an assessment process has been completed and outcome goals have been set. Interventions, then, are integrally connected to how the counselor views the issues being discussed and are chosen as part of a plan to address (and hopefully alleviate) these issues. Although interventions may look like and feel like advanced skills (and to some extent they are), they are used with more sense of where the counselor is headed than are the core skills. Said differently, interventions are chosen specifically because the counselor believes they will assist the client in resolving the issues that have been presented in as efficient and meaningful a way as possible.

Chapters 8 through 11 are divided into the four principal categories of interventions that counselors use: *Affective Interventions, Cognitive Interventions, Behavioral Interventions*, and *Systemic Interventions*. In each chapter, we attempt to help the reader see counseling from that particular orientation and give examples of how this is done. Prior to reading about these different categories of interventions, consider these three introductory points about them.

First, these chapters do not present a full review of the possibilities within each category. The professional literature and now the Internet offer a plethora of possibilities for either fine-tuning interventions for specific populations or expanding one's personal collection of interventions. What we offer here is a sample and some of the most common interventions in the profession. We hope that the reader will use these chapters as a place to begin, not as an authoritative collection of what is available.

Second, although the chapters are divided by major orientations or domains, we view interventions as more flexible than they might appear. Just as a counselor can reflect affect or reflect thought, some of the interventions could be revised easily to attend to another domain. We encourage the reader to consider such possibilities as they gain experience as counselors.

Third, we repeat this point on occasion in the chapters themselves, but here we introduce the idea that a client's dominant method of communicating is not necessarily the best orientation for intervention selection for that client. For example, a client might present with a great deal of emotion. It might be tempting, therefore, for a counselor to stay in the affective realm in working with that client. We believe that this could be an error. Because the client already has access to his or her emotions, it may be other areas that need exploration for feelings to get "under control." Similarly, the highly cognitive client probably needs more than cognitive interventions. Our point is that the client's "strong suit" is not the primary criterion for how counselors choose interventions.

We have ended each of the four intervention chapters with some attention to two popular therapy approaches: Motivational Interviewing (MI; Chapters 8 and 9) and Dialectical Behavior Therapy (DBT; Chapters 10 and 11). Of course, it is not our intent nor is it realistic for us to offer any sort of comprehensive explanation of either of these approaches. Rather, we are attempting to demonstrate the ways that different therapies use interventions and, in the case of DBT, how interventions from all four orientations can be used at different times as therapy proceeds.

Finally, in Chapter 12, *Termination and Evaluation*, we return to the final stage of counseling, termination, as a process in itself rather than an event. What are the ingredients of a successful termination? What ethical issues are raised in the termination process? Who decides when termination is appropriate? How is referral to another helping source part of the termination process? We also discuss the evaluation of counseling as an important task for counselors during this stage so that they can continue to improve.

Each chapter includes exercises and discussion questions that help individual students to integrate the information they have just read. Discussion questions have also been provided to aid in group discussions. At the end of each chapter, we provide video illustrations of the skills that are available at MyCounselingLab, along with suggestions for viewing these videos.

Appendix A offers students more comprehensive practice exercises, along with a Counseling Skills Checklist that can be copied and used for feedback purposes.

Students will find a variety of forms commonly used in counseling practice in Appendix B. These forms may be copied and used by students as they practice their craft.

Also available with MyCounselingLab®

This title is also available with MyCounselingLab–an online homework, tutorial, and assessment program designed to work with the text to engage students and improve results. Within its structured environment, students see key concepts demonstrated through video clips, practice what they learn, test their understanding, and receive feedback to guide their learning and ensure they master key learning outcomes.

- **Learning Outcomes and Standards measure student results.** MyCounselingLab organizes all assignments around essential learning outcomes and national standards for counselors.

- **Video- and Case-Based Assignments develop decision-making skills.** Video- and Case-based Assignments introduce students to a broader range of clients, and therefore a broader range of presenting problems, than they will encounter in their own pre-professional clinical experiences. Students watch videos of actual client-therapist sessions or high-quality role-play scenarios featuring expert counselors. They are then guided in their analysis of the videos through a series of short-answer questions. These exercises help students develop the techniques and decision-making skills they need to be effective counselors before they are in a critical situation with a real client.

- **Licensure Quizzes help students prepare for certification.** Automatically graded, multiple-choice Licensure Quizzes help students prepare for their certification examinations, master foundational course content, and improve their performance in the course.

- **Video Library offers a wealth of observation opportunities.** The Video Library provides more than 400 video clips of actual client-therapist sessions and high-quality role plays in a database organized by topic and searchable by keyword. The Video Library includes every video clip from the MyCounselingLab courses plus additional videos from Pearson's extensive library of footage. Instructors can create additional assignments around the videos or use them for in-class activities. Students can expand their observation experiences to include other course areas and increase the amount of time they spend watching expert counselors in action.

- **Comprehensive online course content.** Filled with a wealth of content that is tightly integrated with your textbook, MyLab lets you easily add, remove, or modify existing instructional material. You can also add your own course materials to suit the needs of your students or department. In short, MyLab lets you teach exactly as you'd like.

- **Robust gradebook tracking.** The online gradebook automatically tracks your students' results on tests, homework, and practice exercises and gives you control over managing results and calculating grades. The gradebook provides a number of flexible grading options, including exporting grades to a spreadsheet program such as Microsoft Excel. And, it lets you measure and document your students' learning outcomes.

ACKNOWLEDGMENTS

Thinking about a new edition begins with the opinions of others—specifically, the persons who serve as reviewers provide invaluable insights into how the user views a text, both its strengths and its weaknesses. Insightful reviewers provide enormous value in this renewal process. We thank Jori Berger-Greenstein, Boston University School of Medicine; Vanessa D. Johnson, Northeastern Univeristy; Gulsah Kemer, Arizona State University; Yu-Fen Lin, University of North Texas, Dallas; and Oscar Sida, University of Nevada, Las Vegas, for their generous and serious attention to this responsibility. Their comments have given us a real advantage in our effort. We also wish to thank Kevin Davis, our editor, for his support in how this edition was to take shape, and to Lauren Carlson, project manager, for her expert choreography of the eighth edition. Special thanks to Mercedes Heston for her careful review of the manuscript and her good humor throughout. Finally, we wish to thank our students, past and present, who consistently give us new insights into the process of learning to become a counselor. Without their help and the help of scholars who continue to wrestle with understanding the counseling process in modern times, no new edition could be in fact *new*.

H.H.
J.M.B.

ABOUT THE AUTHORS

Harold (Dick) Hackney, Professor Emeritus of counseling at Syracuse University, is a nationally certified counselor and a Fellow of the American Counseling Association. Dick is past-president of the Association for Counselor Education and Supervision and former member of the ACA Governing Council, and a past-president of the Center for Credentialing and Education, an affiliate of NBCC. His areas of expertise include counselor training, training of future counseling professors, research methodology, counseling processes, and counseling theory. Hackney's writings draw from his experiences as a school counselor, a marriage and family counselor, and his research on counseling processes. Prior to his appointment at Syracuse University, Hackney was a professor at Purdue University and at Fairfield University.

Janine M. Bernard, Professor Emeritus of counseling and counselor education at Syracuse University, is a nationally certified counselor, an approved clinical supervisor, and licensed as a mental health counselor in New York. Bernard is a Fellow of the American Counseling Association and a long-term member of the American Psychological Association. She is a past-chair of the National Board for Certified Counselors. Her areas of expertise include clinical supervision, counselor training, multicultural aspects of supervision, and life-span human development. Prior to her appointment as department chair at Syracuse University, Bernard held faculty appointments at Purdue University and at Fairfield University.

BRIEF CONTENTS

Chapter 1 Conceptualizing Professional Counseling   1

Chapter 2 The Language of Counseling   20

Chapter 3 The Essential Structure of Counseling   36

Chapter 4 Initiating and Maintaining a Working Relationship   54

Chapter 5 Assessing Client Problems   75

Chapter 6 Developing Counseling Goals   98

Chapter 7 Defining Strategies and Selecting Interventions   116

Chapter 8 Affective Interventions   131

Chapter 9 Cognitive Interventions   157

Chapter 10 Behavioral Interventions   183

Chapter 11 Systemic Interventions   212

Chapter 12 Termination and Evaluation   240

Appendix A Integrative Practice Exercises   259

Appendix B Forms and Guides for Use in Counseling Practice   266

References   284
Index   291

CONTENTS

Preface   iii
About the Authors   viii

Chapter 1 CONCEPTUALIZING PROFESSIONAL COUNSELING   1

What Is Counseling?   2

The Parameters of Counseling   3

Counseling Conditions and Their Effects   8

▶ **Case Illustration of Possible Counseling Outcomes   11**

Characteristics of Effective Helpers   12

The Developmental Nature of Learning to Counsel   16

Summary   18
Exercises   18
Discussion Questions   19
MyCounselingLab Assignment   19

Chapter 2 THE LANGUAGE OF COUNSELING   20

Communication in Counseling   21

Nonverbal Skills of Counseling   21

Basic Verbal Skills of Counseling   23

Advanced Verbal Skills of Counseling   26

Summary   31
Exercises   34
Feedback for Exercise III, Recognizing Different Counselor Responses   34
Discussion Questions   35
MyCounselingLab Assignment   35

Chapter 3 THE ESSENTIAL STRUCTURE OF COUNSELING   36

The Counseling Process   37

The Client's Experience in Counseling   48

Summary   51
Exercises   52
Discussion Questions   52
MyCounselingLab Assignment   53

Chapter 4 INITIATING AND MAINTAINING A WORKING RELATIONSHIP   54

Characteristics of a Therapeutic Relationship   55

Communicating Empathy   59

Relationship-Building Skills   60

Conditions That Convey Genuineness   65

Conditions That Convey Positive Regard   67

Functions of a Therapeutic Relationship   68

Effects of Therapeutic Relationships on Clients   69

▶ Case Illustration of Relationship Building   70

Children and the Counseling Relationship   71

Summary   72

Exercises   73

Discussion Questions   74

MyCounselingLab Assignment   74

Chapter 5   ASSESSING CLIENT PROBLEMS   75

Purposes of Assessment   76

Dimensions of Assessment   77

Clinical Assessment with Children   81

Clinical Assessment with Couples and Families   83

Using Assessment Information   85

Skills Associated with Assessment   85

Effects of Assessment on Clients   90

▶ Case Illustration of the Intake Interview   91

Crisis Assessment   94

Integration of Problem-Definition Information with Treatment Planning   95

Summary   95

Exercises   96

Discussion Questions   97

MyCounselingLab Assignment   97

Chapter 6   DEVELOPING COUNSELING GOALS   98

Functions of Counseling Goals   99

Parameters of Goal Setting: Process and Outcome Goals   100

Three Elements of Good Outcome Goals   101

Obstacles in Developing Specific Goals   102

Skills Associated with Goal Setting   102

Effects of Goal Setting on Clients   107

Goal Setting with Children   107

Crises and Goal Setting   108

Goal Setting and Culture   108

Client Participation in Goal Setting   109

Resistance to Goal Setting   110

Assessing Counseling Goals   111

▶ Case Illustration of Goal Setting   111

Summary   114

Exercises   114

Discussion Questions   115

MyCounselingLab Assignment   115

Chapter 7   DEFINING STRATEGIES AND SELECTING INTERVENTIONS   116

Case Conceptualization Skills   117

Theory and Case Conceptualization   117

Worldview and Case Conceptualization   118

Conceptualizing Presenting Problems   119

Diagnosis and Case Conceptualization   121

Time Orientation and Case Conceptualization   121

Goals and Treatment Planning   122

Strategy Selection   123

Categories of Counseling Interventions   123

▶ Case Illustration of Strategy and Interventions Selection: Angela   125

Defining a Counseling Strategy   126

Strategies for Working with Children   128

Summary   128

Exercises   129

Discussion Questions   130

MyCounselingLab Assignment   130

Chapter 8   AFFECTIVE INTERVENTIONS   131

Theories That Stress the Importance of Feelings   132

Affective Interventions   133

Helping Clients Express Affect   134

Nonverbal Affect Cues   135

Verbal Affect Cues   136

Helping Clients Sort Feelings   140

Focusing Intervention   143

▶ Case Illustration of Focusing   144

Helping Clients Integrate or Change Feeling States   145

▶ Case Illustration of Integrating Feelings   146

Role Reversal   147

▶ Case Illustration of Role Reversal   147

Alter Ego 148

▶ Case Illustration of the Alter Ego 149

The Empty Chair 150

▶ Case Illustration of the Empty Chair 151

Client Reactions to Affective Interventions 152

Applying Interventions to Dialectical Behavior Therapy and Motivational Interviewing 152

Summary 155

Exercises 155

Discussion Questions 156

MyCounselingLab Assignment 156

Chapter 9 COGNITIVE INTERVENTIONS 157

Theories That Stress the Importance of Cognitive Processes 158

Goals of Cognitive Interventions 158

Assessment of Cognitive Problems 159

Eliciting Thoughts 160

Cognitive Interventions 161

▶ Case Illustration of A-B-C-D Analysis 163

▶ Case Illustration of Injunctions and Redecision Work 168

Second-Order Interventions 173

Meaning-Making Interventions 175

▶ Case Illustration of Meaning Making 177

Client Reactions to Interventions 177

Applying Interventions to Dialectical Behavior Therapy and Motivational Interviewing 179

Summary 180

Exercises 180

Discussion Questions 182

MyCounselingLab Assignment 182

Chapter 10 BEHAVIORAL INTERVENTIONS 183

Behavioral Interventions and Theory 184

Goals of Behavioral Interventions 186

Basic Behavioral Skills 187

Using Behavioral Interventions 188

▶ Case Illustration of Skill Training 195

▶ Case Illustration of Anxiety Reduction 201

▶ Case Illustration of Self-Management 206

Client Reactions to Behavioral Interventions   209

Applying Interventions to Dialectical Behavior Therapy   209

Summary   209

Exercises   210

Discussion Questions   211

MyCounselingLab Assignment   211

Chapter 11   SYSTEMIC INTERVENTIONS   212

System Properties   213

Therapies That Stress the Importance of Systems   214

Systemic Skills and Interventions   215

Establishing a Therapeutic Relationship and Assessing System Issues   216

Goal Setting   220

▶ Case Illustration of Reframing for Goal Setting   221

Systemic Interventions   223

Communication Skill Building   223

Altering System Properties   229

▶ Case Illustration of Altering Hierarchy and Boundary Making   231

▶ Case Illustration of Enactment   233

Second-Order Interventions   235

▶ Case Illustration of Prescribing the Symptom   235

Client Reactions to Systemic Interventions   237

Summary   238

Exercises   238

Discussion Questions   238

MyCounselingLab Assignment   239

Chapter 12   TERMINATION AND EVALUATION   240

The Termination Stage   241

Termination as a Process   244

The Referral Process   246

Blocks to Termination   249

▶ Case Illustration of Termination   250

Evaluation of Counseling   254

Summary   256

Exercises   256

Discussion Questions   257

Appendix A   INTEGRATIVE PRACTICE EXERCISES   259

**Appendix B   FORMS AND GUIDES FOR USE IN COUNSELING
PRACTICE   266**

References   284

Index   291

Conceptualizing Professional Counseling

INTRODUCTION TO *PROFESSIONAL COUNSELING*

We have an ambitious goal for the reader of this text. We hope to provide you with the tools to move you from someone who knows little about the actual process of providing professional counseling to someone who is ready to see her or his first client under supervision. Therefore, this book includes discussion of basic skills of counseling but goes beyond this to give you frames of reference that will assist you in knowing *what* skills to use *when* and for *what purpose*. However, before we begin this exciting (and occasionally intimidating) journey, it is important to spend some time trying to deconstruct the term *professional counseling* and to understand a number of concepts and conditions that are fundamental to the counseling process.

PURPOSE OF THIS CHAPTER

In this chapter, we consider some important topics that should be contemplated before you begin to learn specific skills for the process of counseling. Foremost to our discussion is that counseling must be viewed in context. The factors that contribute to that context include philosophy, theoretical premises, and cultural realities—in other words, the intellectual and social milieu. In addition, we address different ways client problems can be assessed and counselor qualities that are universal, crossing theoretical approaches, cultures, and time. Our ultimate objective is to help you, the reader, begin to identify yourself within these parameters and to do some introspection regarding how your thinking and your personal qualities match those of the professional counselor.

Considerations as You Read This Chapter

- How do you view life? Do you believe that most things that happen to people are unplanned and coincidental, or do you believe that life events tend to fit a "larger plan"?
- Is life's challenge a matter of analyzing situations and developing successful responses to those situations? Or is it to become the best person one can be, given the circumstances life presents?
- How do you describe yourself culturally? From whom have you learned the most about yourself as a cultural being? What do you believe is most misunderstood about you culturally?
- As you read about each of the personal qualities required of professional counselors, how does the explanation describe you? How would you edit the explanation to be a better fit to how you see yourself?

This is a text about the process of counseling. In the hands of a skilled and sensitive person, this process can be used to enhance the lives of people who are seeking to cope with difficult life challenges, to change their relationships, or to develop self-understanding. Although it is almost impossible to define precisely what the experience of providing counseling will be for you, some general parameters of the counseling process will certainly be part of your experience. There are several ways to consider the counseling process, beginning with a clear sense of what the process is, how counseling is applied to human problems, how the client and the client's circumstances influence the process, and what constitutes successful counseling. In this chapter, we examine these and other fundamental issues as they relate to the practice of counseling.

WHAT IS COUNSELING?

At its core, *counseling* is the process of offering assistance. It is for this reason that we hear of credit counselors, investment counselors, camp counselors, and retirement counselors, to name just a few. This book is about professional counseling as used by mental health professionals in general and specifically those whose professional home is with the American Counseling Association and its affiliates. In this text, we use the terms *professional counseling* and *counseling* interchangeably. Often, mental health agency settings refer to *therapy,* short for *psychotherapy.* Again, these terms refer to the same processes that we address in this text.

Counseling is a combination of having specialized knowledge, interpersonal skills, and personal dispositions that are required to assist clients in facing or understanding successfully what is interfering with their lives, assisting clients in identifying attainable goals to improve their situation, and offering interventions that assist clients in goal attainment. You might be asking, "What knowledge? What skills? What dispositions?"; we begin addressing each of these questions in this chapter. But we could also include, "What clients?" because clients can be individuals, groups, families, or institutions. As an example of having an institution as a client, when a mental health counselor convinces agency staff to provide service at times more convenient to clients in a community or when a school counselor offers a new psychoeducational program, he or she is using counseling skills to intervene at an institutional level to arrive at a goal the counselor has assessed as worthy. Most counseling, however, is confined to persons in a room where a professional is listening intently, checking in to be sure that the client(s) is understood in both a cultural and psychological sense, and moving toward some outcome that enhances the client's well-being.

The content of professional counseling tends to include both internal and relational concerns. *Internal (intrapersonal) concerns* can range from issues of self-concept or self-defeating habits to severe mental impairment. *Relational (interpersonal) concerns* can range from communication and perceptual problems between the client and others to issues of hostility, aggression, and criminal activity toward others. These problems cross all age groups and developmental stages. It is important to note that these issues, even the "lesser" ones, are diagnostic in nature— that is, the problems must be understood both in their expression (as behaviors, feelings, or thoughts) and in the context in which they are supported (what keeps the problem alive).

Finally, although our definition is generic in nature, this is not to suggest that a professional counselor might be a provider of services for any type of problem. Within the counseling profession are many specialties, including mental health counselors, marriage and family counselors, school counselors, rehabilitation counselors, pastoral counselors, creative arts counselors, and career counselors. Each specialty is based on knowledge that is specific to working within certain institutions or with particular populations. Still, despite differences, the actual process of counseling shares the common elements of relationship, communication, conceptualization, and intervention skills that are covered in this text.

Why Counseling?

It may be necessary to remind some aspiring counselors that the problems of life can be solved in many ways, counseling being only one of those ways. The vast majority of the human race has never experienced professional counseling. Does that mean that they are functioning at some sublevel of life? Of course not. Many people adapt to life's challenges by using personal resources, friends and family, or religious faith. But even with these resources, challenges can sometimes accumulate to the point that an unencumbered and skilled helper can facilitate the process of growth and adaptation to such challenges.

Viewed in this way, counseling can assume the function of change, prevention, or life enhancement. As change, counseling is concerned with situations that, for whatever reason, have become so disruptive that people are unable to continue through the normal passage of life without excess stress, dissatisfaction, or unhappiness. As prevention, counseling is able to take into account those predictable life events that produce stress, cause people to draw on their psychological resources, and, ultimately, demand adaptation to changing life forces. Finally, a third form of counseling, *enhancement counseling,* goes beyond life's challenges and predictabilities. As a counseling goal, enhancement attempts to open clients' experiences to new and deeper levels of understanding, appreciation, and wisdom about life's many potentialities.

THE PARAMETERS OF COUNSELING

Counselors can talk about counseling as change or growth, or they can talk about counseling as a process or product. If counselors go very deeply into an examination of these alternatives, it also becomes apparent that they are beginning to talk about philosophical, cultural, and even spiritual issues as well as psychological or interpersonal concerns. How counselors view these issues and concerns determines at least part of what they do in the counseling interview. If I happen to hold an optimistic view of human beings and how they adapt to life's ups and downs, my view of what should happen in counseling will be quite different from that of the person who holds a cautious, or even pessimistic, view of human beings and how they function. If I have experienced life only in a sheltered or encapsulated environment, then I may view counseling as not involving cultural dimensions, including the extreme conditions when all some clients have known is a culture of little opportunity, survival of the fittest, and violence. If I solve my problems by careful examination and analysis of issues, decisions to be made, appropriateness of outcomes, and so on, then I might naturally assume that others should approach life problems in a similar fashion, especially if I have been fortunate enough to have the resources to make this happen. Or if I see life as a multifaceted adventure, then I might feel less urgency to identify, prescribe and, thus, control the outcomes of counseling. If I am fearful of things going in a negative direction if I make an error, then I may seek "solutions" for my clients and attempt to push these to conclusion. These are just some of the possibilities of how the counselor's worldview can affect counseling when she or he enters the process.

Occurring simultaneously with the counselor's worldview is the presentation of the client's concerns by the client. These concerns may have a strong basis in reality, or they may be self-generated by the client's discomfort or skewed by the client's faulty perceptions. And it is also obvious that clients come as optimists or pessimists, bold or cautious, with personal or environmental resources, or without them. Whatever the case, the counselor must have a healthy appreciation of the very broad range of behaviors, attitudes, self-concepts, histories, cultural contexts, resources, and feelings that their clients represent. In other words, the term *normal* may not be very useful apart from understanding the client's context. For any given client, it may be normal for a child to live with more criticism than love; it may be normal for a woman to live with men who are volatile and occasionally violent; it may be normal for substances to be abused to block out feelings of hopelessness. Regardless of whether something is normal to a particular client, it may not be functional, and this is where counseling can be helpful. *Functional behavior* is that which thwarts dysfunction and opens up new possibilities, including the possibility of growth, problem solving, and an increased ability to cope with life's inevitable stressors. When listening to the personal concerns of clients, counselors must seek to understand life (i.e., what has been normal for them) as clients see it and the reasons they see life as they do. Only then can counselors begin to participate as helpers in the counseling relationship. Only then can clients begin to move toward more functional behavior.

Although we alluded to it earlier, it is important to stress once more that there is no way to understand human existence by separating it from the setting or environment in which existence occurs. Children cannot be fully understood separate from their families of origin, their neighborhoods, or their peer groups; adults cannot be understood separate from their families, ethnicities, social class, belief systems, or careers; and individuals cannot be dissected into intellectual selves, occupational selves, affective selves, or whatever. Each individual is an ecological existence within a cultural context, living with others in an ecological system. One's intrapersonal dimensions are interdependent with others who share one's life space. A keen understanding and appreciation of this interdependence will facilitate your understanding of yourself as a counselor, and of your clients as people seeking to become healthier, to make better choices, to grow, or to enhance their lives.

Counseling and Philosophy

Before we move on to more specific aspects of counseling, including the interface between theory and counseling process, let's step back for a moment and consider philosophical viewpoints. Few people consider themselves to be philosophers, and yet everyone has a philosophical outlook on life. Some people see life as a sequence of events and experiences over which they have little or no control; others view life as a challenge to be analyzed, controlled, and directed. Some see achievement and self-improvement as the purpose of life; others view life as a process to be experienced. Who is right? Everyone. Philosophical outlooks on life are varied, allowing each individual to choose or to identify with that outlook that seems to fit him or her best.

Counseling theory has drawn primarily from four philosophical positions (Hansen, 2004; Wilks, 2003). The first of these, *essentialism,* assumes that human beings are rational by nature, that reason is the natural goal of education, and that the classical thinkers are the chief repository of reason. From this orientation come the problem solvers, the analyzers, those who search for patterns in life.

The second philosophical position, *progressivism,* is concerned with the fundamental question, "What will work?" Knowledge is based on experimental results, truth is identified through consequences, and values are relative rather than absolute. From this orientation come the persons who rely on data and research for their truths, who believe that pragmatic solutions do exist for human problems, and who are committed to the pursuit of logical and lawful relationships in life.

The third philosophical position, *existentialism,* holds that life's meaning is to be found in the individual, not in the environment or the event. Lawfulness (progressivism) and rational thinking (essentialism) are meaningless unless the individual gives them meaning. People who align with this view of life believe that values are real and individually determined, and that experiences are subjective rather than lawful or predictable. Individual responsibility is emphasized; human reactions are the result of choice or potential choice.

Finally, the fourth philosophical position, *postmodernism,* raises the fundamental question, "What is real?" This question is particularly relevant in terms of the client's experience versus an external reality—or more specifically, which reality is more important—the client's reality, or an outside reality to which the client should adapt? Although there are some similarities between postmodernism and existentialism in this regard, the important point is that one can never know a reality outside oneself and, therefore, must focus on personal reality. From this orientation come persons who believe that reality can have only a personal meaning, that reality gains meaning through one's personal perceptions or explanations of experiences.

Obviously, all counselors enter the profession with some variation of these viewpoints. Each counselor's philosophical view is reflected in how he or she reacts to client problems and how those problems are addressed. Similarly, clients enter counseling with some variation of these viewpoints that are reflected in how they view their problems and what they consider to be viable solutions. Keeping these variations in mind, both for yourself and for your relationship with clients, will help you to choose interventions that are relevant to the people you are trying to assist.

Counseling and Theory

Whether you are studying theories of counseling concurrently to learning about the counseling process or at a different time, at some point, you will be asked to consider how theory will inform your work. Stated simply, a *theory* attempts to explain how something came to be or how it works. *Personality theory,* from which numerous counseling theories spring, is an effort to explain the various ways that the psyche emerges, evolves, and matures, both in terms of normal development and in terms of dysfunction. *Counseling theories* move beyond an explanation of dysfunction in relation to normal development, and offer ideas of how corrections to this dysfunction can be accomplished. Said differently, counseling theory not only hypothesizes about how humans operate, but also how to intervene when things appear to be unraveling. What confuses many students of counseling is how differently some theories conceptualize human existence from others. It would be convenient, perhaps, if the mental health disciplines had only one theory, like relativity; however, that is not the case, and every counselor must study the extant theories available and determine which theory or combination of theories resonates with him or her.

Within the context of counseling therapies, more than 400 approaches have been identified. Most of these approaches would be better labeled as *variations* on a much smaller number of theoretical themes. Among the dominant theoretical approaches are *psychodynamic, cognitive/ behavioral, humanistic, systemic,* and *postmodern* approaches, each of which offers a type of map of the counseling process and the route its participants should take to achieve certain goals. Rarely does a counseling theory prescribe what the specific goals of counseling should be. Because there is much room for alternative viewpoints on matters such as normal human functioning, how people change, and what is a desirable outcome, different theories have emerged to reflect these various viewpoints. On a more practical level, counselors use theories to organize information and observations, to explain or conceptualize client problems, and to order and implement particular interventions with clients.

Counselors tend to identify with particular theories for a variety of reasons. Some counselors look for a theory that provides the most utilitarian explanation of the counseling process. Their quest is for a theory that provides concrete guidelines. Other counselors look for a theory that is compatible with their life perspective—that is, a theory that makes similar assumptions about human nature as their own private assumptions. Still other counselors seek a theory that best explains or conceptualizes the types of problems their clients present. Of course, it is possible for a counselor to obtain all three objectives with the same theory, but this realization tends to emerge only as the counselor gains experience.

Over the years, the counseling profession has witnessed an increased convergence among theorists and a growing realization that no single theory can explain or fit all client challenges. The result is an emerging view that theory is meant to serve the user, and when no single theory totally fits the counselor's needs, then a blending of compatible theories is an acceptable practice. This is known as either an *eclectic* or an *integrative* approach. An *eclectic* approach is one where a counselor chooses a theory depending on each client's needs. Hoffman (2006) noted that the challenge with this approach is that it requires that the counselor become expert in applying many theories, a feat that could take many years. Rather, Hoffman suggests that many practitioners adopt an *integrative* approach, where they claim a central theoretical position but pull from other theories as needed, such as a counselor who claimed to be cognitive-behavioral-integrative. Prochaska and Norcross (2014) report that a sizable number of practicing counselors prefer an integrative or eclectic approach.

Despite a variety of theories to draw from, there are common factors that are present across all counseling. The following list presents seven elements about counseling that are operative for all of the major theoretical approaches:

1. Counseling involves responding to the feelings, thoughts, actions, and contexts of the client. Existing theoretical approaches tend to emphasize one of these over the others. However, all counselors must be excellent observers and skilled in their ability to engage clients, to elicit the client's thoughts and feelings, and to respond to these in ways that are helpful.

2. Counseling involves a basic acceptance of the client's perceptions and feelings, regardless of outside evaluative standards. In other words, you must first acknowledge who the client is before you can begin to consider who the client might become. Clients need your understanding of their current reality and concerns before they can anticipate growth and change in a new direction.

3. Counseling is a multicultural experience. This realization affects all aspects of the process, including assessment, goal setting, and intervention selection.

4. Ethical mandates of the profession are relevant across all counseling, and include confidentiality, receiving adequate supervision, avoiding multiple relationships with clients, informed consent, and so forth. All counselors must be familiar with the ethical codes to which they are subject.

5. Counseling must include client buy-in. This is especially important when clients are mandated, but is also true of many clients who come voluntarily but have not yet made a commitment to work toward change. Therefore, counselors must be skilled in "marketing" what it is they have to offer as a first step with some clients. This can take the form of showing respect and interest in the client, even if the client appears to be disengaged; or it can take the form of frank talk of consequences for the client if no change occurs in his or her life. Whatever is the decided approach, buy-in must be accomplished if counseling is to have positive outcomes. Otherwise, the counselor learns that counseling can be a weak intervention with a client who is unable to make a commitment to the process. This, of course, is the client's right, and coercion is never appropriate as a means to continue with a client.

6. Generally speaking, the counselor operates with a conservative bias against communicating to the client detailed information about his or her own life. Although there are times when counselor self-disclosure is appropriate, counselors generally do not complicate the relationship by focusing attention on themselves.

7. One cluster of skills underlying all approaches to counseling is that which makes up communication. Counselors and clients alike continually transmit and receive verbal and nonverbal messages during the interview process. Therefore, awareness of and sensitivity to the kinds of messages being communicated is an important prerequisite for counselor effectiveness.

Counseling and Culture

Increasingly, society is becoming aware of the complex role that culture plays in interpersonal relationships. Furthermore, cultural awareness is endemic to the discussion of theory and philosophy already introduced. As you listen to how clients see the world (often reflecting how their families taught them to see the world and how the world taught them to see themselves), you may begin to see some similarities within cultural groups. As a result, one of your challenges as a counselor is to find a theory (or theories) that reflects your own view of the world but is not inconsistent with how your clients view the world. One of the rewarding parts of counseling is that if you listen intently to how other cultural groups think and feel, you may find that your own views about things evolve.

If you were to look up the word *culture* in a variety of resources, some of the words and phrases that would keep coming up are *beliefs, values, way of life, shared attitudes, morals,* and *characteristics*. For this reason, counseling is best viewed as *multicultural,* because most individuals are members of more than one cultural group. For example, you may be a White, Irish-American, Catholic, working-class, heterosexual woman. Each of these cultural identities includes some shared attitudes and beliefs with many (certainly not all) of other persons of the same profile. And this is only the beginning. You may also be a member of the Alcoholics Anonymous culture as a recovering alcoholic, and you may identify as a feminist. You most certainly find some of your cultural identities more central to how you view yourself than others, and these identities change depending on the context. For example, you may not find yourself focusing on your working-class background (which includes a strong work ethic) much, until you are working with a client who doesn't seem interested in helping him- or herself. Suddenly, you are experiencing a cultural "moment" that you must work through if you are to be helpful to your client. In this example, it's quite possible that you never considered that part of your adopting a strong work ethic is the embedded privilege that was part of your upbringing—that is, it paid off to work hard because you were rewarded for doing so. What if this was not the case? What if you were viewed negatively even when you thought you were doing things correctly? Might this be your client's cultural reality? If so, your awareness of this cultural difference may lead you to implementing appropriate interventions.

In short, the implications for counseling and for the counselor are quite clear: If understanding and acceptance of the client are to occur, then the counselor must understand the cultural factors that have shaped and continue to influence the client's worldview. Even before that can happen, the counselor must understand his or her own worldview and how it is shaped in ways similar to how this occurred for the client, even when the two worldviews are substantially different from one another. To do less is to flirt with what Wrenn (1962) initially termed *cultural encapsulation:* defining reality according to one set of cultural assumptions and stereotypes, being insensitive to cultural variations among individuals, and assuming that one's personal view is the only real or legitimate one. Clearly, counseling cannot go far when the counselor is handicapped by cultural encapsulation.

Finally, the greater the value of a cultural identity to the client, the more important it is to be understood by the counselor. Therefore, race, gender, sexual orientation, religious identity, ability/disability, and social class may be key cultural variables to communicating accurately and empathically with a client. That said, we should also be aware of what may be "lesser" cultural variables and how they help us to understand our clients. Urban culture, corporate culture, Y generation, "geek" culture, athlete culture—all of these may include embedded values and beliefs that enhance the counseling relationship if you take time to learn about them. Furthermore, in attending to what appeared a "lesser" identity, you may learn that it is, by contrast, quite central to how the client views him- or herself.

COUNSELING CONDITIONS AND THEIR EFFECTS

Some clients find seeking counseling to be a major life decision. Apart from the fact that pockets of society continue to associate personal problems with weakness or inadequacy, the process of finding a person who is trustworthy, confidence inspiring, and competent is a daunting challenge. Other clients have a longer history of participating in counseling because of chronic mental health conditions, spiraling consequences of faulty decision making, living in an abusive situation, or any number of other reasons. Many clients are ill informed about counseling. If the experience is new, they may be unprepared to appraise the situation, determine the counselor's ability to be of help, and make the judgment to commit to the process. The counselor must also make an initial assessment of the situation, determine that his or her skills are adequate for the client's presenting concerns, and also determine that counseling holds some promise for improving the client's situation. What conditions or events provide signals to both clients and counselors that the prospective relationship and the counseling process hold promise for success?

Clients are likely to be encouraged by factors such as feeling support and understanding from another person, beginning to see a different and more hopeful perspective, or experiencing a more desirable level of relating to others. Similarly, counselors feel reinforced as they are able to establish those conditions that lead to successful counseling outcomes. Although different theoretical orientations emphasize somewhat different counseling outcomes, most practitioners agree on some rather basic outcomes. When counseling has been successful, clients often experience a combination of the following four types of outcomes:

1. *Clients develop a more useful understanding of problems and issues.* Once clients begin to view the sources of their problems more appropriately, they frequently develop greater understanding or insight into the problem and some of the ways that the problem manifests itself. Although understanding a problem differently is rarely an end in itself, it is an important beginning. There are four avenues for problem understanding that can increase client awareness: feelings and somatic reactions (affect) associated with the problem, thoughts (cognitions) related to how clients perceive or explain their problems, behavior patterns that may be associated or attributed to experiencing the problem, and interpersonal relationships that affect or are affected by the problem occurrence. Understanding these different dimensions of a problem helps clients perceive their reality more clearly and gain or experience more control over their reactions to an issue.

Example: Joseph, a Korean-American college student, was mandated to receive three counseling sessions at the college counseling center as a result of public drunkenness on campus. Joseph noted that he doesn't typically abuse alcohol but decided to get "wasted" when his girlfriend ended their relationship. He reported feeling down, hurt, lonely, and unlovable since the breakup a week ago. He showed no clinical signs of depression (e.g., sleeplessness, weight loss, isolation); rather, his behavior appeared to be more about letting the world (and his former girlfriend) know that he was in crisis. Through counseling, Joseph began to realize that his reaction is similar to how he would respond as a child when his mother would get on his case. Then, he reports, she would start to feel sorry for her effect on him and try to repair the obviously damaged relationship. In other words, Joseph began to understand that his style of dealing with stressful relationship events was to manipulate the other person into repairing the damage. In so doing, Joseph never had to assume any responsibility either for the initial issue or for the solution to the relationship problem. Thus, his reaction involved feelings, how he explained the problem to himself (as someone else's doing), his irresponsible behavior (in this case, getting drunk on campus), and how he would manipulate relationships. Through counseling, Joseph also began to understand the relationship between his problem-resolution style and his resulting behaviors that reflected passivity and inertia. Finally, Joseph came to understand that his interactional patterns with his mother were intruding and controlling his relationships with women. Now that Joseph has a clearer understanding of his issues, he is in a better position to commit to a goal of changing this pattern.

   2. *Clients acquire new responses to old issues.* Many counseling theorists now agree that, for most clients, insight or understanding of problems is not a sufficient counseling outcome. In addition to developing greater understanding of issues, clients must also acquire more effective ways of responding, verbally and/or behaviorally, to problematic situations. Otherwise, they tend to repeat their ineffective coping methods, and fail to make any connection between how they understand their problem and what they do when experiencing their problem.

Example: Maria and Juan see a counselor because of "poor communication" in their marriage. Gradually, they are realizing that part of the problem is that Juan is at work all day in a very intense environment and wants to come home to relax, to sit down with the TV or his iPad, and to be left alone. Maria, however, has been at home alone all day with a young child. She seeks out Juan for some adult conversation until he pushes her away. Maria retreats in tearful anger. Although an understanding of the dynamics of this scenario may be useful to both Maria (she might be able to understand that it is not she, personally, whom Juan was rejecting) and to Juan (he, in turn, might realize that Maria had reasonable and understandable needs), it is unlikely that they will be able to alter or interrupt their reentry behavior patterns through understanding alone. They must also develop new behavioral patterns or interactions that meet each person's unique end-of-the-day needs.

3. *Clients begin to perceive their problems and issues contextually.* Many times, clients have formulated a set of explanations for their problems. Such explanations may reflect cultural factors, societal factors, or familial factors. From an upper-middle-class privileged perspective, the issue might be one of helping clients to "own" their problems. *Owning* means that clients begin to accept responsibility for themselves, their problems, and solutions. However, there are other ways of viewing the source of client problems. Clients who have experienced systematic discrimination because of disability, race, or religion—to name only a few—may not feel empowered to affect change in their lives. Some clients can appear beaten down by their experience as they view it, and muster little energy for counseling; others are angry at life in general for giving them such an unfair hand; still others tend to be in denial and present unrealistic (and often simplistic) views of how easy it will be for things to change. An important goal for the counselor, therefore, is to help clients understand the contextual factors that contribute to their issues, to fairly assess contextual restrictions and opportunities, and to offer clients both support and respect (i.e., to acknowledge discrimination and limited resources when they are apparent, and yet speak to clients' strengths) within the counseling process.

Example: Diane is a 30-year-old White woman who is being interviewed at a community domestic violence center. Diane's cousin convinced her to come; it is clear that Diane is not convinced that she belongs there. Diane's husband, Rick, hit her during a recent argument. Diane tells her counselor that he has never hit her before. When encouraged to tell their history, Diane reveals that Rick is under a lot of stress at work and is very impatient with her. But this has been restricted to verbal insults and once shoving her as he left the room, but never striking her until this recent event. Diane shares that they have a 6-month-old baby and that Rick has been less affectionate since she became pregnant. She also tells the counselor that she understands Rick's reaction as she is still carrying pregnancy weight and feels fat and ugly. In this case, it is clear that Diane has viewed Rick's abuse only in personal and interpersonal contexts. She does not yet appear to be aware of the role that sexism and society's tolerance of violence against woman has played in her relationship with Rick. Between these divergent contexts, the counselor must also learn more about what Diane learned from her family of origin about the role that women play in families and their relative status to the men in the family. Without any appreciation of these broader contexts, Diane is likely to continue to blame herself and Rick's work stress for the situation.

4. *Clients learn how to develop effective relationships.* For a significant number of people who end up in a counselor's office, adults and young people alike, effective and satisfying interpersonal interactions are nonexistent or rare. Because change is often created and enhanced by a social support network, it is essential for clients to begin to develop more adequate relationships with other people. Occasionally, the counseling relationship is the initial vehicle by which this occurs.

Example: Renee, a 17-year-old African-American high school junior was referred to her school counselor after an altercation with another girl. Renee is significantly obese and says that everyone is "nasty" with her because of her weight. Renee also says that, even though she'd like to lose weight because her mother has diabetes, she doesn't care about kids in the school liking her because the school is full of "losers." In talking more to Renee, it becomes clear that her aggressive veneer is a thin shield covering feelings of isolation and rejection. The school counselor has a dual challenge in this case, and may call on the help of other professionals as well. Part of the issue harks back to multiple contexts as Renee's weight may be at least in part due to poor nutrition and unhealthy eating habits in her family and her community. In addition, the counselor must assist Renee in forming relationships that allow her to discard her veneer and be more authentic. Renee and her counselor have their work cut out for them, but it is unlikely that much will change without attention to these issues.

To summarize, counseling usually results in more than one single and all-inclusive outcome for clients. Effective change is multifaceted and comprehensive, and includes keener understanding of the dynamics of problem sources and maintenance, new insights, different and more facilitative behavioral responses, and more effective interpersonal relationships.

CASE ILLUSTRATION OF POSSIBLE COUNSELING OUTCOMES

The Case of Janet

Janet is a 35-year-old, White, single parent of two teenage girls. She has been employed as a bookkeeper for a local auto parts company for 12 years and is considered to be "the glue that holds the operation together" by her colleagues. Within her work context, Janet feels competent and comfortable. At home, her self-confidence disappears and she has overwhelming doubts about her parenting role and her relationship with neighbors "who see what a bad job I am doing." These doubts also invade her relationship with her parents, her ex-husband and in-laws, her church, and her social relationships. The result is that she has been spending increasing amounts of time in her job, thus accentuating her feelings toward her non-work world. These feelings seem locked into a downward spiral from which she cannot escape. Lately, she has been experiencing some physical symptoms involving her digestive system, inability to sleep more than four to five hours, and a nagging sense of despair.

Given an effective counseling experience, Janet might realistically expect to see some of the following kinds of change:

- Development of a more positive perception of herself away from work.
- Increased awareness of the relationship between her satisfying work setting and her overcommitment to time at work rather than at home.
- A more objective (and possibly enhanced) personal view of herself as a mother.
- A more realistic view of how others see her as a single parent and adult.
- Awareness that her physical symptoms might be related to her emotional reactions.
- Awareness of societal gender stereotypes that feed her reduced self-concept.
- A plan that would help her extract herself from the various "traps" she is experiencing at work, at home, in her neighborhood, in her church, and in her social relationships.
- Interactions with her daughters that reinforce their relationship and her view of herself as a mother.

CHARACTERISTICS OF EFFECTIVE HELPERS

Research on the effectiveness of counseling does not provide clear evidence of the relative contributions of factors that influence counseling (Sexton, Whiston, Bleuer, & Walz, 1997). Nevertheless, the professional literature is consistent in its emphasis on counselor characteristics as important to the success of counseling, including the following:

- Self-awareness and understanding
- Good psychological health
- Sensitivity to and understanding of culture as well as the role of "positionality"
- Open-mindedness
- Tolerance for ambiguity
- Clear boundaries
- Competence
- Trustworthiness
- Interpersonal attractiveness
- Ethical behavior

Other characteristics that have been identified include the ability to be empathic, genuine, and accepting (Neukrug, 2007); belief in the personal meaning of another person (Combs, 1986); and power or comfort with having influence with another (Cormier, Nurius, & Osborn, 2013).

Self-Awareness and Understanding

On the road to becoming an effective counselor, a good starting place for most counselors is a healthy degree of introspection and self-exploration. We suggest you might examine and seek to understand the following four specific areas:

1. Awareness of your needs (e.g., need to give or to nurture, need to judge others, need to be loved, need to be respected, need to be liked, need to please others, need to receive approval from others, need to be right, need for control)
2. Awareness of your motivation for helping (e.g., What do you get or take from helping others? How does helping make you feel good?)
3. Awareness of your feelings (e.g., happiness, satisfaction, hurt, anger, sadness, disappointment, confusion, fear)
4. Awareness of your personal strengths, limitations, and coping skills (e.g., things you do well or things about yourself that you like, things about yourself you need to work on, how you handle difficulties and stress)

Self-awareness and understanding are important in counseling for a variety of reasons. First, they help you see things more objectively and avoid "blind spots"—that is, difficulties that may arise because you do not understand some aspects of yourself, particularly in interpersonal interactions. One such difficulty is *projection*. Counselors who do not understand their needs and feelings may be more likely to project their feelings onto the client and not recognize their real source (e.g., "I had a very angry client today" instead of "I felt angry today with my client"). Projection is one example of a process we discuss later in this chapter called *countertransference,* or the emotional reactions of the counselor to the client.

Self-awareness and understanding also contribute to greater security and safety for both counselor and client. Lack of self-awareness and understanding may cause some counselors to personalize or overreact to client messages and respond with defensiveness. For example, a client questions whether counseling "will do her any good." The counselor's need to be respected and affirmed are jeopardized or threatened, but the counselor is not aware of this. Instead of responding to the client's feelings of uncertainty, the counselor is likely to respond with personal feelings of insecurity and portray defensiveness in his or her voice or to portray other nonverbal behavior. In summary, self-awareness and understanding is having a keen knowledge of one's triggers; for counselors, it also means having the ability to moderate one's reactions to triggers so they do not hamper your client's progress.

Good Psychological Health

Although no one expects counselors to be perfect, it stands to reason that counselors will be more helpful to clients when they are psychologically intact and not distracted by their own overwhelming problems. In a classic study of the psychological health of mental health providers, White and Franzoni (1990) report that studies of the psychological health of psychiatrists, psychologists, and psychotherapists in general revealed higher rates of depression, anxiety, and relationship problems than the general population. Even those counselors-in-training at the master's degree level showed evidence of higher levels of psychological disturbance than did the general public (White & Franzoni, 1990).

Unfortunately, some counselors do not recognize when their own psychological health is compromised. It is for this reason that it is generally viewed as good practice for counselors to seek counseling if there is any question of their own issues making it difficult for them to be fully present to their clients. And because we are all sometimes the last to know if we are in trouble, it is also best practice to have supervision available to us, at least at the front end of our careers, and potentially throughout our careers.

Sensitivity to and Understanding of Culture as Well as the Role of "Positionality"

As stated earlier, all clients live in multicultural worlds, as do we. Although psychotherapy began as a profession to examine the intrapersonal, it has evolved to include cultural realities as relevant to achieving psychological health and to functioning and developing as individuals, families, and communities. We have already noted that good psychological health allows the counselor to be more helpful to clients. It is just as true that awareness of one's own multiple cultural identities and how these shape one's worldview contributes to one's effectiveness as a counselor. And as also noted earlier, counselors must afford their clients the space for their cultural identities to emerge.

In addition, it is essential that counselors are aware of how power and privilege play out in counseling. Alcott (1988) was one of the first scholars to use the term *positionality,* a term that has influenced the mental health professions. By *positionality,* we mean that cultural identities are indications of relative positions rather than descriptors of particular characteristics. Therefore, being lesbian or a Muslim or an amputee is *descriptive* largely in relationship to the position it places you in the many contexts of your life. For example, a Muslim may experience his or her position differently in their mosque than at an airport. Frequent experiences of positions, whether they are privileged or put one at a disadvantage, eventually become mingled with one's identity.

The important concepts of culture, power, privilege, and positionality are endemic to most counseling programs at this point in our evolution as a profession, and are embedded in many discussions on many topics. For our purposes here, it is sufficient to say that counselors must become students of the implications of cultural identities and positionality in relationship building, assessment, and all other aspects of the counseling process. This is an inherently challenging aspect of counseling but necessary for its success.

Open-Mindedness

Open-mindedness suggests freedom from fixed or preconceived ideas that, if allowed expression, could affect clients and counseling outcomes. Open-mindedness must include enlightenment and knowledge of the world outside the counselor's world; it must also include an acute understanding of one's inner world and how those internal standards, values, assumptions, perceptions, and myths can be projected on clients if the counselor is not vigilant.

Open-mindedness serves a number of significant functions in counseling. First, it allows counselors to accommodate clients' feelings, attitudes, and behaviors that may be different from their own. Second, it allows counselors to interact effectively with a wide range of clients, even those regarded by society at large as unacceptable or offensive. Finally, open-mindedness is a prerequisite for honest communication.

Tolerance for Ambiguity

Conducting a counseling session is not like balancing your checkbook. No matter how many times you do it, you will never have the feeling that things have been wrapped up in a neat package (and even if you were to feel that way, you would also learn how quickly a package can unravel). This doesn't mean that counseling is a total mystery, because it is not. But it does mean that successful counselors have a healthy tolerance for not knowing what may be around the corner even as they fully engage in a process that is intentional. Said differently, successful counselors are fascinated by the complexity of people and are fully committed to the process of counseling even if the outcome is unclear.

Clear Boundaries

Having a clear boundary between you and the client allows you to be involved with a client and, at the same time, stand back and see accurately what is happening with the client and in the relationship. Carl Rogers' description of empathy alluded to this when he explained that *empathy* is the ability to experience the client's problem as if it were your own while never losing the "as if" aspect (Rogers, 1957). It is extremely important to maintain clear boundaries for the client's benefit. Most clients are bombarded with views and advice from many well-meaning persons, such as friends and family, who are sometimes part of the problem or perceive being helpful as seeing things as the client does. Counselors, however, give the client an additional set of eyes and ears that are needed to develop a greater understanding without the complication of a personal relationship.

When counselors have clear boundaries, they also avoid getting caught up in certain client behaviors or dysfunctional communication patterns. For example, clients sometimes try to manipulate the counselor to "rescue" them, using a variety of well-learned and sophisticated ploys. Counselors who have a clear sense of themselves are more likely to recognize client manipulation for what it is and respond with therapeutic appropriateness.

Also, boundary clarity acts as a safeguard against developing inappropriate or even dysfunctional emotional feelings about or toward a client. Counselors must learn to recognize when countertransference develops in the relationship. *Countertransference* involves either a counterproductive emotional reaction to a client (often based on projection) or the entanglement of the counselor's needs in the therapeutic relationship. Some of the more common ways in which countertransference may manifest itself include the need to please one's clients, overidentification with certain client problems, development of romantic or sexual feelings toward clients, need to give constant advice, and a desire to form friendships with clients (Corey, 2011). Astute counselors gradually learn to identify certain kinds of clients who consistently elicit strong positive or negative feelings on their part, and also certain kinds of communication patterns that entice the counselor into giving a less helpful response.

Competence

Ethical standards of all mental health professions call for maintaining high standards of competence. According to Egan (2014), *competence* refers to whether the counselor has the necessary information, knowledge, and skills to be of help, and is determined not by behaviors but by outcomes. The profession generally agrees that counseling competency includes knowledge in areas such as psychological processes, assessment, ethics, and other areas relevant to professional work, as well as clinical skills, technical skills, judgment, multicultural competence, and personal effectiveness.

Counselor competence is necessary to transmit and build confidence and hope in clients. Clients must develop positive expectations about the potential usefulness to them of the counseling experience. Competent counselors are able to work with a greater variety of clients and a wider range of problems. They are more likely to be of benefit to their clients and to make inroads more quickly and efficiently. Sometimes referred to as *expertness,* competence is often associated with a model of counseling known as the *social influence model,* the two basic assumptions of which are as follows:

1. The helper must establish power or a base of influence with the client through a relationship composed of three characteristics or relationship enhancers: competence (expertness), trustworthiness (credibility), and attractiveness (liking).
2. The helper must actively use this base of influence to effect opinion and behavior changes in the client.

An increasing amount of evidence on this model suggests that clients' respect for the counselor increases in direct proportion to their perceptions of the counselor's expertness or competence.

Trustworthiness

Most of us like to think that we are trustworthy. Within professional counseling, *trustworthiness* includes such qualities as reliability, responsibility, following ethical standards, and predictability. Counselors who are trustworthy safeguard their clients' communications, respond with energy and caring to client concerns, and never let their clients regret having shared information. This last point is key—trustworthiness includes providing a client with a safe space to share their true thoughts and feelings. Safety includes not only a promise to honor confidentiality, but also working hard to understand the client's world in as many contexts as possible.

We ask a lot of clients in asking them to trust us, especially because many clients have had their trust violated in the past. Trust can be hard to establish, and it can be ruptured relatively easily. For this reason, if any rupture of the therapeutic alliance occurs, we must stop the process and attempt to make repairs by reviewing what happened to diminish the client's trust in us, sharing perspectives and motives on both sides, and (hopefully) inching toward a new working relationship with reinforcements where the break occurred. Another essential component of trustworthiness can be summarized in one sentence: Do not promise more than you can do, and be sure you do exactly as you have promised. Trustworthiness is essential, not only in establishing a base of influence with clients, but also in encouraging clients to self-disclose and reveal often very private parts of their lives. Counselors cannot *act* trustworthy; they must *be* trustworthy.

Interpersonal Attractiveness

We are all familiar with the adage that attractiveness is in the eye of the beholder. This is true in counseling as well, with a caveat or two. Clients perceive counselors as interpersonally attractive when they see them as similar to or compatible with themselves. Clients often make this assessment intuitively, although it is probably based on selected dimensions of counselors' demeanor and attitude, particularly their likability and friendliness. In other words, it is helpful for counselors to be down to earth, friendly, and warm, rather than formal, stuffy, aloof, or reserved. Yet, here we add the caveat that counselors must take into account what knowledge they have of the history and cultural contexts of their clients. For a family used to formality, being too "down to earth" would run the risk of being seen as less professional. Male counselors must learn how to appear warm with female clients without appearing to be flirting. Supervision as one begins to work with a variety of clients is most helpful for learning how to strike the right balance. This is an important goal because counselors who are perceived as interpersonally attractive become a positive source of influence for clients and may also inspire greater confidence and trust in the counseling process.

Ethical Behavior

How the counselor performs under conflicting or challenging conditions affects all of the other conditions. But what determines ethical behavior? The American Counseling Association (ACA) has established guidelines for ethical counselor performance in a variety of settings and under a broad spectrum of problem situations. *Ethical behavior* is primarily a self-determined adherence to these standards. However, there are conditions in which failure to perform ethically could lead to malpractice and lawsuits. The ACA Ethical Standards may be found and downloaded at their website: www.counseling .org. For counselors who belong to counseling divisions or affiliates (e.g., American School Counselor Association, American Mental Health Counseling Association), their ethical standards must also be followed. Finally, those counselors certified by the National Board for Certified Counselors must follow its code. All ethical standards for counselors are very similar; still, it is good practice to read all of those that are relevant to your practice and to be aware of those for which you are held responsible.

THE DEVELOPMENTAL NATURE OF LEARNING TO COUNSEL

Over the years, counselor educators have participated in a recurring debate regarding the experience of learning to counsel. The two poles of this debate are (1) that potential counselors already possess the "skills" of counseling but must learn how to differentiate these skills and use them selectively with clients; and (2) that the skills of counseling have been rather specifically defined and can be taught to potential counselors with a reasonably high degree of success, regardless of whether they possessed the skills initially. Obviously, most counselor preparation programs fall somewhere between these two poles. Regardless of the source of those skills, whether they are inherent in the candidate's personhood or are embedded in the curriculum of the preparation program (or both), the process of bringing them into dominance is worthy of attention.

Almost everyone has known someone who was untrained and yet was a "natural" counselor. In getting to know such people, one often finds that they assumed the helper role as children. They may even have been identified by their families as the peacemaker, the facilitator, the understanding one, or the one to whom other family members could turn. Such a role emerges both from temperament and from expectations. Such helpers evolve into the role as their sensitivities, skills, and confidence grow over time. (We should note that some of these helpers have also adopted the role of *hero* or *overachiever* in their families, and these roles are not always conducive to professional counseling.) Similarly, students entering counselor preparation programs find that the process is a developmental experience. That is to say, early in the training, the focus tends to be on professional issues external to the person and the context for helping. Gradually, the focus of preparation turns to the personal qualities of helpers, and the process then becomes more personal. From this, attention turns to the skills of counseling— what effective counselors are doing and thinking as they work with clients. Finally, preparation begins to integrate these skills with the practical experience of counseling clients in professionally supervised settings.

In a seminal contribution to the professional literature, Loganbill, Hardy, and Delworth (1982) suggest that the developmental process for counselors included stagnation, confusion, and integration. *Stagnation* is typically seen as reliance on established social responses when learning to counsel (e.g., trying to make the client feel better rather than listening deeply to what the client is saying). *Confusion* follows as counselors learn professional counseling skills but do not yet feel comfortable directing the counseling process. Once counselors begin to feel more sure of themselves and to see the counseling process benefit their clients, they begin to experience some *integration*. This learning curve is not a speedy one; it is our experience that success occurs for students of counseling who are patient with themselves, are open to feedback, and are willing to take risks (i.e., make mistakes from which they can learn).

In summary, few beginning helpers feel prepared, either technically or personally, to begin working with clients. In part, this is a matter of developing self-confidence in the new skills that have been learned, but it is also associated with their personal growth as human beings. Experienced counselors find that they learn much about themselves and about the process of living through their work with clients. We have certainly found that to be true in our own experience. Each new client introduces us to ourselves in another way. Each client also expands our world in a new way. Very often, the experience reveals aspects of our own life views and adjustment that merit attention and exploration. When this happens, we become increasingly aware of both our strengths and our limitations. It is around those personal strengths that effective counselors build their approach to helping, and it is around those personal limitations that effective counselors attempt to structure growth experiences.

Summary

In this chapter, our aim has been to describe the various parameters of the counseling process; to relate the process to philosophy, counseling theory, and culture; to illustrate the purposes of effective counseling; to highlight the major personal characteristics of effective counselors; and to underscore the developmental nature of learning to be a counselor. The counseling relationship has certain features that set it apart from other professional or social relationships or even friendships. One of the most significant features of the counseling relationship is that the counselor is a trained professional capable of providing assistance in a competent and trustworthy manner.

In Chapter 2 we examine the skills of counseling, including the basic skills of communication that occur intentionally or unintentionally between counselor and client, and the more advanced verbal and nonverbal skills that the counselor uses as interventions into the process and the client's experience.

Then, in Chapter 3, we take a more focused look at the landscape of the counseling process. Subsequent chapters examine portions of this landscape in greater detail. The larger intentions of this text are to provide the skills dimension of the learning process and to offer some structure for the implicit and explicit interactional nature of these skills. Each chapter concludes with suggested exercises as well as discussion questions to assist your integration of the content.

Exercises

I. Cultural factors and countertransference

Two client case descriptions are presented in this activity, and you have two tasks: First, based on the case description for each client, identify as many cultural factors as you can speculate may be operating for each case. Second, does either case stimulate a more personal reaction in you than the other? To what do you attribute your reaction? You may wish to share your responses with your instructor or another student.

A. Ben is in his early fifties. He has been fairly happily married for 25 years and has two grown children. Ben ran a successful business for 20 years; however, his business recently took a nosedive. He has had to lay off several employees and take a 50% reduction in his own salary. Going to work each morning has become a punishing experience, because each day seems to bring only more bad news. Ben is very nervous about his ability to hold on to the company and his marriage during this stressful time.

B. Margaret is an older woman (in her late seventies). Her hearing has begun to deteriorate and she finds that often she must ask people to repeat themselves when they speak to her. She has also had a couple of bad falls in the past year, one of which resulted in a severe back sprain. Margaret lives alone in a two-room apartment and receives only a Social Security check. Public transportation is her only means of getting around. She often complains of loneliness and boredom.

II. Qualities of effective counselors

Listed next are the nine qualities of effective counselors described in this chapter. With a partner or in a small group, discuss what you believe is your present status with respect to each quality. For example, how open-minded are you? What makes it easy (or difficult) for you to be open-minded and relatively tolerant of different values and ideas? Then identify several areas that you may need to work on during your development as a counselor. Refer to the case description about Margaret in Exercise I.B. Which factors do you believe would have the greatest impact on Margaret's psychological health?

1. Self-awareness and understanding
2. Good psychological health
3. Sensitivity to and understanding of culture as well as the role of "positionality"
4. Open-mindedness
5. Tolerance for ambiguity
6. Clear boundaries
7. Competence
8. Trustworthiness
9. Interpersonal attractiveness

Discussion Questions

1. Counseling has been described by some as a *purchase of friendship*. Do you agree with this statement? How do you believe counseling differs from a close friendship?

2. Do you know someone who possesses the qualities to be an effective counselor? What are some of this person's qualities? How do you suppose these qualities were acquired?

3. Considering your age, background, and life experiences, what do you think you have to offer to clients that is different from what they would receive from their friends or family members?

4. What are the most important reasons why you want to be a counselor? How might a typical client react to your reasons for choosing counseling as a career?

5. How likely are you to see a counselor yourself? In what ways do you think counseling could help you in your own development as a person and as a counselor? For which reasons might you resist getting involved in this experience?

MyCounselingLab® Assignment

Go to the Video Library under Video Resources on the MyCounselingLab site for your text and search for the following clips:

- **Video Example: What is a Counselor?** In this exchange between a counselor and a client, the counselor attempts to explain how she is different from a psychiatrist or a psychologist. How would you describe your professional identity to someone new to receiving counseling?

- For the following clips, two with adults and one with a child, identify characteristics of that counselor that make him or her "attractive" as mental health professionals? Would you want to be this person's client? Why or why not? Would you be comfortable recommending this counselor to another? Why or why not?

Video Example: Attending, Joining, and Active Listening
Video Example: Goal-Setting Skills: Dayle
Video Example: Helping Client "Construct Their Own Story"

2

The Language of Counseling

PURPOSE OF THIS CHAPTER

What do counselors do? How do they do it? We listen. And we talk. And then we listen some more. The simplicity of that answer belies the complexity of the process—otherwise, why would so many beginning counselors panic at the thought of meeting that first real client? And why would national standards for training exist?

Although we could argue that the most essential element of counseling is how counselors think, the focus in this chapter is on the more observable aspects of counseling—that is, verbal and nonverbal communication. There is a way of using language that counselors acquire as they learn how to counsel. To some extent, the media has given us a stereotype of that language, including head nods, "Uh-huh," "I see," "How do you feel?" "What I hear you saying is . . .," and other minimally representative expressions. In fact, the language of counseling is both broad and effective when used intentionally. In this chapter, we introduce a range of verbal and nonverbal skills that have demonstrated their importance and usefulness with clients.

Considerations as You Read This Chapter

- How do different counselor responses change the discussion?
- How does silence affect the client? How does silence affect you?
- What is it that you are doing when you listen to someone? ("Just sitting there" is *not* the right answer!)
- What communication challenges might exist among persons of different ethnicities, genders, and age groups?

Counseling is not for everyone who might want to be a helper. Not everyone is a good listener. Not everyone can help people share their private thoughts and feelings. Not everyone can keep the discussion going for 30 minutes, or 40 minutes, or (heaven forbid!) 50 minutes. And it isn't because some people are "born" counselors, although a few are. Rather, the skilled counselor has learned helping skills that lead clients to explore and take risks, and to confront old beliefs and generate new ones. Helping skills incorporate basic communication skills and advanced therapeutic skills, all within the context of a positive relationship with the counselor and safety for the client. These skills have been part of the counselor's repertoire for decades and have been studied for their effect on client behavior.

COMMUNICATION IN COUNSELING

Before going further, we must attempt to define communication and how it occurs. In human discourse, *communication* occurs when messages are encoded (by communicators) and decoded (by receivers). The skill of encoding and the accuracy of decoding are obvious concerns. Both you and your clients encode and decode continuously. Not all encoded messages are intentional. For example, our body language may communicate more loudly than our words, and this might be what others "hear." Even if our message is consistent, that does not ensure that the receiver hears what we intend. Consequently, miscommunication can occur, either as a result of inaccurately composed messages or by unrecognized or misperceived messages. Cultural differences can contribute significantly to errors in encoding and decoding. It is for this reason that counselors must keep cultural factors in mind from the very beginning of counseling.

Communication in counseling is both verbal and nonverbal. From the moment you and your client first meet, messages are sent and meanings are inferred. Counselors communicate self to others through physical appearance, initial behaviors or gestures, the comfort or awkwardness of the first moments, the use of verbal expressions, and the appearance of nervousness or comfort. In the early moments of a first meeting, a journey begins, often vague and of uncertain meaning, but significant and to be remembered by both. At this point, you begin to work by deciphering (decoding) the client's messages, by facilitating the client's comfort, and by encouraging the client to enter into a "helping world."

From your client's perspective, this entry is somewhat different. The client's focus is twofold: How to read and interpret your meanings and how to monitor his or her own. It is too early to trust and maybe too soon to hope, and your client is too vulnerable to discard caution. Your sensitivity to what messages you are sending, the messages your client is sending, and how both are being received and decoded is critical in this initial period of the relationship.

NONVERBAL SKILLS OF COUNSELING

Much research has been conducted on how our nonverbal behavior affects communication, particularly in intimate settings. Early studies examined the impact of space and distance (e.g., how near or distant two persons are), arrangement of furniture (e.g., seating around a table in a restaurant, at a bar, or in a living room), appearance of the room (professional or casual), psychological warmth, cultural effects, physical appearance (how one is dressed), and conversational distance. One pioneer in the field of communication concludes that nearly two thirds of the meaning in any social situation is derived from nonverbal cues (Birdwhistell, 1970).

So what aspects of nonverbal communication are particularly important in the counseling office? Research suggests that we should be sensitive to placement and comfort of furniture, including its movability; whether the room suggests confidentiality and professionalism; facial expressions and eye contact; and vocal cues (paralanguage) such as verbal rhythm and tempo, loudness or softness, and use of minimal verbalizations such as *"umm," "uh-huh," "huh-uh,"* or *"oh."* That said, some of these recommendations belie work conditions for many counselors ("Comfort of furniture? Yeah, that would be nice.") Still, regardless of work environment, the counselor's role is to maximize the potential for meaningful interactions with clients at whatever level is possible.

Physical Conditions

Space matters; physical barriers also matter. If you have a choice, we recommend that you sit close enough to your clients to encourage a sense of professional intimacy but at enough distance that ensures psychological safety as well. The age of your client(s), gender, and certain cultural characteristics may influence how close is too close and how far is too far. If you have an office with a desk, you shouldn't use your desk as a barrier. Clients shouldn't feel like they've been sent to the principal's office. If your conditions for conducting counseling are far from ideal, we suggest that you speak to the obvious. "It's louder in the corridor than I'd like, but you'll notice that I have a white noise machine going. That ensures that even though we can hear them, they can't hear what we're saying." "It's a little tight in here for all of us. Is it getting in the way for anyone? If so, I'll do what I can to find us another meeting place." "I know it's hot in here. I wish we could regulate the heat better. Please feel free to get a cold drink before we begin."

Body Language

How we sit or stand communicates our comfort with the setting. Our physical movements, head nods, and facial expressions all have a place and convey a meaning in the counseling room. For example, sitting back in one's chair and leaning away from the client can imply escape, whereas sitting forward and leaning toward the client can imply intensity. Sitting with arms or legs crossed can imply guardedness or disengagement. Visible tension in the counselor's body can suggest nervousness, self-doubt, and discomfort with the process, but sitting with an open and relaxed posture communicates comfort with the process.

One of the more common nonverbal behaviors of counseling is the head nod. When used selectively, it communicates an acceptance or understanding of the client's message. Like most counseling skills, however, it can be overused and can thus lose its power to communicate; its overuse can even cross the line from effective to annoying. Similarly, an appropriate smile (not a grin) can communicate warmth and acceptance, but this can also be overused.

As individuals we fall somewhere on a continuum of very nonverbally expressive on one end to very hard to read on the other end. Unlike some behaviors, this characteristic appears to be less likely to change with training. If you are told that you are easy to read, you may want to be sure that what your clients are reading is what you intend. For those who are difficult to read, clients are more likely to "read in" something to explain what they see (and what they don't see). In either case, it is probably wise to check in on occasion and use words to supplement nonverbal behaviors so that misunderstandings are kept to a minimum.

Silence

Intentional silence is one of the most important skills a counselor can use. It goes without saying that without silence, your client won't have space to talk; however, silence is more than a convenience that provides the client with talk time—it is also a tool in the counselor's repertoire. Used judiciously, silence can communicate counselor expectation to the client; the message is, "I want you to talk." Silence can also induce mild anxiety in the client, and overly long silences can have the undesirable effect of inducing extreme self-consciousness, anxiety, or even resentment in a client. It is probably better to think of silences as 5- to 10-second pauses in conversation. Pauses have several potential effects, such as:

1. They can give the client an opportunity to think about and integrate a newly discovered insight or awareness.
2. They can be an invitation to continue a line of discussion or exploration.
3. They can communicate to the client the importance of taking some responsibility in the counseling relationship.

4. They can encourage the client to focus on self-exploration. (See Exercise I, Exploring Silence, at the end of this chapter.)

Cultural Factors

Researchers have also been interested in the multiple effects of nonverbal communication across cultures. The contribution that culture makes to nonverbal behavior is mixed. In the 1970s, much research was conducted on the meaning of nonverbal communication across cultures. Ekman (1973) concludes that there is a universality of facial expressions across cultures, but later work by Knapp (1978) reports that the meanings attached to specific nonverbal gestures was, in fact, culturally determined and not universal in nature. Counselors, then, must be aware that some of their nonverbal behaviors may be misunderstood and learn to check in with clients if they pick up any dissonance from their clients. It is also important for counselors to take responsibility and learn what they can about cultural nonverbal norms.

How different cultures respond to space and touch is another matter that has been widely studied. Research has found that cultural differences tend to be defined by comfort levels related to physical closeness and touch when communicating. Generally speaking, North American, northern European, and Australian communicators prefer greater interaction distances (3–5 feet) and less touch than many Latino, Middle Eastern, southern European, and Asian cultures, who are more comfortable with closer physical distances and physical touch (Barnland, 1975; Klopf, Thompson, Ishii, & Sallinen-Kuparinen, 1991; Sussman & Rosenfeld, 1982). Although research like this is somewhat helpful, we advise caution in applying these findings because of individual differences among cultural group members. (See Exercise II, Personal Space/Personal Comfort, at the end of this chapter.)

Summary

Now that we may have made you completely self-conscious, let's look at how all of this nonverbal insight plays out in the counseling session. First, awareness of and insight into the effect of nonverbal communication is crucial. Much is at play in those early moments of a counseling relationship, when silence, gestures, postures, and facial expressions are part of the client's hypersensitive awareness. Much that is communicated risks misinterpretation or miscommunication; consequently, the counselor's messages must be intentional and clear. Second, it is important to realize that nonverbal communication is your friend, not your enemy. It is a useful component in your creation of a comfortable, safe, and workable environment.

BASIC VERBAL SKILLS OF COUNSELING

Verbal behavior of counselors was an important area of study during the 1960s and 1970s. Using a variety of methodologies, researchers identified some 15 different types of counselor responses that were present in therapy sessions across different counseling theories (Hackney, 1974; Tepper & Haase, 1978; Zimmer & Anderson, 1968; Zimmer & Park, 1967; Zimmer, Wightman, & McArthur, 1970). Their effect was measured for impact on client verbal participation, degree of perceived counselor empathy, level of topic exploration, and other relevant counseling effects. Today, these counselor responses are still seen as essential counselor communication skills (Cormier & Hackney, 2012; Hill, 2014; Ivey, Ivey, & Zalaquett, 2014; Okun, 2015; Young, 2012). Each counselor response has an intended outcome in the interaction between counselor and client. A number of counselor verbal responses—minimal response, restatement, paraphrase, and clarification—can be classified as facilitating and act to return the topic focus to the client, much as the tennis player returns the ball to the opponent's side of the court. The result is to keep the focus on clients, their concerns, and their reactions.

Minimal Responses

Counselors communicate their involvement in a client's story in many ways, ranging from attentive expressions to brief statements, including the familiar "*OK*," "*mmm*," and similar minimal expressions. All serve to communicate the counselor's attentiveness or interest in what the client is saying. When used intermittently, they encourage the client to continue talking, but if they are overused, they become distracters. For example, in the following excerpt from a counseling session, the client is describing a discussion he had with his employer. The counselor listens and occasionally responds with a minimal response (noted in bold).

> CLIENT: I guess Mike was just having a bad day yesterday. As soon as I got to work he started in on me, **[mmm-hmm]** how I hadn't finished the material the day before, and how I was slowing up the project. **[Oh?]** Yeah, and I had done everything he had told me to do. I don't know what was going on, but he got over it later and apologized to me.

Restatement

The *restatement,* or repeating a phrase or thought uttered by the client, is the simplest response to the content of a client's message.

> CLIENT: I don't know what I would do if he stopped trying.
>
> COUNSELOR: You don't know what you would do.

Restating serves to emphasize a thought, to bring the client's attention to the statement, and perhaps even to challenge the client to reconsider what was just said. The restatement is particularly effective in response to an exaggerated or foreclosing statement by the client.
Consider the following statement:

> CLIENT: No matter how hard I try, I will never be happy with him.

What are some possible restatements you could make that would either mirror the client's hopelessness or would challenge the client's conclusion?

Restatement 1: No matter how hard you try.

Restatement 2: You'll never be happy.

Restatement 1 encourages the client to continue talking about her effort; restatement 2 invites the client to consider her predetermined future unhappiness.

Paraphrase

Rephrasing the client's response using the counselor's own choice of words is called a *paraphrase.* This rephrasing of the client's message neither adds to nor detracts from the client's meaning. Its effect is quite similar to the restatement, except that it uses the counselor's vocabulary rather than the client's. As a result, it communicates that the message has been (accurately) received, but avoids parroting what the client said. For example:

CLIENT: It's going to be a little tricky to leave work early tomorrow in order to go to the interview.

COUNSELOR: You're not sure about leaving work in order to try to get a new job.

Unlike the restatement, a paraphrase allows the client to modify the message if the counselor misunderstood the original statement, an equally important outcome. However, it also allows the client to hear his or her own message as someone else has heard it, and that often adds to the client's perspective.

The Question

The *question* is a statement beginning with "Who," "What," "How," "When," or "Where." There are two types of questions in the counselor's repertoire: the closed question and the open question. Questions (sometimes referred to as *probes*) achieve different results and are used in different situations.

CLOSED QUESTIONS.   *Closed questions* ask the client to respond with a minimal statement, usually yes or no, or a bit of information. It is the most overused and underproductive of all responses made by beginning counselors and is the primary reason why they can't get their clients to talk freely. After all, a closed question, such as, "Do you abuse drugs?" doesn't require elaboration. Consequently, when clients are peppered with closed questions, their tendency is to give a minimal response and wait for the counselor to come up with another question. This shifts complete responsibility to the counselor to make the session flow. However, the closed question is valuable in an intake interview, where specific information about the client is required. And occasionally, the counselor needs a specific bit of information to understand the client's narrative, in which case the closed question is also appropriate. (See Exercise III, "Recognizing Different Counselor Responses," at the end of this chapter.) Following are examples of closed questions typically used in a counseling session or intake interview (note the boldface probe in each question).

- **How long** have you been married?
- **When** did you and your husband separate?
- **Who** was your other counselor?
- **What** would be a good time to meet next week?
- **Do you** have difficulty sleeping?

OPEN QUESTIONS.   *Open* or *open-ended questions* seek elaboration without specifying precisely what information is being sought. These questions cannot be answered with a simple yes or no response. Counselors use open-ended questions to understand how the client perceives the problem, relationships, conditions, and so on. Examples of open-ended questions include

- What happens when you say that to her?
- How would you like your classmates to react to you?
- What are you doing when you get this feeling?
- How are things different when you get to work on time?

In addition to giving the counselor different kinds of information and insight into how the client perceives the world, the open question also teaches the client how to observe, how to process reactions, how behaviors are connected to feelings and thoughts . . . all important skills for clients to accrue.

Interjecting

Some clients appear to need someone to listen and that's all—or, at least, that's all that happens if the counselor doesn't know how to interrupt the client by interjecting oneself into the flow of the session. Although some counselors find this difficult to do because it appears "rude," we list it as a basic skill because without doing so, the session will be the client talking to the counselor's nonverbal expressions and mmm-hmm's. Please note that when interjecting is called for, it usually is because the client thinks he or she is doing what is expected. It's up to the counselor to teach the client what the counseling process is like.

There is no one way to interrupt. We've all developed some cues that we give out when we want our turn to speak. It is when these do not work with clients that we must learn how to stop the flow of words and interject. Comments such as, "I really want to be sure that I'm catching all that's important, so let me summarize what I've heard thus far," or, "I can understand how you are feeling overwhelmed; I'm feeling a bit overwhelmed right now too. Can we review highlights, and can I ask you some questions around some of what you've said?" Still, these only work if you can manage to get the client's attention. If that's a bigger task than you expected, share this with such clients and ask them to tell you how to interrupt them. It may be as obvious as a hand gesture. Although perhaps not what you are comfortable doing, this is still better than doing nothing and having your counseling time be little more than clients getting things off their chests.

Clarification

As already noted, communication occurs only when the message has been accurately perceived; otherwise, it is *mis*communication. Consequently, the counselor must sometimes seek confirmation from the client that what the counselor is hearing (decoding) is what the client is trying to communicate (encoding).

Clarifications seem like restatements, but their intention is more than communication of understanding and interest. Instead, they are phrased to solicit a confirmation or correction. The clarification often is initiated with a statement of the counselor's intent. For example, the counselor might say, "Let me see if I am following you accurately," "If I'm hearing you correctly, . . . ," or "I want to be sure I understand." Notice that the counselor is being careful not to assume the client's intent and is offering the response tentatively so the client is comfortable making a correction if necessary.

> Counselor: Before we go further, let me just be sure I'm understanding you. You want to say to Danielle that she should back off and give you some space, but if you do that, she may take it wrong, and you'd rather not say anything than to risk damaging the relationship. Is that right?

SUMMARY.   Basic verbal skills are frequently used components of the counselor's repertoire, especially at the beginning of the counseling relationship. Although very important, they must eventually be combined with more advanced skills to fully establish rapport, communicate empathy and positive regard, and begin building a working alliance with the client.

ADVANCED VERBAL SKILLS OF COUNSELING

Although we refer to these skills as *advanced,* we do not see them as difficult to learn. They are only advanced because they have more potential to move the counseling process forward. Advanced skills involve intentionality beyond that of facilitating discussion or soliciting information. These skills nudge the client toward self-exploration, gaining new insights, considering alternative perspectives, setting goals, and planning for change. In other words, they reflect the counselor's counseling plan as well as the client's immediate issues. The first of these counselor responses is the summary statement.

The Summary Statement

The *summary statement* typically follows a client discussion of events or circumstances. It may include content that the client has been discussing for 5 minutes or for an entire session. The obvious effect of the summary statement is confirmation that the counselor is following the client's narrative, but it also has more subtle effects. It can pull together aspects of the client's statements that reveal contradictions in the client's thinking, feelings, or assessments, or it can wrap up a discussion, permitting a transition to a new topic or concern. The summary is always selective—that is, the counselor is not trying to collect all details of the discussion. Rather, it focuses on, or highlights, aspects of the client's narrative.

> COUNSELOR: You've been describing a lot of reactions to your meeting with your probation officer. At first, you resented having to check in with him. But while you were waiting to see him, you talked yourself into a positive attitude that this was part of getting your life back on track. When you met, I think you're telling me that it was a major downer because, from your perspective, he didn't even seem mildly interested in you. Finally, after the meeting, you were mad at yourself for hoping that things could be better and that people would give you a second chance. [At this point, the counselor stops to let the client consider the implications of the emotional trip the client has put herself through.]

Reflections

Reflections are different from either restatements or paraphrases because they attempt to capture the essence of what the client is saying. Carl Rogers was a master at reflection. Although many of his responses to his clients appeared simple enough, they almost always reflected meaning that moved the client just a bit closer to the goal of self-actualization. It is because of the apparent simplicity of his approach that many beginning counselors mistakenly believe that it is the "easiest" of counseling approaches, not realizing how expert Rogers was at this technique.

No one expects you to demonstrate reflections in a manner that reminds anyone of Rogers—at least, not at first! Learning how to reflect either feeling or thought, however, is essential for counseling, because it assists clients in understanding themselves at a deeper level and perhaps how others may be experiencing them.

REFLECTION OF FEELING. A *reflection of feeling* is an attempt to help the client get in touch with affect that is often right below the surface. Even when the client is using emotional language, there may be other feelings that the counselor senses have not been explicit in the session. If the counselor reflects accurately, a deeper or clearer exploration of feeling may follow; however, if the counselor reflects inaccurately, the client can correct the counselor or the counselor often can sense that their comment is not resonating with the client. Rogers often used metaphor in his reflections, such as, "I get the sense of someone who is trapped in a dark room and can't find the door." Although no "feeling words" are used in this reflection, it conjures up someone who is feeling fear or even panic. Indeed, the picture of this reflection may be more powerful than the counselor saying, "You feel some panic in this situation."

CLIENT: I am just sick to death of their fighting. I get home from work and it's always chaos. It's not like I have anyone else to help me. I've told them that I can't take it anymore and they don't seem to care. Well, maybe the little one does, but not the others. I just can't take it anymore.

COUNSELOR: You sound pretty discouraged, even desperate. I get the picture of someone drowning with no lifeguard in sight.

REFLECTION OF CONTENT.   *Reflection of content* is different only in focus. The purpose of the content reflection is to uncover meaning that may be slightly beyond the reach of the client, but is embedded in what the client has been saying. Using the same client comment that we used for reflection of feeling, a reflection of content could be as follows:

COUNSELOR: You're a single parent and you have your limits. The kids just don't offer you the support that you expect.

We find that beginning counselors sometimes conflate reflections with interpretations. For this reason, we address interpretation next.

The Interpretation Response

Whereas the intention of a reflection is to offer the client a slightly different view (and hopefully one that adds clarity) to what they have said, the *interpretation* goes beyond what has been said and proposes additional meaning. The meaning might be suggested by the counselor or the counselor can ask the client to interpret the meaning. In using interpretation responses or requests, the counselor's intent is to take the client's awareness or understanding of a situation, person, or process and move it in a different direction or beyond the current level. This is considered an advanced communication response because it requires the counselor to reconceptualize the condition while at the same time remaining consistent with the details of the client's narrative—a demanding task. When the interpretation is counselor-initiated, it is framed as a possible meaning or a speculation that the client can accept, modify, or reject. Interpretation responses can be framed as questions or statements—for example:

CLIENT: When I try to talk to Nancy [daughter], she immediately flares up and pushes me away. It's so frustrating.

Possible Counselor-Initiated Interpretations:

- Is it possible that Nancy thinks it's time to become more independent?
- Perhaps Nancy is trying to be responsible and figure it out herself.
- Is it possible that you are coming on too strong because you are anticipating Nancy's reaction?

When the counselor asks the client to assign meaning, it is made in the form of a question.

COUNSELOR: What do you think is going on with Nancy when you initiate and she pushes away? What does it mean?

Clients may not be able to assign meaning at first, but as the topic is explored further, the counselor can again ask what meaning the client might read into the interaction.

Generally speaking, the interpretation response has four qualities or conditions that must be met:

1. It must be as logical an explanation as one that the client has rendered.
2. It must be potentially true.

3. It must change the perspective from a negative valence to a positive valence.
4. It must provide the client with a way of responding to the problem in a manner that effectively eliminates the problem.

It is our belief that interpretations should be used conservatively by new counselors; otherwise, they run the risk of attempting to "guess" at the reasons for particular client situations. That said, a well-timed interpretation that has come after an adequate amount of time has been spent listening and reflecting can be highly fruitful to the counseling process.

The Encouraging Response

The *encouraging response* is meant to be supportive, to suggest that the client has the skill or potential to do something, to feel a particular way, or to think in a different way. What makes this a more sophisticated verbal response by the counselor is how and when it is used. The most critical element is timing. A counselor should not suggest that the client could be different in some way when, in fact, the client is not prepared to be different; that only sets the client up for disappointment or failure; so, knowing that the client is ready or able to respond in a particular way is crucial. A second consideration is knowing that if the client responds in the way the encouragement suggests, the suggestion would make a positive difference for the client; therefore, it is important for you to know both that the client is ready and able to respond as the encouragement suggests, and that the suggestion would make a difference.

Encouraging responses are typically phrased as statements that imply or suggest that the client has the ability or potential to act in a different way. Here are some examples:

- You could ask her to accompany you to the doctor.
- I think you could manage that by yourself.
- Of course, you could consider changing your schedule.
- You are probably ready to take on some new responsibilities now.

In the following exchange, the client is considering a plan of action but reflects some uncertainty. The counselor offers encouragement in response.

> CLIENT: I've been thinking about looking for a different job, but then I worry if I will like it. Or if I will like the people as well. Or what if I take a new job, and they don't like me?
>
> COUNSELOR: You could deal with this if you had a pretty good idea of what jobs best fit your skills and interests.

The Confrontation or Challenge

Beginning counselors tend to avoid confronting a client because it deviates from what they have been taught is polite behavior; therefore, they fear that doing so might damage the relationship. If confrontation occurs too early in an emerging relationship, the effect could be negative. However, once the counselor has been found to be caring and trustworthy, clients are able to receive confrontation as a necessary part of the process. In fact, when a confrontation is rooted in a condition the client can recognize as true, it is often welcomed by the client.

The *confrontation* is effective in those instances when the client is experiencing but not acknowledging a condition, belief, or feeling that is part of the presenting problem. In other words, like everyone else, clients have blind spots in their thinking and experiencing. Those blind spots can become troublesome when they support or maintain dysfunctional thoughts and behavior. Blind spots can be recognized in the client's narrative through contradictions, missing logic, or lack of awareness. When a client speaks of her shyness but describes it to you in an outgoing manner, the moment for confrontation is present. If a client presents himself as unlikable but is surrounded by a support group, confrontation may be appropriate.

Often, the confrontation addresses the client's misinterpretation of others' behaviors or feelings. One of the most obvious opportunities for the counselor to confront is when the client is immobilized by a problem or doesn't see how to address a problem. Here are two examples of confrontations:

- Sheri, you keep telling me that Toni isn't your friend and that you don't trust her. Yet, once again, when the chips are down, Toni seems to be the one who is there for you. How do you make sense of that?
- To hear you, Greg, there is absolutely no way for you to be treated fairly in your family. Is it really that bleak? Is there no one who cares about you? (Obviously, the counselor only challenges in this way if he or she is convinced that there is indeed support for Greg in his family.)

Using Immediacy

Fritz Perls was instrumental in stressing the "here and now" in therapeutic situations (Perls, 1969/1976). His intent was to take the psychological noise that was shoved into the background and bring it into the foreground, where it could be addressed. Similarly, *immediacy* is the act of addressing what is observed directly by the counselor, but wouldn't be addressed in a social situation. Therefore, like confrontation, immediacy is difficult for counselors to learn because of the social mores it seems to violate. If you are talking to an acquaintance who appears to be edgy, you are not likely to say anything. In fact, we've learned that we might embarrass the person if we said something; we've even been taught to convince others that we didn't notice the behavior. Of course, this is all perfectly appropriate outside of counseling, but within counseling, what we observe is often best addressed. Cormier, Nurius, and Osborn (2013) identify three purposes that are served by counselor use of immediacy statements:

1. It brings out into the open something that you feel about yourself, the client, or the relationship that has not been expressed directly.
2. It may generate discussion or provide feedback about some aspects of the relationship or verbal interactions as they occur.
3. It is useful to facilitate client self-exploration and to keep the focus on the client or the relationship rather than on the counselor. (p. 166)

When to use immediacy is, of course, a judgment call, but speaking to the obvious in a way that invites honest sharing is usually a good idea. Jacobs, Masson, Harvill, and Schimmel (2012) refer to making internal thoughts external. So, if you find yourself thinking, "She's not herself today," or "I think my last comment was too direct and I pushed him away," it might be a good idea to address this openly. Another kind of immediacy is sharing one's own emotional reaction to the client and what the client is saying. What follows are some examples of counselors using immediacy.

- You know, Evie, I was a little nervous too wondering what you'd be like after last week. I was looking forward to seeing you. I just didn't know what to expect.
- Tom, something about you feels different today . . . new energy, or confidence, or something. Am I making it up, or are you in a better place than you've been lately?
- I know that you were pretty upset when Barbara left the agency and you were transferred to me. I decided to give it some time. If it's OK with you, I'd like to see where we are, because I still see you being careful with me and I worry that it's because you know I'm an intern and will be leaving at the end of June.

The Directive Response

Directive responses involve assignments to do or to think in a specified manner. The most frequent use of the directive response is when the counselor uses a homework assignment designed to help the client develop or strengthen a particular skill or thought response. It carries an instructional message, usually with a plan for implementing the instruction. Examples of the directive response include the following:

- Between now and our next session, I'd like you to keep a record of when and where you are each time you start feeling discouraged and down.
- This week, when you start feeling isolated and lonely, I want you to get away from your computer and go for a walk where other people are, maybe the library, or the park, or the grocery store.
- When you start to feel your anxiety rise, I want you to find a quiet place and use the relaxation exercises we recorded.

Providing Information

Counselors provide information primarily when information is missing that the client requires in order to act or think in a particular way. It is instructional in nature, but it is not giving advice. For example, the counselor may wish to suggest alternatives regarding relationships, actions, or plans; for example, it may involve information about referrals for services, sources for self-help materials, and career information. The giving of information is not frequently used in counseling because it sets the counselor up as an authority. Examples of information giving include the following:

- If you do a computer search for "hypertension," you probably could get some good information on reasonable activities.
- Relaxation exercises have been found to be of help for persons experiencing high anxiety.
- There's a class on effective parenting coming up that you might find helpful.

Summary

The nonverbal and verbal messages of counseling are a step beyond mere conversation; they reflect intentionality or purpose on the counselor's part. That purpose is determined by what the counselor believes is the client's current need(s) or by the goal or objective currently being addressed. Nonverbal counselor messages can either facilitate or inhibit the counseling atmosphere, whereas verbal responses have a more intentional role. Basic verbal responses are most common—heavily used early in the process— but they continue to be useful throughout the counseling relationship. Advanced verbal responses are tied to specific interventions or purposes and require greater skill in use, are heavily dependent on timing, and require good clinical judgment about when they are appropriate.

Table 2.1 summarizes the 16 responses described in this chapter and indicates how they relate to content of different topic domains in the counseling process. For example, the open-ended question, which is a basic verbal counseling skill, is useful in several ways: It can invite the client to explore feelings, thought processes, behavior patterns, or interpersonal relationships. The danger is that open-ended questions can be overused, so it is important that the counselor vary his or her responses. All 16 response categories are discussed in greater detail as we proceed through the chapters on counseling stages and interventions.

TABLE 2.1 Verbal Responses in Counseling Domains

Counselor Response	Affective Domain	Cognitive Domain	Behavioral Domain	Interpersonal Domain	Cautions
Minimal Reinforcer	Encourage client discussion	Encourage client discussion	Encourage client discussion	Encourage client discussion	Can be overused
Restatement	Bring focus to client feeling comments	Bring focus to client thought comments	Bring focus to client behavior comments	Bring focus to client relationship patterns	Can sound like parroting if overused
Paraphrase	Let client hear feelings differently	Let client hear thinking differently	Let client hear behaviors differently	Let client hear systems differently	Can be overused
Closed Question	Not as helpful with feeling domain	Obtain specific thought responses	Obtain specific behaviors/reactions	Obtain specific relationship data	Can be overused; keeps responsibility on counselor
Open Question	Explore feelings	Explore client thinking processes	Explore client behavior patterns	Explore client relationships	Should be used in combination with other responses
Interjection	Stops a spiraling report of feelings	Stops client litany of events	Stops distracting or unhelpful behaviors	Stops unhelpful interactions with counselor or others present	Must interject without chastening
Clarification	Seek to verify client feelings	Seek to verify client thinking	Seek to verify client actions/behaviors	Seek to verify client relationships	Must listen for client corrections
Summary	Help client connect feeling statements	Help client connect thoughts	Help client identify behavior patterns	Help client identify interpersonal patterns	Can have important missing elements
Reflection of Feeling	Can help client gain insight into feelings	Can give client insight into how feelings affect thoughts	Can give client insight into how feelings affect behavior	Can give client insight into how feelings affect relationships	Avoid interpretation; pace depth of reflection to client readiness
Reflection of Content	Can help client see relationship between thoughts and feelings	Can give client insight into thoughts	Can give client insight into how thoughts affect behavior	Can give client insight into how thoughts affect relationships	Avoid interpretation; reflection may miss the mark
Interpretation	Provide new or alternative meaning about feelings	Provide new or alternative meaning about thoughts	Provide new or alternative meaning about behaviors	Provide new or alternative meaning about relationships	Be cautious not to overinterpret

Basic Verbal Skills of Counseling

Advanced Verbal Skills of Counseling

	Feelings	Thoughts/Cognition	Behavior	Relationship	Limitations
Encouraging	Point out potential for feeling differently	Point out potential for thinking differently	Point out potential for acting differently	Point out potential for changing relationship	Can be unrealistic
Confrontation/ Challenge	Point out competing feelings	Point out irrational thoughts	Point out self-defeating behaviors	Point out ineffective relationship patterns	Can be introduced too soon; relies on working relationship between counselor and client
Immediacy	Addresses feelings in the present	Addresses thoughts in the present	Addresses behavior in the present	Addresses relationship between counselor and client(s) in the present	Should not be used only to confront; relies on safe atmosphere
Directive	Assignment to modify feeling reactions	Assignment to modify thought patterns	Assignment to modify behavior	Assignment to modify interaction patterns	Client must be ready to comply
Information Giving	Provide information/ resources having to do with feelings	Provide information/ resources having to do with cognition	Provide information/ resources having to do with behavior	Provide information/ resources having to do with relationships	Can be unhelpful if situation is misunderstood

Exercises

I. Exploring Silence

As a way to explore and expand your comfort with silence, have a conversation with a member of your class or a colleague. Discuss whatever you wish for about 10 minutes. The only ground rule is that each of you wait 5 to 15 seconds before responding to the other.

II. Personal Space/Personal Comfort

With a colleague, determine your personal space requirements. Begin a conversation standing (or sitting) about 10 feet apart. Move closer and continue talking. Move closer again. Keep moving closer until either of you becomes uncomfortable with the proximity. Then find the optimum space that accommodates personal comfort for both of you. Discuss the implications of this exercise with each other. Do you think your preferences are cultural? Gender-related? Age-related?

III. Recognizing Different Counselor Responses

In the following list of counseling responses, label each response using these categories:

O = Open-ended question   E = Encouraging
CL = Closed question   IG = Information Giving
CR = Clarifying response   IM = Immediacy
R = Restatement   C = Confrontation
P = Paraphrase   INT = Interpretation
IJ = Interjecting   D = Directive
S = Summary
RF = Reflection of feeling
RC = Reflection of Content

_____ 1. How would you respond if she asked . . . ?
_____ 2. Let me be sure I understand. You would like to change jobs, right?
_____ 3. You really wouldn't want to move to another city.
_____ 4. You could look up the cost-of-living index for Seattle.
_____ 5. I have a friend who lives in Bellingham, and she says that it isn't expensive.
_____ 6. How much would they pay you?
_____ 7. You say you want to move, but you aren't doing anything to make it happen.
_____ 8. Tonight, I want you to go to the library and look up Places Rated Almanac.
_____ 9. You seem to walk right up to the edge of making a decision and then you back off. I wonder what that's about. Do you have any idea?
_____ 10. It feels to me like you've gotten less comfortable talking about this in the last few minutes.
_____ 11. Can I stop you there? I'm getting lost in some of the details.
_____ 12. This is all more terrifying than you expected.

Share your responses with a class member, and resolve any differences you might have with your ratings.

IV. The Counseling Session Typescript

Record a 10-minute counseling role-play with another class member. Transfer all comments made by both you and the client to a typescript of the session, then label each of your responses according to the type of response it is. Note the effect that different responses have on the client's response.

Feedback for Exercise III, Recognizing Different Counselor Responses

III. Recognizing Different Counselor Responses

1. O
2. CR
3. R or P (depending on client statement)
4. E
5. IG
6. CL
7. C
8. D
9. INT
10. IM
11. IJ
12. R or P or RF (depending on client statement)

Discussion Questions

1. Discuss the conditions that make a difference between *miscommunication* and *successful communication*.
2. Some counselor responses ask the client to elaborate, whereas others lead the client to a deeper level of exploration. Identify two responses that do both.
3. Following is a client narrative from a counseling session. At each point where the typescript has an asterisk [*], provide a counselor response and identify what type of response it is.

When I went back home last weekend, my parents told me that they had decided to separate and maybe divorce [*] and it really threw me. [*] Then they watched me the entire weekend, I guess to see how I was reacting to them. [*] Anyhow, I just pulled in and didn't give them anything to react to. I couldn't. I didn't know what to say. [*] I mean, I knew that they had been having some trouble, but I never expected this. So they just unloaded and what was I to do with that? [*] What would you do? [*] By Saturday night, I had to get out, get away from the house, because all I was doing was staying in my room and crying, [*] so I called a friend and we went out and really got wasted. I haven't been so drunk in a long time. [*] Then Sunday morning, I was, like, really feeling it, and that's when they chose to try to have a conversation with me about their reasons for deciding to separate. I mean, I just couldn't hack it and so I packed up and left early to come back to school.[*]

Discuss your choice of responses with a class member. Together, consider what other responses might have been appropriate, and how the discussion might change if different responses were used.

MyCounselingLab® Assignment

Go to Video Library under Video Resources on the MyCounselingLab site for your text and search for the following clips:
- **Video Example: Gina: Individual—Childhood Experiences**
- **Video Example: Example of Active Listening in Session**

- **Video Example: Youth: WDEP: Wants**

As you view these videos, how many different counselor nonverbal and verbal responses can you identify and label?

3

The Essential Structure of Counseling

PURPOSE OF THIS CHAPTER

The overall objective of this chapter is to present the structure of the counseling process and how that structure helps you determine what the counselor should be doing. The beginning point of counseling is a time when you and your client must decide, both independently and mutually, whether a working relationship is feasible. Beyond that decision, you must reach agreement on what the problem is, how counseling might assist in changing problematic circumstances, what counseling activities would help produce that change, and finally, when counseling should conclude. The chapter then examines this process from the client's perspective, which will interface with your own perspective but will be unique as well.

Considerations as You Read This Chapter

■ How do you approach new relationships? Do they make you nervous? Do they offer excitement?

■ What do you suppose other people observe in you when they are meeting you for the first time?

■ Put yourself in the role of a client meeting your counselor for the first time. What does the counselor look like? What if the counselor was very different from what you expected? What differences might be interesting or even pleasing to you? What differences might be a barrier, at least initially? Can you explain these reactions?

■ How much structure do you prefer in most situations? What type of structure do you tend to need in new situations? What kinds of structure make you comfortable in the counseling relationship? How can you accommodate your client's needs for structure if they are different from your own?

For many years, counseling was viewed as a process that did not lend itself to concrete analysis. For this reason, some people began to think of counseling as having indefinable, almost mystical, qualities. In the 1970s, through the work of Robert Carkhuff, Allen Ivey, Stanley Strong, and others, this mystical character began to disintegrate and be replaced by more specific explanations of what counseling entails. Since that breakthrough, counseling has taken on a much more defined character.

In this chapter, we consider how counselors and clients meet and begin to establish understandings that gradually evolve into a meaningful and productive therapeutic relationship.

These instrumental elements of counseling and the skills indigenous to them are presented as a conceptual base for the chapters that follow.

THE COUNSELING PROCESS

Counseling is often described as a *process*. The implicit meaning of this label is a progressive movement toward an ultimate conclusion, that conclusion being the resolution of whatever precipitated the need for help. This movement may be described as a series of stages through which the counselor and client move, including the following:

Stage 1   *Assessing* or defining the presenting problem and initiating a working relationship.

Stage 2   Identifying and setting *goals* while maintaining a working relationship.

Stage 3   Choosing and initiating *interventions* while maintaining a working relationship.

Stage 4   Planning and implementing *evaluation* and *termination.*

Each stage leads logically to the next subsequent stage—that is, one must establish the reason that the client has sought or been referred to a counselor before counseling goals are established. The process is not totally linear, however. It is not uncommon to have to retrace one's steps to a prior stage when new material emerges that affects the previous stage. Therefore, a possible counseling experience might look like this: assessment ⇨ goal setting ⇨ interventions ⇨ goal setting ⇨ interventions ⇨ assessment ⇨ goal setting ⇨ interventions ⇨ termination.

Even when stages are not revisited, each becomes part of the next stage. That is, once assessment and establishing a relationship are accomplished and the counselor is attending to goal setting and maintaining the relationship, assessment remains open to refinement under the light of setting concrete goals. Whether counselor and client must do a full return to assessment or simply clarify the issue at hand depends on what becomes apparent during goal setting that was not apparent before. Figure 3.1 is a visual depiction of the essential structure of counseling.

Establishing a Positive Working Alliance

Before we discuss the first "stage" of counseling, we want to introduce a concept that is the foundation for any successful counseling process and that is the therapeutic working alliance. Bordin (1979) proposed a three-factor model for thinking about the working alliance that is still used (and researched) today. Bordin proposed that for counseling to be successful, there must be an agreement between therapist and client on goals and the tasks (interventions) to meet those goals. The third essential element of the working alliance is a positive emotional bond between the counselor and the client. At this point, we have considerable evidence of the importance of the working alliance for successful counseling outcomes (e.g., see Norcross & Wampold, 2011). So strong is the empirical evidence that Castonguay, Constantino, and Holtforth (2006) assert that

> *Empirically, the alliance appears to be the most frequently studied process of change . . . . Clinically, the alliance occupies such an important place in our conceptualization of what good therapy entails that not paying attention to its quality during practice . . . could be viewed as unethical.* (p. 271)

What Bordin referred to as establishing an *emotional bond* with the client is more frequently referred to as *establishing a positive relationship* or *building rapport.* Unlike the stages of counseling, a positive relationship between counselor and client must be evident from start to finish. Therefore, we begin discussion of the role and importance of a positive relationship in

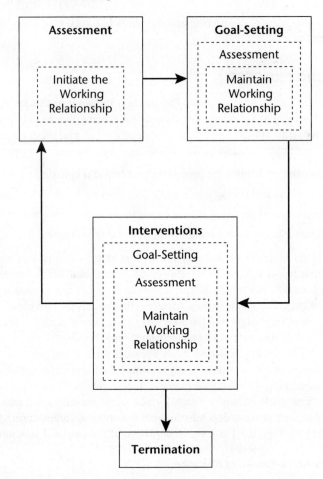

FIGURE 3.1 Stages in the Counseling Process

what follows. Second, as we discuss each stage of counseling, we briefly comment on relationship dynamics for that stage. Finally, we devote Chapter 4 to the use of counseling skills to build and maintain a positive working relationship with the client.

The term *relationship* has many meanings, including the ties between two people in love, kinship within a family, the bond between close friends, and the understanding that can develop between humans and animals. In the counseling setting, *relationship* takes on a specific meaning: When the counselor establishes rapport with a client, the relationship includes factors such as respect, trust, psychological comfort, and shared purpose. *Rapport* refers to the psychological climate that emerges from the interpersonal contact between you and your client. Consequently, good rapport sets the stage for the client's positive psychological growth, whereas poor rapport leads to undesirable or even counterproductive outcomes.

Obviously, this psychological climate can be affected by several factors, including your personal and professional qualifications and the client's interpersonal history and anxiety state—in other words, even the best-trained and best-adjusted counselor still faces a variety of challenges when meeting a new client. Many of these preexisting conditions can be anticipated. For example, few people like the prospect of asking others for assistance; thus, when people are forced to admit to themselves that they need help or feel they have been forced by others to do so, they approach the situation with two sets of feelings: (1) "I guess I need help and will feel better when I get it," and (2) "I wish I weren't here." This conflict is quite common in the early stages of counseling, and is particularly evident in the assessment phase.

Other preexisting client conditions relate to the client's previous experience with sharing personal information or interacting with authority figures, with older persons, with the opposite sex, with people of very different cultural backgrounds, and with other mental health professionals. In Chapter 1, we refer to some of these factors within the context of interpersonal attraction, trustworthiness, competence, and sensitivity to and understanding of cultural factors in oneself and others. The culturally or psychologically sensitive client may read your nonverbal and verbal messages and make inferences about these qualities. These first impressions influence rapport building and may need to be reexamined later, when you and your client have reached a more comfortable level with each other.

Sometimes these interpersonal reactions can assume overriding importance and may influence or even control the process of counseling. When this happens, professionals refer to the psychological dynamic as *transference* or *countertransference*. *Transference* occurs when the client associates certain qualities with the counselor. For example, if the counselor's demeanor reminds the client of his or her nurturing mother, demanding boss, or bigoted neighbor, the client may decide that the counselor is like that person, or, in extreme cases of transference, is that person. Transference can be either positive (favorable comparison) or negative (unfavorable comparison). *Countertransference*, which we refer to briefly in Chapter 1, describes the same psychological condition, except it is the counselor who is associating imagined qualities with the client. This might seem less likely, but in fact, it is not uncommon.

Assessing the Problem and Initiating a Positive Working Relationship

Assessment is a rather sterile word for an obvious fact—clients seek, are referred, or even mandated to counseling for a reason, and that reason often has layers. For example, "I need to get sober" sounds pretty straightforward. However, the conditions that have maintained substance abuse, the barriers to a healthier lifestyle, the individual and environmental resilience for each client—all these make assessment more complicated (and more interesting). One outcome goal is still the same, that is, sobriety; however, the counseling process to get there can only be successful if the counselor has conducted a careful assessment at the outset and is open to refining the assessment as the client becomes better known.

In a similar vein, Seligman (2004) proposes that the assessment process should be a way of recognizing the importance and uniqueness of each person, a way of saying to the person, "You are special, and I want to get to know you and understand why you are the way you are." In actual practice, it is important to assess problems in more than one way to avoid the constraints of personal bias, theoretical encapsulation, or a stereotyping of particular problems. This also includes thinking of the problem in the client's social and cultural context as a way of manifesting Seligman's advice.

Other terms used for assessment are *problem identification* or *diagnosis*. The problem with the latter term is that it is often driven by third-party payers and is a particular classification of symptoms that can shut down the assessment process. We encourage counselors to remain open to the assessment process even if a diagnosis has been established. Said differently, diagnoses are important because they guide treatment; however, they are not necessarily the end of the assessment process.

Assessment is not independent of counselors and clients as individuals. First, assessment reflects the counselor's theoretical and philosophical view of human problems. Second, assessment depends on the conditions present in the client's situation and the counselor's understanding of those conditions. And third, assessment depends on the client's cultural frame of reference and the conditions that frame of reference imposes on the client's worldview. (See Section E, Evaluation, Assessment and Interpretation, ACA Code of Ethics, 2014, http://www.counseling.org/docs/ethics/2014-aca-code-of-ethics.pdf?sfvrsn=4.)

Likewise, client problems may be conceptualized in different ways: as needs ("Something is missing in my life and its absence is disturbing the way my life is unfolding"); stressors ("Something unpleasant has entered my life and its presence is producing distress and distraction"); life conditions ("Conditions outside my control are limiting my potential happiness and success in life"); misinterpretations ("I am told that the way I am thinking about my life limits my alternatives"); dysfunctional social patterns ("I am a worse person with some people than I am with others, and it is a source of distress and unhappiness"); or, more likely, some combination of these factors. Counseling theories tend to classify these client conditions as affective, behavioral, cognitive, or systemic in origin. In other words, the client's problems emerge from emotional sources, undesirable behavioral contingencies, cognitive misrepresentations of reality, or systemic/contextual contingencies. Of course, problems rarely sit in one of these categories exclusively; theories, however, assist counselors by giving them an entry point from one of these major sources. In addition, despite where problems originate, they may manifest as feelings, worries, undesirable consequences, fear, missing or unsatisfactory interpersonal relationships, or unfair discrimination (see Chapter 5).

At first, assessment is an information-collecting time. You should open all your communication channels to receive information that the client is communicating. Initially, you may see no patterns and no meaning to the information. As you continue to work with the client, however, patterns emerge, and you begin to understand how the client perceives and tries to affect reality. You also begin to see your client in the larger context of his or her environment, social setting, or world of relationships. And as the subtleties become increasingly obvious, either by their repetition or by their inconsistencies, you begin to recognize how you can help your client.

There are many views concerning how assessment should be conducted. Our view is that you should have some blueprint to follow. Otherwise, the amount of detail begins to overwhelm the process, and you either overlook important information to solicit and consider or you become distracted from your purpose, which is to determine just what the problem is before you begin to set goals for counseling. In Chapter 5, we offer an approach to assessment that is widely used in clinical settings.

The process of clinical assessment involves several specific skills, including observation, inquiry, making associations among facts, recording information, and forming hypotheses or clinical hunches. *Observation* includes

- Taking notice of the client's general state of anxiety or discomfort
- Establishing some sense of the client's cultural context
- Noting behaviors that suggest either emotional or physical dysfunctions
- Hearing the manner in which the client frames or alludes to his or her problems (e.g., some tend to diminish whereas others inflate aspects of a problem)
- Noting verbal and nonverbal patterns

What may appear to be an insignificant detail at the moment can prove to be part of a significant pattern over time. Thus, observation—mental attentiveness to the persona of the client—is a significant component of the assessment process.

Inquiry is equally important. Beginning counselors have a tendency to ask a lot of initial questions but few follow-up questions, whereas experienced counselors pursue certain topics in much greater detail, for example, issues related to health, medication, feelings of despair or depression, positionality, self-destructive thoughts, and interpersonal conflicts. *Inquiry* is the skill of asking for the finer points, the details behind the event, or the information that provides the meaning to an event or condition. Open-ended questions explore processes; closed questions provide specifics. Both of these important inquiry tools are discussed in Chapter 2.

Collected information must somehow be organized and recorded. Some counselors take notes as they acquire information, and others record sessions. Some do neither, but allow time immediately following the session to write down observations and impressions. The recording of information is a disciplined process. If recording is not done systematically and promptly, information is lost, and therefore useless. It is a common counselor lament that information previously given is unavailable because it was not recorded promptly.

When the counselor uses observation and inquiry to collect information related to the client's presenting problem, the result is a substantial quantity of material. The more observant the counselor is, the greater the amount of data that is collected. Somehow, this information must be synthesized so it is usable. This synthesis is conducted within a context. The context may be a counseling theory, or it may simply be the counselor's view of life. Whatever the case, the process involves associating facts and events, constructing possible explanations for events, and making educated (or intuitive) guesses. This assimilation process condenses a large quantity of information into a more usable form. These hypotheses, hunches, and educated guesses become the foundation for the next stage—identifying and setting counseling goals. At this time, it is vital that you incorporate multicultural perspectives into your assessment. Early in our understanding of the importance of cultural data, Pedersen (1991) cautioned, "Behavior [or feelings, or cognitions, or social systems are] not data until and unless [they are] understood in the context of the person's culturally learned expectations" (p. 9). You might ask the client, "What do you think the problem is?" or, "How do you think your family would explain your problem?" or even, "Is this a common problem among your family and friends?" These simple questions often elicit the most important information, especially if followed by questions that seek the meaning of events from the client's cultural position. It is surprising that counselors often fail to ask such contextualizing questions. We explore the assessment process more fully in Chapter 5.

INITIATING A POSITIVE WORKING RELATIONSHIP DURING ASSESSMENT. From the very onset of counseling, assessment is taking place. Similarly, from the outset of counseling, the counselor is establishing a working relationship. Skillful counselors develop a self-congruent style for meeting clients—a style that reflects both the counselor's personal qualities and counseling experience. Even though there is no set formula for establishing rapport, some guidelines and skills are associated with this stage of counseling.

The relationship begins with adequate social skills. Introduce yourself. Hear the client's name and remember it. Invite the client to sit down and see to it that he or she is reasonably comfortable. Address the client by name. If he or she appears highly anxious, initiate some social conversation and watch to see if the anxiety begins to dissipate. Notice nonverbal behavior and use it to try to understand the client's emotional state. Invite the client to describe his or her situation that has led this person to counseling. Allow the client time to respond. This behavior is often described as *attending* or *active listening*. It communicates to the client that you are interested in the person and in what she or he has to say, and that you will try to understand both the spoken and the unspoken message in the communication.

Just as assessment is rarely done in a single session, the working relationship is not established in a single contact. During early sessions, clients become comfortable with you and begin to accept you into their more private world of thoughts and feelings. This condition represents the initial phase of therapeutic relationship building. At this time especially, consistency is an important quality. Your behaviors, your attitudes and opinions, your promptness and attentiveness to detail, and your acknowledgment of the client's personal and cultural realities—all may be noted by the client. If you vary from session to session in these details, the client may find you less predictable and may find it more difficult to become comfortable with you. Equally important is your sensitivity to cultural similarities and dissimilarities between you and the client. It is a time for you to be hypersensitive to the many legitimate ways people can be different from you.

Although it is not the same as friendship, the counseling relationship shares some qualities with good friendships, and this may prove confusing to some clients. Sometimes the counselor may also find this aspect of relationship to be problematic. This is primarily a boundary issue and a balancing act. If you place too much emphasis on being professional, you may find that the role doesn't fit what you feel about yourself or about your client, and thus lacks authenticity. At the other end of the spectrum is the temptation to be yourself fully and compromise the professional character of the relationship that is so important in facilitating client change. Finding a balance on this continuum is one of the early challenges in building a therapeutic alliance. Poor boundaries established during the assessment stage compromises all stages that follow. (For ethical guidelines regarding boundaries, see ACA Code of Ethics, 2014, Section A.6 Managing and Maintaining Boundaries and Professional Relationships, found online at www.counseling.org/resources/aca-code-of-ethics.pdf.)

Finally, note that some clients make forming a positive working relationship difficult. Mandated clients may especially be aloof, defensive, or even rude or hostile. In this case, we suggest two primary rules of thumb: (1) Do not react predictably—that is, do not get angry or show frustration. Rather, keep attempting to empathize with the client's situation and to communicate interest in the client; (2) Do not allow yourself to be abused. This is an example of "What we allow, we teach."

In summary, initiating a positive relationship does not happen before or after assessment, but during the assessment process. This might make this the most challenging stage of counseling, because counselors must attend equally to two vitally important tasks. Our recommendation, therefore, is to take it slowly and not rush to goal setting before the client is known adequately by you and you are trusted adequately by the client.

Setting Goals and Maintaining a Positive Working Relationship

Setting goals is extremely important to the success of counseling, and yet some clients and even some counselors are resistant to this stage of the process. The act of setting a goal involves making a commitment to a set of conditions, a course of action, or an outcome. Sometimes the highly stressed or disoriented client may find goal setting difficult to do. Even in this situation, the goal ultimately becomes one of setting goals!

Why are goals so important? The best answer is a simple one: Goals are set in order to know how well counseling is working and when counseling should be concluded. Isn't it enough to let the client decide these questions? Yes and no. The client is an important source of information and reaction to counseling; however, because clients may not be aware of the relationships of some of their behaviors to a multitude of consequences, it is only with the counselor's assistance that goals are identified that have the power to get the client where they want to go.

To this extent, goals are also important as a sort of teaching process. Some of the problem for some clients is that they are ambiguous about how to get from one place to another. For example, they may say that they keep finding themselves in abusive relationships; however, they have not yet seen a way clear of this pattern except to "hope" that the next relationship will be different. After a thorough assessment, one goal may be to become more assertive in non-intimate relationships so as develop one's interpersonal style *before* the next possible intimate relationship presents itself. A similar progression is appropriate for clients who are targets of unfair and discriminatory behavior of others. The goal isn't to cope or to hope, but to determine what new skills are needed that allow one to advocate for oneself.

In short, the process of setting goals is mutually defined by the counselor and client. The counselor has the advantage of greater objectivity, training in normal and abnormal behavior, and experience in the process. The client has the advantage of intensive experience with the problem and its history, potential insights, and awareness of personal investment in change. Thus, the client must be involved in the thinking as well as the decisions about what should happen.

The skills involved in goal setting are basically threefold: First, the counselor must be able to translate the client's goal into something that can be measurable down the road. As alluded to earlier, the counselor must be able to take something nebulous and help the client consider more concrete outcomes that help both counselor and client measure progress. This process does not reject the clients' goals; rather, it offers a map to help clients see how different aspects of their lives are connected. For example, a client may say that he or she wants to have higher self-esteem. With the counselor's help (and after careful assessment), the client may be able to identify those conditions that maintain a low self-esteem. These, then, become the targets for goal setting, and if adequate progress can be made, higher self-esteem should follow.

The second skill involves differentiation among ultimate goals, intermediate goals, and immediate goals. Most people think in terms of ultimate goals (e.g., "When I grow up . . . ," "When I graduate from college . . . ," "When I get sober . . . ," "When my boat comes in . . ."). But if a person is to accomplish ultimate goals, he or she must be able to think in terms of intermediate goals ("In the next six months, I plan to . . .") and immediate goals ("I will do the following things tomorrow: . . ."). Intermediate and immediate goals provide the strategies necessary to accomplish ultimate goals and are the real vehicle for change in counseling.

The third skill of the goal-setting process involves teaching clients how to think realistically in intermediate and immediate terms—in other words, it may be necessary for the counselor to teach clients how to set goals that are attainable. The negligent parent will certainly be set up for disappointment if she believes that one good encounter with her children will erase years of neglect. A common role for counselors, especially those working with clients with limited impulse control, is to prepare them for incremental progress and support them through their disappointment when change is slow. For this parent, her immediate goal may be to call her child at the same time for five days in a row. In Chapter 6, we discuss ways in which you can use these three sets of skills to help clients set realistic goals for counseling.

Finally, it should be emphasized that counseling goals are never chiseled in stone. Goals can be altered when new information or new insights into a problem call for change. Sometimes a goal is identified inappropriately and must be dropped. It is important to remember that the major function of goals is to provide direction to the counselor and the client.

MAINTAINING A POSITIVE WORKING RELATIONSHIP DURING GOAL SETTING. In the counseling setting, goal setting is where the proverbial rubber meets the road. Just as a boat isn't really tested until it hits the water, the working relationship between counselor and client isn't really tested until it's time to move from assessment to goal setting. Asking clients to commit to goals can stimulate all sorts of transference and countertransference reactions. Internally, the client may be experiencing feelings that could be attached to the following words if they were adequately aware: "You're just like my father. You only approve of me if I do what you want me to do!" On the counselor's side, the countertransference might look like this if it had words: "You're just like other failed relationships I've had. Everything is just fine until it's time to commit."

What counselors must realize and prepare for is that moving to goal setting introduces a new vulnerability into the process for the client. Therefore, discussions should be as empathic and attuned to what is going on for the client as were the first minutes of the first session. Reflections of feeling and immediacy statements can be important. The counselor's objective is to communicate to the client that he or she understands the vulnerability and is committed to provide the necessary support to help the client through it. Usually, this is enough. Without it, goal setting and the stages that follow are in jeopardy.

Initiating Interventions and Maintaining a Positive Working Relationship

There are different points of view concerning what a good counselor should do with clients. These viewpoints are primarily related to different counseling theories. As you may be aware from Chapter 1, there are a variety of counseling theories, each of which can be used by counselors to organize information, define problems, set goals, and select intervention strategies. For example, a cognitive behavioral counselor intervenes by introducing conditions that invite cognitive dissonance or disrupt static cognitive states. The multicultural counselor uses a variety of approaches and intervenes by understanding the client's cultural milieu and helping the client take charge of his or her life within that milieu (Ivey, D'Andrea, & Ivey, 2012). Thus, all counselors, regardless of theoretical orientation, have a therapeutic plan that they follow, a plan that is related to the assessment of the presenting problem, to their view of human nature and change processes, and to the resulting goals that have been agreed upon.

The real issue in talking about interventions is change and how it occurs. The whole object of counseling is to initiate and facilitate desirable change. Thus, when you and your client are able to identify desirable goals or outcomes, the next logical question is, "How do we accomplish these goals?" In Chapters 8 through 11, we discuss specific types of interventions used in counseling. For the moment, let's consider briefly the process a counselor goes through in identifying counseling interventions based on the assessment and goal setting process.

Having defined the problem and set a goal, the first thing you should do is ask clients what solutions or remedies they have already tried. Most of the time, clients are able to describe one or more things they have done that were not productive or only minimally successful in alleviating the problem. This information not only saves you from suggesting alternatives that will be rejected, it also gives you a sense of clients' past efforts to remedy difficulties and clients' resourcefulness as problem solvers. Occasionally, clients report that something they attempted did work, but for one reason or another, they discontinued the remedy. Client-induced interventions that were temporarily effective can sometimes be modified and made more effective. Such answers might also broaden your definition of the problem to include clients' inability to stay with a solution until it succeeded.

Assuming all client-induced interventions have been ineffective, the next step is to relate goals to interventions, depending on the character of the goal. Goals to alleviate problems that appear to be a result of how a client is viewing a life situation may be defined as cognitively determined goals. This suggests that interventions directed toward cognitive change should be considered. If the goal is related to the client's social environment (e.g., family, work, friends, community), then interventions designed to alter interdependent social systems should be considered. If the goal is to address emotional states such as hurt, sadness, or anger, then it may be affectively based, in which case interventions that facilitate affective disclosure and exploration should be included. However, if the goal relates to the client's actions or efforts to affect others, the goal is behaviorally based. Then the most effective interventions may be designed to help clients achieve more successful behaviors. The intervention strategies described in Chapters 8 through 11 are grouped around these dimensions of client problems. Chapter 8 examines affective interventions, Chapter 9 presents cognitive interventions, Chapter 10 addresses interventions for behavioral change, and Chapter 11 explores interventions designed to bring about system change.

At this point in the counseling process, your own theoretical preferences will most certainly emerge (although it is more likely that they have emerged during earlier stages). We all tend to have a preferred lens for viewing life. One person might emphasize the importance of feelings; another may view life as a behavioral to-do list; someone else may see the cultural implications of most situations; and yet another may see life as a set of challenges to be thought out and planned for. Although these do not appear to be theoretical, they are. We have found consistently that students who favor the feelings world also identify with humanistic theories, and those who identify with thinking out problems prefer the cognitive theories. There is nothing wrong with this, except that problems are rarely confined to a specific theory; rather, a problem usually can be assessed through several theoretical lenses. Similarly, clients have a habitual perspective for dealing with their problems, which may be why their solutions consistently miss the mark.

Choosing the right intervention is often a process of adaptation. Not all interventions work with all clients, or as well as one might predict. Sometimes the "perfect" intervention turns out to be perfectly awful. It is important that you approach selection of interventions judiciously and be prepared to change strategies when the intervention of choice is not working. This process is similar to the treatment of medical problems. When one treatment does not produce the desired response, the practitioner should have an alternative treatment in reserve or reevaluate how the problem is defined.

The four skills related to initiating interventions are

1. Competency in using a specific intervention
2. Knowledge of appropriate uses of a specific intervention
3. Knowledge of typical responses to that type of intervention
4. Observational skills related to the client's response to the intervention

Developing the skills necessary to use different interventions requires that the counselor be able to practice in safe surroundings under expert supervision. Typically, this kind of practice occurs in a counseling practice course or supervised clinical field practice. Interventions can be deceptively more difficult to use than they appear. Counselors who try interventions on clients without the benefit of supervised practice may do more harm than good.

The counselor must also know how clients normally react to a specific intervention. Usually, this is expressed in terms of a range of typical reactions. The object is to recognize the abnormal reaction, the unpredictable response, the result of which might intensify the problem rather than alleviate it. For example, the "empty chair" (discussed in Chapter 8) is a gestalt technique often used to help clients recognize and expand their awareness of alternative feelings or reactions. It can be a powerful technique, one that sometimes provides access to hidden and possibly frightening feelings. Occasionally, this technique unlocks an overwhelming amount of emotion for the client. In this case, the counselor must be able to recognize that the client's reaction is more than the typical response to this intervention.

This kind of dramatic reaction is, however, more rare than the alternative, which is a nebulous reaction because the intervention is used without adequate skill. Interventions are like playing musical pieces. They have a tempo and particular notes that should be emphasized. When they are presented and executed with skill, something happens that the counselor can evaluate. Whether the outcome is reaching or partially reaching a goal or moving the counseling process back to the assessment stage, the intervention has done its work. Prior to suggesting interventions that fall in the four major theoretical categories in Chapters 8 through 11, we offer more detail about the selection of interventions in Chapter 7.

MAINTAINING A POSITIVE WORKING RELATIONSHIP WHILE INITIATING INTERVENTIONS. By the time interventions are introduced, there is an assumption of a fairly solid working alliance between the counselor and client. In fact, as interventions require clients to put in additional effort or take risks, they are unlikely to be successful if the therapeutic relationship is weak. Still, even though the relationship may be adequate, counselors must attend to it when introducing interventions. Just as people may balk in our personal relationships if they feel we are taking them for granted, clients too need us to acknowledge that interventions may be hard or scary or inconvenient, and so forth. Obviously, interventions should be explained and clients must agree to them prior to implementation, and perhaps most importantly, clients should not be shamed if they are unable to complete or engage in an intervention. Rather, counselors must communicate that their relationship is strong enough to adjust to such bumps in the road. An intervention failure is a time for everyone to regroup, reevaluate, and move forward. It should be noted that this process in and of itself is often highly therapeutic, because clients may not have been given support in the past when they failed. By contrast, the strong working alliance between counselor and client should offer a healthy combination of accountability and support.

Planning Termination, Evaluation, and Follow-Up

It is difficult for beginning counselors to think of termination, because they are so much more concerned with how to conduct counseling that ending the process seems a distant problem. However, all counseling has as its ultimate aim the successful termination of the client. Furthermore, counseling often must end without a successful resolution (e.g., end of an intern's semester; end of mandated treatment days). Whether termination is ideal or much less so, let's consider the significance and subtleties of the termination process and what is realistically in the power of the counselor to control.

How does a counselor terminate a counseling relationship without destroying the gains that have been accomplished? When done optimally, it must be done with sensitivity, with forethought, and by degree. As the client begins to accomplish the goals that have been set, it becomes apparent that a void is being created. The temptation is to set new goals, create new activity, and continue the counseling process. Eventually, however, the client begins to realize that the original purpose for seeking counseling no longer supports the process. At this point, a creative crisis occurs for the client.

Long before the client reaches this awareness, the counselor should be recognizing the signs, anticipating the creative crisis, and laying the groundwork for a successful termination. As a general rule, the counselor should devote as many sessions to the active terminating process as were devoted to the assessment process. This is what is meant by *termination by degree.* When it is apparent that the counseling relationship may not last more than a few more sessions, it is time for the counselor to acknowledge that the process will end in the near future. This can be done simply by saying, "I think we are going to be finished with our work soon."

It is not uncommon for an early acknowledgment of termination to provoke denial or even a temporary crisis. Up to this point, the client may not have been thinking about facing his or her problems alone. If the client denies, allow it—denial is part of the recovery process and will dissipate. However, if the counselor resists the denial by assuring the client that he or she is much stronger, it may only intensify the crisis. It is important to remember that the client must get used to this new thought. In succeeding sessions, the opportunity may arise to introduce the thought again. Gradually, most clients come around, begin to let self-resourcefulness fill the void, and ultimately "decide" that counseling can end soon.

Occasionally, clients need a bit of security to take with them even though they feel ready to terminate. This can be accomplished by making a follow-up appointment 6 weeks, 3 months, or even 6 months in advance. It may be a good idea to ask clients to decide whether they feel the need to keep the appointment as the date approaches. If they do not, they can call and cancel and let the counselor know that they are doing well. However, it is also important to communicate to clients that if new counseling needs arise, they should feel free to call before the appointment date. (See Section A.11, Termination and Referral, ACA Code of Ethics, 2014, www.counseling. org/docs/ethics/2014-aca-code-of-ethics.pdf?sfvrsn=4.)

We must acknowledge that what we have described is termination that is orderly and more or less satisfying; clearly, this is not how termination always plays out. In some cases, termination is only partially a useful concept. For example, school counselors may end individual or group counseling with a student, but the student knows that the counselors are still accessible to them. Other clients have such complicated life issues and chronic diagnoses that termination may occur because of a hospitalization or falling off the wagon or losing transportation to the counseling center, to name just a few. In these cases, termination is a far cry from satisfying for either client or counselor. For this reason, counselors who work with clients who have chronic and often acute mental health issues should seek out regular support for themselves lest they become discouraged.

Although termination is a given in the counseling process, unfortunately, evaluation is not. As a result, the mental health professions lack credible knowledge of what works and what does not work in counseling (Tracey, Wampold, Lichtenberg, & Goodyear, 2014). Occasionally, satisfaction surveys are given to clients, and these are of some benefit. But we must do more. A form following assessment that lists symptoms quantifiably (e.g., number of incidences of anxiety that are debilitating in a week) and then asks the client to record improvement may be enormously helpful, especially if counselors find over time that one set of interventions appears to result in more success than another set. For school counselors, a form could be given to a referring teacher and ask for the same kind of pre and post data. As counselors argue for positions across settings, these kinds of data can go a long way to help decision makers understand the value of counselors. We discuss termination and evaluation more fully in Chapter 12.

MAINTAINING A POSITIVE WORKING RELATIONSHIP DURING TERMINATION. Counseling, and especially good counseling, can be a highly significant event for clients. Occasionally, the relationship to the counselor is the most important relationship in the client's life at that moment. Some counselors find this flattering; others may find it uncomfortable. Some may find it incomprehensible that they could become so important to a stranger in so short a time. However, the fact that the relationship is important does not negate the fact that the relationship must eventually end. This fact poses a *relationship paradox*—that is, putting significant effort into developing a relationship that is time-limited. By contrast, our hope typically is that those relationships we invest in will be long lasting. Yet, good teachers and coaches and others engage in this kind of relationship paradox all the time. Perhaps the only difference is that they often hear from former students and athletes, whereas counselors may not hear ever again from former clients. This latter fact may be the biggest termination challenge for counselors, especially when the relationship with the client has been a meaningful one to the counselor.

From the standpoint of the client, what is crucially important is to navigate termination without making it feel like rejection, especially as many clients have had far more than their fair share of rejection in their lives. Even if rejection is not a theme in the client's life, termination represents a significant transition, and these are difficult for many people, clients included. It is for this reason that the idea of termination should be introduced early, and referred to throughout the counseling relationship. Beyond this, termination can be a time of "relationship review" with some discussion of implications.

> COUNSELOR: "I still remember when I met you. You were pretty angry at the world, and I was included in that world."
>
> CLIENT: (Chuckling) "Yeah, I wasn't very nice."
>
> COUNSELOR: "Well, I didn't see it as you not being nice, just that you weren't going to give me much help in getting to know you. I'm glad we got beyond that. I'm glad you took the risk."
>
> CLIENT: "Me too."
>
> COUNSELOR: "And what probably makes me gladdest of all is hearing about you taking more risks to let people know you in your life outside of this room."

Finally, as noted earlier, terminations are not always ideal or even planned. When this is the case, terminations become representative of the fragility of relationships for both client and counselor. If the counselor believes that he or she will not have an opportunity to work with the client in the future, at the very least the counselor should seek an opportunity to process the abrupt termination with a colleague or supervisor.

THE CLIENT'S EXPERIENCE IN COUNSELING

Most people have been in a position at some point in their lives when it would have been useful to seek counseling. Perhaps you can identify such a time in your life. Did you enter into a counseling relationship as a client? If you did, where you frightened? Hopeful? Desperate? It's not easy for some people to ask for help. For others, it may be relatively easy to see oneself as in need, but expectations for change are low. In short, clients enter counseling for many reasons and from a variety of positions of strength and weakness. Not all clients come to counseling empowered to take full advantage of the process. Some discover that counseling offers more than they had thought possible; others leave counseling disappointed or disenfranchised. Although not all clients can be helped, we believe that careful attention to the client at each stage of counseling is the counselor's best opportunity to make a difference. Sometimes the difference is profound.

Assessment and the Client's Experience

Clients who seek counseling of their own volition have typically muddled along for long periods of time in a state of dissatisfaction or even chaos. By choosing to seek professional assistance, they are giving up some control in order to gain control. Most do not yet appreciate this paradox.

They are often, however, very aware of the front end of the paradox—that is, giving up control by sharing important personal information with someone outside of their personal relationships. For very understandable reasons, therefore, most clients have some ambivalence entering counseling, ranging from mild to significant.

Inexperienced clients enter counseling without knowing exactly what to expect or what is expected of them. Because of this information deficit, they may feel uncertain, vulnerable, or guarded and doubtful. Individual and cultural differences between the client and counselor are accentuated at the front end of the process. "She looks like she comes from a nice neighborhood." "He looks pretty conservative. I wonder what his reaction will be when he learns that I'm gay." "She seems nice enough but kind of naïve. My life may shock her." "He can't possibly be old enough to have kids. How on earth is he going to help me with mine?" These internal thoughts are not resistance; they are fair and reasonable for persons who do not know about counseling and possibly have had little positive experience with others outside of their social and cultural context.

Not all clients react tentatively to the newness of the situation or with reservations. Some task-oriented clients begin as though it were already the third session and give little indication that they are anxious or uncertain; others are what we refer to as "experienced clients"—those who have had multiple counseling experiences in their past. This does not mean that rapport has been established with these clients. The issues of trust, respect, and safety have been suspended temporarily as the client rushes into the process. Those issues may arise later as the process heads toward goal setting and interventions.

Some clients have a strong interest in determining what or who "caused" their problems. Very often, this question is pursued with such vigor that one might expect the answer to be the solution. In fact, the cause of most human concerns is rarely the solution to the problem. There are exceptions to this, of course, but knowing why a set of conditions exists usually, in and of itself, doesn't make them go away. This knowledge *is,* however, important for some of the goals of counseling.

Finally, we must appreciate that some clients enter counseling because they have been referred or mandated to counseling by someone else. For these clients, assessment must begin slowly, and the relationship aspect of assessment must be emphasized more than is typical. In short, the counselor must help the client make his or her own decision to commit to the counseling process, even if this means that only modest goals will be forthcoming. Otherwise, goal setting and interventions are unlikely to produce any positive outcome.

Regardless of where clients fall on the continuum from eager and prepared to mandated and resentful, perhaps the most universal client reaction to assessment—if it is done well—is that it takes longer than the client would have predicted. This may in and of itself stimulate frustration in some clients. They came to counseling for solutions that they needed yesterday! When will this person have enough background to be satisfied? For this reason, it's important for counselors to be transparent about the process and about their reasons for doing what they are doing. It goes without saying that counselors must *know* why they are doing what they are doing. Gathering information is not an end in itself; rather, it must be connected to the problem as presented and must assist the counselor and client to move toward goal setting.

Goal Setting and the Client's Experience

As noted earlier, goal setting is the point in the process where the proverbial rubber meets the road. Some clients are eager for this stage to have arrived; others, much less so. It may seem counterintuitive to a counselor that clients would push back as the counselor is attempting to help them set goals related to alleviating their stated problem, but this misses what may be underlying what looks like resistance. Many clients have experienced more disappointments in their lives than successes; therefore, goal setting represents yet another opportunity to fail or to be disappointed by others. Even if the working alliance was moderately strong during assessment, goal setting requires even more trust in the counselor to "have the client's back." Therefore, counselor patience and giving adequate attention to growing a positive working relationship are required.

When clients approach goal setting eagerly, counselors have opportunities to be more collaborative. This is potentially a very rewarding and hopeful time for both counselor and client. It signifies that the client is engaged and empowered by the process and sees counseling as personally and culturally relevant. Such a situation is ideal for this stage and those that follow.

Most clients fall somewhere between eager and highly reticent in terms of setting goals. If the counseling process is all new to them, they may be somewhat intrigued as to how problems that felt overwhelming or at least intractable just a few weeks ago are now being translated into what appear to be attainable goals. The goals, especially the first goals discussed, may in fact appear too modest, and clients may need the counselor to reassure them that change is usually a series of small steps and not huge leaps. With some explanation, understanding of the client's misgivings, and support, clients can most often be helped to identify goals that are meaningful to them personally. As a byproduct, they are also learning a life skill for challenges that present themselves in the future.

Interventions and the Client's Experience

When counseling is working optimally, the intervention stage is characterized by an infusion of new energy into the process. That being said, counselors must be vigilant during this stage to assess client reaction to each intervention, as these reactions may be varied. For example, it may be relatively unthreatening for a client to be given an intervention to track social contacts for a week. However, a systemic intervention that involves approaching a parent or an employer differently might get the client back in touch with their vulnerability or their anger, and so forth. Even though interventions are directly related to goals that clients have endorsed and have been explained beforehand, they still may cause reactions in the client that are challenging, even frightening. This is one of the times when immediacy is an important skill for the counselor to use, as well as reflection and comments of support.

Some interventions may not be threatening, but they may be hard work and require discipline on the part of the client. Clients must be reminded on occasion that change is rarely a linear process. A *progress assessment* of the intervention stage is often helpful to clients when they are discouraged. A mother may be distraught that she engaged in a screaming match with her adolescent daughter during the past week. It's helpful for the counselor to remind her that 5 weeks have passed since the last fight with her daughter, whereas when she arrived at counseling, these kinds of scenes were happening a couple of times a week.

As clients recover from fairly predictable setbacks, they regain their confidence, and new patterns become more stable. By this time, some clients can begin to anticipate a new kind of crisis—the crisis of termination. They are feeling better about themselves, about their ability to handle problems, and about the counseling process. A cognitive dissonance may emerge, which may be conceptualized as follows:

Through counseling I am stronger, more satisfied, more in control. Thus, I soon may
need to end that which has proven so helpful. But I'm not sure I would be as strong,
as satisfied, as in control without counseling. However, I will never know if counseling
is propping me up or if I have really changed unless I leave counseling.

The resolution of this conflict is critical to the success of the counseling process. Only
when the client decides to take the risk of ending counseling can it ever be established that
counseling helped. It is critical at two levels: First, counseling gains must be supported and
maintained in the client's real environment. Second, the client must be able to view him- or
herself as a changed person.

Termination and the Client's Experience

Counseling is no more permanent than any other life condition. When termination occurs as a
result of successful counseling, the process is one of both accomplishment and regret. Feeling
self-confident, more integrated, and forward-looking, the client experiences a sense of optimism
about the future. At the same time, the client is saying goodbye to a significant relationship,
unique in that it allowed the client to be the center of attention, concern, and effort. One does not
give up such relationships easily. Thus, there is also a sense of loss blended into the termination.
These two emotional undercurrents surface as the client and counselor discuss the ramifications
of terminating. The client benefits if both sets of feelings are affirmed and normalized by the
counselor as counseling comes to an end.

Perhaps the most difficult of termination situations is that in which counseling has been
partially successful but cannot be continued. This might occur as a result of the counselor or client changing residence, of funds for counseling ending, of the academic year ending for an
intern, to name just a few. Clients in such situations may experience loss even more intensely
than when counseling was successful. That loss may be justifiable, and anger or fear may emerge.
Such negative emotions are important to acknowledge with concern and a lack of defensiveness
on the part of the counselor. Although an imperfect termination, it is the counselor's duty to
attempt to conduct as therapeutic a termination as possible.

We want to acknowledge once more that termination as a stage of counseling is not always
assured. An adolescent is suspended from his school or a client in an outpatient mental health counseling clinic is terminated by the agency for missing two consecutive appointments. These are endings, but not terminations. They leave all parties feeling loss and sometimes discouragement at the
limited role counseling can play in people's lives. In such cases, we must hope that the work that
was done prior to such an abrupt ending bears fruit for the client somewhere down the road.

Summary

All relationships have structure. That structure may
take the form of roles that the participants play, rules
that they follow as they interact with one another, or
concepts about what different types of relationships are
like. Until an individual understands the structure of a
relationship, he or she will find it difficult to understand
how to be part of that relationship. In this chapter, we
provide a structure for viewing the counseling relationship. Beginning with assessment and building the
helping relationship, the counselor then moves on to
goal setting, planning and initiating interventions, and
finally, termination and evaluation. These stages are
never accomplished without the participation of the
client. Within each stage, there is much to be considered.

Often, two stages overlap. Occasionally, the counselor and client must take stock and move back to an earlier stage. Throughout these stages, evaluation of the process is an important activity, whether it is considering how well the relationship seems to be developing; whether the problem has been correctly identified; whether the goals that have been identified are appropriate (or achievable); how well the interventions seem to be working; and, of course, what needs are part of the process of ending the relationship.

Finally, we consider the client's part in this experience. How does the typical client react to this passage from initiation to termination? What are normal expectations? These many facets of the counseling experience are important, but often intangible. Thus, while you attend to the progress of counseling, it is also important that you attend to the client's experience, listening for the intangible, the unique, and the nonconforming aspects of each client's passage.

Exercises

I. Stages of the Counseling Process

Select a partner and role-play a counseling relationship. Determine in advance which of the four stages (i.e., assessment, goal setting, interventions, termination) you will illustrate in the role-play. Have other class members observe and then identify the stage. Continue this exercise until you have illustrated all four stages, then discuss the following question: Are the counselor's verbal behaviors the same across all stages or do they change? Describe any changes you would expect to see.

II. Cultural Identity of Client

Using the same partner, develop a role-play in which you are attending to the relationship in the assessment stage. One of you should assume the identity of a person of a distinctly different culture than the other. After the enactment, discuss what dynamics you experienced in the role-play. What insights did you gain? What problems did each of you experience? What implications for learning did you discover? Share your experience with other members of your class, and ask them if they can offer additional insights.

III. Termination of Counseling

Select a partner and determine who will be the counselor and who will be the client. Then enact the following role-play:

You and your client have been working for 5 months and have reached a plateau. Most of the client's presenting problems at the outset of counseling have been resolved. In your judgment, based on the client's report, the client is functioning well and could terminate counseling at this time. The client both agrees and disagrees with this assessment. He or she has no new problems to address, but deeply regrets (and perhaps fears) to see counseling end. You have no desire to terminate prematurely, but your concern is that the client realize and accept that he or she is functioning well and is not in need of further counseling.

Following the role-play, discuss among yourselves the dynamics that seemed to arise during the session. What were your feelings? The client's feelings? Were you able to stay on task? Could you see the client's ambivalence? Could you help the client with that ambivalence? Where do you think the relationship was heading? What does the ACA Code of Ethics say about this dilemma?

Discussion Questions

1. How is *assessment* different from *goal setting*? What counseling activities are part of assessment but not part of goal setting? What activities are common to both?
2. Discuss the ramifications of initiating and maintaining a positive working relationship with the client. How does it affect assessment? Goal setting? Intervention? Termination?
3. If counseling interventions do not seem to be working, what might be the problem? How would you know?
4. What do you think is the most important stage of the counseling relationship? Why? How does your choice reflect your theoretical biases? Your own cultural background and values? Your gender? Would you consider yourself more attuned to what people do, to what people think, or to how people feel? How much of people's reactions can be attributed to their personal qualities? How much to their current environment? How much to their cultural background?
5. How does one know when counseling should terminate? Is there more than one way of knowing? Explain.

MyCounselingLab® Assignment

Go to the Video Library under Video Resources on the MyCounselingLab site at www.pearsonmylabandmastering.com/northamerica/mycounselinglab for your text and search for the following clips:

- **Video Example: Reflecting Meaning: Dayle**   As you watch this video, notice how the counselor is both patient and deliberate in her attempts to understand the client's issues. She does not rush the process; therefore, she is less apt to come to a faulty assessment.
- **Video Example: Reflecting Meaning: Mark**   Mark presents a different style from Dayle, and yet there is no question of his concern and investment in the client. Again, the counselor takes care to be sure that he understands the client and doesn't jump to conclusions.

Both video examples depict counselors as they are meeting clients for the first time; therefore, they are still in the assessment and building a working relationship stage. Do you think these videos are balanced between assessment and providing a safe space for the client? Can you see any goals beginning to formulate for either client?

Initiating and Maintaining a Working Relationship

PURPOSE OF THIS CHAPTER

Because a positive relationship between counselor and client is one of the three requirements of a strong working alliance, this chapter is devoted to the topic of building and maintaining a therapeutic relationship. Throughout all the stages of counseling, the working relationship is central to all counselor/client interactions, and the focus of this chapter is counselor and client characteristics and skills that enhance relationship.

Considerations as You Read This Chapter

- You have known many relationships. What have your relationship experiences been like? Which were supportive, helpful, or meaningful to you? What personal needs did they satisfy in you?

- Which of your relationships have had the same effect on the other person? What is it about you, or the things you do in a relationship, that would prove supportive, helpful, or meaningful to another person?

- How well do you know yourself as a person? Where did you get your eccentricities? Your values? Your ways of viewing yourself and others?

- With what social, cultural, or ethnic group did your family identify?

- What are your relationships with persons culturally different from you? Have you ever found yourself adjusting your individual tendencies to accommodate a relationship? Was this a positive experience?

- What were the values of your family? Did your family value closeness or separateness? Organization or disorganization? Confronting or avoiding? Touching or distance? Inclusiveness or exclusiveness?

If counseling is to be successful, clients must know that we are listening to them, understand what they are trying to communicate, and are genuinely interested in working with them. The actions that lead to these conditions are subsumed under rapport and relationship, heavily used concepts within the context of professional counseling. Each has acquired an impressive array of meanings and importance. *Rapport* refers to conditions of "mutual trust and respect" within the relationship (*The American Heritage Dictionary of the English Language*, 2012).

Rapport is the entry point into a therapeutic relationship—that is, it must be minimally present before the therapeutic relationship can take form. It might also be conceptualized as the synoptic root of a relationship.

CHARACTERISTICS OF A THERAPEUTIC RELATIONSHIP

Carl Rogers was among the first American therapists to provide the conditions of a humanistic therapeutic relationship. Early in his career, he proposed the counseling conditions that he considered both necessary and sufficient to produce constructive client personality change (Rogers, 1957). Those conditions included two persons in *psychological contact,* one of whom was in a state of *incongruence* (the client) and the other of whom was *congruent* or integrated in the relationship (the counselor). Beyond these primary states, the relationship also required that the counselor experience *unconditional positive regard* and *empathic understanding* for the client, and that these two conditions be *communicated* to and *perceived* by the client.

Conditions that generally have been identified as important in the establishment of an effective counselor–client relationship include accurate empathy, counselor genuineness, and an unconditional caring or positive regard for the client. Proponents of diverse theoretical orientations tend to join on this one issue: Effective counselors are personally integrated and self-aware, value the client as a unique person with a unique cultural background, and are able to understand (or at least strive to understand) how and what the client is experiencing.

A constructive counselor–client relationship serves both to increase the opportunity for clients to achieve their goals and as a potential model of a healthy interpersonal relationship, one that clients can use to improve the quality of their relationships outside the counseling setting. It is a condition that is generally accepted by most theories of counseling as an important component of therapy.

Entry Behavior: An Initial Barrier

Before we go any further in describing how a therapeutic relationship is formed, we must acknowledge a barrier that is virtually always present when strangers meet: *entry behavior,* or what could be referred to as *image management.* Most of us have some superficial layers that have been formed over many years that allow us to remain "safe" as we encounter people. These layers are part of who we are, but typically say more about how we want others to see us than how we feel internally. We call these layers *entry behavior* because they tend to fall away after we have "entered" and feel safe within a relationship. Entry behaviors can be perceived as positive or negative. The adolescent who is hostile or seemingly unperturbed by negative events is displaying a certain form of entry behavior. The person who diffuses with humor or is "slow to warm up" or is markedly friendly or self-discloses easily. All these are behaviors that are designed to manipulate others to see the person as he or she wishes to be seen.

The fact that these behaviors are intended to manipulate does not mean that they are conscious. Instead, they are habits that have been formed by experiences and the subsequent reinforcement, punishment, or extinction, that followed. For example, the hostile adolescent may have found that she was virtually ignored when she wasn't causing some trouble, or she may have been hurt deeply at pivotal times in her development by people she trusted. Therefore, her "layer" may be a way to connect to people ("Notice me!") or a way to stay hidden ("I'm not about to let you know me so you can hurt me too").

Counselors also have entry behavior. Some want to be seen as bottomless pits of empathy and display behaviors that we think communicate this image; others have a need to be viewed as competent or smarter than anyone else in the room or funny or in control—and the list goes on. Our first task, then, is to understand our own entry behavior and perhaps compensate a bit for it when needed. Again, we are not suggesting that entry behavior is not part of who we are—it is! But typically it has been formed to serve some needs that may not be therapeutic. To the extent that this is the case, we must push some of our layers aside and seek a more authentic person to present to our clients.

What do we do with client entry behavior? At the front end of counseling, we observe, but it is usually best not to react to the behavior directly. Instead, try to respond to the person. Using our hostile adolescent again as our example, responding to the behavior might be to insist that the client show respect, to be annoyed, or to assume this is a waste of time. Rather, responding to the person might be to tell yourself that this entry behavior is a legitimate result of this person's life experience. This recognition alone goes a long way to calm your frustration with the behavior. Then go about your business of attempting to form a relationship and to begin assessment, which may include speaking to the obvious: "I can see that you're not too happy to be here. I think I can understand why that would be the case. No one likes being forced to do something. I'd like to work with you, but I'm not going to force you to do anything you don't want to do." Words such as these are not magical. If change occurs, it will be incrementally. Some entry behaviors have worked so well that they have become more longer lasting than is typical. Still, they are only part of the person we see. What follows in this chapter is essential if we are to see more of the person than entry behavior.

Empathy

Rogers (1989) noted that accurately experienced empathy means

> the therapist senses accurately what the client is experiencing and communicates this accept-ant understanding to the client. When functioning best, the therapist is so much inside the private world of the other that he or she can clarify not only the meanings of which the client is aware but even those just below the level of awareness. Listening, of this very special active kind, is one of the most potent forces of change that I know. (p. 136)

The emphasis on communicating empathy has introduced the concept of the *language* of empathy. Welch and Gonzalez (1999) propose that this requires that counselors communicate on two levels. First, counselors must demonstrate that they understand "the narrative—the situations, events, and people in the story [and] the sequence, the connections, and the themes apparent in clients' life stories. This is the content of the narrative" (p. 141). Beyond understanding content, empathic counselors must also understand the meanings clients attach to their narrative. Welch and Gonzalez (1999) refer to this as "the significance of the story, its meaning in the life of clients" (pp. 141–142).

How will you know when this communication has occurred? Clients often give you the answer through their responses. It isn't unusual for a client to react with some surprise or relief when you accurately understand both the content and meaning of the client's narrative. Expressions such as, "Yes, exactly!" or, "Yes, that's it" or simply a look that tells the counselor that he or she hit a chord . . . all indicate recognition of the level of your understanding.

Empathy has also been seen as a two-stage condition. Gladding (2012) identifies these stages as *primary empathy,* which involves communicating a basic understanding of what the client is feeling and the experiences and behaviors underlying these, and *advanced empathy,* which reflects not only what clients state overtly, but also what they imply or state incompletely.

One of the early researchers on empathy was Robert Carkhuff. To facilitate his study, he developed a 5-point empathy scale to assess how well the counselor was able to identify and communicate back to the client. The scale emphasizes movement to levels of feeling and meaning deeper than those communicated by the client and that are additive in nature. Thus, level 1 reflects the lowest level of interpersonal functioning, and level 5 characterizes responses that go beyond what the client was able to express (advanced empathy). The Carkhuff Scale was used primarily by researchers/observers as they rated counselor responses:

1. The counselor's responses either do not attend to or *detract significantly* from the expressions of the client.
2. The counselor responds to the expressed feelings of the client, but does so in such a way that it *subtracts noticeably* from the affective communication of the client.
3. The counselor's responses are essentially *interchangeable* with those of the client in that they express essentially the same affect and meaning (basically, restating what the client just said).
4. The counselor's responses *add noticeably* to the expressions of the client in such a way as to express feelings at a deeper level than the client was able to express.
5. The counselor's responses *add significantly* to the feelings and meanings of the client in such a way as to express accurately feelings some levels beyond what the client was able to express (Carkhuff & Berenson, 1967, pp. 9–10).

Carkhuff considered level 3 to be the beginning level for helpful, effective, empathic communication.

There is some question as to whether empathy is a learned counseling response, a personal quality, or some combination of the two (Hackney, 1978). Quite possibly, all human beings are born with a capacity to relate to others and their tribulations. If that is so, it is also possible that early life experiences bring out that capacity, leave it dormant, or manage to extinguish it. Whether this is the explanation, it is a fact that not all would-be counselors are able to listen with an empathic ear or project themselves into their clients' narratives in such a way as to experience, vicariously, each client's world. It is for this reason that admission into a counselor program often requires some evidence of having empathic potential. The role of training is to enhance natural empathy so it can be used appropriately and therapeutically.

Chung and Bemak (2002) observe that Western or traditional views of empathy fail to incorporate sufficient knowledge, awareness, or understanding of the complexities in negotiating cultural differences. To develop *cultural empathy* skills, they recommend that you help the client understand that (1) you have a genuine interest in learning more about his or her culture, (2) you have an awareness and sensitivity about some aspects of the client's culture but not necessarily all areas, (3) you have a genuine appreciation for cultural differences between yourself and the client, and (4) you make an effort to use culturally appropriate help-seeking behaviors and expectations in the counseling process. To this, it should be added that *cultural empathy* requires the same conditions as those laid out originally by Rogers (1957). Use the following exercise to see how well you can insert yourself into another person's world:

What does it mean to be a woman? What does it mean in the Muslim context to be a woman? What does it mean in the Detroit Arab American context to be a woman? What does it mean in the Irish context to be a woman? What does it mean in the Boston Irish context to be a woman? Does the Boston Irish woman see her world any differently than does the Detroit Arab American woman? Do their views of the role of women affect their views of themselves? Of their values? Of their world?

Learning to understand empathically is not an easy process, even if you are a naturally empathic person. It involves the capacity to switch from your set of experiences to that of the other person as though you actually viewed the world through that person's eyes. It involves accurately sensing that person's feelings, as opposed to feelings you had or might have had in a similar situation. It involves skillful listening so you can hear not only the obvious, but also the subtle shadings of which perhaps even the client is not yet aware. Counselor empathy contributes to the establishment of rapport, the conveying of support and acceptance, and the demonstration of respect and civility. It helps the counselor and the client clarify issues, and contributes immensely to the collection of client information (Egan, 2014).

Genuineness

Genuineness refers to the counselor's state of mind. It means that the counselor can respond to the client "as a full human person and not just in terms of the role of therapist" (Holdstock & Rogers, 1977, p. 140). Genuine people tend to be comfortable "in their own skin," and thus more likely to be congruent and open to their own experience. Genuine people are less likely to be reactive to others, as they have fewer "buttons" that can get pushed. In short, being genuine is being who you really are, without pretenses, fictions, roles, or veiled images. It positions you well to begin to know another person because you are unencumbered by internal "noise."

If you are uncomfortable with who you are as a person, you will find it very challenging to be genuine with your clients. Your first task is to find ways to become more comfortable with yourself. Many aspiring counselors accomplish this by entering into a counseling relationship as clients.

When applied to the counselor role, *genuineness* is often referred to as *congruence,* which means that your words, actions, and feelings are consistent—that what you say corresponds to how you feel, look, and act. Helpers who attempt to mask significant feelings or who send simultaneous and conflicting messages are behaving incongruently. For example, if I say that I am comfortable helping a client explore his or her adjustment to a disfiguring injury but show signs of my discomfort in his or her presence, then I am in a state of incongruence. Such incongruence can contribute to client confusion, mistrust, or even shame. It is for this reason that multicultural self-awareness, along with self-awareness on other fronts, is essential for counselors.

The word *spontaneous* is also used in reference to genuineness. This is the ability to express oneself easily and with tactful honesty without having to screen your response through some social filter. It does not mean that you verbalize every passing thought to your client, nor does it give you license to blurt out whatever is on your mind. Spontaneity communicates your "realness" to the client and provides the client with a basis for understanding you and establishing a meaningful relationship with you.

Helpers who are genuine are often perceived by clients as more human. Clients are more likely to discuss private views of themselves when the counselor possesses a degree of non-threatening self-comfort. Counselor genuineness also reduces unnecessary emotional distance between the counselor and the client. This is why it is referred to as a *facilitative condition.*

Positive Regard

Unconditional positive regard was one of the original conditions identified by Rogers as necessary and sufficient for positive personality change to occur, and he defined it as prizing the client as a person with inherent worth and dignity, regardless of external factors such as the client's behavior, demeanor, and appearance. In a contemporary context, we think of it as a positive affirmation for the client as a human being. The counselor who experiences a positive regard for clients reflects not only his or her view of who that client is, but also embraces the client's worldview. This incorporates the client's ethnic and cultural sense of self, as well as other aspects of the client's life experiences that have shaped his or her worldview and his or her understanding of change.

COMMUNICATING EMPATHY

It has already been noted that empathy is both experienced by the counselor and communicated to the client. The counselor's success in perceiving the client's world becomes important in the relationship only as it is communicated back to the client. Two sets of conditions are associated with the empathy experience: (1) conditions that allow the counselor to experience the client's world and (2) conditions that allow the client to understand that his or her world has been accurately experienced by another person.

Conditions That Affect the Experiencing of the Client's World

Focusing and relating are two necessary conditions if one is to experience another's world. By *focusing,* we refer to the suspension of all self-directed thinking and, instead, turning one's full attention to the other person. Only as you let go of your own concerns can you become free enough to experience another person's immediate concerns. And as you let go of your agendas, you can begin to relate to the other person's experience as though you were experiencing it yourself.

This is not an easy transition for most counselors. Kottler (1991) describes the challenge from the experienced therapist's perspective:

> There is not a single client I see with whom I do not, at periodic intervals, tune out what they are saying and go off into my own mental world. Most of the time, these are fleeting moments—flash images that are provoked by something the client said or did. Yet with some clients who I find especially difficult to be with, I leave the room more often than I would like to admit. I am, of course, uncomfortable about these self-indulgent lapses that, while excusably human, are nonetheless unprofessional. (p. 99)

Clearly, focusing is a self-disciplinary experience. It must be practiced as one might practice meditation.

Once you have achieved some self-control over your attention span so that the client's narrative can be followed closely, the second aspect of the empathic experience involves *relating* to the other person's experience in meaningful ways. This is much more than having an emotional experience—it involves being so attuned to your client that you are able to imagine how the client's experience must be affecting him or her, choosing from the full range of human emotion. It was noted earlier that advanced empathy involves recognizing even what the client may only be implying. In such cases, the empathic experience may require that the counselor interpret, or at least infer, what the client is trying to communicate. When the counselor must move beyond concrete communication to inferred communication, the risks of error multiply significantly.

Skills Associated with the Communication of Empathy

It is important to establish that we are really talking about a relationship in which two people are relating to one another at an intimate level of meaning. It is important not to think of this process as the mere implementation of skills. However, there are also skills associated with such relating: How you sit as you listen to a narrative of pain unfolding, what you say in response, and how you feel as the client draws you into his or her very private world—all of these reactions are accompanied by outward and visible reactions, too. Just as you are asked to impose self-discipline on your attention span, you must also impose self-discipline on the outward manifestations of your experience in the moment. Yet beyond this, you must respond to your client and help your client know that you are very present, sensitive, understanding, and accepting of the person your client is describing, even if some of the behaviors that the client is describing are unacceptable. The nonverbal and verbal attending responses discussed next help build the relationship between you and your client by communicating your compassion and understanding.

RELATIONSHIP-BUILDING SKILLS

How does one create a positive relationship with a new client? Is it a matter of social competence? Self-comfort? Professional bearing? Although all these qualities are important, they do not address what you will be *doing* as you are talking to your client. The *what* that contributes to constructing a positive working relationship includes the following nonverbal and verbal skills.

Nonverbal Attentiveness

As noted in Chapter 2, clients often determine whether a counselor is attentive by observing the counselor's nonverbal behavior. In fact, even if a counselor states, "Go head and talk—I'm listening to you," the client may not believe this verbal message if the counselor is looking away, leaning back in the chair, or generally appearing disinterested or distracted. Whereas verbal communication is intermittent, nonverbal communication is continuous. When verbal and nonverbal messages contradict one another, the client usually believes the nonverbal message (Gazda, Asbury, Balzer, Childers, & Walters, 1984). In part, this is because so much of the communication that occurs between people is expressed nonverbally rather than verbally. Effective nonverbal attentiveness includes the use of appropriate eye contact, head nods, facial animation, body posture, and distance between speaker and listener.

Ivey, D'Andrea, and Ivey (2012) studied the differential effects of nonverbal behavior for different cultural groups and found that the skills normally associated with "therapy" tend to include nonverbal gestures that are more typical of a Western orientation. That makes sense, of course, because most theories of psychotherapy originated in either Europe or the United States. However, this does not reflect the realities of the 21st century, in which multiculturalism is the norm rather than the exception. For example, the Western communication pattern includes things such as increased eye contact when listening and less frequent eye contact when talking, which has been found to be generally different for African Americans, who are more likely to hold eye contact while speaking and look away while listening. This pattern has also been found to be true for many Arabic cultures, who expect prolonged eye contact in order to establish trustworthiness. Similarly, a comfortable physical distance between two people having a personal conversation tends to be arm's length or greater among Anglo cultures, but it can be as close as 6 to 12 inches among Arab and Middle Eastern cultures.

The concept of time varies considerably among cultural groups as well. Northern European and Western cultures in general tend toward a more linear view of time, with an emphasis on a more constant awareness of what time it is, what must be done at a certain time, and whether a time commitment must be honored literally. Mediterranean and South American cultural groups take a more casual view of time commitment and may not consider it as important to get to a 10:00 appointment no later than 9:59.

Although these examples are generalizations about cultural groups, and certainly every cultural group has a range of behaviors, they can be helpful as background information to help a counselor avoid making errors interpreting behavior. In addition, it makes comments heard in other contexts, such as, "Look at me when I talk to you!" sound as culturally insensitive as they most likely are.

How might you know which behaviors would be understood and which might be misinterpreted by clients of different cultural origins from your own? The most obvious answer is to study cultures and become more aware of patterns of communication. However, this could be a life's study in itself. The next best thing is to become highly sensitive to cultural variations among people, attempt to identify with their patterns of communication, and, in doing so, acknowledge or respect their uniqueness. Be conservative about interpreting the nonverbal behavior you observe, especially if your client is very different from you culturally. Learn to be comfortable with a wider range of nonverbal communication than you are used to in your social circles. Moreover, if something truly baffles you, respectfully ask for clarification. Sometimes this effort becomes the subject of an eye-opening and rewarding discussion between you and your client.

Verbal Attentiveness

Nonverbal attentiveness is supported by *verbal attentiveness*—what is said to clients demonstrates an interest in them. There are different ways of expressing verbal attentiveness. One obvious way is to allow clients to complete sentences. Cutting off a client's communication by interrupting discourages full expression—unless, of course, the client is rambling or telling stories, in which case an interruption may be useful.

The most common way to communicate verbal attentiveness is through the occasional use of short *verbal encouragers,* such as *mm-hmm, I see*, and *go on*. When used selectively, these short phrases can clearly communicate your interest and encourage expression. Overuse of these responses, however, can become a distraction and can impede client expression.

Another aspect of verbal attentiveness is verbal following or *attending* (Ivey et al., 2012). A person engages in attending by following the content and actions expressed in the client's communication. The counselor is nonintrusive and leads by following, accepting, and encouraging the client's communication rather than initiating or changing topics.

Attending can be used in a variety of ways; it is not restricted to just one type of response. It may be a statement or a question, and it may take the form of any number of different verbal responses, such as clarification, paraphrase, reflection of feeling, and open-ended question (see Chapter 2). The critical element in attending is to support the direction your client's communication is taking.

The voice can also be a very powerful tool in communicating with clients. It is important to learn to use your voice effectively and to adapt the pitch, volume, rate of speech, and voice emphasis to the client and to the situation. An important concept to consider in using your voice is that of *verbal underlining*—the manipulation of volume and emphasis (Ivey, 1994). Verbal underlining is a way of using the voice to match the intensity of your nonverbal behaviors with those of the client. For example, if the client is speaking loudly about a situation that caused anger, you can also add energy and emphasize key words in your response with your voice.

Finally, Ivey et al. (2012) introduce *focus* as an aspect of verbal attentiveness. Focus is better described as selective attending, because the counselor is choosing which aspects of a communication to respond to. This is illustrated with a specific client statement, such as the following:

> CLIENT: I really wonder what he might be thinking when I refuse to argue with him. He knows that my family never argues. We always discuss our issues and then find a compromise somehow.

To which the counselor might respond by focusing on the client, the client's partner, the client's family background, the "problem," the counselor's reaction—a *we* focus that communicates communal effort on the part of the client and counselor, or a cultural/environmental context. Ivey et al. also believe that when the counselor is working from multicultural counseling theory, focus should reflect a balance among the individual, family, and cultural issues.

Restating Client Messages

Sometimes the best way to communicate one's attentiveness is to give back to the client what you heard. This can be a brief restatement of the client's communication, or it may be a paraphrasing of the client's message. Generally speaking, your response will not be as complex as the client's message. Client messages may contain an objective or cognitive component and a subjective or affective component. The *cognitive* component includes thoughts and ideas about situations, events, people, or objects; it answers the question, "What happened?" The *affective* component refers to the client's emotions or feelings that accompany the cognitive component. Affective messages answer the question, "How does the client feel about what happened?" Notice the cognitive and affective portions of the following client message:

> I really care for and respect my husband. He gives me just about all I need in the way of security, comforts, and so on. If only he could let himself give me affection, too. Sometimes even when I'm with him, I feel lonely.

The cognitive part of this message—what happened—is fairly obvious. The client thinks her husband is a good provider but does not express his feelings. The affective component—how she is feeling about the situation—refers to her emotional experience of loneliness.

Not all client messages contain easily recognized cognitive and affective components. Some messages have only a cognitive component, as when a client says, "I think my professors here are just average." Other messages may contain only the affective portion; for example, a client might state, "I feel lousy about this situation." In both of these examples, the other component was omitted from the message and must be discovered through indirect inquiry or inference.

Paraphrasing Client Messages

Empathy may also be communicated through the use of verbal responses that rephrase to clients the essential part of their communication. As noted in Chapter 2, the response used to rephrase client messages is the *paraphrase*.

Paraphrasing involves selective attending (focusing) on the cognitive part or affective part of a message—with the client's key words and ideas rephrased into other words in a shortened and clarified form. Thus, an effective paraphrase does more than simply restate or parrot what the client has said. In the example that follows, the counselor has offered a tentative ("It sounds like") response, which softens the paraphrase. The counselor has also rephrased the client's

"I can't seem to stop" to "You aren't able to control," which may invite the client to think more critically about his or her reaction. When a paraphrase is on target, the client is likely to say something to the effect of, "Yes, that's exactly how it is." Well-targeted paraphrases often draw clients into exploring the topic in greater depth, in addition to feeling successful in communicating their message.

The Paraphrase

CLIENT: I know I shouldn't be so hard on myself, but I can't seem to stop second-guessing everything I do.

COUNSELOR: It sounds like you'd like to stop beating up on yourself, but you aren't able to control your reactions.

Formulating an effective paraphrase has four steps: recall, identification of content, rephrasing key words and constructs, and perception check. First, listen to and recall the entire client message. This process helps to ensure that you have heard the message in its entirety and that you do not omit any significant parts. Second, identify the part of the message that seems central to what the client is trying to communicate. Third, rephrase the key word(s) and construct(s) the client has used to describe this concern in fresh or different words. Be as concise as possible in your paraphrase. Long paraphrases border on summarizations—a skill we described in Chapter 2. Finally, include a perception check that allows the client to agree or disagree with the accuracy of your paraphrase. The perception check often takes the form of a brief question. However, counselors also check their perceptions of client messages by phrasing their statements in a tentative manner (e.g., "It sounds like . . .") and by identifying client nonverbal reactions to their paraphrases.

Some counselors are hesitant to paraphrase for fear they might be wrong, yet this is part of active listening and, therefore, part of counseling. It is more important to communicate a desire to understand what the client is saying than to always be right. As long as clients are given an opportunity to correct any misperceptions, most appreciate your effort to listen and understand.

Reflecting Client Thoughts and Feelings

As noted in Chapter 2, reflections attempt to capture the meaning of a client's statement. Because virtually all of us wish to be understood, reflections are a powerful tool in deepening the therapeutic relationship.

The Affective Reflection

CLIENT: I have been working on this project for six months now. It seems like each time I get close to the solution, something comes up that takes me away from it. I can't tell you how sick I am getting with it.

COUNSELOR: It must be really frustrating to get right up to the solution and then have everything fall apart.

The Cognitive Reflection

CLIENT: I was early for work every day this week except Thursday, when the bus was late so I clocked in late. My boss told me if it happened again, he'd fire me. How can I control the buses?!

COUNSELOR: You're wondering if it's worth the effort if you don't have total control over things.

Learning to reflect involves four steps. The first step is to recognize the client's feelings or thoughts and involves being very attentive to both inflection and other nonverbal cues. For example, note the different ways that the following simple sentence can be stated and how each statement carries with it a somewhat different meaning:

"I'm really worried about finding the time to write."

1. I'm really *worried* about finding the time to write.
2. I'm really worried about *finding the time* to write.
3. *I'm* really worried about finding the time *to write*.

The second step involves choosing whether to reflect feelings or content (thoughts) or attempt to reflect both (which we generally discourage). This second step is perhaps the most important, as it directs the session, at least for a bit. Using the client described earlier who was late because of a late bus, the counselor could have reflected the feelings (frustration, anger), but the client is probably already aware of those feelings. By choosing to reflect content, the counselor may be offering the client a challenge to look at these thoughts more closely and determine if they are productive or self-defeating. Said differently, it's unlikely that the feelings are new to the client; it's possible that this reflection of content could open a new door for counseling.

The third step in reflection involves choosing the words to describe the feelings or thoughts. These words should hold onto the generic meaning of the client's statement, but introduce more nuanced meanings. Finally, the fourth step is to give your perception back to the client in a manner that is reflective rather than prescriptive.

REFLECTING AT AN ADVANCED LEVEL. As suggested by Carkhuff and Berenson (1967), the more advanced level of empathy adds significantly to the feelings or thoughts of the client. It was at this level that Carl Rogers often worked; for us mere mortals, it is less often that the insight for such a reflection presents itself. When it does, however, it can do a great deal to advance the counseling relationship. Most seasoned counselors have heard a former client say, "Do you remember when you said . . .?" Often, the counselor does not remember, although occasionally he or she does. The point, however, is that the comment (and often it was an advanced reflection) was so accurate that the client changed perspective because of it. In other words, advanced reflections not only mirror the implied feeling or thought, but also reflect greater intensity of feeling or thought. These types of reflections emphasize what the client is concealing in his or her message and that is usually outside of the client's awareness. The result is an "Aha!" moment for the client, and a deepening of the relationship between counselor and client.

Occasionally, an advanced reflection attends to the counselor/client relationship directly. Consider, for example, the implied feeling in the following message:

CLIENT: I don't know why you just sit there and let me stew.

COUNSELOR: It upsets you *when I don't take better care of you.* [reflection of implied message]

Notice that the reflection at a deeper level not only mirrors the implied feeling, but also reflects greater intensity of feelings. The most effective reflection is one that emphasizes what the client is concealing in his or her message. You may wonder if this sort of challenging reflection will enhance or hurt the therapeutic relationship; in fact, it could do either, depending on what follows. If, however, the counselor delivers this message with concern and caring rather than judgment and maintains such a stance, we may be hopeful for a positive outcome.

As one final caveat, Ivey, Ivey, and Zalaquett (2014) observe that while it is important to look for opportunities to reflect at this level, it may not be appropriate to react or comment on your observations at a particular moment. The authors go on to emphasize the importance of timing to the process of helping a client acknowledge feelings in particular. This caution is an important one, especially at the front end of counseling. Yet, it is our experience that new counselors in particular are more likely to be too timid than too bold in terms of reflecting at a level that would parallel what we have discussed in this section.

CONDITIONS THAT CONVEY GENUINENESS

Genuineness is also communicated through the counselor's verbal and nonverbal behaviors. Three classes of behavior, in particular, communicate genuineness—or the lack thereof:

1. Congruence
2. Openness and discreet self-disclosure
3. Immediacy

Congruence

Congruence means that your words, actions, and feelings all match or are consistent with one another. For example, when counselors become aware that they find a client's loquaciousness to be directionless, they acknowledge this—at least to themselves—and do not try to feign interest when it does not really exist; otherwise, they must conceal their reactions, and this inevitably leaks out nonverbally to the client in one way or another. Instead, the counselor can use the many skills available to him or her to redirect the session and get things back on track.

The sensitive client will find counselor incongruence to be confusing or distracting, and may view the incongruence as an indicator of the counselor's lack of competence or sincerity; thus, counselor incongruence impedes development of the therapeutic relationship. In contrast, counselor congruence is related to both client and counselor perceptions of therapeutic helpfulness.

Openness and Discreet Self-Disclosure

Openness is what Rogers originally referred to as *transparency* (Meador & Rogers, 1984). It is a willingness to let a client see through the counselor's intentions, motives, and agendas.

Self-disclosure, however, is more intentional, because it involves a decision to reveal information of a personal nature to the client. Many counselors believe that openness is a critical dimension of the therapeutic relationship, because it communicates to the client a sense of equality and confidence in the client's power to change. Self-disclosure is a sharing of information that is not necessarily required by the client, although it may be seen as helping the client understand how change occurs or how the client's expressed problem is one shared by others.

The nature and degree of self-disclosure have ethical and professional implications. Conflicting results have been reported among the numerous studies on the effect of self-disclosure. Donley, Horan, and DeShong (1990) conclude that "our data do not support the supposition that counselor self-disclosures have a favorable impact on either counseling process or outcome [and that] counselors ought to be quite circumspect about its use" (p. 412). Conversely, Knox, Hess, Petersen, and Hill (1997) report that "clients perceived self-disclosures to be important events in their therapies" (p. 280). Knox and colleagues do make a distinction between immediate and historical self-disclosure, noting that clients cite personal, non-immediate self-disclosures as most meaningful. These authors conclude, however, that, "even helpful therapist self-disclosures have the potential for some negative impact" (p. 281).

As a result of these and other research findings, it seems wise to use self-disclosure discreetly, emphasizing the counselor's historical rather than immediate events, and measuring carefully the apparent effect that such revelations have on each client.

Counselor openness is related to counselor genuineness. For example, clients sometimes ask counselors such questions as, "Are you married?" "Why did you decide to become a counselor?" and "Are you a student?" Such direct questions are best handled with a direct, brief, and honest answer. You may then return to the discussion that preceded the questions. The point is that clients do have some need to know about their counselor. Not all of what they may wish to know is appropriate information for them to have, but some information is or may be necessary to help the therapeutic relationship grow.

If the request for personal information seems to be excessive, then there are some better ways to respond to the client's queries. For example, it may be more helpful for you to speak to the obvious by saying something like:

- "You seem anxious about talking about yourself today." [Reflecting on the client's feelings of anxiety]
- "You've been asking a lot of questions about me." [Reflecting on the process]
- "Does it feel good to get off the 'hot seat' for a moment?" [Focusing on the reversal of roles]

The verbal skills associated with empathic understanding described earlier maintain a primary focus on the client; in contrast, self-disclosure shifts the focus to the helper. If the counselor uses self-disclosure as an intentional intervention, such as illustrating to the client that there are alternatives to how the client is reacting, then self-disclosure has a therapeutic purpose. However, there are two hazards to using self-disclosure: (1) shifting focus from the client to the counselor alters the working alliance, and (2) it may suggest to the client that the counselor's reaction is the proper one or the "normal" response (Moursund & Kenny, 2002, p. 62).

The most effective self-disclosing responses are those that are similar in content and mood to the client's messages and is referred to as *verbal linking* or *parallelism,* meaning that the helper's self-disclosure is closely linked to the client's preceding thematic response. Consider this example:

CLIENT: I just wish my father was more understanding and less critical of me. He always seems to want me to do better than I can or to be someone I'm not.

COUNSELOR: I do know what it's like to feel like you don't measure up to your parents' expectations. I can remember feeling that way sometimes when I was your age. [Parallel response]

COUNSELOR: I don't like it either when people disapprove of me or my actions. Sometimes I wish people would try to be kinder. [Nonparallel response]

Immediacy

As discussed in Chapter 2, *immediacy* involves sharing a thought or feeling as it occurs in the counseling session. Because immediacy is always about what has been occurring in the presence of only the counselor and client(s), its use always has relationship implications.

Cormier, Nurius, and Osborn (2013) provide some guidelines for using counselor immediacy with clients:

1. The counselor should describe what she or he sees as it happens rather than waiting until later in the interview, when the impact might be lost.
2. The immediacy statement should be in the present tense (e.g., "I'm starting to feel uncomfortable about this") to reflect the here-and-now nature of the response.
3. The counselor should be aware that using immediacy in an early session could be anxiety-producing for some clients.
4. The counselor should be cautious to base an immediacy response on what is actually happening in the relationship, and not to use immediacy responses to reflect countertransference issues.

Counselors may tend to avoid immediacy issues even when raised directly by clients. This may be especially true for beginning counselors, who are unaccustomed to talking about relationship qualities as they are occurring. Unfortunately, counselors who avoid using this response are likely to contribute to the development of a more cautious relationship.

CONDITIONS THAT CONVEY POSITIVE REGARD

Although unconditional positive regard involves an expression of caring and nurturance as well as acceptance, this condition can be conveyed to clients through the appropriate use of certain behaviors, including supporting nonverbal behaviors and enhancing verbal responses, both of which may convey a sense of relationship warmth to clients.

Nonverbal Behaviors Associated with Positive Regard

When one person has a warm and caring regard for another, the clearest communication of that is through the person's nonverbal behaviors. Tone of voice, facial expression, eye contact, manner of using one's body, touch . . . all are assumed to be tools to engage with clients, some of which are used judiciously. As underscored in Chapter 2, nonverbal behavior is also culture-bound; in fact, there are cultures that are far more attentive to nonverbal behavior than to what is said. Therefore, all good counselors must become students of culture, especially those cultures represented by their clients. In this way, counselors are more apt to use nonverbal behavior to enhance the therapeutic relationship rather than to offend or to send incorrect messages.

Even within cultural groups, there can be wide variation of what each client may find comfortable. A client's attachment history may change how he or she reacts to touch, for example. Because of these occasionally dramatic differences among clients, we suggest that counselors watch very closely to see how their clients react to their nonverbal behavior. If the counselor notices any apparent discomfort in the client, it is best to adjust nonverbal behavior to make the client more comfortable. Later in the relationship, these differences can be processed using immediacy.

Acceptance and Enhancing Responses

There is one thing that all clients need from the counselor, particularly in the initial stages of helping: *acceptance*. Counselors convey acceptance by responding to client messages with nonjudgmental or noncritical verbal and nonverbal reactions. Thus, when a client states, "I know I'm pregnant again. It will be my fifth abortion. But I don't know who the father is, and I can't stand to use contraceptives," the typical reaction might be disapproval. However, if you hope to establish a relationship with your client that allows you to be a positive influence through counseling, such a response would be self-defeating. You do not have to agree with or condone the client's behavior.

A verbal skill related to the communication of affirming respect and acceptance is the use of *enhancing statements*—those that comment on some positive aspect or attitude about the client and provide encouragement or support to the client in some fashion.

The Enhancing Response

The enhancing response provides positive feedback to the client, usually on process rather than on outcome criteria. Referring to the earlier client statement, the following are examples of enhancing responses:

"I can see that finding yourself back in a familiar situation is upsetting to you."

"The fact that you're here talking about this says to me that you'd like things to be different."

Enhancing responses can have a strong effect on the client and on the relationship and are most effective when used selectively and sincerely. You know the feeling you have about someone who is always saying nice things about you—these statements lose their effect when used too often.

FUNCTIONS OF A THERAPEUTIC RELATIONSHIP

The core conditions and associated skills we describe in this chapter are derived from the person-centered approach to helping. Most other helping approaches or theoretical orientations also stress the importance of a sound therapeutic relationship in effective helping, even though some approaches differ in the nature and degree of importance they attach to the role of relationship in counseling. Adlerian counseling, for example, emphasizes the necessity of establishing a democratic and egalitarian relationship with the client. Behavioral approaches identify the importance of a good relationship as a potential reinforcing stimulus to the client. One of the key ingredients of Reality Therapy—that of *involvement*—is based on the concept of the counselor's ability to relate to clients effectively. Some family therapy approaches appear to put less emphasis on relationship, but all systemic approaches speak of joining with the client or family as a prerequisite to therapeutic work.

At least three primary functions are associated with a strong relationship bond between counselor and client: First, the therapeutic relationship creates an atmosphere of trust and safety for the client. This reduces client cautiousness, suspicion, or hesitancy to take risks, thus facilitating the client's disclosure of very personal and sensitive material without the fear of aversive or punitive consequences. Without such disclosure, counseling is likely to have little impact on clients because pertinent issues are not being explored.

Second, the relationship provides a medium or vehicle for intense affect. It permits and protects the client who needs to express strong feelings. Often, expression of such feelings is the initial step in diminishing their intensity and developing a greater sense of self-control.

Third, an effective therapeutic relationship allows the client to experience a healthy interpersonal relationship. Such an experience can assist clients in identifying and enhancing the quality of their relationships with others in their world. For example, clients may learn that it is all right to say how one feels, ask for what one needs, and share thoughts and feelings with others within the context of cultural restraints. They develop more effective forms of communication that are consistent with their worldview.

EFFECTS OF THERAPEUTIC RELATIONSHIPS ON CLIENTS

Clients' reactions to the counselor's level of involvement can range over several dimensions. Initially, some clients may feel pleased and satisfied with the quality of this interpersonal relationship. They may experience relief that someone finally seems to understand, giving them the opportunity to get burdensome or painful issues out in the open. They may also feel hopeful that someone seems to care enough to become involved in their lives.

Not all initial client reactions will be this positive, however. Some clients, unaccustomed to the informality or intimacy of the setting, may feel threatened, intimidated, or claustrophobic by the therapeutic relationship. They are uncomfortable with so much attention directed at them, with the counselor's expression of caring and concern, and with what they perceive as an insufficient amount of role distance.

Other clients may question the counselor's motives or sincerity, and view the counselor and the relationship with a degree of skepticism. They may have trouble believing that the counselor's intentions are good. They may wonder how committed the counselor really is to them and to working on their behalf. These clients are often looking for assurance that counseling will not exploit in any way their vulnerability, and often express their concerns with indirect or mixed messages designed to collect data about the counselor's trustworthiness. If counselors fail to respond to the underlying issue of trust and skepticism, the relationship may deteriorate or even terminate, with the counselor still unaware that the real issue was lack of trust.

Counselors may want to be careful about assuming that the conditions and quality of the therapeutic relationship always produce favorable client reactions. Current interpretations of empathy, for example, view it as a multistage process consisting of multiple elements (Egan, 2014). As such, empathy may be more useful for some clients and less effective with others. Gladstein, a leading authority on the person-centered approach once observed that, in the counseling process, empathy "will be helpful in certain stages, with certain clients, and for certain goals." At other times, however, it "can interfere with positive outcomes" (Gladstein, 1983, p. 478).

When clients respond to therapeutic involvement with apprehension or skepticism, it does not mean that the counselor stops reacting therapeutically or that the counselor denies involvement with the client or withdraws from the relationship. It means that the counselor makes a concerted effort to pay close attention to the client's reactions and attempts to relate to the client in a way that matches or tracks the client's feelings and frame of reference. Initially, this might mean moving a little more slowly, not pushing as much, or not conveying implicit or explicit demands for client progress and change. Your understanding of the skills and concepts of the therapeutic relationship may be enhanced by reading the following case. (Case illustrations are provided throughout the book to illustrate the major stages and strategies of the helping process. The case examples should help you in the application of the material you read.)

CASE ILLUSTRATION OF RELATIONSHIP BUILDING

The Case of Amy

Amy is a 45-year-old woman referred to you by her physician after he failed to find any organic basis for her frequent headaches and depression. He thought her symptoms could potentially be complicated grief, a condition resulting from the untimely death of her husband 14 months earlier. Her physician did prescribe an antidepressant and continues to monitor its effect.

Amy is an elementary school teacher and is highly regarded in her community. She is viewed as competent, very child-centered, and dutiful to all the tasks that relate to good teaching. At home, Amy is barely able to manage her schedule, which includes her children's activities, a large house, and daily family management. When he was alive, her husband assumed responsibility for many of these duties.

Amy has finally agreed to seek grief counseling, but she does not seem particularly receptive in the first interview. She sits in the most distant chair in your office, keeps her eyes down rather than making eye contact with you, and speaks in monosyllables during the first half-hour of the session. Finally, you ask her an important question: "Amy, would you tell me about your children?" She raises her head to make eye contact, and answers, "I have two children: Max, who is 17, and Jennifer, who is 12."

Because this is her first display of responsiveness in the session, you choose to stay with the topic. Your thought is that anything that gets Amy involved is an important first step in establishing a

relationship, so you proceed to ask her questions about the children. It quickly becomes obvious that they are her prized reality at this point, and she is able to talk about them. At the same time, you know that Amy was unable to talk earlier because the presenting problem, the loss of her husband, was simply too painful to talk about.

At the end of this session, you ask Amy if she is willing to meet again and if she is willing to bring pictures of her children. She is obviously reluctant to commit, but with some gentle urging, she agrees. As she is putting her coat on to leave, you remind her again to bring pictures to the next session and ask her if she would like an e-mail reminder. She says, "No, but thank you."

Amy arrives at the second session 10 minutes late and apologizes, saying something came up at the end of the school day that delayed her. The two of you sit in the same chairs as earlier and discuss how her school assignment is going. She replies that parent conferences are starting soon and she is feeling pressure from that. In addition, the father of one of her students died in a car accident and she has been quite involved with the child and her mother. You listen carefully to the story as Amy explains it, but you do not ask probing questions. Instead, you use your basic verbal and nonverbal counseling skills to help Amy describe the situation. You note that it is stressful for her to discuss this topic, but she seems to need to describe it. You avoid bringing up Amy's loss at this time, thinking that she will be able to get there as she discovers that it is a safe place to talk about such traumatic conditions. At the end of this session, as Amy prepares to leave, you ask for another session because you did not get to see her children's pictures or hear about their activities and school situations. Amy reluctantly agrees, and a third session is planned.

At the third session, Amy arrives promptly but appears exhausted. You enquire about this, and she says that she hasn't been sleeping the past couple of nights. You remember that she had said in the second session that parent conferences were coming up, so you take a chance and ask, "Have parent conferences started yet?" She says, "Yes, this week." You look at her and ask, "Is that where the stress is coming from that is keeping you awake?"

At this point, Amy begins to weep softly and pulls herself back in her chair. Finally, she says in an almost inaudible voice, "I guess so." You do not respond, choosing instead to let her gather her thoughts and emotions. Finally, Amy looks up and says, "It's all so hard," and begins to sob. During this time, you respect her need to cry by offering tissues and support. "Go ahead and cry—don't rush this—take some time and let these feelings and tears come out." You attempt to respond with both warmth and spontaneity to her and to let her know that you are not uncomfortable with the intensity of her feelings, even though she might be uncomfortable. "Sometimes feelings can be pretty overwhelming, especially if you have been holding them in for a long time. It may be helpful to try to express them any way that you can."

As the session winds down, Amy begins to talk about her own situation, her loss, and her feelings of inadequacy. Time and again, she indicates how incompetent she feels. You take this opportunity to direct her attention to her children, asking if she remembered the pictures. She nods and pulls them out of her briefcase. At this point, you move over to the chair beside her to look at them. Four or five pictures later, you remark about how much Jennifer looks like her. She smiles and adds, "Max looks just like his dad, too." She agrees to schedule another session, this time without the same reluctance as before, although she isn't exactly enthusiastic. As she leaves, she turns and says, "Thank you. I feel a little better."

Case Discussion

In this case, the counselor quickly recognizes that the client is very fragile, and needs to be given as much emotional space as possible if a counseling relationship is to emerge. At the same time, the counselor knows that a relationship cannot emerge until some verbal interaction does occur. Finally, she is given an entry when the client mentions her children. This proves accurate when the client responds willingly to a question about the children. The counselor uses this information by asking the client to bring pictures of the children to the next session. At no time in the first session does the counselor bring up Amy's loss. She focuses instead on those concrete conditions of her present life: school, students, schedule. In the second session, Amy ventures into the world of feelings and talks a bit about her student who lost her father. The counselor does not try to use this as a bridge to get Amy to talk about her own situation, fearing that it is too soon and that Amy might retreat into her overwhelmed state. Instead, the counselor listens sympathetically and with understanding, hoping that this will help Amy realize that the counselor is a "safe" person to talk to. At the end of this session, the counselor reminds Amy that a goal of this session— viewing the pictures of her children—was unmet. This further reinforced the notion that the counselor was attentive to, cared about, and able to react to Amy in ways that Amy valued.

CHILDREN AND THE COUNSELING RELATIONSHIP

Thus far, we have discussed rapport and relationship in an adult context. Much of what we have observed may also apply to adolescents, although the issue of trust is inherently more complex with these clients, who are actively seeking to differentiate themselves from parents. For younger children, however, the matter of relationship is more variable. Children may be referred to counseling when they are exhibiting difficulty with peers, with responsibilities, or with adults. Sometimes parents seek counseling for children when the family is undergoing stress—for example, the death of a family member or moving to a new community. With younger children, the trust issue is more likely to be whether to trust a stranger. Henderson and Thompson (2011) observe

> Counseling seems to work better if children can control the distance between themselves and the counselor. Adults are often too aggressive in trying to initiate conversations with children. Children prefer to talk with adults at the same eye level, so some care needs to be given to seating arrangements that allow for eye-to-eye contact and feet on the floor. A thick carpet, comfortable chairs, floor pillows, puppets, dollhouses, and other toys to facilitate communication are also recommended for the counseling room. (p. 45)

Other developmental issues should be taken into account: The younger child has not learned many of the subtleties of adult communication, but at a less-subtle level, younger children also lack the vocabulary of the adult world. It is important that you modify your adult behavior and vocabulary to match that of the child without making the common error of talking in a singsong lilt to a child.

A second concern is the physical domain. To young children, adults look like giants. Their appearance serves as a reminder of the child's powerlessness and vulnerability.

Third, it is important to remember that the child's attention span, which is briefer than that of adults, has two implications: First, younger children are not be topic-bound for more than a couple of minutes at a time (they may return to a topic several times during a session). Second, the counseling session is not as long as an adult or adolescent session. You may want to think in terms of 20-minute counseling sessions for younger children unless you are using play therapy, where the session can be somewhat longer, but there is usually more play than therapy. Beyond these immediate concerns, the establishment of rapport and a relationship with younger children also involves understanding, acceptance, a liking of children, and genuineness. Genuineness is especially critical. If young children sense that you are being disingenuous or not taking them seriously, their basis for trusting you will be destroyed and rapport will not occur.

These suggestions only scratch the surface in terms of working with children. For those who will counsel children primarily or exclusively, we recommend contributions such as Halstead, Pehrsson, and Mullen (2011) and Henderson and Thompson (2011) to supplement the information found in this text.

Summary

Several conditions and ingredients contribute to building and maintaining a therapeutic relationship with clients. Accurate empathy, counselor genuineness, and supportive respect are three counselor qualities that form the foundation of therapeutic relationships. These qualities are conveyed through the counselor's attitudes, and they are also expressed by certain helping skills, including facilitative nonverbal behaviors and verbal skills such as paraphrasing, reflecting, self-disclosure, immediacy, sharing, and enhancing responses.

With all this information as background, it is important to appreciate that clients' entry behaviors are at work at the front end of the relationship; it's also important to be sensitive and responsive to each client's worldview, which is composed of ethnic/racial, cultural, gender, lifestyle, physical, and age parameters. These unique qualities play an important role in shaping the nature of helpful counseling relationships.

Exercises

I. Attentiveness and Empathy

This exercise involves you and a partner in two interactions, each of which lasts about 5 minutes. After both have been completed, assess the impact of each interaction. Ask for your partner's reactions to each situation. In which interaction did he or she feel most comfortable? In which did he or she feel like stopping or leaving?

A. You are to listen carefully to what your partner is saying, but you will send your partner nonverbal signals that indicate boredom: look away, doodle, appear distracted, and so on. If your partner accuses you of being uninterested, insist that you are interested—you may even review what has been said—but continue to send nonverbal signs of boredom. Do not discuss or share these instructions at this time.

B. In the second exercise, listen carefully to what your partner is saying and send nonverbal signals that indicate your interest and attentiveness—eye contact, head nodding, facial animation, and so on. Make some attempt to ensure some synchrony between your partner's nonverbal behavior and your own.

II. Identifying Nonverbal and Verbal Affect Cues

To give you practice in identifying nonverbal and verbal affect cues, complete the following exercises:

A. Pick a partner. One of you is the speaker; the other is the respondent. After you complete the exercise, reverse roles and repeat the exercise. The speaker should select a feeling from the following:

Contented, happy
Puzzled, confused
Angry, hostile
Discouraged, depressed

Do not tell the respondent which feeling you have selected, and portray the feeling through nonverbal expressions only. The respondent must try to identify the feeling you are communicating as well as the behaviors you use to express the feeling. After he or she has done so, choose another feeling and repeat the process.

B. The speaker should select a feeling from the following list:

Surprise
Elation or thrill
Anxiety or tension

Sadness or discouragement
Seriousness or intensity
Irritation or annoyance

Do not inform the respondent which feeling you have selected. Verbally express the feeling in one or two sentences, being certain to include the affect word itself. The respondent should try to identify the feeling in two ways:

1. Restate the feeling using the same affect word as the speaker.

2. Restate the feeling using a different affect word but one that reflects the same feeling, for example:

SPEAKER: I feel good about being here.
RESPONDENT: a. You feel good?
b. You're glad to be here.

Choose another feeling from the list and repeat the exercise.

III. Paraphrasing and Reflecting

Respond in writing to each of the following three client messages.

A. Client: "I'm tired of sitting at home alone, but I feel so uncomfortable going out by myself."

1. Cognitive part of message: _____

_____

2. Affective part of message: _____

_____

3. Paraphrase of cognitive part: _____

_____

_____

4. Paraphrase of affective part: _____

_____

_____

B. Client: "I don't know why we got married in the first place."

1. Cognitive part of message: _____

_____

2. Affective part of message: _____

_____

3. Paraphrase of cognitive part: _____

_____

_____

4. Paraphrase of affective part: _____

_____

_____

C. Client: "The pressure from my job is a lot to contend with, but I expected it" (said with strained voice, furrowed brow, twisting of hands).

1. Cognitive part of message: _____

_____

2. Affective part of message: _____

_____

3. Reflection of content: _____

_____

_____

4. Reflection of feeling: _____

_____

_____

IV. Self-Disclosure and Immediacy

Listed next are four client situations. For the first two, develop and write an example of a self-disclosure response you might make to this client. For the second two, develop and write an example of an immediacy response you could use with this client. Share your responses with other students, colleagues, your instructor, or your supervisor.

A. The client hints that he wants to tell you something, but he is reluctant to do so because it is something he feels very ashamed of.

B. The client believes she is the only person who has ever felt guilty about a particular issue.

C. You experience a great deal of tension and caution between yourself and the client. You both seem to be treating each other with kid gloves. You are aware of physical sensations of tension in your body, and you observe signs of similar sensations in the client.

D. You and your client like each other a great deal and have a lot in common. Lately, you have been spending more time swapping life stories than focusing on or dealing with the client's presented concern of career indecision.

Discussion Questions

1. How do you approach a new relationship? What feedback have you received about your entry behavior? What conditions do you require to be met before you are willing to disclose personal information?

2. What are the unwritten rules in your family about interactions with non-family members? How do you think these unwritten rules will affect the way you relate to clients?

3. If you were a client, what kind of relationship would you expect and value? What conditions would you probably put on the relationship?

4. What role has culture played in some of your past relationships with teachers, coaches, counselors? Have your past experiences given you any insight into how culture may influence your interactions with clients?

5. Do you view culture as operating in all your interactions or only those with persons visibly different from yourself? If the former, what might you be missing? If the latter, what dangers are embedded in this approach to culture?

6. We quoted Gladstein's (1983) counterintuitive comment that empathy can, at times, interfere with a client reaching his or her goals. What do you make of this assertion? Can you think of an example when this might be the case?

MyCounselingLab® Assignment

Go to the Video Library under Video Resources on the MyCounselingLab site for your text and search for the following clips:

• **Video Example: Invitational Skills**   In this brief segment, what counselor behaviors did you observe that were discussed in this chapter?

• **Video Example: Confronting Client's Resistance and Responses**   In this segment, the counselor challenges the client regarding some of his self-defeating patterns. Is the counselor able to maintain a positive working relationship with the client while doing so? If your answer is "Yes," how does the counselor accomplish this? If your answer is "No," what might the counselor have done differently?

• **Video Example: Reflecting Feelings: Bryce**   In this segment, the client addresses trust issues. Is it typical for clients to be wary of trusting others? How do you assess this beginning working relationship between Bryce and his client?

• **Video Example: Being Straightforward with Parent and Child**   In this segment that depicts a counselor challenging a client, what do you think are the benefits and risks of the counselor's directive approach?

Assessing Client Problems

PURPOSE OF THIS CHAPTER

In this chapter, we examine the general process by which counselors can assess the client's presenting problems, a process that involves the collection of information relevant to problem definition, conceptualization of that information into a cogent contextual picture of the client, and consideration of client resources.

Clinical assessment in counseling may occur at an intake interview prior to assignment to a counselor, or it may occur during the assigned counselor's sessions with the client. When it occurs prior to counselor assignment, it may include paper-and-pencil assessment instruments in addition to information gathering in the interview(s).

Drummond and Jones (2010) describe two approaches to clinical assessment: the psychodiagnostic method and the psychometric method. In this chapter, we examine the psychodiagnostic approach, which has as its purpose the evaluation of client problems and contextual conditions in order to determine what type of counseling is needed, what types of interventions should be used, and how counseling is likely to progress. Therefore, although the word *assessment* is often used to refer to a test or psychometric instrument, here we use it in its more generic form, meaning the gathering and analyzing of information from the client to arrive at appropriate counseling goals.

Considerations as You Read This Chapter

- Defining a "problem" is a difficult process because different people see problems differently. How does a professional counselor view problems?
- How does the professional counselor separate his or her worldview from that of the client to arrive at a definition of the problem that the client can relate to?
- What kinds of information are useful in understanding a stranger's problems?
- How do you determine the difference between seeking information that is significant in your client's life and merely going on a "fishing" expedition?
- How do the differences between crisis counseling and other forms of counseling reveal themselves?

T hese questions are at the root of the clinical assessment process. They affect the counselor and client alike. For this reason, it is useful to have some sort of guideline or outline to follow as one collects information and then assimilates that information into an understanding of the client's presenting problem, the context in which that problem exists, and the alternatives available to the client in problem resolution. Although this appears to be a straight-forward process, assessment is probably the biggest challenge for counselors, especially counselors who are at the front end of their professional life. For this reason, we include in this chapter two commons errors in assessment: (a) conceptual foreclosure and (b) an assessment style that follows "plot" (i.e., the story line) rather than "process."

In most instances, clients seek a counselor (or are encouraged to seek one) to help resolve concerns or problems that are interfering with their daily functioning or causing discouragement or despair; consequently, clients often come to counseling with a sense of vulnerability, yet hoping that counseling will lead to improvement in their lives. Most beginning counselors enter new therapeutic relationships with similar feelings of hope and vulnerability. For the counselor, the vulnerability comes from self-expectations to do something to ease or improve the client's situation. This need can lead to thinking that, unless the counselor is always *doing* something— usually *for* or *to* rather than *with* the client—counseling will not be successful. Given such pressures, beginning counselors often have difficulty with the discipline of the assessment process. They may have a tendency to move as quickly as possible toward a solution; or the counselor may feel a strong need to establish a nurturing relationship to ease the client's distress, thus neglecting to identify parameters of the problem, a tendency we refer to as *conceptual foreclosure*. Just as in the developmental literature were *foreclosure* refers to making a decision of life path without full exploration (Erikson, 1968), *conceptual foreclosure* on the part of the counselor refers to making a decision about what the client's issue is without a full assessment of all aspects of the client's situation and background. Like developmental foreclosure in choosing a life path, there are occasions when the counselor gets it right even without a full assessment—but this is more about luck than skill. It is far more likely that goal setting will be premature and even nonproductive when assessment has been shortchanged.

Seligman (2004) observes, "The assessment process should be a way of recognizing the importance and uniqueness of each person, a way of saying to the person, 'You are special and I want to get to know you and understand why you are the way you are'" (p. 85). Therefore, of all the stages of counseling, assessment is the most challenging because the counselor must be the most patient, the most inquisitive, the most engaging, and the most insightful to get it right. That said, each counselor comes to the task with a host of resources that can help in assessment. This chapter covers only the fundamentals; we suggest that counselors actively build a library of resources that, over time, enriches their understanding of human behavior in a variety of contexts. We also suggest that counselors continue to learn what they can about the presenting issues they encounter most often—for example, substance abuse, PTSD, or anxiety. In this way, their counseling will represent a synergy between their expert knowledge base and their developing skills in assessment.

PURPOSES OF ASSESSMENT

Assessment has many functions within the counseling process. It provides a systematic approach to soliciting and organizing relevant client information. It also aids in the identification of significant individual and cultural conditions that contribute to or interface with a client's presenting problems.

Assessment is a means by which the counselor seeks to understand the client's world, both in terms of how the client perceives that world and how the client is able to report the factual world. This involves a process of exploring the conditions the client is experiencing—other persons, contexts, and time sequences that are part of that experience, as well as efforts to change those conditions or events the client would like to change.

It is also important to note that assessment can be *reactive;* that is, the process of obtaining specific information about problems may also cause some change in the problem. For example, a male client who reports that he is self-conscious around women may find that some of his self-consciousness dissipates as he begins to explore his behavior with the counselor and to monitor it more closely outside the counseling sessions. Thus, assessment can also contribute to desired client changes or outcomes.

DIMENSIONS OF ASSESSMENT

Assessment refers to anything counselors do to gather and reflect on information and draw conclusions about client concerns. Although most of the major components of assessment occur early in the counseling process, some assessment actually goes on continuously during counseling, because counselors are always seeking to understand their clients more fully as they engage in goal setting and selecting interventions.

Formal Intake Interviews

We refer here to *formal intake interviews* because not all counseling relationships begin with such an intake process. Some settings—for example, school counseling settings—tend to rely on accumulated knowledge of a child and the family when issues emerge rather than conducting a formal intake. This is not to indicate that an assessment process is not important in these settings, but assessment as we consider it here relates more to settings that conduct formal intakes (an *intake*), sometimes completed by someone different than the person the client ultimately sees as a counselor.

During an intake, counselors are interested primarily in obtaining information about the range or scope of the client's problem(s) and about aspects of the client's background and present situation that may relate to the problem. An assumption behind the intake interview is that a counseling relationship will follow the intake; therefore, intakes are not appropriate if there is any reason to think that the client will not return for subsequent counseling. Most counselors try to limit intake interviews to one hour or ninety minutes. To do this, the counselor must assume responsibility and control over the interview. There is no overt attempt to make the session therapeutic for the client (although having an opportunity to be heard is in and of itself therapeutic for many). In this way, the intake interview is like an appendage that precedes the process of establishing a relationship with the client.

Because the intake session is different from a regular counseling session, it is helpful if the counselor gives the client an explanation about the purpose and nature of the initial session. You might say something like, "DeShawn, before counseling begins, I would like to get some preliminary background information about you. So today, I'm going to spend the hour getting to know you and asking you some questions about your schooling, your work, your family, and so on. I'll also get some information about the specific concerns that brought you to counseling. Do you have any questions about this?" If it is unknown if the intake counselor will be the client's assigned counselor, this, of course, is necessary to communicate to the client as well. If the client is in crisis during this first interview, a typical intake is not conducted; rather, an assessment of the crisis is conducted and the goal is to establish physical and psychological safety for the client until a regular intake can be conducted.

Forms and the Written Intake

Intake forms vary widely, especially as dictated by the mission of the counseling office or agency for which they are used. For a full-service mental health agency, intake forms collect data in a comprehensive manner, including medical history; mental health history; family history (medical and mental health); work history; current and prior use of substances; current or prior legal involvement; current living situation, including co-habitants; sexual identity and history; and so on. In other words, the intake not only presents a description of the client's presenting problem and conditions that surround it, but a more general picture of the client and the client's current and former situation(s) as well.

A counseling office that serves a distinct population (e.g., on a college campus, students who have been referred because of alcohol- or drug-related issues, or an office that provides services to students who have been assaulted sexually), intake forms are more targeted. Furthermore, they may take the form of a checklist rather written in script format. Using the college student exhibiting alcohol- or drug-related issues as an example, the intake counselor should ascertain if there are comorbid conditions like anxiety, depression, eating disorders, or aggressive behaviors, each of which might have several subcategories that the intake counselor might check. Of course, there is also some information gathered on psychological or psychiatric treatment history, family history, social relationships, and academic standing. Finally, as is typical for any intake when a client exhibits serious concerns, a risk assessment is conducted, specifically risk of suicide or homicide.

When writing the results of the intake interview, a few cautions should be observed. First, avoid using a diagnostic term unless you are making a diagnosis. If you say that a client seemed "depressed," this should be supported by the markers listed in the *DSM–5* for depression; otherwise, such non-diagnostic language as, "The client reported feeling chronically sad" is appropriate. Also, avoid elaborate inferences. Remember, an *inference* is a guess—sometimes an educated guess, but still a guess nevertheless. An inference that is incorrect can be a distraction in the early stages of counseling. Try to prevent your own biases from entering the report. Remember, assessments must be defensible, both psychologically and sometimes legally. It is important to know what your agency or counseling office guidelines are regarding client assessment and to stay within those constraints while giving an accurate picture of the client's world to the extent that you can.

The information gained through intake interviews takes on added significance at the worst times. Far too many counselors have confronted a client crisis lacking the information they needed to address the situation. Because beginning counselors are torn between relationship building and information gathering, they can neglect gathering that vital bit of needed information should the client became suicidal, severely depressed, or dangerous to someone else. In those moments, critical information about the client's medications, support network, and previous similar crises are vital to making decisions in the client's and others' best interests.

I. **Identifying Data**
   A. Client's name, address, and telephone number at which the client can be reached. This information is important in the event that you must contact the client between sessions. The client's address also gives some hint about the conditions under which the client lives (e.g., large apartment complex, student dormitory, private home, inner-city project).
   B. Age, sex, relationship status, occupation (or school class and year), those living in household. Again, this is information that can be important. It lets you know if the client is still legally a minor, and provides a basis for understanding information that will come out in later sessions. For children, it is essential to know what adult supports are available to the child in the home.

II. **Presenting Problems, Both Primary and Secondary**
   It is best that these problems are presented in exactly the way the client reports them. If a problem has behavioral components, they should be recorded as well. Questions that help reveal this type of information include the following:
   A. How much does the problem interfere with the client's everyday functioning?
   B. How does the problem manifest itself? What are the thoughts, feelings, and so on, associated with it? What observable behavior is associated with it?
   C. How often does the problem arise, and how long has the problem existed? When did it first appear?
   D. Can the client identify a pattern of events that surrounds the problem? When does it occur? With whom? What happens before and following its occurrence? Can the client anticipate the onset of the problem?
   E. What caused the client to decide to enter counseling at this time?

III. **Client's Current Life Setting**
   What is the background or context for the client's daily functioning?
   A. How does the client spend a typical day or week?
   B. What social, religious, and recreational activities does the client undertake?
   C. What is the nature of the client's vocational and/or educational situation?

   D. What special characteristics about the client—cultural, ethnic, religious, lifestyle, age, and physical or other challenges—must the client address on an ongoing basis?

IV. **Family History**
   A. Father's and mother's ages, occupations, descriptions of their personalities, family roles, relationships of each to the other and each to the client and other siblings.
   B. Names and ages of brothers and sisters, their present life situations, relationships between client and siblings.
   C. Is there any history of mental illness in the family? Substance abuse? Domestic violence?
   D. Descriptions of family stability, including number of jobs held and number of family moves (and reasons). This information provides insights during later sessions when issues related to client stability and/or relationships emerge.

V. **Personal History**
   A. Medical history: Include any unusual or relevant illness or injury from the prenatal period to the present.
   B. Educational history: Include academic progress through high school and any post-high school preparation. This includes extracurricular interests and relationships with peers during schooling.
   C. Military service history. Did the client serve in combat? What kind of assessment did the client undergo upon return to the United States? Did the client see action? Was the client wounded? Is there any indication of posttraumatic stress disorder (PTSD)?
   D. Vocational history: Where has the client worked? At what types of jobs? For how long? What were the relationships with fellow workers?
   E. Sexual and relationship history: With what sexual orientation does the client self-identify? Has sexual orientation been an issue in one's family, cultural group, or community? What is the client's history of committed relationships? Is the client currently in a committed relationship? Does the client have children or stepchildren?
   F. What experience has the client had with counseling, and what were the client's reactions?

G. Alcohol and drug use: Does the client currently use alcohol or drugs? Has the client used alcohol or drugs in the past? To what extent?

H. What are the client's personal goals in life? To what extent are these complicated by the presenting problem?

VI. Description of the Client during the Interview
Here you could indicate the client's physical appearance, including dress, posture, gestures, facial expressions, voice quality, tension; how the client seemed to relate to you in the session; the client's readiness of response, motivation, warmth, distance, passivity, and so on. Did you observe any perceptual or sensory characteristics that intruded on the interaction? What was the general level of information, vocabulary, judgment, and abstraction abilities displayed by the client? What was the stream of thought and rate of talking? Were the client's remarks logical? Were they connected to one another?

VII. Summary and Recommendations
In this section, acknowledge any connections that appear to exist between the client's statement of a problem and other information collected in this session. What type of counselor do you think would best fit this client (assuming that you are responsible only for the intake)? What is your understanding of the client's rationale for seeking counseling at this time? To what extent is this client an appropriate fit for the services offered at your agency? How long do you think counseling might require?

Problem Definition

Beyond the intake interview, clinical assessment involves a more extensive definition of the problem. This may begin as part of the intake, but continues into the next one to two sessions and even beyond in some cases. Problem definition differs from intake information because specific details regarding the nature and context of the presenting problem(s) are explored. These details may include not only the one(s) presented initially by the client (referred to as the *presenting problem*), but may also include any others that might have been mentioned during the intake or during subsequent sessions.

Frequently, clients identify a presenting problem as their reason for seeking help and then, during the subsequent sessions, reveal something else that they realize is even more germane to their angst. This can be a surprise to them, because they have spent a significant amount of time distracted from the core of their issue by some more superficial concern. In addition, clients often have trust issues, some of which are outside of their awareness. Therefore, as counseling progresses and they believe the counselor to be trustworthy, they may find themselves divulging very hurtful moments in their past that continue to haunt them. It is for this reason that we underscore the importance of the therapeutic relationship from the onset of counseling to its conclusion. It's also why we suggest that assessment be a continuing function in counseling and that the counselor resist conceptual foreclosure, thus making it more difficult for the client to share deeper levels of concern. The following are areas to explore in reaching a useful understanding of the client's problem(s):

I. Components of Problem (ways in which the problem manifests itself primarily and secondarily)

A. Feelings associated with the problem (major feeling or affect categories to assess include confusion, depression, fear, anger).

B. Cognitions associated with the problem (including thoughts, beliefs, perceptions, internal dialog, ruminations, and self-talk).

C. Behaviors associated with the problem (specific actions observable not only by the client but also by others, including the counselor).

D. Physical or somatic complaints associated with the problem.

E. Interpersonal aspects of the problem (effects on significant others and on the client's relationships with others, including family, friends, relatives, colleagues, peers; also the effects that significant others may have on the client or his or her problem).

II. Pattern of Contributing Events (Can the client identify a pattern or sequence of events that seems to lead up to the problem and also maintains it?)
   A. When does the problem occur? Where? With whom?
   B. What is happening at the onset of the problem?
   C. What is happening just prior to occurrence of the problem?
   D. What typically happens just after its occurrence?
   E. What makes the problem better? What makes it disappear?
   F. What makes the problem worse?

III. Duration of Problem (extent to which the concern disturbs the client and/or interferes with the client's everyday functioning)
   A. How long has the problem existed?
   B. How often does the problem occur?
   C. How long does the problem last when it does occur?
   D. What led the client to seek counseling at this time regarding the problem?
   E. In what ways does the problem interfere with the client's daily functioning?

IV. Client Coping Skills, Strengths, Resources
   A. How has the client coped with the problem? What has worked? What has not worked?
   B. How has the client coped successfully with other problems?
   C. What resources, strengths, and support systems does the client have to help with change efforts?
   D. What is the client's cultural worldview? Sociopolitical histories of the groups the client identifies with? Language(s) spoken? Impact of gender? Neighborhood the client grew up in? Religion the client practices, if any? How do each of these effect the problem(s) from the client's perspective?

In addition to this kind of information collected from problem-definition interviews, counselors can also obtain additional assessment information about clients and their problems by using *adjunctive data,* such as psychological tests and self-ratings.

Finally, problem definition can be approached in numerous ways, as determined by one's theoretical orientation, the use of the American Psychiatric Association's *Diagnostic and Statistical Manual,* 5th edition (*DSM-5*; American Psychiatric Association, 2013), and/or by contextual realities. Contextual realities are important to recognize because not all human problems originate within the individual; rather, they can be imposed by the environment in ways that impel the client's reactions. For example, the Americans with Disabilities Act recognizes the environment as the source, thus the target for change, of problems that persons who have disabilities experience related to their physical disabilities. Similarly, many persons representing disenfranchised cultural groups experience degrees of discrimination that, if remedied, could have a major effect on the client's "problem." Young children also experience problems imposed by environmental or contextual conditions. In these cases, the environment may be the source, thus the target for intervention, as well as the client.

CLINICAL ASSESSMENT WITH CHILDREN

Children pose a unique assessment challenge to the counselor. On the one hand, children are less inhibited than adults in talking about their concerns to a trusted counselor. On the other hand, children, especially young children, lack the cognitive development to describe problems with causal or contextual clarity. As a consequence, you must phrase questions so that you draw out the kinds of information that allow you to conceptualize the child's world.

Intake information for children and adolescents who are minors are almost always completed by an adult who is legally responsible for the child. Within a school counseling setting, the "intake" may be composed of school records, teacher referral information, and a conversation with a parent. For children seeing a counselor outside of an educational setting, the intake most likely covers a host of areas including medical and mental health history; school success; disruptions in living arrangements for the child; history of trauma, including the witnessing of domestic violence; and the discipline practices of the parent(s).

Beyond intake, the obvious first task in child assessment is the establishment of a positive relationship with the child. Such relationships require a special sensitivity to the child's world. For example, children who live in a threatening environment are much more reluctant to engage in new relationships with strangers. However, once children have begun to accept you as a "safe" person, they often are more open and genuine than adults tend to be.

Once you have established a safe and trusting relationship with a child, you can begin the problem-definition process, using intake information as appropriate. Thus, the first contact with the child may find you already involved in problem-definition questions that draw out the child's perspective, emotional state, environmental factors contributing to the child's problem, self-views, and significant relationships with others. The highly verbal child is able to respond to open-ended questions about self, family, friends, and environment. However, the less-verbal child may need structured questions (Who? What? Where? How? When?) in order to respond to the counselor. Some child counselors prefer to avoid these types of questions because they also restrict the child's response and thus the range of information that is gained.

Given the special nature of communicating with children, it is important that the counselor have a plan before entering into the assessment process. This plan must take into account the child's developmental language level and ability to respond to concrete or abstract concepts. Younger children may not understand questions that are framed abstractly. It is also important to the process that you ask questions in a way that provides specific rather than general responses. All of this must be done in a time span that fits the child's attention span. For younger children, play therapy is often used both as an assessment tool and counseling approach (e.g., Schaefer, 2011). Play therapy requires specialized training in its use.

Finally, with older children and adolescents, it is important to recognize the pressures the young person is experiencing from family members, siblings, or peers. Such pressures only make it more difficult for the child to respond cooperatively to the counselor. Assessment techniques such as a genogram with a theme that tracks an issue throughout the family and social network (e.g., substance abuse) may be of help in such instances.

Issues Related to Child Clinical Assessment

A number of concerns have been raised by state legislatures, social service agencies, and the helping profession regarding the welfare of children. Many of these concerns are revealed in the child counseling process, including child abuse, the effect of divorce on children, the single-parent home, and poverty. The counselor is faced with a fundamental question when he or she works with a child: Given the child's familial and socioeconomic status, how is the child functioning? Is the child thriving adequately, or is there a worrisome developmental lag? Do parents have resources available to them that are necessary for adequate parenting? How can their resources be improved? In short, a child's situation simply cannot be assessed without a parallel assessment of the child's context. Furthermore, although counselors must always advocate for social justice, they must also adjust expectations in particular assessment tasks so that they are both empathic and realistic. Parents who are burdened with poverty and unsafe neighborhoods need support from counselors, not judgment.

In addition to assessing environmental context, counselors must be prepared to diagnose children who are not functioning using *DSM-5* criteria. This resource is used by all service providers who conform to guidelines for repayment for psychological/psychiatric services by health insurance companies and government programs. It addresses wide-ranging behaviors, such as oppositional behavior, cruelty to peers or animals, destructiveness, chronic lying, stealing, inattentiveness and failure to learn, eating disorders, suicide risk, and autism. In addition to criteria, the *DSM-5* includes a discussion of subtypes, diagnostic features, prevalence, development of the problem and its typical course, culture-related information, and functional consequences of the particular problem, all of which helps mental health professionals make an accurate diagnosis and broaden the counselor's understanding of the factors associated with a diagnosis.

Depending on the diagnosis, the counselor's role may include involvement with others: physicians, psychologists, psychiatrists, social workers, marriage and family therapists, the court system, or the state child welfare system. The counselor is often the person to initiate these other services. When this happens, it is rarely the end of the counselor's role. The more likely outcome is that the counselor remains involved, either as a primary or secondary service provider to the child and family. As a primary provider, the counselor continues the counseling relationship with the child, using the other resources as consultant or adjunct services. For school counselors, the role is likely to be that of coordinating the school's participation in the larger therapeutic plan.

CLINICAL ASSESSMENT WITH COUPLES AND FAMILIES

Most professional literature on marital and family therapy emphasizes a systemic approach to working with couples and families (see Chapter 11). This approach represents a qualitative shift in the conceptual framework toward data about interactions among individual members rather than characteristics of each individual member. In other words, the question changes from what is the individual thinking, doing, or feeling, to what is going on between persons and how the interaction is shaping or supporting a particular outcome. Thus, the approach is referred to as *systemic* because it is concerned with how the system is functioning and whether persons within the system are having their needs met.

Given this systematic perspective, the types of questions that characterize the intake and problem-definition interview address verbal and nonverbal interaction patterns between members of the identified system (e.g., family, couple, peer group). Although it is still important to obtain demographic information and medical information about each member of the couple or family, the counselor must refocus quickly on systemic factors—for example, the ways that each person's behaviors are both cause and effect of the behaviors of others. Interpersonal sequences are central to systemic assessment. Questions that reflect this orientation include the following:

"Whenever Antonio does this, how are you likely to respond, Nia?"

"When Nia reacts, what is the next thing you are likely to say, Antonio?"

Note that the counselor does not ask, "Why do you respond this way?" because that suggests to the clients that intention is more relevant than how the system actually functions.

The Family Genogram

One way to identify family structure and interaction data is the genogram. This type of diagram uses symbols to represent family members, typically over three generations. Figure 5.1 includes many of the symbols used most often in genograms. This exercise begins by explaining to family members how the genogram is drawn. Then the counselor begins to solicit information about various family members, beginning with the immediate family—for example, father and mother, each child, and the birthdates of each person. Children of the immediate family constitute the third (present) generation, whereas parents (mother and father) constitute the second generation. Added to this are the maternal and paternal grandparents (first generation) and any other family members who play active roles in the family's functioning.

Once the genogram has been drawn, it may be used to develop insights into family dynamics, including how family members perceive their relationships within the family, how they perceive their personal family role and the roles of other family members, how members are included or excluded verbally and nonverbally, who the protagonist is, who the peacemaker is, who hides, and so on. At the very least, the genogram can indicate where close relationships reside in the family and where overinvolvement or conflict is present. The review of the family genogram yields a family picture, both literally and systemically. It may be used to help individual family members gain insight into the family's functioning, to repair relationships where a family member may have been cut off by other family members, and to make adjustments in systemic patterns. The genogram is probably most used by Bowen-oriented counselors, but it is a useful intervention exercise for all schools of family therapy as well as for individual counselors.

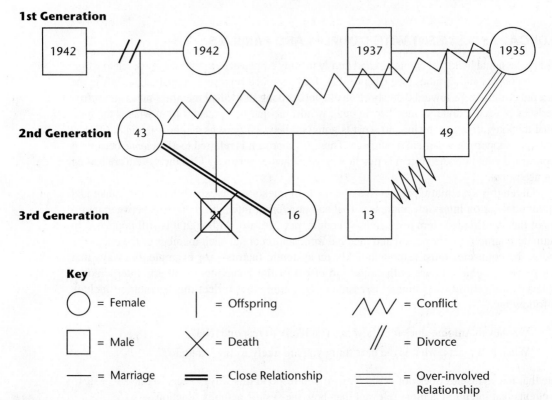

FIGURE 5.1   The Family Genogram

Thomas (1998) describes a multicultural genogram that incorporates cultural origins as well as family history. It includes all of the traditional information found in the family genogram, but it adds "assessment of worldview and cultural factors that often influence behaviors of members [such as] differences in cultural values between family members" and spirituality/religion (pp. 25–26). Genograms can be used in assessment across a multitude of themes including a variety of cultural factors, gender roles, work history (as used by career counselors), and military involvement (McGoldrick, Gerson, & Petry, 2008).

USING ASSESSMENT INFORMATION

Counselors develop different approaches to using the information collected from intake and problem-definition sessions. Some counselors look primarily for patterns of behavior. For example, one counselor noted that his client had a pattern of incompletions in life, including a general discharge from the Army prior to completing his enlistment, dropping out of college twice, and a long history of broken relationships. This observation provides food for thought: Are these events revealing a pattern of functioning? What happens to this person as he becomes involved in a commitment? What has this client come to think of himself as a result of his history? How does he anticipate future commitments?

The information that counselors collect during assessment is also invaluable not only in moving toward goals in counseling but also in planning relevant counseling strategies and approaches to use with problems. For example, a client who reports depression describes the problem primarily in cognitive terms: "I'm a failure; I'm not good at anything. I can't stand it when people don't approve of me. When something goes wrong, it's all my fault." Has this client internalized a self-defeating set of beliefs and self-perceptions that are erroneous and not likely to be based on data or facts? The counselor would probably decide to use an approach or strategy with this client that deals directly with cognitions, beliefs, and internal dialog.

In contrast, suppose another client is depressed because of a perceived inability to make friends, to form new relationships, and to maintain existing ones. In this instance, the counselor might look at the client's behavior in interpersonal relationships and use behavioral strategies that emphasize acquisition of social skills and interpersonal or systemic strategies that deal with relationships between people.

Counselors who fail to conduct assessment interviews are more likely to formulate erroneous conclusions about client problems, arrive at equally erroneous goals, and pursue irrelevant or non-workable counseling approaches and strategies. As a result, not only is more time spent on hit-or-miss counseling, but ultimately clients might leave with the same set of problems they brought to the first session.

To help you tie together the information revealed from assessment of a client with corresponding counseling interventions, the intervention chapters (Chapters 8 through 11) are organized around the four components of a problem (i.e., feelings, cognitions, behavior, relationships). For example, interventions that deal primarily with feelings or have an affective focus are presented in Chapter 8. Cognitive-based interventions are described in Chapter 9, and Chapter 10 presents behavioral interventions. Interventions with an interpersonal or systemic focus are discussed in Chapter 11.

SKILLS ASSOCIATED WITH ASSESSMENT

Assessment is an intentional process. Each question, each clarification, each line of discussion by the counselor has a purpose. The process of assessing client concerns is both current and contextual. Details surrounding the client's presenting issues are important to understand, but equally important are background details that shape how clients understand and define their world (Seligman, 2009).

In assessing client concerns, the counselor relies on all of the rapport and relationship skills described in Chapter 4 as well as data-gathering skills. Some of the skills most frequently used during intake and problem-defining interviews include verbal and nonverbal attending, paraphrasing content, and using a variety of questions to facilitate the assessment process. Of these skills, questioning and exploration become the intentional instruments for introducing, leading, facilitating, and inferring what the client brings to the counseling event. Each of these types of skills is examined in greater detail to explain how they differ and how they produce different types of information. Before we move to these skills, however, we introduce the reader to a critical difference in the object of such skills. It is our experience that many beginning counselors are enamored with the "plot" (i.e., the story line) that clients describe rather than the implications of their story. Their questions and comments, therefore, miss much of the *meaning* that events and interactions with others have for clients. Rather, we encourage assessments that are centered on the client rather than the plot. We offer the following to underscore the difference:

Plot-Centered Counseling Example:

> CLIENT: I had a real rough week.
>
> COUNSELOR: I'm sorry to hear that. What happened?
>
> CLIENT: My bossed yelled at me and told me he'd fire me if he could.
>
> COUNSELOR: What did you do to get that reaction?
>
> CLIENT: Well, I was late a few times and I messed up on a major account.
>
> COUNSELOR: How did you mess up? *(Staying with plot rather than the client)*
>
> CLIENT: Well, I was supposed to call this guy as a follow-up and I forgot to do it and he called my boss and complained. I don't think it was such a big deal, but my boss is afraid that he'll take his business elsewhere.
>
> COUNSELOR: Is there anything you can do to make things better? *(Skipping to intervention before finishing assessment or goal setting)*
>
> CLIENT: I don't know what that would be. It's not like I can go back in time.
>
> COUNSELOR: Are you really afraid that your boss may fire you?
>
> CLIENT: Nah. I think he was just blowing off steam.
>
> COUNSELOR: Oh, so did anything else make it a hard week? *(Dropping one theme and seeking additional plot.)*
>
> CLIENT: Well, my girlfriend broke up with me.
>
> COUNSELOR: She did? How did that make you feel? *(An attempt to be empathic but not a great one. How does the counselor think he feels?!)*
>
> CLIENT: Not great, that's for sure. I thought we were doing better.
>
> COUNSELOR: What did she say was the reason she was breaking up? *(Again, seeking more plot and ignoring the client.)*
>
> And on and on . . . .

Client-Centered Counseling Example:

> CLIENT: I had a rough week.
>
> COUNSELOR: I'm sorry to hear that. What was rough for you? *(Although only slightly different from the previous example, it communicates that the client is the central focus, not the plot.)*

CLIENT: My bossed yelled at me and told me he'd fire me if he could.

COUNSELOR: That sounds unpleasant. Can you remember your thoughts when all of this was happening? *(Moving toward a cognitive lens. Staying with the client.)*

CLIENT: You mean other than thinking he was an a number 1 jerk?? (Laughs)

COUNSELOR: Yeah, I mean other than that. Sometimes our thoughts at difficult moments are a good place to begin. *(Provides rationale to client for the question.)*

CLIENT: Well, I don't know exactly what I was thinking, but I know I was actually freaked for a moment because I need this job. I don't want things to go south. I've been there before and I don't want to go back.

COUNSELOR: You've been there before. *(Restatement to underscore what seemed important.)*

CLIENT: Yeah. *(Looks pensive but doesn't say any more.)*

COUNSELOR: *(Choosing to stay with the present.)* So, although you can't remember exact thoughts when your boss got mad at you, you can recall feeling threatened because this job is important to you. It also seems like you were a little afraid that you might be repeating something from your past that you don't want to repeat. *(Reflection of feeling.)*

CLIENT: That about sums it up.

COUNSELOR: With a little more distance, does either of those feelings, being threatened or fearing that you are repeating old mistakes, still feel real to you? Try to give yourself a minute to get in touch with your feelings. *(Here the counselor is moving toward an affective focus.)*

CLIENT: (After a pause.) I don't really feel threatened; I think my boss was just blowing off stream. But I do feel like I continue to do stupid things. My girlfriend broke up with me too this week and I didn't see it coming. This has happened before. So, I'm starting to feel like a loser, you know? I can't impress my boss and I can't keep a girlfriend.

COUNSELOR: That sounds pretty heavy. You're right. You have had a bad week. I wonder if we could look at both of those more closely, the way you approach the job and the way you are in relationships to see if there's something in all of that you might want to work on changing. *(Rather than moving quickly and asking for more plot, counselor encourages client to reflect on what has already been shared.)*

And so on . . . .

In summary, although counselor statements should always emphasize meaning for the client over tracking the plot, this is especially important to keep in mind during assessment, because it is so easy to fall into the latter pattern at that time.

Clarifying Questions

Sometimes a client's responses sound cryptic or confused and the counselor is left wondering just what the client is trying to say. It is important to seek clarification in these moments rather than guess or assume that the communication is unimportant. The *clarifying question* asks the client to rephrase the communication and can be stated in several ways.

Clarifying questions are self-explanatory; the important point is that they can be over- or underused. When overused, they become distractors. When underused, the reasons are typically that

---

Key Assessment-Related Skills

Clarifying Questions

Questions that ask the client for greater detail (e.g., "Can you tell me more about how that happens?")

- "Could you try to describe that feeling in another way? I'm not sure I am following what you mean."
- "When you say 'fuzzy,' what's that feeling like?"
- "I think I got lost in that. Could you go through the sequence of events again for me?"
- "Is there another way you could describe what that meant to you?"

Open-Ended Questions

Questions that require more than a minimal response from the client, usually seeking for more detail (e.g., "How?")

- "What is there in all of this that has special meaning to you?"
- "How do you react when she [he] says that sort of thing to you?"
- "What is keeping you from asking him [her]?"
- "What is the piece that would unlock the puzzle?"

Closed Questions

Intake questions that ask for specific data (e.g., "When?" "Where?" "Who?")

- "How old were you when your parents died?"
- "Are you an only child, or do you have brothers and sisters?"

- "Are you taking any medications now?"
- "Have you ever received counseling or therapy?"

Linking Statements

Statements that ask the client to make connections, explain relationships, and so on.

- "So when you withdraw, he's more likely to overreact, right?"
- "You said earlier that your husband is 'high maintenance.' Is this an example of high maintenance?"
- "It sounds like you feel you overreacted both times that you were challenged. Is that right?"

Confirmatory Statements

Statements that seek to verify what the client has described to ensure accuracy of understanding (i.e., the "flip side" of clarifying questions).

- "Let me be sure I understand. You say that . . . ."
- "I assume you were serious when you described the relationship between you and your siblings as 'hostile'?"
- "Let me be sure I'm on the right page with you. You definitely want to be less angry with your kids, right?"

---

the counselor is reluctant to seek clarification lest it impede or distract the client from the topic or the counselor believes that it somehow reflects on him or her as a poor listener if clarification is needed. If you are simply unable to follow the client's train of thought, it is important to seek clarification before you encourage the client to proceed; otherwise, you run the risk of drawing inaccurate conclusions. Furthermore, seeking clarification reflects well on you as a counselor, not poorly.

Open-Ended Questions

Open-ended questions require more than a minimal one-word or factual answer by the client. They are introduced with the words *what, where, when, who,* or *how.* "What?" questions solicit facts and information; "How?" questions are used to inquire about emotions or sequences of events; certain "Where?" "When?" and "Who?" questions can invite answers that give context surrounding an issue. (We should note that these words can also introduce closed questions.) It is important to vary the words used to start open-ended questions depending on the type of material you want to focus on and solicit from the client. The minimal restatement is a softer way of asking an open-ended question. It is a one- or two-word restatement of what the client just said:

CLIENT: "I'm beginning to think I am burned out."

COUNSELOR: "Burned out?"

A good open-ended question offers new energy into the session and helps open clients up in a different way. Three specific instances when open-ended questions are particularly useful during counseling sessions include the following:

1. *Beginning an interview*
   "What would you like to talk about?"
   "What brings you to counseling?"
   "How have things been this week in relation to _____?"
   "Where do you want to begin today?"

2. *Encouraging client elaboration*
   "What happens when you lose control?"
   "Who else is invested in this problem?"
   "When do you notice that reaction?"
   "How could things be better for you?"

3. *Eliciting specific examples*
   "What do you do when this happens?"
   "Exactly how do you feel about it?"
   "Where are you when you feel this way?"

Closed Questions

As noted in Chapter 2, a *closed question* narrows the area or focus of discussion. Thus, when you need a specific piece of information (e.g., "Are you taking any medications now?"), it is best obtained by a closed or targeted question. Closed questions may be answered with yes or no or a specific piece of datum. The closed question can also work against the counselor because it is the easiest to ask, and yet it provides the most limited amount of discourse. For this reason, the closed question should be used sparingly except when specifics are needed.

The Linking Statement

Part of the counselor's task is to understand background factors that may have spawned patterns that are operating in the client's life. Such patterns often play a significant role in how the client reacts or how the client interprets events. These connections can be subtle or even unrecognized by the client. Consequently, an important aspect of counseling is to identify and examine the connectors between events, thoughts, feelings, and circumstances. Only by recognizing and consciously challenging these patterned connections can the client regain control over them. Not to be confused with interpretations, *linking statements* are exploratory and even hypothetical in nature. Their purpose is to invite the client to take an event, thought, feeling, or circumstance and look for connections between it and other events, thoughts, feelings, or circumstances. A good linking statement has the potential for an "Aha moment" for the client early in the counseling process.

Confirmatory Statements

Confirmatory statements serve as a flip side of a clarification question and are an important tool in the counselor's repertoire of responses. Rather than ask for clarification of what the client has just said, the counselor offers his or her understanding of the client's situation.

Thus, *confirmatory statements* demonstrate that the counselor is hearing the client accurately and that they are engaged in the session, something that can be very important to the client. From the counselor's perspective, such statements may also lead the client into further or deeper exploration of a topic, feeling, or condition. When this happens, the client is open to greater self-examination and self-understanding. From an assessment perspective, confirmatory statements not only confirm what the client is saying, they may also confirm the counselor's hypotheses or speculations about the client's world.

EFFECTS OF ASSESSMENT ON CLIENTS

The assessment stage of counseling is likely to have a number of possible effects on clients. Although each client's reaction to an intake or problem-definition interview(s) is unique, it is also possible to describe some fairly predictable client patterns of reaction. Some of these patterns are positive; some are negative. On the positive side, assessing client concerns helps clients experience various feelings, which they reveal in responses such as the following:

Understanding: "I believe someone finally understands how terrible these last few months have been for me."

Relief: "Well, it does feel good to get that off my chest."

Hopefulness: "Now maybe something can be done to help me feel better and get a handle on things."

Motivation: "Now that I have someone to talk to, I feel like I can stick with a plan."

On the negative side, assessment can result in such client reactions and feelings as the following:

Anxious: "Am I really that bad off? This is a lot to deal with all at once. Can I do this and still keep up with everything else?"

Defensive: "Boy, do I feel on the spot. There are so many questions being thrown at me. Some of them are so personal, too."

Vulnerable: "How do I know if I can trust her with this? Can she handle it? She seems awfully young. Will she keep what I say to herself?"

Evaluated: "I wonder if she thinks I'm really messed up? Crazy? Stupid? Maybe something really *is* wrong with me?"

Given these possible reactions, it is important to assess client concerns carefully and with much sensitivity. The ideal outcome is when the client's positive reactions to assessment outweigh the negative reactions. When this occurs, assessment has become a useful and productive part of counseling without jeopardizing the working relationship between the counselor and client that is being established. Client reactions to assessment are likely to be more positive when the counselor uses questions that are directly relevant to the client's concerns and are also used in proportion to other skills and responses.

Nothing can make a client feel defensive and interrogated more quickly than asking too many questions. Sometimes the same information can be gleaned by nonverbal attending behaviors, verbal underscoring, or statements that paraphrase or reflect content or affect. Inexperienced counselors seem to have a natural tendency to use questions more frequently than any other response, and they must be especially careful during assessment not to let this skill take over while their other newly learned skills go by the wayside.

CASE ILLUSTRATION OF THE INTAKE INTERVIEW

The Case of Angela

Angela is a middle-age female who works full-time as a teacher. She reports that she is divorced and has not remarried, although she maintains custody of two teenage children. Angela states that the reason she is seeking counseling at this time is to learn to have better control of her moods. She indicates that she often "flies off the handle" for no reason with her own children or with her students in the classroom. She also reports that she cries easily and "feels blue" much of the time.

The Intake Interview

The intake/history interview with Angela revealed the following information:

I. Identifying Data

Angela is a 45-year-old White woman. She lives with her two children (ages 14 and 16) in a mobile home outside a small town. She has been divorced for 6 years. She teaches English to high school juniors.

II. Range of Problems

In addition to the problems first presented (feeling out of control and blue), Angela also feels that she is a failure as a wife and mother, primarily because of her divorce and her mood swings. Her self-description is predominantly negative.

III. Current Life Setting

Angela's typical day consists of getting up, going to work, coming home, making sure her kids have had something to eat, and then grading papers or watching TV. On weekends, she stays at home a great deal unless she needs to take her 14-year-old somewhere. She has few neighbors, only one or two close friends, and does not participate in any recreational, religious, or social activities on a regular basis. Occasionally, she reports checking her Facebook page. Often, however, this is a mixed experience as most of her childhood friends are still married and

she finds it difficult to hear about their lives. Angela reports a great deal of difficulty in carrying out her regular routine on days when she feels down. Occasionally, she calls in sick and stays home and sleeps all day.

IV. Family History

Angela is the youngest of three children. She was raised Roman Catholic in a second-generation Italian American family. She describes her relationship to her two older brothers and to her mother as very close. She is not as close to her father, although she reports that he was always good to her. The family remains close and gathers whenever there is an occasion, a birthday, or a celebration. Angela also reports that, as the youngest child and the only girl, she was protected and pampered a great deal by her parents and her brothers while growing up. Currently, she lives a day's drive away from both her parents and her brothers and looks forward to seeing them on family occasions. To her knowledge, none of her immediate family members has had any significant mental health problems, although she thinks that one of her aunts is chronically depressed.

V. Personal History

A. Medical: Angela reports that in the last year she has undergone surgery for the removal of a benign lump in her breast. She also indicates that she has been diagnosed as having Addison's disease and is on medication for it, but she frequently forgets to take the medication as prescribed. The medication is prescribed by a general practitioner.

Angela reports some sleeping problems, primarily when she is distressed. At these times, she has difficulty falling asleep until 2:00 or 3:00 A.M. She has reported her sleep disturbance and mood swings to her physician, who has suggested that she may be experiencing early perimenopausal symptoms. Her weight fluctuates by 5 or 6 pounds during a given month. When she is upset, she often eats little or nothing for a day or two.

When asked about suicidal ideation, Angela states that she has never wanted to kill herself. Even at her lowest point during the divorce, she never contemplated ending her life.

B. Educational: Angela has a bachelor's degree in English and a master's degree in education. She appears to be of above-average intelligence and describes herself as a conscientious teacher to the point of worrying excessively about performance and evaluation. She occasionally takes graduate courses to renew her teacher certification.

C. Military: Angela has never served in the military.

D. Vocational: Angela has been a high school English teacher ever since graduating from college, although she reports that she "dropped out" of her teaching after her first child was born 16 years ago. She resumed teaching when she was divorced 6 years ago when her children were 8 and 10 years old. She describes her present job as adequately challenging but not very financially rewarding. She stays with it primarily because of job security and because of the hours (summers off). She reports satisfactory relationships with other teachers, although she has no good friends at work.

E. Sexual and marital: Angela's first sexual experiences were with her former husband, although she reports she received adequate sex education from her parents and her older brothers. She asserts that this is a difficult subject for her to discuss.

She states that although she felt her sexual relationship with her husband was satisfactory, he became sexually involved with another woman prior to their divorce. Angela indicates that before her marriage, she had only two other love relationships with men, both of which were terminated mutually because of differences in values. She describes her marital relationship as good until the time she discovered through a friend about her husband's affair. She has very little contact with her ex-husband, although her two children see him every other weekend. She reports that the children have a good relationship with their father and that he has been helpful to her by taking them for periods of time when she is feeling depressed and overwhelmed by her life situation. Angela repeatedly indicates that she blames herself for the failure of the marriage.

F. Counseling: Angela reports that she saw a counselor for depression during her divorce (about 12 sessions). She terminated the counseling sessions because she thought she had things under control. She was never on antidepressant medication, nor does she want to be. She is currently concerned about her ability to manage her feelings and wants help to learn how to deal better with her moods, especially with feeling upset, irritable, and blue.

VI. **Counselor's Observations of Angela**
During the intake interview, you observe that Angela generally seems to have little energy and is rather passive, as evidenced by her slouched body position, soft voice tone, and lack of animation in facial expressions and body movements. Angela appears to be in control of her feelings, although she cried much of the time while describing her marital and sexual history.

Integration of Material from Intake

Following an initial interview, it is important to tie together the information obtained from the client in some meaningful fashion. In Angela's case, you know that she is a 45-year-old female who, although she has been divorced for 6 years, has not ever really resolved the divorce issue in her mind. Her concern with mood fluctuations and feeling so blue appears to be substantiated not only by her nonverbal demeanor, but also by her verbal reports of symptoms and behaviors typically associated with mild to moderate depression:

- She perceives herself as a failure, particularly in her role as a wife and mother.
- She communicates some responsibility for the divorce because her husband "needed" to find another woman to make him happy.
- She describes herself negatively.
- She experiences a reduced level of energy and rate of activity when distressed.
- She has very few close relationships with others.
- She experiences some sleeping difficulties and loss of appetite when distressed.
- She does not appear to have any concrete goals or plans for the future apart from her role as mother and teacher.

This picture is complicated by Angela's health. She has undergone a surgical procedure that was undoubtedly worrisome. She suffers from a fairly complex endocrinological problem that, because of her lack of compliance in taking prescribed medication, may make her mood fluctuations and depression more intense and more frequent. There is also a possibility that perimenopause is contributing to sleeplessness, if not mood issues.

Angela's family is a strength. She is on good terms with her family and enjoys the occasions when they get together. Knowing that strong family ties are characteristic of the Italian American family, this is likely to be a source of significant support. However, the distance between her home and that of her family poses a problem.

Beyond the intake interview, it is important for the counselor to continue developing an understanding of the presenting problem. This involves assessment of the components of the problem, intensity, and possible controlling variables associated with Angela's feelings of depression. Some of the information she gave during the intake session serves as suggestions on which to build during the process of problem definition.

Problem-Definition Analysis

COMPONENTS OF THE PROBLEM.

Feelings.   Angela describes her predominant feelings as irritable, upset, and "down" or "blue." Primary somatic reactions during times of stress include loss of appetite and insomnia.

Cognitions.   When you ask Angela to describe specific things she thinks about or focuses on during the times she feels down, she responds with statements such as, "I just think about what a failure I am," "I wish I had been a better wife [mother]," and "I should have been able to keep my marriage together and because I didn't, I'm a failure." Her cognitions represent two areas or trouble spots often associated with feelings of depression—"shouldism" and perfectionism. She does not report any thoughts or ideas about suicide.

Behaviors.   Angela has some trouble specifying things she does or does not do while depressed. She finally says that she often withdraws and retreats to her room or that she becomes irritable, usually to her students or children. She also cries easily at these times. During leisure time, she reports passive activities such as watching TV or checking in on her Facebook account.

Interpersonal Relationships.   Angela notes that once she feels down, no one around her can pull her out of it, but she also says that she does not have close friends with whom to share her feelings or problems. She believes her depressed feelings interfere with her relationship with her children because they tend to avoid her when she gets into a period of depression. However, she also acknowledges that she can use her feelings to get her children to do things "her way."

PATTERN OF CONTRIBUTING EVENTS.   When Angela describes what seems to lead up to these feelings, she notes the following:

- Failure to take her medication
- Being reminded or reminding herself about her divorce
- When she's had a bad day at work
- Hassles with her children and/or ex-husband

In describing what seems to stop the feelings or make them better or worse, she observes:

- Taking her medication
- Doing something pleasant with her children
- Having to go to work (most of the time)
- Having telephone or other contact initiated by her brothers or parents

INTENSITY OF THE PROBLEM.   With depression, it is important to assess whether it is a long-term, chronic condition or a short-term response to a situation or event. Angela reports that she has felt depressed more frequently for the past 6 years since the divorce than she ever did before. However, she acknowledges that even during her marriage, she was occasionally blue for several days at a time and was not responsive to her husband's attempts to make her feel better. Eventually, she reports, "he just stopped trying." It's during these current bouts that can last up to a week that she is most apt to call in sick or to become irritable with her students and her children.

CLIENT COPING SKILLS, STRENGTHS, RESOURCES.   Angela is not readily aware of anything she does to cope effectively with her depressed feelings. She seems to believe that the onset and termination of these feelings are mostly out of her control. She does describe herself as having been a good student and currently a good teacher. Her strengths are her reliability and dependability. She does indicate that she has a lot of perseverance and tenacity when she decides she wants something to work out. Angela's family of origin is a resource to be explored.

CRISIS ASSESSMENT

Crisis has become a very common condition in our world. For the individual, crisis can be composed of a life-threatening medical diagnosis, a divorce, a death, or a job loss. A crisis may also be a new state that follows unrelenting stress—PTSD falls in this category when a person is experiencing acute symptoms. Crises can also include a variety of personal losses (real or imagined), physical or sexual abuse, natural disaster, or any combination of these. Another point to remember is that a crisis is in the eye of the beholder. For one client of relatively low resiliency, a neighborhood robbery might instigate a crisis; for another client of high individual resiliency, even a robbery in their own home would not push them beyond their ability to cope. Therefore, crisis is integrally tied to the overall emotional and psychological strength of the individual.

The point, then, is that a crisis is a condition where persons have used the psychological resources and coping strategies that they typically use when a problem occurs, and yet the situation doesn't seem to get any better. This can be frightening and results in the person feeling out of control. When clients come to counseling in crisis, therefore, there is an urgency that presents unique challenges.

Crisis assessment requires that the counselor perform three tasks: (a) seek to understand the nature of the client's perception of the crisis event, (b) determine the needs and strengths of the individual in crisis, and (c) determine the strengths and deficits of the client's recovery environment (Collins & Collins, 2005, p. 10). Making this assessment involves most of the stages described in Chapter 3. It is important to assess whether the client is in emotional or physical jeopardy. In addition, issues such as goal setting and intervention planning take on a much shorter-term focus.

Consider Angela's case. Is she in crisis? More specifically, is she in danger of self-harm or emotional collapse? What is the intensity of her presenting problem(s)? What coping skills, strengths, and resources can she potentially mobilize?

In closing this brief section, note that crisis counseling is a specialty within counseling with its own literature (e.g., Collins & Collins, 2005; James & Gilliland, 2012; Kanel, 2011; Wright, 2011). However, every practicing counselor is apt to come across a client in crisis on occasion; for this reason, some rudimentary comments about crisis assessment are included here. We urge all counselors to gather additional resources for their work with persons in crises.

INTEGRATION OF PROBLEM-DEFINITION INFORMATION WITH TREATMENT PLANNING: ANGELA

The information obtained from this problem-definition session and initial session is of direct value in selecting and planning relevant counseling interventions to help Angela. In her case, the depression seems partially maintained by two potential physiological sources—Addison's disease and, at least potentially, perimenopause. Therefore, part of your planning should involve having her health assessed and monitored by a physician. It is evident that the cognitive and interpersonal spheres are major components and contributing causes of her feelings. Thus, it is important to select counseling interventions that focus on the cognitive and interpersonal modalities. Interventions such as cognitive restructuring, reframing, irrational thought analysis, systemic analysis, assigning homework to increase social life, and family counseling are all useful possibilities. (These interventions are described in Chapters 9 through 11.) It is also possible that some of Angela's difficulties stem from dissonance she feels with the cultural values of her childhood and family. All of these are preliminary treatment planning hypotheses; however, they assist Angela's counselor in moving toward goal-setting once a diagnosis has been established.

Summary

Assessment is invaluable for seeking pertinent information about clients and their presenting problems. In addition to the value of information garnered, assessment can also be reactive—that is, it can initiate the process of change for clients. Assessment is often started by intake sessions that gather information about the client's background and history. Assessment is very important in the early stages of counseling to help counselors formulate hypotheses, but it is also an ongoing process during counseling because presenting problems and accompanying conceptualizations of issues often change. Specific assessment interviews obtain information about components of the problem, patterns of contributing events, intensity of the problem, and client coping skills. Skills used to obtain such information frequently include paraphrasing content, reflecting content and affect, summarizing, and asking a variety of questions with an emphasis on open-ended questions.

Exercises

I. Intake and History Interviews

A. Identify a current or existing problem in the life of a member of your family. It might be a family or relationship conflict, an intimacy issue, a financial problem, or a work- or school-related concern. Select someone with whom you feel comfortable discussing this problem. Your task is to discuss how your relative's background and history have affected the development and maintenance of this concern. Refer to the intake and history outline in this chapter to guide your discussion.

B. Using triads, identify one person as the Client, another as the Counselor, and one as an Observer. The assigned tasks are as follows:

Client. Describe a present or ongoing concern or issue in your life.

Counselor. Conduct an intake or history session with this client following the outline given in the chapter. If possible, record the session.

Observer. Be prepared to give feedback to the counselor following the role-play and/or to intervene and cue the counselor during the role-play if he or she has difficulty and gets stuck. Rotate the initial roles so that each person has an opportunity to be in each role once. Time requirement: 1 hour.

II. Problem Definition

A. Using the same problem you identified for Exercise I.A, identify the following:

1. Various components of the problem
2. Contributing conditions
3. Intensity of the problem
4. Client's resources, strengths, and coping skills

You may wish to do this alone or in conjunction with a partner, colleague, instructor, or supervisor. It may be helpful to refer to the outline in this chapter to jot down some key words as you go through this process.

B. Read Chapter 16, "Italian Families," by Joe Giordano, Monica McGoldrick, and Joanne Giordano Klages (2008), in M. McGoldrick, J. Giordano, and Nydia Garcia-Preto (Eds.), *Ethnicity and Family Therapy,* 3rd ed., pp. 616–628. New York, NY: Guilford. Then do an analysis of Angela's intake interview within the context of her family of origin. What insights about Angela may be gained through an understanding of her cultural background? How might her background and her family be utilized as part of her counseling?

III. Questions

A. In this activity, identify whether each of the questions listed is a Clarifying, Open-Ended, or Closed question. Use the key below to record your answers in the blanks provided.

C = Clarifying
O-E = Open-ended
Cl = Closed

_____ 1. "What is it like for you when you get depressed?"

_____ 2. "Have you had a physical exam in the last two years?"

_____ 3. "Are you saying you don't give up easily?"

_____ 4. "How does this job affect your moods?"

_____ 5. "Do you mean to say that you have difficulty letting go?"

_____ 6. "Do you have any children?"

B. In this activity, you are given five client statements. Practice formulating a question for each client statement. Share your questions in your class or with your instructor or a colleague.

1. *Client (a teenager):* "I've got to graduate with my class. If I don't, everyone will think I'm a real screw-up."

2. *Client (an elderly man):* "It's just so hard to make a living on a fixed income like I do. If I had it to do over, I'd do it a lot different."

3. *Client (a young girl):* "I hate my dad. He's always picking on me."

4. *Clients (a couple married for 4 years):* "It's just not turning out the way we thought. We wanted our marriage to really work. But it's not."

5. *Client (a middle-age person):* "There are just so many pressures on me right now from all sides—family, work, friends, you name it."

Discussion Questions

1. Intake interviews and the problem-definition process are time-consuming and may seem to delay the counseling process. Assume you are the clinical director for a private mental health agency. How do you justify the use of these assessment interviews to the administrative director or to the agency's board of directors?

2. Suppose you are seeing a client who presents a crisis situation (e.g., recent sexual assault, involved in a car accident that included a fatality, one's child diagnosed with serious chronic condition). You probably will not have the luxury of devoting a session or more to conduct a complete intake/problem-definition process. What information about the problem and about the client's background and history would be most important to obtain in a 15- to 20-minute time period? Discuss with other class members.

3. Assessment with young children (ages 6–10) calls for a different type of interaction. How should you modify your approach for this age group? What kinds of information should you solicit? What do you know about yourself that either facilitates the assessment process or provides obstacles to your success with this age group?

4. How do you think the assessment process may be viewed differently by women and by men? Can you also think of instances in which the effect of assessment may vary with the cultural/ethnic background of the client?

MyCounselingLab® Assignment

Go to the Video Library under Video Resources on the MyCounselingLab site for your text and search for the following clips:

- **Video Example: Barbara: Parenting—Identifying the Program**   What did you learn in this video clip that you could use in your counseling during the assessment phase?

- **Video Example: Identifying a Specific Problem**   This segment depicts work with a child. Does the counselor use different skills here than he might use with an adult? How does this segment exemplify what you read in the chapter about assessment with children?

- **Video Example: Paraphrasing: Nicole**   Although this segment emphasizes paraphrasing, note how the counselor uses this and other skills to track the problem. By requesting specific examples, she is able to gain a clearer understanding of the client's presenting issue.

- **Video Example: Listening Cycle**   As this counselor gathers information, what counselor skills are evident?

Now that you have seen some different counselors attempting to understand the client's issues, how do you think you will incorporate any of what you viewed in your own counseling?

Developing Counseling Goals

PURPOSE OF THIS CHAPTER

When the counselor and client first meet, there are two stories to be told. The client's story is whatever he or she is bringing to counseling: a troubled relationship, a history of personal crises, a failing career, a cycle of abuse, a sense of impossibility. The counselor's story is about what happens in counseling: How success or failure in life is understood; who is responsible for client change and improvement; what the counselor is actually *doing* as the client engages and explores; the role of counseling in the bigger picture of the client's life itself; and, of course, achieving a desirable outcome. This chapter examines the process by which the counselor and client can work collaboratively to define what that desirable outcome might or will be.

Considerations as You Read This Chapter

- There is a great divide between needs and wants. In the context of counseling, how can we differentiate between *needs* and *wants*?
- Who is best able to judge what are wise wants or goals? The counselor, or the client?
- How does one make these decisions?
- What is the impact of one's choice of goals on the counseling process?

Often, counselors (or sometimes clients) will complain, "The session didn't go anywhere," or "I felt like we were talking in circles." Once the assessment process has resulted in a reasonably solid understanding of the client's issues, it is important to translate general client concerns into specific desired goals. Goals give direction to the therapeutic process and help both the counselor and the client to move in a focused direction with a specific route in mind. They represent the results or outcomes the client wants to achieve at the end of counseling. Without goals, it is all too easy to get sidetracked or lost. Goals help both the counselor and client specify exactly what can and cannot be accomplished through counseling. In this respect, goal setting is an important extension of the assessment process. Recall that during assessment, clients focus on specific concerns and issues that are difficult, problematic, or not going very well for them. In goal setting, clients identify, with the counselor's help, specific ways in which they want to resolve these issues and specific courses of action they can take for problem resolution.

The word *goal* can sound quite behavioral, and indeed, behavioral counselors consistently refer to goals. We argue, however, that *all* counseling is goal-driven. *Goal* simply refers to an outcome for the counseling process that alerts both counselor and client that counseling has been successful. Although it is certainly the case that, when possible, goals are best described as behaviors because these are easiest to measure, goals may also include emotional states, insights, and even existential calm. As we describe in this chapter, goals are negotiated between the client and counselor, must provide some direction for the counseling, and should lead to appropriate counseling interventions.

FUNCTIONS OF COUNSELING GOALS

Goals serve four important functions in the counseling process. First, goals can have a *motivational effect*. When clients are encouraged to specify desirable changes in their lives, they are more likely to work toward accomplishing those outcomes. This is particularly true when clients actively participate in the goal setting process.

Goals also have an *educational function* in counseling. Over and over again, counselors realize that clients have not been successful in managing their lives or their internal life because they do not know how to set positive, achievable goals. Such goals can help clients acquire new life responses. By going through a goal-setting process, clients learn not only how to structure their lives but also what changes in behavior or thinking may be involved in the new vista. Dixon and Glover (1984) explain the benefits in this way:

> Once a goal is formulated and selected by a problem solver, it is likely to be rehearsed in the working memory and stored in long-term memory. A goal encoded in this way, then, becomes a major heuristic for the problem solver as he or she interacts with the environment. (pp. 128–129)

This is quite evident in the performance of highly successful performers, including athletes, who set goals for themselves and then use the goals to rehearse their performance repeatedly in their heads. For example, concert pianists cognitively rehearse the way they want a particular passage to sound; champion divers visualize themselves performing a particular dive in a desired fashion both before the competition and on the platform.

Goals provide an *evaluative function* in counseling. The type of outcomes or change represented by the client's goals helps the counselor select and evaluate various counseling interventions that are likely to be successful for a particular client pursuing a specific goal or set of outcomes. Goals also contribute to the evaluative function in counseling, because a goal represents a desired outcome, a point at which counseling can be deemed successful. Thus, when outcome goals are established, both the counselor and the client can evaluate client progress toward the goals to determine when they are being attained and when the goals or the counseling intervention may need revision. But goals must be defined so that clients can measure their progress. As already stated, goals that are easily observable and measurable are the easiest to use. When goals are observable and measurable, clients can recognize when efforts are succeeding or when efforts must be revised because they are not succeeding. Further, even internal states can often be paired with external behaviors. For example, a client may assert that she wants more self-esteem, at which point the counselor then engages this client in a discussion about how she will recognize increased self-esteem in herself. If her response is that she will "feel better," the counselor can inquire about what the client tends to do when she feels better. In other words, although not all goals are *behaviors* in the strictest sense, it is enormously beneficial, especially for evaluation of the counseling process, for goals to be linked to something that the client (and perhaps the counselor) can recognize as indicating that a goal is met.

Finally, goals serve a *treatment assessment function* in counseling. As the impact of third-party payers on counseling practice continues to grow, peer review of the effectiveness of treatment becomes increasingly important. In this context, goal setting by the counselor becomes part of the formal treatment plan. (See Chapter 7 for a more extensive discussion of treatment plans.) Typically, these goals are derived from the goals that have been identified in the counselor–client discussion. Other goals are developed by the counselor after reviewing and interpreting data from the assessment phase of counseling.

PARAMETERS OF GOAL SETTING: PROCESS AND OUTCOME GOALS

The counseling process involves two types of goals: process goals and outcome goals. *Process goals* are the responsibility of the counselor and include establishing a therapeutic relationship so that a client is met with the conditions necessary for change. Thus, establishing rapport, providing a nonthreatening setting, and possessing and communicating accurate empathy and positive regard can all be considered process goals. These can be generalized to all client relationships and can be considered universal goals. Most of what was discussed in Chapters 4 and 5 are process goals. Once the client is better known and a working relationship is established, process goals are more fine-tuned for each client—that is, for Terry, it may be important that the counselor stay focused on his emotional responses, whereas for Glenn, a focus on his dichotomous thinking may be the process goal. In other words, counselors approach each counseling session with process goals, some of which are universal and some of which are specific, but all are related to the client's outcome goal once that has been established.

Outcome goals are also different for each client. They are the goals directly related to the changes your clients hope to accomplish through counseling. As you help each client understand his or her concerns, you help each client understand how counseling can be useful in responding to those concerns. The two of you begin to formulate tentative outcome goals together. As counseling continues, the original goals may be modified through better understanding of the problems and through the development of new attitudes and behaviors that will eliminate or reduce problems. Goal setting should be viewed as a flexible process, always subject to modification and refinement. Most important, outcome goals are *shared goals*—goals that both you and your client agree to work toward achieving.

We stated earlier that outcome goals that are visible or observable are easier to evaluate. And even though goals may first be stated as internal states (e.g., "I want to be happier"; "I don't want to be angry all the time"), the counselor can assist the client in pairing those internal states to behaviors. As most of us know, people do not divorce their emotional selves from their thinking selves and from their behavioral selves. We are complex beings, and we count on behaviors to give us cues about each other (e.g., "You look upset"; "You're not being yourself; what's going on?"). However, when our thoughts are too confused to sort out or our emotions are drowning out everything else, we may need the help of a counselor to link part of our reality to another part. Therefore, helping clients look for behaviors that are evident when their problems are under control or receding does not necessarily make us behavioral counselors. It's simply an important part of the goal-setting process that gives both client and counselor a GPS of sorts for knowing that counseling is going in the right direction.

As an example of our point, you may understand your client's issue as a lack of self-esteem. She may express feelings of worthlessness on a fairly regular basis. Whether you adhere to cognitive–behavioral approaches to counseling or phenomenological approaches, at some point the observable universe will be used to reflect the client's internal universe. Rogers (1977) believed that the goal of person-centered counseling was to help clients become more integrated so they could solve problems in their future. From this theoretical position, counselors did not set goals for clients, but helped clients establish their own goals. For the client with low self-esteem, a Rogerian approach is to offer a therapeutic pathway through empathy and unconditional positive regard that allows the client to discover herself in a way that eventually extinguishes her low self-esteem. Although it is unlikely that Rogers would make lists of behaviors to be accomplished, the goal was still clear and the counseling was intentional. Furthermore, the client would inevitably point to new feelings and behaviors to document the change. Our point is that goals are endemic to good counseling. For most counselors, having observable behaviors can be attached to the elimination of virtually all problems ("How would the people around you know that you weren't angry?"). Identifying these markers is an important part of goal setting.

When outcome goals are stated precisely, both you and your client have a better understanding of what is to be accomplished. This better understanding permits you to target your client's problems or concerns more directly and reduces tangential efforts. Equally important are the benefits you are able to realize in working toward specific goals. You are able to enlist the client's cooperation more directly because your client is more likely to understand what is to be done. In addition, you are in a better position to select appropriate interventions and strategies when your client has specific objectives. Finally, both you and your client are in a better position to recognize progress when it happens—a rewarding experience in its own right.

THREE ELEMENTS OF GOOD OUTCOME GOALS

Having differentiated process goals from outcome goals and wrestling with the issue of how goals "fit" counseling that is more phenomenological than concrete, we present elements of "good" outcome goals for the majority of counseling situations.

First, a well-stated outcome goal includes what is to be changed, the conditions under which the change(s) will occur, and the level or amount of change. One client may want to halt a pattern of being in dysfunctional relationships; another may wish to reduce negative self-appraisals; yet a third may wish to earn back the trust of a parent. In each of these situations, behaviors (including changing cognitive behaviors) can be identified as targets of improvement.

The second element of an outcome goal indicates the conditions under which the desired behavior(s)—clients might say *desired outcomes*—will occur. It is important to weigh carefully the situations or settings in which a client will attempt a new behavior. Don't set your client up to fail by identifying settings in which there is little hope for success. For example, a client who is working on changing his strained relationship with his father may not want to start doing so over the Thanksgiving holiday, when he knows his father will be "uptight." It would make much more sense to identify a more neutral time to begin his work.

The third element of outcome goals involves the choice of a suitable and realistic level or amount of change. A couple who has fought consistently for a decade needs a plan to avoid contentious interactions and to learn to communicate differently. A plan for a "getaway weekend" to rekindle the spark is probably not the first level of progress that would be realistic for such a couple. This is not to say that the getaway weekend will be forever unrealistic; rather, it's an acknowledgment that most goals are reached in increments, and the role of the counselor is to help the clients determine what are plausible next steps toward their ultimate goals. These in-between steps are referred to as *successive approximations* and are very important. They allow a client to set more attainable goals, experience success more frequently, and ultimately make what might be dramatic changes, one step at a time.

OBSTACLES IN DEVELOPING SPECIFIC GOALS

As noted earlier, most clients are unaccustomed to thinking in terms of specific, concrete goals. Instead of saying, "I want to be able to stand up for myself without getting in a fight," the client is likely to say, "I have a temper." In other words, a personal characteristic has been described rather than the ways in which the characteristic is expressed. It then becomes the counselor's job to help the client describe the ways in which the characteristic is expressed, under what conditions it is expressed, and consequently, how it could be expressed differently. Taking nonspecific concerns and translating them into specific goal statements is no easy task for the counselor, who must understand the nature of the client's problem and the conditions under which it occurs before the translation can begin.

What can you expect of yourself and your clients in terms of setting specific goals? First, the goals that are set can never be more specific than both your and your client's understanding of the problem. This means that, at the outset of counseling, goals are likely to be nonspecific, and perhaps even nebulous. But nonspecific goals are better than no goals at all.

Clients tend to move from nonspecific to intermediate goal setting and then from intermediate to specific goal setting as they move through the process. In other words, a client does not jump from "I want to be happy" (nonspecific) to "I want to learn how to make friends" (specific). Rather, the client will probably move to the intermediate level of goal setting, as in, "I want to have a social life."

As you and your client explore the nature of a particular problem, the type of goal(s) appropriate to the problem should become increasingly apparent. This clarification permits both of you to move in the direction of identifying specific behaviors that, if changed, would alter the problem in a positive way. These specific behaviors can then be formulated into goal statements; as you discuss the client's problems in more detail, you can gradually add the circumstances in which the client will perform the behaviors and how much or how often the target behaviors might be altered. (Again, we remind the reader that these behaviors can include cognitive behaviors as well as tracking feelings.)

SKILLS ASSOCIATED WITH GOAL SETTING

Two kinds of skills are associated with goal setting activities in counseling: the *verbal skills* the counselor uses to open and guide discussions about client goals, and the *structuring skills* that the counselor uses to help the client formulate or conceptualize goals. The counselor should be informed during the assessment stage about the client's ability or insight into the process of goal setting. Some clients are able to take verbal guidance in the process, whereas others require visual aids to help them conceptualize goals. We should add that visual aids might help the counselor as well as the client. It is our experience that learning the verbal skills of goal setting is easier for most counselors than learning the structuring skills. Breaking down problems into their parts and planning progress based on increments is a learned skill, and one that is relatively new to many counselors.

Verbal Goal-Setting Skills

Counselors use all the verbal skills presented in preceding chapters when working with clients in the goal-setting process, including verbal attentiveness, reflections, paraphrases, enhancing statements, and various types of questions. In addition to these core responses, counselors also use visualizing, confrontations, and encouraging responses to facilitate goal setting.

Goal-Setting Skills

Verbal skills

Counselor responses that allow clients to examine and assess their short- and longer-term objectives include the following:

- Visualizing activities help clients define changes they would like to introduce into their lives.
    1. "Imagine how it would be different if you and Bob could agree on how to raise the children."
    2. "Can you describe how you would like your life to be different in a year from now?"
    3. "You've mentioned three or four things you would like to see change. Which of these would make the greatest improvement in your life?"
- Verbal confrontations challenge clients to face issues they may not recognize or may be avoiding.
    1. "You say school isn't very satisfying, but your grades are excellent." [Discrepancy between stated conditions and behavior]
    2. "You indicated that you have resolved that conflict, but are you aware of the emotion in your voice when you talk about it?" [Discrepancy between stated feeling and communicated affect]
    3. "A while ago, you said you never want to see Patrice again, and now you say she's your best friend." [Discrepancy between two verbal messages]

- Affirming responses communicate the counselor's confidence or a client's potential for accomplishing a particular objective.

    1.   CLIENT: I'd like to be able to tell him what I really feel, but if I do, he'll get upset.

        COUNSELOR: Perhaps you could find some positive ways to tell him, if you think about it.

    2.   CLIENT: I can't imagine how I could ever feel positive about myself.

        COUNSELOR: I think if you had a plan for facing this problem, you could make some real headway toward liking yourself.

Structuring skills

Aids that help clients to plan and organize their thinking, activities, and self-assessments.

- The goal-setting map provides a visual hierarchy of achievable, interconnected goals and how they lead from one level of attainment to another.
- Timelines help clients organize activities in reasonable and achievable order.
- Successive approximation helps clients order their goals in the most achievable sequence of objectives.

VISUALIZING.   *Visualizing* invites clients to consider how their world might be different or how they would wish to make their world different. It is usually introduced as a targeted question, such as, "When you finish school next year, what would be the ideal job to move into?" Asking about "ideal jobs" is akin to asking about dreams, so the counselor is really asking the client to dream a bit about the future, or his or her relationships, or self-perceptions. Visualizing can be used with almost any topic, and often yields information that clients might be reluctant to share at first; indeed, some clients find it almost impossible to visualize a different world, perhaps because their reality is so bleak that visualizing something more positive seems like a dangerous activity.

CONFRONTATION.   One of the most useful counselor responses is the confrontation. The word *confrontation* has acquired some excess emotional meanings. It is sometimes misconstrued to mean "lecturing," "judging," or "punishing." It is more accurate to view the confrontation as a response that enables the client to face that which is being avoided, be it a thought, a feeling, or a behavior. Avoidance is usually expressed as one part of a discrepancy present in the client's message. Thus, the confrontation helps the client identify a contradiction, a rationalization or excuse, or a misinterpretation. The discrepancy or contradiction is usually one of the following:

1. A discrepancy between what the client is saying and how the client behaves (e.g., the client says that he is a quiet type, but in the interview he talks freely).
2. A contradiction between emotions and behaviors that the client presents (e.g., the client says that she is comfortable, but she continues to fidget).
3. A discrepancy between two verbal messages (e.g., the client says that he wants to change his behavior, but in the next breath he places all blame for his behavior on his parents and others).

Operationally, the confrontation is a compound sentence. The statement establishes a "You said—but look" condition. In other words, the first part of the statement is the "You said" (a paraphrase or affective reflection). It repeats a message given by the client. The second part of the statement presents the contradiction or discrepancy—the "but look" of the client message. Sometimes the "You said" part can be implied rather than said, particularly if the discrepant message has just occurred. For example:

> CLIENT: I just can't talk to people I don't know.
>
> COUNSELOR: But you don't know me all that well. [Implied]

The confrontation describes client messages, observes client behavior, and presents evidence; however, the confrontation is not meant to accuse, evaluate, or solve problems. Use of the confrontation serves four important purposes:

1. It assists in the client's effort to become more congruent by helping the client recognize when discrepancies exist.
2. It establishes the counselor as a role model for direct and open communication; if the counselor is comfortable acknowledging contradictions, perhaps the client can become more comfortable challenging them as well.
3. It is an action-oriented response. Unlike the reflection that mirrors the client's thoughts or feelings, the confrontation mirrors the client's behavior. It is useful in initiating action plans and behavior change.
4. It is useful for exploring conflict associated with change and goal setting.

THE ENCOURAGING RESPONSE. The *encouraging response* is intended to say to the client, "I know you have within you the capability to do this" or "to be this." It is often introduced with such phrases as "You could . . ." or "You might . . . ." It is an important statement from the counselor and should be used cautiously; that is, it should not be used if the counselor has any doubts about the client's potential to carry out an activity. Although the encouraging response can sound like advice, it can be used effectively as a way to identify alternatives available to the client. It is misused when, in oversimplification, the counselor attempts to suggest or prescribe a solution; the effect is to negate or ignore the client's concerns.

Structuring Goal-Setting Skills

Structuring skills are particularly useful tools when clients need help in understanding the goal-setting process. We mentioned earlier in the chapter that clients often don't know how to set goals or, more precisely, how to set appropriate goals. They may literally need to be taught how to select goals that are achievable and that serve as an antidote to the issue at hand. Structuring skills often involve visual aids, such as a goal-setting map, a timeline, or successive approximation.

GOAL-SETTING MAP. A goal-setting map is a useful tool to help clients learn how to set goals (Figure 6.1). The map provides a visual representation of the goal-setting process and requires the client to focus on the steps that lead to change. The first task is to help your client establish a desired outcome (main goal). Next, encourage your client to identify three (or more) changes that have to happen for this goal to be realized (subgoals). Finally, the client must identify two or three behaviors that he or she must do for each of the subgoals to happen (immediate tasks).

When several subgoals are identified, they are usually arranged in a sequence or hierarchy, from easiest to attain to most difficult. Similarly, the immediate tasks related to each subgoal are arranged in a logical sequence and are accomplished in that order. The client completes one subgoal before moving on to another. By gradually completing the activities represented by the subgoals and immediate tasks in a successful manner, the client's motivation and energy to change are reinforced and maintained. Successful completion of subgoals always represents actions that move clients in the direction of the desired goal. There are several ways to ensure that counseling subgoals are effective:

- Build subgoals on existing client resources and assets
- Base subgoals on client selection and commitment
- Make subgoals congruent with the client's values
- Identify subgoals with immediate tasks that the client can reasonably be expected to accomplish

Main Goal	Subgoals	Immediate Tasks
	1. ________	1. ________ 2. ________
	2. ________	1. ________ 2. ________
1. ________	3. ________	1. ________ 2. ________
	4. ________	1. ________ 2. ________
	5. ________	1. ________ 2. ________

Step 1: Choose a *main goal* (long-term or short-term).
Step 2: Write five steps you must take toward achieving this main goal. These are your *subgoals.*
Step 3: For each subgoal, write down two specific things you must do to achieve the subgoal. These are your *immediate tasks.*

FIGURE 6.1 The Goal-Setting Map

Subgoal 1:

Immediate Task 1:	Immediate Task 2:	Immediate Task 3:
By date: _____	**By date:** _____	**By date:** _____

FIGURE 6.2 The Timeline

TIMELINE. The timeline is another visual aid that helps clients gain a time perspective for their goals. Clients often can't visualize potential progress and have unrealistic expectations for what they can accomplish. The timeline involves a discussion between the counselor and the client that introduces reality checks for how quickly something might happen (Figure 6.2).

SUCCESSIVE APPROXIMATION STAIRS. *Successive approximation* is a way to define change by breaking down the process into a logical sequence of easily achievable steps. It is how humans first learned to walk, talk, read, play, socialize, work, and so on. Even though everyone has had these experiences, many adults cannot analyze goal attainment in terms of steps or stages. They may need to be taught the concept, and may need help in defining the steps that are inherent in a particular goal. One way this lesson may be presented is with a visual drawing of the process, such as the one shown in Figure 6.3, which often helps the client visualize the process more easily. By asking the client to help you fill in the blanks for each step in the process, the client becomes involved in the goal-setting procedure.

These are suggestions for structuring goal setting, but they are not the only ways to structure the process. Counselors may find additional ways that make sense to them and appear to appeal to their clients. For example, if a problem can be deconstructed by the counselor and client into its various contributing parts, then each part can be reconstructed in a more desirable way and, in doing so, goals and subgoals are established. We've already mentioned a GPS as a metaphor for goal setting. Most times when identifying where one wants to end, a GPS gives more than one route to get there. There are different reasons for taking each route, and there are roads or highways that must come before others. What is important is that the driver has some confidence that the route is intentional and leads to the desired outcome. So too is it important that counseling has an agreed-upon end point, and that the counselor and client are working together to find ways to get there effectively.

My ultimate goal!
_____

Where I will be in three weeks.
_____

Where I will be in two weeks.
_____

Where I will be next week.
_____

Where I am now.
_____

FIGURE 6.3 Successive Approximation Stairs

EFFECTS OF GOAL SETTING ON CLIENTS

The process of setting goals can have important effects on clients. Most are positive or helpful, although an occasional client may resist the goal-setting process. The advantages of establishing concrete goals are several: Clients feel clearer about themselves and their wants and needs; it helps clients sort out the important from the unimportant and the relevant from the trivial in their lives; and it encourages clients to make decisions and choices that represent their most significant values and priorities. As a consequence, clients often feel more enlightened and clearer about what they really want for themselves.

Goal setting is often the first time during counseling that clients begin to take specific action in response to a problem or issue. Sometimes the problem has existed for a long time. Through goal setting, clients can feel better about themselves by overcoming a sense of inertia, by mobilizing their forces, and by setting in place a chain of events that leads to problem resolution. As a result, clients often feel a great sense of accomplishment during and after the goal-setting process.

Goal setting affords clients a different view of their problems and concerns. The process of establishing specific goals can be *reactive*—that is, the act of selecting and defining results can contribute to desired changes in itself. This is particularly true when clients are heavily invested in the goal-setting process.

It is generally agreed among professional counselors that clients progress more rapidly when they have been involved in the goal-setting process and have a clear understanding of how achievement of those goals would enhance their lives. When clients understand and commit to outcomes in counseling, they become co-participants in that process of growth and change.

Research into client perceptions of various aspects of the counseling relationship supports the importance of goal setting (Halstead, Brooks, Goldberg, & Fish, 1990). In the results of their research, they observe

> that clients perceived the goal portion of the alliance as being stronger than their counselors did. A possible explanation for this finding, again, may be associated with the nature of the client's personal investment. One would expect the counselor and client to have a common understanding of the explicit goals that help to guide the counseling process. These goals, from the counselor's frame of reference, serve as a beacon by which to set a course to help the client. To the client, however, the goals of counseling, especially in early sessions, may be associated directly with a way to relieve emotional pain. The goals in counseling may represent a real sense of hope for the client. Therefore, it is likely that clients form stronger personal attachments to their goals in that goals can serve to create solutions to what may look like overwhelming situations. (p. 216)

GOAL SETTING WITH CHILDREN

As noted earlier in the chapter, counseling children imposes certain special conditions that alter the goal-setting process, and foremost among these is the need to recognize the child's developmental level. At the very least, this includes *cognitive development* (Is the child able to think abstractly because many goals have an abstract future dimension?); *affective development* (Is the child able to identify and discuss levels of feelings?); and *moral development* (Is the child able to discriminate between socially appropriate and inappropriate goals?). Assessment of developmental stage is a critical precursor to goal setting for these reasons. When appropriate assessment has been made, however, the counselor still must accommodate and adapt to the child's developmental level of functioning.

Children can be amazingly good about goal setting. Perhaps this is because they do not play mental games with their world; instead, they go straight to the heart of the matter and are very concrete about what they would like to be different. Further, they are used to having adults play an important role in suggesting what activities they engage in. That said, some children are slow to trust adults for a variety of reasons. Therefore, counselors should not assume that setting goals will be natural for all children.

CRISES AND GOAL SETTING

When clients are in crisis, the notion of goal setting might seem to be the least likely of all activities; however, crisis dictates that certain goals must be achieved. Even if the contact is to be a single session (which is often the case in crisis counseling), Collins and Collins (2005) assert that counselors must attend to certain process goals, including establishing that the client is safe and that any danger posed by the crisis is reduced; that the client is stable enough and that the environment is stable enough to avoid harm; and finally, that the client is connected to formal resources and informal supports to again assure the short-term well-being of the client. To accomplish these three goals, the counselor must solicit appropriate information about the client's cognitive, affective, behavioral, and environmental conditions during the intake portion of the contact.

Beyond these important process goals, goal setting is still a function of attempting to identify a desirable outcome and assisting the client in taking steps to achieve it. When clients are in crisis, the "goals" may appear unrelated to the real "problem," but they are essential, nonetheless. For example, a man who is functioning poorly a month after his wife was killed in a car accident may be assisted by the counselor to start taking some responsibility back for his children rather than let his relatives do it all. He may also be assisted in identifying a friend in his social circle that he *could* talk to when he eventually felt the need. Neither of these address his grief directly, the cause of his crisis, but both help rebuild a structure within which his grief can start to be faced. In addition, because this person is in crisis, such tangible goals are more appropriate and more therapeutic than setting goals that attempt to direct him to life after grief. Said differently, goal setting for persons in crisis is intended to help them deal with the crisis itself, not necessarily deal with a post-crisis life.

GOAL SETTING AND CULTURE

Goal setting is meant to give direction to the counseling process. In establishing goals, it is important that counselors consider the cultural context within which the client lives. Even here, however, naïve errors can be made. Many well-meaning counselors have imposed stereotypic assumptions about the culture of their clients without doing the more sensitive work of checking out their assumptions. When involved in the goal setting process, what does it mean if your client is Italian American, or African American, or an immigrant from Mexico? The answers to these questions are difficult to know without a complete assessment process that includes inquiry into these layers of identity. For example, the developmental literature as a whole emphasizes individual development over family development. Even family development models can stress what is called *individuation* (Bowen, 1978)—that is, the ability to be one's own person even while staying connected to one's family of origin. It is easily conceivable, therefore, that individuation might be a goal for a young woman who appears too dependent on her family of origin. Still, traditionally, some ethnic groups have been identified as having lesser individuation as the norm than other ethnic groups (McGoldrick, Giordana, & Garcia-Preto, 2005). Even here, however, counselors who operate on these assumptions can become examples of "A little knowledge is a dangerous thing." Rather, as the counselor gets to know his client (let's say, for the purposes of this discussion, that she's Latina) and her issue(s), it is important to ask how—or even *if,* in the client's view—being Latina affects her as she struggles with her issue. What, if anything, did her family teach her about being Latina that interfaces with the issue? In addition, and most important to our discussion here, how does her identity as a Latina affect goal setting and what goals she can commit to? This is equally important to investigate if the client is Irish American, or an immigrant from Bosnia, or any number of other equally likely scenarios. We must also be clear that ethnicity is not unique in carrying cultural layers. It might be more important that the client is Catholic or transsexual, or a person with a physical disability, or from a professional family. In fact, ethnicity is so diffuse for some persons that it does not carry much cultural capital at all. Furthermore, the family may not even be the primary source of cultural identity. Instead, the community one grew up in may be more powerful in defining values and beliefs than the family; an example that comes to mind is the urban youth whose parents struggle to keep him out of trouble, but whose cultural identity is primarily dictated by harsh neighborhood conditions. In this case, culture is not a friend to the client, and may in fact be something to target in the goal-setting process.

In summary, cultural identity and individual identity are integrated in ways that are complex. We do not adhere to the notion that some goals (e.g., insight) are appropriate for some cultural groups but not for others; rather, the counselor must be invested in discovering how culture influences how a client sees the world, and how this is relevant to the issue at hand and to the goal-setting process. There is no magical way of accomplishing this process goal. The skills described in this text, however, are adequate to acquire the necessary perspective to be of help to the client during goal setting in a manner that honors cultural identity.

CLIENT PARTICIPATION IN GOAL SETTING

Some counselors may construe goal setting to mean that they listen to the client, make a mental assessment of the problem, and then prescribe a solution or goal; in fact, such a procedure is likely to be unsuccessful. The nature of counseling is such that the client must be involved in the establishment of goals. Otherwise, the client's participation is directionless or, even worse, counterproductive. The following example illustrates this point.

A beginning counselor was seeing a client who was overweight, self-conscious about her appearance, reluctant to enter into social relationships with others because of this self-consciousness, and very lonely. Realizing that the problem of being overweight was an important factor, the counselor informed the client that one goal would be for her (the client) to lose 1 to 3 pounds per week, under a doctor's supervision, of course. With this, the client became highly defensive and rejected the counselor's goal, saying, "You sound just like my mother."

Goal setting is highly personal and requires a great deal of effort and commitment on the client's part. Therefore, the client must select goals that are important enough to make sacrifices to achieve. In the preceding example, the client's reaction could have been prevented if the counselor had moved more slowly, permitting the client to identify for herself the significance of her being overweight and the importance of potential weight loss. At this point, both the counselor and the client could then work together to determine the specific goals and subgoals that, when achieved, might alleviate the client's concerns. As with other aspects of the counseling relationship, goal setting should be an interactive process for which both counselor and client assume responsibility.

RESISTANCE TO GOAL SETTING

We use the word *resistance* with some trepidation because it connotes a deliberate pushing back on the part of the client (resisting arrest comes to mind). Sometimes clients simply can't or won't participate in goal setting or seem highly reluctant (our preferred term) to making a commitment to change. In these cases, it is easy for the counselor to slip into a mindset that they have a resistant client on their hands. Rather, what is often referred to as "resistance" can be a host of things, and counselors must discover what dynamics are occurring for the client in these instances.

In dealing with client reluctance to setting goals, it is helpful to realize that such behavior is purposeful—that is, what the client does or avoids doing achieves some perceived desirable result for the client (regardless of whether the client realizes it). You might find that the client who resists setting goals could be protecting the very behavior that is in need of modification because that behavior is also serving some purpose. One example is the chronic smoker. Although an individual may recognize the negative consequences of smoking, including its addictive properties, he or she also clings to the habit, believing that it helps him or her relax during stressful moments, or fearing the moodiness he or she recalls the last time an attempt to quit was undertaken.

It becomes your task to get clients to identify what they gain from their current behavior or what they fear in changing their current behavior. In so doing, you may help clients determine whether what they want can be achieved in more desirable ways than how they are presently going about their business. For example, a young student may reject the teacher's authority in order to gain attention from peers. Gaining attention may be a desirable outcome; it is the method that is the problem. Therefore, finding more appropriate ways of gaining increased attention is a functional goal for counseling.

Sometimes clients resist attempts to establish goals because they believe that the counselor (either overtly or subtly) is pushing them in a certain direction. Unless clients can determine some personal goals for counseling, the probability of any change is minimal. You can avoid creating client resistance to goals by encouraging active participation by clients in the goal-setting process.

Finally, some clients are reluctant to set goals because they are genuinely confused about their desired priorities, needs, and wants. They know what is wrong in their lives, but they cannot visualize how to achieve a better life. These clients may resist goal setting because it puts them in touch with their confusion, and also because there is an implicit demand for them to sort things out and look beyond their current reality. With such clients, it is often very helpful to acknowledge their confusion directly.

COUNSELOR: Lawanda, I can see you trying and I do know that it's really difficult to imagine a different or an improved situation.

If you give clients permission to move at their own pace, the pressure to set goals does not compound their already building sense of frustration and powerlessness. Indeed, the process of identifying desired priorities, needs, and wants is a goal in itself.

Three other possible strategies to help clients set goals include the following:

1. Language work. Ask the client to complete open-ended sentences, such as, "I want . . . ," "I do not want . . . ," "I need . . . ," "I do not need . . . ," "I choose to . . . ," and so on.
2. Imagery and visualization. Ask the client to imagine him- or herself in a better situation and describe it. (We refrain from using such terms as *ideal situation* because it can lead the client into the world of make-believe rather than a world that is attainable.) Alternatively, the client can be asked to visualize someone else who embodies the qualities and behaviors the client desires. What are those qualities?
3. Role-play and enactment. Ask the client to attempt to reenact the problem through a role-play.

Some clients may be very conflicted about competing priorities and needs. They may identify several possible directions or options, but they may still be in conflict and thus unable to choose which course of action is the best one to pursue. These clients resist goal setting because it exposes the conflict, which often feels uncomfortable or painful. It looks easier to mask or avoid than to deal with the issue head-on. With such clients, it is often helpful to use confrontation (described earlier) to point out the apparent conflict:

> COUNSELOR: Lucy, on the one hand, you're saying that you want to have some stability in your life. At the same time, you're saying you are considering a job that requires an additional two nights a week away from your family.

It is important that such internal conflicts are brought out at the goal-setting stage (or earlier). Otherwise, counseling interventions that follow are unlikely to be effective.

ASSESSING COUNSELING GOALS

The obvious reasons for setting goals are to determine the direction counseling should go *and* to determine when counseling has been successful. An unmet goal can mean numerous things—it may indicate that counseling was unsuccessful, that the client was not able to change, or that the goal was somehow inappropriate—for example, it may be immeasurable, unrelated to the problem, or culturally insensitive.

People tend to think of goals in broad, global terms rather than concrete, measurable terms. Global goals are almost impossible to achieve. Concrete goals are *observable* and thus *measurable*. The following case of Angela illustrates how concrete goals may be conceptualized using the goal-setting map in Figure 6.1.

CASE ILLUSTRATION OF GOAL SETTING

In this example, we illustrate how the counselor can help Angela (see Chapter 5) identify desired outcome goals for counseling. Recall that Angela described her problem as a depressed state in which she perceives herself as a failure; engages in few meaningful activities or relationships; and, in general, lacks a purpose in life apart from her role as parent. Also, recall that part of Angela's depressed moods seems to be precipitated and/or maintained by a physiological condition—Addison's disease.

After you and Angela probe the facets of her concerns, you can consider the specific changes Angela would like to make. Gradually, these changes can be translated into an outline of desired goals (see Figure 6.1). Angela and the counselor discuss goals and identify the following:

Continuation of the Case of Angela

I. *Outcome Goal 1* Angela wishes to become significantly more positive about herself over the next 3 months. (Not measurable)

A. Angela must learn to recognize when she is involved in negative and self-defeating thoughts or self-talk about herself each day.

1. Angela will start noting the number of times each day that she says or thinks something negative about herself. (Observable and measurable)

2. Angela will begin to keep a list of general topics she tends to use in putting herself down. (Observable and measurable)

3. Angela will start noting what time of day she finds herself involved in negative and/or self-defeating self-talk to determine if she is more vulnerable at certain parts of the day or night. (Observable and measurable)

B. Angela must develop a list of positive or self-enhancing statements about herself.

1. Angela will begin focusing on her positive qualities with the counselor's help. (Measurable)

2. Angela will write each positive quality statement she identifies on 3 × 5 cards and keep these cards handy during those parts of the day that seem to be her most vulnerable times. (Measurable)

3. When Angela gets negative, she will faithfully read a positive-quality card and focus on it until she has overcome the negative surge. (Measurable)

C. Angela will examine the setting(s) in which she is most likely to become self-defeating or negative to determine the effect of setting on her moods.

1. With the counselor's help, Angela will look for a time-of-day pattern to her tendency to become negative or self-defeating. (Observable and measurable)

2. With the counselor's help, Angela will look for other conditions that might be associated with her moods (e.g., being alone, having a lot of tasks). (Measurable)

3. With the counselor's help, Angela will identify settings to avoid and develop a list of alternative activities when she finds herself in a self-defeating setting. (Measurable)

II. *Outcome Goal 2* Angela wishes to control any negative effects from the Addison's disease that might contribute to her moods. (Not measurable)

A. Angela will make an appointment with her physician (which she has been avoiding) for an examination and consultation on the possible progression of her Addison's disease.

1. She will call within 3 days and will make the appointment within 2 weeks. (Measurable)

2. Between now and the appointment, Angela will keep a record of her bouts with the blues, including day, time, situation, and duration of the feelings. She will take this record with her when she goes for the appointment. (Measurable)

B. With the physician's help, Angela must determine what changes of behavior, use of medication, and so on, would counteract any effects of Addison's on her moods.

1. With the counselor's help, Angela will use this information to identify how her daily habits must change. (Measurable)

2. Angela will begin a preventive program based on the plan she and her counselor develop. (Measurable)

3. Angela will keep a daily record of her new activities until they become part of her normal routine. (Measurable)

4. Angela will monitor the intensity of her moods on a 1–10 scale in at least three different time periods on a daily basis over the next 3 months. (Measurable)

III. *Outcome Goal 3* Angela wishes to be more aware of her daily activities and relationships and their meaningfulness or value to her. (Not measurable)

A. Angela will determine the relative importance of her work and leisure activities and relationships. (Not measurable)

1. Angela will monitor and log all daily work and leisure activities for a week and, with the counselor's help, will categorize these activities into "Pleasant" or "Unpleasant" categories. (Measurable)

2. Angela will determine which of the unpleasant activities are within her control to change or reschedule. (Measurable)

3. With the counselor's help, Angela will attempt to reframe the meaning of those unpleasant activities so they become at least neutral, and perhaps pleasant. (Measurable)

4. Angela will do the same analysis with her relationships. (Measurable)

B. Angela will establish a more positive balance between negative and positive work/leisure activities and relationships. (Not measurable)

1. With the counselor's help, Angela will analyze her typical weekly schedule to determine whether it includes a disproportionate number of negative activities and relationships. (Measurable)

2. With the counselor's help, Angela will identify new sources of positive activities and relationships associated with her work and leisure time. (Measurable)

3. With the counselor's help, Angela will seek to establish and maintain a positive balance in her weekly work/leisure activities and relationships. (Measurable)

IV. *Outcome Goal 4* Angela would like to have a sense of meaning for her life and some sort of "plan" for the next 2 to 5 years, and she would like to feel like she is working toward fulfilling that plan. (Measurable or not measurable?)

A. Angela knows that she must have a better understanding of her values and must determine what kinds of goals and accomplishments are really important to her.

1. With the counselor's help, Angela will do some values clarification activities to get a better sense of her life priorities. (Measurable or not measurable?)

2. Angela will begin to look at her present activities and priorities to see if they match her life priorities. (Measurable or not measurable?)

3. With the counselor's help, Angela will consider how her family background relates to her situation (how well or poorly her family would function if they were in her present circumstances). (Measurable or not measurable?)

4. With the counselor's help, Angela will consider what "family solutions" could be prescribed for her present circumstances. (Measurable or not measurable?)

5. With the counselor's help, Angela will look for any value conflicts between her present worldview and the worldview she was taught as a child by her family. (Measurable or not measurable?)

6. With the counselor's help, Angela will attempt to resolve any value conflicts she discovers. (Measurable or not measurable?)

B. Angela would like to feel more independent of her ex-husband.

1. Angela will attempt to be more resourceful about taking responsibility for the children during times when she is feeling blue. (Measurable or not measurable?)

2. Angela will try to view the children's relationship with their father as a positive factor in her life rather than as a potentially threatening factor. (Measurable or not measurable?)

Notice the process by which these outcome goals are established. First, they begin as overall goals (Roman numerals) that are directly related to the client's specific or general complaints. Then specific and observable changes (subgoals; capital-letter items) are identified, which must occur if Angela is to succeed in accomplishing each overall goal. Finally, specific tasks (numbered items) are identified that will allow Angela to accomplish each of the subgoals. In this way, goal setting moves from general goals (related to the presenting problem) to specific subgoals and then to specific tasks.

Summary

Goal setting is such a central part of the change process that people often take it for granted. Yet many people (including many counselors) are not very skilled at setting their own goals or helping others to identify and set goals. In this chapter, we differentiate two types of goals that are part of the counseling process: process goals and outcome goals. Process goals are those that the counselor identifies for each counseling meeting; outcome goals are meant to describe the desired results of counseling, and they also dictate the specific counselor interventions to be used in counseling. Goals can help motivate clients to make desired changes, and can also prove useful as the counselor attempts to evaluate therapeutic progress. Parameters of effective goal setting include identification of what broad changes the client wishes to accomplish, specific situations that must change if this broad goal is to be achieved, and specific tasks the client must undertake if the intermediate objectives are to be realized. Goals are affected by the ability of the client and the counselor to imagine the change process and by the values and beliefs embedded in the client's cultural context. Cultural factors always play a central role in goal identification and attainment; however, sometimes these factors are so familiar to both counselor and client (e.g., being self-sufficient) that the cultural precursors are virtually invisible. Counselors who view culture as affecting *all* counseling relationships are less likely than others to miss these indicators of cultural beliefs.

Exercises

I. Labeling Goals as Measurable or Not Measurable

Notice that for the fourth outcome goal for Angela, we did not indicate whether the goal or subgoals were measurable or not measurable. With classmates, determine which of these are measurable and which are not.

II. Identification of Client Goals

Martin is a mandated client being seen at the special office for campus disturbances at a large university. Martin is a sophomore and was arrested this past weekend for public drunkenness. In addition to being drunk, he instigated a fight with another young man because he thought he saw that man looking at Martin's girlfriend with more than a little interest. Although Martin was initially resistant to the idea of counseling, Martin's counselor, Frank, has helped him appreciate that his behavior was not acceptable, even for a college student (his initial defense). At this point, Martin agrees that he has a "short fuse" and that he is overly controlling of his environment, including his relationship with his girlfriend. He reports that he drinks to get more comfortable, but knows that after a couple of drinks he gets aggressive. Asked if he is happy with himself when he doesn't drink, Martin's answer is: "Not really. My girlfriend and I fight a lot. I don't like some of her friends. It bugs me that she's still friends with the guy she dated last year. She tells me to get over it, which just pisses me off." Although Frank will most assuredly identify goals with Martin, making sure that he is committed to each as they progress, use Martin's situation to see if you can respond to the following:

A. Put yourself in Martin's position. Identify a few goals that you think might be appropriate, using the suggested goal outline in Figure 6.1.
B. Are the goals in your list specific or vague? How would Martin know when he had achieved these goals? How would achieving them affect Martin's concerns?

C. As Martin's counselor, what process goals would you set for yourself? How would these process goals relate to Martin's presenting problems?

III. Culture and Goal Setting

Jaime Huang is a young (late twenties) Asian American who lives in a large urban environment. He was referred to you by a friend who knows you as an acquaintance. His friend thought you could help Jaime because he has had difficulty in both seeking and obtaining employment that pays enough to support his family (wife and child), support he feels a strong obligation to provide. In the first session, Jaime is somewhat reluctant to talk about his situation. He appears to be reserved and polite, but not trusting. He is willing to talk about the mutual acquaintance who referred him and, to some extent, he is willing to talk about his employment history and skills.

A. As Jaime's counselor, what process goals would you set for yourself? How would these process goals be affected by Jaime's cultural background?

B. Put yourself in Jaime's position. Using the suggested goal outline in Figure 6.1, identify a goal that Jaime might think is appropriate in the counseling process, and include subgoals and immediate tasks.

C. Is your goal statement specific or vague? How would Jaime know when he had achieved this goal? How would achieving this goal help Jaime?

D. Finally, look at your list of goals and now assume that Jaime is a member of your ethnic group. Would your goals change? If yes, can you justify your list for Jaime? If not, reconsider your goals to determine if they are adequately sensitive to culture.

Discussion Questions

1. In this chapter, we discuss possible reasons for client resistance (reluctance) to goal setting. Identify some reasons why counselors might also resist developing outcome goals with clients.

2. In what ways do outcome goals help the counselor assess client progress? Describe what you think it would be like to assess counseling progress when no goals have been formulated.

3. Identify a recent problematic situation that you or a close friend experienced. What kinds of solutions came to mind for the person? Was goal setting part of the process? What are the pros and cons if goal setting had been part of the process?

4. Consider the differences between a "typical" counseling session and a session in which the client is in crisis. How would you handle goal setting with the client in crisis?

MyCounselingLab® Assignment

Go to the Video Library under Video Resources on the MyCounselingLab site for your text and search for the following clips:

- **Video Example: Goal-Setting Skills: Linda** Notice that the counselor does not ask the client to specify what it is that has become an issue between her and her boss. Counselors do not always need to know all the details surrounding an issue to be of help. Note also that the counselor asks the client which area she wants to work on first. Identify what verbal skills the counselor is using to get the client to start talking about goals.

- **Video Example: Using Reflective Questions** In this short segment, the counselor asks the client how things would look if her goals were met. How is this question helpful as part of goal setting?

- **Video Example: Using Re-authoring to Reframe a Narrative** This video follows the child video we suggested for Chapter 5 with the boy who experiences taunting. How does the process you see here lead the counselor to goal setting? How much client "buy-in" do you think is operating at this point?

- **Video Example: Proposing a Treatment Plan to a Client** This video depicts a very different counselor style with a highly intellectual client. We enter the point in the session where the counselor is suggesting a treatment plan. What are the benefits of the counselor's approach? How do you think you would react to this counselor if you were his client?

CHAPTER 7

Defining Strategies and Selecting Interventions

PURPOSE OF THIS CHAPTER

Once you and your client have collaboratively established goals for counseling, the next step is to develop a therapeutic plan for counseling that is tailored to the client's goals. This process involves identification of a case strategy (often referred to as a *treatment plan*) and identification of counseling interventions that both serve the strategy as well as address the therapeutic and contextual issues present in the case. This represents the third prong of the working alliance between counselor and client(s)—that is, agreement on tasks or approaches in counseling that assist client(s) in attaining agreed-upon goals.

Considerations as You Read This Chapter

- Planning is a major part of every complex activity. What are you like as a planner?
- When you become involved in a complex activity without a plan, what do you do?
- When you form new relationships with friends and colleagues, what do you find yourself mainly focusing on? What they talk about? How they think? What activities they are involved in? Or who they seem to be when they are in a particular social environment?
- Are the people you get to know best more like you, or very different from you?
- How might these questions relate to you as a counselor?

Thus far, we have described a process in which the counselor and client meet, a therapeutic relationship begins to take form, and an assessment of the parameters of the problem occurs; from this, goals to be accomplished in the counseling relationship begin to emerge. In this chapter, we examine the case conceptualization process that supports the counseling plan. In other words, identifying a problem and even setting a goal does not necessarily dictate an approach for the counselor to take; rather, the counselor considers different perspectives on how the problem might have originally occurred and how it may be maintained. These perspectives are conceptual lenses that provide the direction for a strategy; the strategy leads to intervention options for the counselor to consider.

Most models of case conceptualization involve three components: (1) the plan organizes a broad range of client information into a small number of categories, (2) the product is a concise understanding of the client, and (3) the plan facilitates the processes of diagnosis and treatment planning (Seligman, 2004, p. 280). Each of these components is, in itself, a thoughtful process involving the counselor's understanding of theory, the worldviews of both client and counselor, mutually agreed-upon therapeutic goals, the diagnosis of the presenting problem, the time orientation, the identification of appropriate treatment strategies and interventions, and client characteristics that either contribute to or impede therapeutic progress. Thus, case conceptualization is a thought process the counselor uses when preparing to work with the client.

CASE CONCEPTUALIZATION SKILLS

Theoretical Bases

Counselors work from theoretical orientations that can be broadly classified as affective, behavioral, cognitive, or systemic in nature. These orientations are not in themselves theories, but most theories of counseling are situated primarily in one of these orientations. For our purposes here, it is enough for the reader to consider these broad orientations as theoretical bases.

Worldview

How we view and interpret life experiences plays a major role in how we understand and define our problems. It is as true for the counselor as it is for the client that worldview shapes how counseling will proceed and be experienced.

Diagnostic Acuity

Case conceptualization must include the identification or ruling out of psychopathology.

Therapeutic Goals

Solutions are an obvious component in the definition of counseling. Solutions, or objectives, should be realistic, appropriate to the level of the problem, and acceptable to both the client and the counselor.

Time Orientation

The counselor must be able to assess the time dimension of the problem, how long it has persisted, how long might be required to change, and whether the client is in a crisis state.

Treatment Interventions

The interventions selected by the counselor should have some demonstrated effectiveness with problems similar to those with which the client presents and should be consistent with the overall strategy. The counselor must be able to assess the effectiveness of a selected intervention and alter the treatment plan (strategy) when necessary.

Client Characteristics and Context

The client's background, interpersonal history, and current living situation may just as easily work against the counseling process as facilitate it. The counselor must be able to assess the client's resources and barriers to counseling. In addition, client individual characteristics, such as low impulse control or anxiety, should also be included in case conceptualization.

THEORY AND CASE CONCEPTUALIZATION

Counseling theory attempts to provide explanations about (a) why people live their lives in productive and sometimes unproductive ways and (b) how people can change their lives when change is needed. Theory can be used by the counselor as either foreground or background in the counseling process. Used as foreground, the counselor embraces a specific theory, uses its guidelines to understand and explain client behavior patterns, and projects ways in which those patterns could change. When theory is used as background, counselors are more likely to emphasize cognitive consistency as their guide in working with cases—that is, they tend to draw on a theory that "makes sense" to them as they consider what they understand to be the client's presenting issue. Either way, the counselor is using theory as one of the components for conceptualizing each client's world. In Chapter 1, we discuss the range of theories that represent the counseling profession. These theories, although numerous, reflect a finite number of philosophical viewpoints, personality development patterns, change processes, and relationship alternatives.

One could argue that all human beings embrace five forces—feelings, thoughts, behaviors, interpersonal relationships, and something in the realm of the existential or spiritual, some sense of wonderment at existence itself—and that would be accurate for the most part. However, each person also tends to be more pronounced in one of the five areas, relying on the other areas when human understanding calls for it. Thus, one person views feelings as the core of being. Another person believes that it is not what one says, but what one does that matters. Yet another person believes that it is the meaning one makes of experiences that matters most; a fourth person views interaction with others and with nature as most important; and a fifth person views the soul and one's purpose in life as the source of meaning. Finding one's theory is partly determined by finding oneself in the context of theory choices. It is also determined by the nature of one's professional training and the orientation of one's professional models. As noted earlier, although some of the interventions that we discuss are identified with a particular theory, we are attempting to paint as broad a picture as possible so that the reader can practice a wide range of interventions, even though (or *if*) she or he has not yet identified a theory (or theories) of choice.

WORLDVIEW AND CASE CONCEPTUALIZATION

The counselor's theoretical orientation is influenced by his or her worldview. In Chapter 1, we describe *worldview* as the total perception one has of self, others, environment, and relationships. One's view of others includes a very wide range of culturally based differences. As has been long argued by multicultural specialists, all counseling is multicultural in nature. This seems obvious if one considers the many effects that factors such as race, ethnicity, religion, social class, gender, sexual orientation, and physical ability have on human experience.

This multicultural perspective can be approached from *culture-specific* orientations, in which the counselor is aware of and responding to the unique cultural qualities of the client, or it can be approached from a *culture-general* perspective that emphasizes similarities across cultures. Which is the better direction to take remains an issue of discussion in the counseling profession. Some fear that the culture-specific approach might lead to overlooking the individual characteristics and the universal humanness of the client, whereas others argue that only a culture-specific approach can fully reflect the nature and qualities of a person.

We favor a "both/and" approach, even though it is far more challenging than either a culture-specific or a culture-general approach. The mental health professions have produced many authoritative resources that can educate counselors to worldviews that are, at least historically, endemic to different ethnic groups (e.g., McGoldrick, Giordano, & Garcia-Preto, 2005). Even so, counselors must resist making assumptions about any individual client and that person's worldview. Both individuals and cultural groups evolve. Worldview, therefore, is fluid.

Still, as part of assessment, goal setting, and strategy/intervention selection, we offer three rather straightforward issues that have been identified as having cultural overtones. The first of these is what has been described as an individualistic orientation versus one that is more family- or community-centered. How we might view a young adult in his 30s living at home with his parents might reflect our worldview on this dimension. Therefore,

When working with clients of different cultures, it is important to determine where the client's identity emphasis lies—within the individual or within the family/community.

For the young man discussed earlier, his residence with his parents might be the result of financial expedience, and might cause him frustration and embarrassment (thus indicating a stereotypic Western individualistic view), or it might be the result of family values that he holds dear. The fact of his residence doesn't tell us much in and of itself.

Second, ethnic groups have been identified as differing on verbal expressiveness and on willingness to share one's emotional life. Of course, all cultural groups have introverts and extroverts, and even in a therapy-friendly environment such as the United States, many persons have great difficulty sharing emotions. However, some differences within a counselor's caseload could be cultural as much as individual. Therefore,

> When working with clients of different cultures, it is important to determine the client's orientation toward verbal expressiveness and cultural values regarding emotional expression and disclosure.

Finally, it has been noted that many psychotherapies rely heavily on client insight as one of the goals of counseling. This too apparently may be influenced by culture. For example, Sue and Sue (2008) note that the traditional Asian advice for handling such feelings as anger, frustration, or depression is to "keep busy and don't think about it," an orientation that goes in the opposite direction from insight. Therefore,

> When working with clients of different cultures, it is important to determine the client's orientation toward introspection and insight as opposed to taking action on the external problem.

CONCEPTUALIZING PRESENTING PROBLEMS

Although the conceptualization of presenting problems is mostly accomplished during assessment, we return to the topic here because successful strategies and interventions are related to the conceptualization of the client's presenting problem. Best results are achieved when selected interventions match the components of the problem. Thus, if the client's presenting problem appears to be predominantly affective or emotional in nature, interventions should be targeted to the affective complaints. Similarly, if a client seems to be using his thought processes to sabotage himself, then the counselor should select interventions that address the cognitive sources. However, it is important to realize that most client problems are multidimensional. A problem with negative self-talk ("I'm constantly telling myself I'm no good") is not just cognitive; it also reflects an affective dimension ("I feel lousy about myself"), a behavioral dimension ("I choose to stay home and watch a lot of TV"), and a systemic or interactional dimension ("When I do go out, I avoid contact with others because they find me strange, or I behave strangely and others react to me accordingly").

In addition, determining where a problem is situated is not obvious at first blush. A client who displays a significant amount of emotion is not necessarily a candidate for affective interventions. One could even argue that this is the *last* thing such a client needs, because emotions are quite accessible to the client. Rather, after exploration, it may be clear that cognitive, systemic, or behavioral interventions will be much more helpful in helping this client achieve stated goals.

Another important dynamic of counseling is that although problems tend to have multidimensional aspects, the counselor need not address all aspects for counseling to be successful.

Frequently, a cognitive aspect, if altered, leads to different social consequences that, in turn, alter the client's interactional aspect as well ("If I am able to think more kindly about myself or my problem, I may find that I worry less and behave less self-consciously"). This ecological interconnectedness suggests that positive change can occur regardless of how the problem is experienced by the client. However, it may prove less efficient and less effective if the helper chooses to intervene behaviorally when the client is experiencing the problem affectively (or if the client is culturally disposed toward one aspect and the counselor uses an intervention reflecting a different aspect). Figure 7.1 illustrates how a problem can be explored from different perspectives. Even though these several perspectives yield different information about the problem, the larger context of the problem is the same.

How does one plan a strategy for counseling intervention if multiple choices exist and "all roads lead to Rome"? Beyond theoretical bias for going in one direction or another, a general guideline for selecting counseling strategies is that clients are more receptive when the choice of strategy matches their cultural history and how they understand the problem (which includes how the counselor has helped them understand the problem). Inconsistency between the client's understanding of the problem and the counselor's counseling strategy can lead a client to conclude that the counselor has failed to understand. This is not to suggest that the counselor's interventions would be exclusively in one domain. As counseling proceeds and as the multiple dimensions of the problem become apparent to the client, counseling can begin to address these other dimensions. For example, affective reactions are often reinforced by the client's self-talk. An affective strategy focuses on the client's affective reactions but might include cognitive interventions that address the negative self-talk. In this example, the base

1. How does the problem make your client feel? How do her feelings affect her effort to change the problem? How might her feelings maintain the problem? What different feelings might change the problem? What is your client's cultural perspective toward feelings associated with the problem?	2. What kinds of things does your client do when the problem is "in charge"? How do these behaviors support or maintain the problem? What behaviors could she change and thereby reduce the effects of the problem? What are her cultural predispositions toward *doing* as opposed to *feeling*?

CLIENT'S PRESENTING PROBLEM
Your client is in her second semester at a community college. She is the first in her family to go to college. She was in counseling for depression, and her counselor helped get her into school. For a while, things were good; lately, however, she is starting to feel hopeless and is considering dropping out. She doesn't know what she might do, but her boyfriend wants her to drop out and marry him.

3. What kinds of things is your client saying to herself? How might her messages be part of her problem? What cultural messages are part of her self-talk? What roles do her cultural values play in the self-statements that she makes, and what alternative self-statements are available?	4. What are your client's relationships with other students like? What is her relationship with her boyfriend like? How do her teachers fit into the picture? How has her family functioned while she has attended school? In what ways do relationships support the problem? What are the cultural expectations on her to marry?

FIGURE 7.1   The Various Ways to Approach a Client's Problems

for this working alliance is the affective domain. In a different counseling case, the client's experiencing of the problem might be behavioral (e.g., excessive drinking), thus suggesting that the counseling plan should be behaviorally based. This would involve behavioral interventions, with cognitive, affective, and systemic/interactional excursions from the behavioral component as appropriate.

Sometimes the client's presentation of a problem fails to produce the best understanding of how that problem should be confronted, and so the counselor chooses a strategy that yields only qualified success. When this occurs, you should reexamine your rationale for selecting a particular strategy. For example, if a woman presents a problem of poor self-concept, the counseling strategy may be to address her cognitive self. As she begins to feel and to become more competent, however, her new self may lead to a crisis in her marriage, causing her to back off her recent gains. It may be that her husband's expectations are for her to remain less competent, thus maintaining a relationship in which he is superior. In this situation, the problem may have been experienced as a cognitive and/or affective issue, yet the underlying issues really represent a systemic/interactional problem.

DIAGNOSIS AND CASE CONCEPTUALIZATION

It cannot be assumed that your clients will always be free of pathology, even if you work outside of the mental health delivery system, such as in a school. This reality emerges with increasing frequency as stress and violence grow in the school, the community, and the family. Consequently, it is important that you be able to identify or rule out client psychopathology early in the counseling relationship (Nelson, 2002). Regardless of whether it is your professional role to treat clients who carry a diagnosis, all counselors must be able to recognize psychopathology when it exists, either to arrive at appropriate treatment plans or to make appropriate referrals to other clinicians. The standard source for diagnostic direction is the *Diagnostic and Statistical Manual of Mental Disorders, 5th ed. (DSM-5*; American Psychiatric Association, 2013).

Depending on the diagnosis, a counselor may be working in concert with a psychiatrist or engaged in consultation with other mental health practitioners. When other therapists are involved, it is very helpful to consult not only about the diagnosis but also about the treatment plans. Identifying alternative approaches for a particular diagnosis can make therapy more efficient. In addition, when different strategies are discussed, different members of a therapeutic team can focus on a particular intervention, thus avoiding "bumping into" the work of another member of the team but truly working in concert. This can be especially helpful when, for example, a client is receiving both individual counseling and group counseling. Each of these modalities has a potential for providing distinct interventions, thus increasing the benefits to the client.

TIME ORIENTATION AND CASE CONCEPTUALIZATION

Time is an extremely important part of the working alliance. It includes the amount of time devoted to each session, the amount of time devoted to the process, how long the problem has been experienced by the client, and the amount of time required to address the problem fully. If the client comes to counseling in crisis, time may be seen as a critical aspect of the problem. Time also has its cultural dimensions. In some cultures, time is a friend; in others, time is a factor to be controlled.

Time also enters into the equation when goals of counseling are considered. Some goals are short-term, whereas others may have lifetime implications. Client tolerance for ambiguity and process is a direct reflection of the client's view of time. Generally speaking, clients choose goals that represent either choice or change, or a combination of the two. Clients who commit themselves to choices usually have the prerequisite skills and opportunities to take a particular course of action but have not yet committed themselves to do so. Clients who commit themselves to changes may very well lack the necessary skills, opportunities, or behaviors needed to achieve those changes. Thus, the fundamental alternative between choice goals and change goals has time ramifications because change will likely require more time than choice.

Questions about how long counseling should take are probably on the mind of most clients as they enter the process: What is a reasonable amount of time for me to solve my problems? Will a "good" counselor speed up that process for me? How patient must I be in waiting for the good feelings to return (or the bad feelings to fade)? How long should I wait before deciding that counseling isn't the right solution for me? Such questions are rarely verbalized but are often thought by clients.

Counselors think of time issues, too: How much time should I devote to building rapport? To assessment? To the process of goal setting? How long will the client commit to counseling? Are my chosen interventions efficient? Are they the most effective in light of how I understand the problem? What is a reasonable amount of time to wait before seeing some evidence of progress? How long should most counseling take? These are important questions. They reflect the counselor's theoretical underpinnings, tolerance for ambiguity, belief in the process, understanding of interventions, and understanding of client differences.

GOALS AND TREATMENT PLANNING

As already noted, goals are directly related to the counselor's choice of strategy and intervention. Goals may be classified as immediate, intermediate, or long term (Cormier & Hackney, 2012). Generally, a combination of these goals is reflected in the treatment plan. There are exceptions, of course. When working with clients in crisis, most goals must be short term and crisis mediating in character. Once goals have been identified through counselor–client discussion, the treatment plan is developed.

Treatment planning has long been part of the counseling process, but in recent years, as third-party reimbursement has become a consistent dominant concern for many mental health practitioners, the treatment plan has become an essential step in case conceptualization. Although this may not be necessary for counselors who do not rely on third-party reimbursement, the practice of preparing treatment plans is nonetheless good counseling practice.

Treatment plans include four types of information: the goals that have been established to address the problem or diagnosis; the kinds of interventions (including a rationale for each) that are designed to assist clients in realizing their goals; the anticipated length of time (or number of sessions) it would reasonably take to achieve success; and the format or milieu that will be used to deliver interventions, usually referred to as the *mode of treatment*. Although this can appear to be fairly straightforward, many other variables are considered in forming a successful treatment plan, including client characteristics that might make particular interventions optimal or a challenge, the skill, knowledge and resources of the therapist, the client's support system for treatment, and the research evidence regarding a particular treatment versus other competing treatments. We offer a template for a treatment plan in Appendix B. It is, however, beyond the scope of this text to addresses treatment planning in any comprehensive fashion and we refer the reader to other resources for a comprehensive discussion of this important topic (e.g., Cormier, Nurius, & Osborn, 2013; Seligman & Reichenberg, 2014).

STRATEGY SELECTION

In addition to choosing strategies that reflect client expectations and preferences, counselors also must consider available client resources and characteristics. For example, does the client have sufficient self-discipline to carry out a particular intervention outside of counseling? Does the client live and work in an environment in which support from others is fully given or withheld? Does an intervention require the client to do something (such as engage in imagination), and is the client capable of doing this? Are certain types of interventions outside the clients' experience or worldview? Is the intervention developmentally or age appropriate?

Proposed strategies must also take into account previous client attempts to solve their problems. When dealing with problems, clients often arrive at solutions that are both inadequate and irrelevant. When this happens, an all-too-common situation arises: The solution becomes part of the problem. This can be illustrated by the person whose world contains so many pressures that relaxation is very difficult. Seeing the need to escape from the pressures and routines, the client embarks on a course of action that includes hobbies, travel, and reading. Soon, the client realizes that these diversions have taken on the same character as the original problem. Hobbies have become compulsive activities, travel necessitates extraordinary planning, and reading has become a quest to absorb more books than last month's record. In other words, the solutions only added more pressure; consequently, the problem is exacerbated by the solutions. A counselor's strategy, then, must include interventions that cut below this dynamic and do not add to it.

It is vitally important for the counselor to understand, as much as possible, the client's world. It is also important to understand the frustrated needs the client is experiencing in that world. Finally, it is critical to understand what the client has been doing or thinking to find a solution. From the insights gleaned during this process, a strategy can be formed that leads to intervention selection.

CATEGORIES OF COUNSELING INTERVENTIONS

Counseling interventions may be described within the major categories through which problems are enacted: affect-centered problems, cognitive-centered problems, behavior-centered problems, and problems that are interactional/systemic in nature. Some interventions have some relevance for more than one domain; still, for the most part, they can be situated primarily in one of four categories.

Affective interventions (Chapter 8) elicit and respond primarily to feelings and emotions. They may also involve body awareness activities that focus on somatic components of a problem, because emotional states often involve the musculature and the expenditure of physical energy.

Cognitive interventions (Chapter 9) deal with thoughts, beliefs, and attitudes one has toward self and others. Such interventions are intended to help the client think differently about a situation, person, fear, boss, spouse, and so on.

Behavioral interventions (Chapter 10) are used to help the client develop new behaviors or skills and/or control or eliminate existing behaviors that are counterproductive. They may be used to modify habits, routines, or interaction patterns with others.

Interactional/systemic interventions (Chapter 11) address relationship patterns with other persons. The source may be one's family, work setting, neighborhood, church, or any social setting in which interactional patterns have been established, especially if the patterns are rigid and appear to be blocking development for the individual.

Table 7.1 describes therapeutic interventions used by counselors to accomplish these tasks. They are classified under the four orientations mentioned here and include examples of client

TABLE 7.1 Counseling Interventions and Corresponding Client Manifestations[a]

Affective	Cognitive	Behavioral	Systemic
Person-centered therapy; Gestalt therapy; Body awareness therapies; Psychodynamic therapies; Experiential therapies	**Rational–emotive therapy; Cognitive therapy; Reality therapy; Adlerian therapy**	**Skinner's operant conditioning; Wolpe's counterconditioning; Bandura's social learning; Dialectical behavior therapy**	**Structural family therapy; Strategic family therapy; Intergenerational systems therapy; Feminist therapy**
Interventions	*Interventions*	*Interventions*	*Interventions*
Empathic responses; positive regard; awareness techniques; empty chair; fantasy; bioenergetics; biofeedback; free association; transference analysis; focusing techniques	A-B-C-D-E analysis; homework assignments; bibliotherapy; media tapes; brainstorming; identifying alternatives; reframing; script analysis; problem definition; prescribing the problem (paradox)	Guided imagery; role playing; self-monitoring; physiological recording; behavioral contracting; assertiveness training; social skills training; systematic desensitization; contingency contracting; action planning; counterconditioning	Addressing triangulation, alliances, and coalitions; role restructuring; clarifying interactional systems; prescribing the problem (paradox); altering sequences; genogram analysis; coaching; defining boundaries; shifting triangulation patterns
Manifestations	*Manifestations*	*Manifestations*	*Manifestations*
Lack of understanding of feelings; confusion about feelings; fear of affect; closed off to feelings; highly defensive	Dichotomous (right/wrong) thinking; irrational thinking; conflicting or limited explanations for events	Lack of skills in key areas; lack of experience in key areas; limited ability to follow through on action plans	Enmeshed or disengaged relationships; rigid relationship boundaries and rules; dysfunctional interaction patterns

[a]The list of therapies does not include those that cross categories regularly, such as Multimodal therapy and Existential therapy. Also, *all* therapies cross categories to some extent.

Case Illustration of Strategy and Interventions Selection: Angela

Based on information derived from an intake interview with Angela, the counselor summarizes Angela's complaints using the four domains discussed here (Figure 7.2). Next, the counselor examines six factors for establishing a counseling strategy for this case:

1. The counselor's theoretical orientation. The counselor prefers an affective approach, with elements of person-centered theory and existentialism. The counselor also subscribes to systemic explanations of human problems.

2. Counseling experience. The counselor has practiced for about 4 years and has taken several training workshops since completing her formal counselor preparation program. She has worked with several depressed clients.

3. Character of the problem. Angela's problem may have a medical dimension in addition to affective, cognitive, behavioral, and systemic dimensions. Her presenting concern is how to have better control over her moods.

4. Typical responses to her problem. Based on her training and experience, the counselor knows that clients who feel inadequate must examine their support system, identify what

outcome their moods may be serving, and develop alternative and more facilitative behavior patterns.

5. Character of the goal. Angela identifies four main goals (Chapter 6) that she would like to achieve in counseling: (a) to become significantly more positive about herself over the next 3 months, (b) to control any negative effect that the Addison's disease may be contributing to her moods, (c) to become more aware of the meaningfulness of her daily activities and relationships, and (d) to have a sense of meaning for her life and some sort of "plan" for the next 2 to 5 years, and she would like to feel like she is working toward fulfilling that plan.

6. Client's characteristics. Angela appears to be functioning at a minimal level, both personally and socially. She was raised in a family in which she was not expected to be responsible for attending to her needs. She does not seem to be able to create social support. In addition, she quickly feels overwhelmed when life's demands begin to accumulate. In her former marriage, her husband took responsibility for "cheering her up."

presentations (manifestations) that might call for their use. This categorization system is based on previous classification systems, particularly Hutchins's (1982) thought-feeling-action (T-F-A) model and L'Abate's (1981) emotionality-rationality-activity (E-R-A) model.

Recall from Chapter 5 that client problems typically are multidimensional (including any combination of feeling, thinking, behaving, and interacting with others). In categorizing counseling interventions along these dimensions, the intent is to illustrate how selected interventions may be suitable for specific expressions of client problems. The intent is not to oversimplify the therapeutic process, but rather to lay out the range of options that counselors have when working with specific client problems. In addition, of course, affective interventions may be functional with more than affectively expressed problems, and so, as well, with the other three categories. In fact, if one views human beings as total persons rather than parts to be added together, then interventions in any of these four domains produce effects in all of the other domains of the problem. Let's revisit Angela, our fictional client from Chapter 5, to illustrate how the working alliance and intervention selection might be implemented.

Affective	*Behavioral*
Angela often feels irritable, upset, or depressed; feels sorry for herself when things go wrong; feels inadequate; feels abandoned by her ex-husband.	Angela retreats into her room when she feels blue; takes out her feelings on her children and students; occasionally has sleep problems; avoids social contact; has no regular recreational activities.

ANGELA'S PRESENTING PROBLEMS

Angela (Chapter 5) is seeking counseling to learn how to have better control over her moods. She indicates that she often "flies off the handle" for no reason with her children or with her students in the classroom. She has occasional difficulty sleeping. She feels like a failure as a wife and mother, primarily because of her divorce and her mood swings. Her self-description is primarily negative.

Cognitive	*Systemic*
Angela has a lot of negative self-talk; thinks her divorce was primarily her fault; blames herself for her inability to control her moods; thinks she is not giving her children the atmosphere they need.	Angela seems to have little in the way of positive relationships; has little contact with her family of origin; "uses" her children to avoid others; asks ex-husband to take children when she is overwhelmed, thus continuing her dependence on him.

FIGURE 7.2 Four-Domain Analysis of Angela's Case

DEFINING A COUNSELING STRATEGY

The first step in developing a counseling strategy is to synthesize what is known about the case and define a plan of action that is consistent with those factors. This synthesis should take into account both the four-orientation analysis and the six factors for establishing a counseling strategy. We note that (a) Angela presented her problem as affective (mood swings, feelings of inadequacy) and the counselor is predisposed toward an affective approach; (b) the presence of possible medical concerns should be addressed by a physician; (c) Angela set as a goal to become more positive about herself, which corresponds to her cognitive negativity; (d) Angela tends to retreat from others (behavioral and systemic) as well as from her problem (cognitive) and hides in her affective self when stress builds up; and (e) Angela's problem has spilled over to interpersonal relationships (children, students, social life), which relates to the counselor's systemic interests. In addition, she continues to lean on her ex-husband for help when she is in emotional distress, and this tends to both continue their systemic dysfunction and undermine her self-confidence even more.

Possible Strategies

The counselor has several viable choices of direction to take. The counselor might choose to work from an affective context because of a hypothesis that Angela is carrying several unresolved issues from her former marriage (failure feelings) and her mood swings, the effect of which produce increased stress, interpersonal issues, and possible exacerbation of her perimenopausal symptoms and Addison's disease. This seems to be a promising approach, particularly because the counselor has an affective predisposition and Angela's initial complaints are affective in nature.

Angela's problem could support a different strategy as well. Rather than address her emotional baggage from her former marriage, the counselor might choose to examine how Angela presently places herself into situations that remind her of her former marriage. In other words, the counselor might address the systemic and cognitive links that connect Angela's present to her past and, in so doing, seek to establish more facilitative cognitive responses. In addition, with the counselor's aid, Angela might challenge her self-defeating thinking about her past, her potential, and her interpersonal relationships. This approach might allow Angela to reassess her priorities, view her unchangeable life factors in a more positive light, and identify new goals and activities that would support a more desirable lifestyle. Because the counselor has not shown a strong inclination toward cognitive counseling approaches, this strategy could be more difficult to implement.

A third way that the counselor could conceptualize the case is to focus on Angela's behavior patterns, both in terms of how she responds to herself and to her children, students, and adults. The fact that Angela withdraws when she feels depressed probably exacerbates her affective response and becomes self-defeating. It was noted that Angela appears to be functioning at a low level, personally and socially. It may be appropriate to help Angela identify and strengthen certain behavior patterns that she could turn to when she begins to feel overwhelmed, depressed, or self-negative, the rationale being that if she can intervene in this downward spiraling pattern, then she might be spared the undesirable emotional consequences.

Finally, there seem to be clear links between Angela's present functioning and her role in her family of origin and in her relationship with her ex-husband. The counselor may wish to explore this linkage with Angela by seeking to clarify how her interaction patterns reflect her family's views of interdependency and family unity, how she manifests these patterns with her children and her students, and how her interactions with her family are similar to her interactions with other adults. The counselor might encourage Angela to examine how this pattern has repeated itself with her reliance on her ex-husband, and could help Angela address issues of individuation and differentiation versus connectedness. One might also wonder if Angela is in conflict with her ethnic (family) values. The counselor may wish to include the children in the counseling process as a means of revealing patterns of interaction, assumptions, and family rules, roles, and structure. This might logically lead to a systemic reassessment of Angela's approach to family and social groups through the use of one of the systemic family therapies. Because the counselor does subscribe to systemic explanations, this is an attractive approach, especially if the counselor has had adequate experience using systemic interventions.

Selecting Interventions

Each of the four strategies described here embraces a repertoire of counseling interventions that are consistent with the assumptions of each strategy. For example, the affective approach emphasizes exploration of feelings in a safe and understanding environment, the development of insight into and mindfulness of one's feelings, and ultimately the acceptance of those feelings and of oneself. Counselor activities such as empathic understanding of the client's situation and acceptance are endemic to this strategy. Similarly, the cognitive, behavioral, and systemic approaches also identify counselor interventions that support the objectives of these respective strategies. Chapters 8 through 11 examine these interventions and illustrate how they complement the strategy in question.

Choosing the Preferred Strategy

The character of the problem may be addressed through any one of a variety of counseling strategies, including behavioral, cognitive, affective, systemic, or any combination of these (e.g., cognitive–behavioral, cognitive–systemic). Your choice of strategy probably will reflect your personal explanation of human problems and how they can best be resolved (your personal theory). However, multiple or sequential strategies may be needed to work with the entire character of the defined client problem. For example, anxiety may be experienced behaviorally (inability to complete a task), cognitively (anticipatory worrying), affectively (depression), and systemically (emotional distancing from others). When more than one component is involved, usually more than one intervention is also necessary. You may still approach the case from your preferred vantage point for case conceptualization, but you may find that your interventions should address all aspects of the problem.

STRATEGIES FOR WORKING WITH CHILDREN

Children pose special issues in the counseling relationship because they have little power or control over their environment. How children view themselves (self-esteem) is bound to have environmental linkages. Similarly, how children behave is interconnected to the behaviors of others in the world. A child's potential to change that environment—be it the home, the neighborhood, or the school—is highly problematic without the involvement of significant others. Consequently, any effort to intervene in a child's problems necessarily involves relationships with siblings, parents, friends, teachers, and other adults. For this reason, a systemic view of the problem, if not a systemic strategy, is appropriate. The systemic view involves relationship patterns and their concomitant behavioral and cognitive components. The counselor can work with the child on an individual basis and seek to produce systemic change through the child, or the counselor can involve other participants in the child's system and seek to invoke direct change in the interactional patterns of the system.

The school counselor may include in this systemic counseling process three other systems: other children; the teacher and the child; or the parents, teacher(s), and the child. If the problem, and thus the goal, is primarily learning-related, then the process may be contained totally within the school setting. However, if the problem is familial, then the counselor's goal may be to generate parental awareness and responsibility for the problem, at which time a referral to a family counselor would be appropriate. Counselors working with children in community settings probably will seek to include the key family members in the counseling process, because family participation is required if successful resolution of the presenting problem is to be achieved.

Summary

Counseling strategies constitute the plan within which most therapeutic work and change take place. The strategic plan of action must reflect a number of divergent factors, including those related to the counselor's theory, experience, and expertise, as well as the client's presenting problem, goals, and environmental contingencies. In the case of children, the other significant players in the child's world assume a particularly significant role. Counselors must work with clients to identify interventions that address both the character of the problem and the goals that have been identified. Client expectations, preferences, capabilities, and resources are other important criteria to consider in choosing workable strategies.

Exercises

I. Choice or Change Issues and Related Counseling Strategies

A. By yourself or with a partner, list four to six issues or problems you are currently experiencing in your own life. Identify whether each is a choice issue or a change issue. Remember, *choice issues* are those in which you have the skills and opportunities to follow a course of action but feel conflicted about which direction to follow. *Change issues* are ones in which you must develop new options and behaviors or modify existing ones. Finally, note whether the choice or change for each issue is under your control and can be initiated by you. If it is not, identify the other people in your life who are also part of this choice or change.

B. With a partner or in a small group, brainstorm possible strategies that might be suitable interventions for one of the issues or problems from your list in part A. Next, evaluate the probable usefulness of each strategy. In your evaluation, consider the six guidelines for selection of counseling strategies described in this chapter.

1. Is the strategy consistent with your theoretical orientation (which may be fledgling at this point)?
2. Do you have any expertise and experience in working with this strategy?
3. Are you knowledgeable about typical responses to and effects of this strategy?
4. Does the strategy fit the character or nature of the problem?
5. Does the strategy fit the character or nature of your desired goal?
6. Does the strategy meet your expectations and preferences, and does it avoid repeating or building on prior unsuccessful solutions?

   (*Note:* You do not have to select complex or sophisticated counseling strategies. If you have not yet been exposed to counseling theories and techniques, rely on commonsense approaches and interventions, because the emphasis in this activity is on the process of strategy selection rather than on the actual strategies you select.)

C. Continue this activity with your partner or group. For the strategy your group selected in part B as the best or most effective one, generate the following information about the strategy:

1. A rationale—how it might work
2. A description of the counselor's role in the strategy
3. A description of the client's role in the strategy
4. Possible discomfort, negative effects, or spinoffs from the selected strategy
5. Expected benefits of the strategy
6. Estimated time involved in using this strategy

D. Role-play the strategy information in part C. One person assumes the client's role and presents the issue. The other person assumes the counselor's role, suggests the recommended strategy, and provides the client with enough information about the strategy to help the client make an informed choice about accepting or rejecting the suggestion. Additional members of the group function as observers, and should take notes and provide feedback to the counselor after the role-play. Follow up with a group discussion of the exercise.

II. Relationship of Problem Components to Strategy Selection

In this exercise, we present three client cases. For each case, determine the component(s) of the problem that must be addressed during the intervention phase of counseling. There may be more than one significant component. Also, keep in mind that each client presents aspects of him- or herself that are individual, aspects that are cultural, and aspects that are universal. Identifying which lens one is using to view the situation helps the counselor to keep the other two in mind as well.

A. Dante is a 16-year-old eighth-grader who has been in and out of trouble for the past 5 years. He belongs to a street gang known to be involved with drugs, and he has been to county jail twice for "aiding/abetting in drug activity." In the past year, he has been considering leaving the gang and as he puts it, "starting all over again." Leaving the gang is not so easy, however, because the gang does not allow members to leave and enforces this rule heavily. Dante is caught between the desire to start over and the probable consequences if he tries.

Primary Components

Affective: _____

Cognitive: _____

Behavioral: _____

Systemic: _____

Preferred strategy(ies): _____

B. Marguerite is a 28-year-old single woman who has been diagnosed with multiple sclerosis, a progressive disease. Her mobility has become increasingly constricted in the past 6 months, to the point that she has encountered increasing situations in which she has limited access. This has both frustrated and angered her. At the same time, she knows that the disease will only get worse, and that she should be using her energies to try to accept and adapt, a position that has been challenged by some of her friends and family. She lives at home with her parents, who give her too much sympathy (she thinks) or turn their frustrations on the society that is so "insensitive" to such situations.

Primary Components

Affective: _____

Cognitive: _____

Behavioral: _____

Systemic: _____

Preferred strategy(ies): _____

C. Heather and Steve have come for marriage counseling. During the first session, Steve dominates and Heather sits passively while he describes their "problem." When he refers to their problem, he stares at her and she looks down at her hands in her lap. Finally, Heather explodes and shouts that the problem is that Steve is having an affair with her best friend. At this point, Steve becomes enraged and leaves the therapy room. Heather begins to cry and says that she is at her wits' end. She doesn't want a divorce, but she doesn't think the marriage can be saved. You ask Heather if they ever discuss their problems at home, and she shakes her head no. You ask if Steve is ever physically abusive, and she says quietly, "Sometimes he pushes me." When you ask if she has ever shared this with her family members, she says that they just wouldn't understand because they are traditional Catholics and believe that she should stick it out.

Primary Components

Affective: _____

Cognitive: _____

Behavioral: _____

Systemic: _____

Preferred strategy(ies): _____

Discussion Questions

1. Identify and discuss the attributes of both a good counseling strategy and a poor counseling strategy. From your perspective, what factors make a strategy good or effective?

2. How much influence do you believe a person's cultural values have? How aware do you think people are of their cultural values?

3. Identify a problem situation that you have experienced (or have observed in a close relationship) in which the attempted solution became the new problem or made the existing problem worse. To what extent was the person in question aware of this complication? How was the problem finally resolved?

MyCounselingLab® Assignment

Go to the Video Library under Video Resources on the MyCounselingLab site for your text and search for the following clips:

- **Video Example: Challenging Clients' Thoughts and Behaviors**   This family session with a mother and her little girl touches on all four orientations/domains as the dimensions of the problem unfold. Which of the four domains (i.e., affective, cognitive, behavioral, or systemic) strikes you as being more

promising? Which of the four do you think the counselor in the video is leaning toward? What is your evidence for this?

- **Video Example: Reflecting Feelings: Mark**   Similar to the first video, this brief clip indicates that issues can be positioned in more than one domain. How would you proceed with this client? What is your reaction to the client's perception of her problem?

CHAPTER

Affective
Interventions

8

PURPOSE OF THIS CHAPTER

Ask someone why people seek counseling and you are likely to get an answer that identifies emotion as the cause. We hear terms like *emotional imbalance, emotionally disturbed,* or *emotionally upset* as conditions that get people into psychological difficulty. Although feelings certainly are not the source of all human difficulties, it is nonetheless true that strong negative emotions are often a cue that something is not going well and that outside intervention may be helpful. This chapter discusses the role that emotions play in the process of counseling and describes counseling interventions that are specifically used to help clients identify emotions; modify troublesome feelings; and, when appropriate, accept feelings that are present.

Considerations as You Read This Chapter

■ Feelings have been described as basic to all human experience, yet many people do not seem to understand their feelings. Some disavow having certain feelings, whereas others treat their feelings as an embarrassment or a sign of weakness. Some ethnic groups treat feelings as private events.

■ What are your views? Would you be described as "wearing your heart on your sleeve," or as the stoic type? On a continuum from highly emotional to unemotional, where would you place yourself?

■ What role does emotion play in people's problems? Is it the source? The result?

■ How do people change the way they feel about something? If a feeling changes, for example, from indifference to liking, will that be reflected in the person's perceptions of his or her world?

People feel happy when things are going well, sad when they experience loss, angry or frustrated when their desires are blocked, and lonely when they are deprived of contact with others. Many times, feelings can be accessed only indirectly through a person's verbal expression or behavior. A client may feel depressed, but only through verbal and nonverbal communication, physical cues, or acting out can the counselor make contact with that feeling state. However, feelings cannot be manipulated in the same fashion as thoughts or behaviors. We can discipline ourselves to be civil with someone we dislike, but that doesn't necessarily lead to a change of feelings about the person. To conflate constructs, feelings seem to have a mind of their own! Perhaps it is this seeming lack of control over our affective life that leads so many people to hide, deny, and even to discount their affective life until it "feels" quite foreign to them.

The role that feelings play in counseling and psychotherapy is an unsettled issue. Feelings can be viewed as peripheral phenomena that accompany but do not affect therapeutic change, or they can be viewed as essential to or evidence of change. Whichever is the case, most, if not all, of human thought and behavior have a feeling dimension. Perhaps because this is so, feelings can be the source, or a significant part, of the problems one experiences. Some clients may lack access to feelings. This bottling up of feelings may be the result of one's early training or to the intensity of an emotion that threatens to overpower the person. Boys are often taught to deny those feelings that are associated with weakness, failure, or powerlessness. Similarly, girls are often taught to deny feelings associated with characteristics such as dominance, control, power, or even intellect. Consider the child who is raised in a perfectionist environment. If that child internalizes the environmental demands, then the need to be perfect without the skills to do so may lead to excessive threat and emotional difficulties throughout childhood and into adulthood. When these unacknowledged or even undetected feelings begin to build up, some people are ill equipped to find release, and counseling becomes an appropriate recourse.

Still, we do not want to imply that gender roles dominant our affective lives or that people who appear more cerebral than emotional are "hiding." People are different, and the role that feelings play in each of our lives is unique to us. Counselors who stress the affective world to the exclusion of thoughts and behaviors may simply be a bad fit for some clients, and for this reason, counselors should have multiple options when they choose their interventions.

When you have assessed that the client's relationship to his or her affective life is part of the problem at hand, there are resources available to you as counselor. Helping the individual develop the capacity to find release of emotional difficulties and cope better with life demands are central goals of many therapeutic approaches. The affect-oriented theories have made major contributions to the counselor's repertoire of interventions. Generally speaking, those theories with an affective orientation rely heavily on the development of affect awareness, exploration, and integration of feelings. They do not discount thought processes or behavior patterns; rather, they emphasize the emotional context in which thought patterns, beliefs, and behaviors occur.

THEORIES THAT STRESS THE IMPORTANCE OF FEELINGS

Most affective or emotion interventions derive from the phenomenological therapies. Phenomenologists make a distinction between what is (objective reality) and one's perceptions of what is. This inner world of perceptions becomes one's personal reality. By far the most dominant of these therapies is Carl Rogers's person-centered therapy. Rogers described a progression in counseling that follows the client's relationship to affect. This description became formalized as the Process Scale (Rogers & Rablen, 1958) and was used for many years to study client change. The scale describes seven kinds of client reactions as change occurs. Typically, the client begins counseling by talking about externals (work, relatives, etc.). This is probably the client's way of controlling his or her commitment to an as-yet-uncertain venture. Next, discussion gradually changes to include references to feelings, albeit past feelings or those that are external to the client—again, a careful step toward commitment. In the third stage, the client elaborates on feelings, but these are historical in nature rather than current feelings (e.g., "I was really hurt by her comment"). At the fourth level, the client begins to talk about present feelings and acknowledges ownership of those feelings (e.g., "I'm still upset with her for what she said to me!"). The fifth stage is one in which the client allows him- or herself to experience current feelings in the presence of the counselor (e.g., "Every time I think about it, I get the same rush of emotion" [begins weeping]). In the final two stages, the client begins to (a) experience previously denied feelings and (b) accept and become comfortable with those feelings. Rogers never forced this development. Rather, he allowed the client to move at whatever speed was comfortable through this developmental process.

Although most dominant, person-centered theory is not alone in its recognition of the importance of affect. Probably next in its impact would be the contributions of gestalt therapy, followed by the existential approaches of Binswanger, Boss, Frankl, and May. Other therapeutic approaches sometimes identified as affective therapies include Kelly's psychology of personal constructs; Gendlin's experiential counseling; psychoanalytic therapy; and the body work therapies, such as bioenergetics and core energetics.

Wellness models of counseling encompass a number of dimensions, including intellectual, emotional, physical, social, and spiritual wellness (Myers & Sweeney, 2005). This approach has been labeled *holistic*, meaning that the entirety of the individual is considered and used in the process of counseling. Wellness also emphasizes prevention as a tool toward healthy living. For our purposes, emotional and spiritual wellness are considered to be conditions residing within the affective or feeling dimension of counseling. Other areas of wellness are addressed in Chapters 9 through 11.

AFFECTIVE INTERVENTIONS

In one respect, referring to affective interventions is a philosophical contradiction. The affect-focused counselor is more likely to emphasize the personhood of the client and the interpersonal relationship between counselor and client rather than the techniques used. Nevertheless, the affective counselor is doing something in this process, and these counselor behaviors are the focus of this chapter. We discuss basic skills that attend to affect in Chapter 4; here we apply those skills and provide additional focus for their use as part of our discussion of affective interventions. As we explore these interventions, keep in mind that the interventions become gimmicky and ineffective if the therapeutic relationship between the counselor and the client has been given a lesser priority.

Affective Intervention Skills

Sorting Out Feelings

Helping the client identify the type of feeling to be explored

- Emotions inventory. A checklist of feelings that the client can use (even during intake) to identify feelings that are present.
- Emotions balloons. An exercise that children are able to use.

Focusing Technique

Using the wisdom of the physical body to help the client get in touch with feelings that interfere with daily living

Role Reversal

Allowing the client to experience interactions from another person's perspective, thus helping the client to get beyond a "stuck" affective state

Alter-Ego Exercise

Helping the client recognize alternative or competing emotions within him- or herself

Empty-Chair Exercise

Using a dialoging exercise in which the client is able to carry on a conversation or even an argument with him- or herself or with another person in order to become more aware of affective states

The Goals of Affective Interventions

The primary goals of affective interventions are to (a) help the client express feelings or feeling states; (b) identify or discriminate between feelings or feeling states; (c) alter or accept feelings or feeling states; or, (d) in some cases, to contain feelings or feeling states.

Some clients come to counseling with awareness that something is wrong in their lives but are unable to articulate or discuss that condition. Talking about problems or feelings may be a new experience for them. This is often the case for the person who grew up in a family or culture in which problems were never discussed openly, or the expression of feelings was discouraged or forbidden through such injunctions as, "Don't be angry," "Don't cry," or "Don't feel." Child clients may not have reached the developmental stage at which skills and affect sensitivity are acquired; consequently, they may lack both the skills of expression and the awareness that expression of feelings can be helpful.

On the other end of the affective spectrum, the client may come to counseling flooded with emotional reactions. When this happens, it is experienced as an emotional overload, and the protective response often is to tune out the emotions, to become emotionless; alternatively, the response may be confusion or disorientation. This client must be helped to recognize and to sort out or contain the variety of affect responses that are being experienced. This condition is frequently found when a person has experienced a long period of emotional turmoil, such as occurs in a divorce, death of a family member, poor physical health, posttraumatic stress disorder (PTSD), or other life tragedy, or it may be a more serious psychopathologic blocking of affect. We offer a caveat here that, depending on how the client is "flooded" by emotion, affective interventions may or may not be called for. Affective interventions are used when clients are not aware of their emotions or cannot sort them out. These interventions are not necessarily an appropriate intervention when the client is in touch with feelings but gets no relief from them. In this case, interventions from other orientations may be more in line with the client's needs.

At the most complex level of affect intervention, the counselor and client are involved in the integration or alteration of feeling states. This may include acceptance of hitherto unacceptable feelings, reconsideration of old feelings, or even redefinition of feeling states. This process is common when the client is beginning to differentiate self from family, self from job or career, self from circumstances, self from culture, or is otherwise laboring with the question, "Who am I?"

In this chapter, we describe and illustrate some common affective interventions that facilitate the expression and examination of feelings, including feeling inventories, dialoging and alter-ego exercises, identifying affect blocks, differentiation among competing feelings, role reversal, the empty chair, and affect focusing. This list is not meant to be exhaustive, but can equip you with some tools with which to approach affective concerns with clients.

HELPING CLIENTS EXPRESS AFFECT

Experiencing a feeling, even knowing that somehow feelings are related to one's problems, does not lead naturally to the expression and examination of the feeling. Part of your role is to help clients find ways to express feelings, in ways that both capture the meaning of the feeling and convey that meaning to others. Your task may be a matter of setting the stage and creating the proper conditions for a reticent client to open up.

Many authors have described the conditions that are necessary for such an involvement. These conditions—an accurate understanding of the client's situation and an unconditional valuing of the client—were discussed in Chapter 4. Beyond the conditions that create the atmosphere of helping, the counselor becomes involved in the client's process of emotional exploration through selective attention and reflective listening, also described in Chapter 4.

The exploration of emotions is a process more than a set of verbal responses, and involves your conceptualization of what the client is trying to understand and the acknowledgment of that effort. Sometimes the process also serves to focus the client's awareness on what he or she seems to be saying. In addition, the process usually involves sharing the satisfaction of having accomplished the task. Given that it is a process rather than a series of behavioral events, you must rely nonetheless on verbal interaction with the client and close observation of nonverbal communication.

Earlier we noted that there are gender differences and personality differences regarding comfort with affect or the expression of affect. The professional literature also indicates that there can be distinct cultural differences. There are various resources for you to consult to become somewhat prepared for ethnic differences related to affect expression (e.g., McGoldrick, Giordano, & Garcia-Preto, 2005; Sue, Gallardo, & Neville, 2014). Still, you cannot practice expert multicultural counseling by using stereotypic shortcuts. Each person represents his or her culture uniquely, and this includes the person's relationship to affect. Counselors learn to draw from resources when useful, but to balance this with their sensitive and unbiased interactions with their clients.

NONVERBAL AFFECT CUES

A major way in which clients show feelings is through nonverbal cues or body language. Early work by Ekman and Friesen (1967) indicates that nonverbal information can be inferred from elements of the client's communication, such as head and facial movement, body position, movements and gestures, and voice qualities. Although no single nonverbal cue can be interpreted accurately in isolation, each does have meaning as part of a larger pattern or gestalt; thus, there are relationships between nonverbal and verbal characteristics of client messages. In addition to these relationships, nonverbal cues may also communicate specific information about the relationship between individuals involved in the communicative process, in this case, the counselor and client. Some nonverbal cues convey information about the nature and intensity of emotions more accurately than verbal cues. The nature of the emotion is communicated nonverbally primarily by head cues—for example, setting of the jaw, facial grimaces, or narrowing of the eyes. The intensity of an emotion is communicated by both head cues and body cues, such as muscular rigidity.

The counselor may or may not choose to acknowledge these nonverbal cues. In some cases, acknowledging them ("You've been looking very tight since you started talking about this matter") can invite the client to share the intensity of the emotion. At other times, the counselor's observation may be rejected outright or may bring out a defensive response. Thus, timing as well as accuracy of perception is a factor in what the counselor chooses to say. As you get to know your client, you will be able to determine how to respond to nonverbal cues.

Accuracy of perception must also be considered a culturally relative term, at least for some nonverbal cues. We learn cues within a cultural context, and must constantly check out our assumptions of what a nonverbal cue means. Is a smile a statement of superiority, or a sign of nervousness? Is shutting down after an expression of sadness an act of resistance, or a sign of shame? Counselors who interpret with a great deal of caution and who are open to meanings that are outside of their own experience make fewer erroneous assumptions. That said, Ekman (1993) emphasizes that "no one to date has obtained strong evidence of cross-cultural disagreement about the interpretation of fear, anger, disgust, sadness, or enjoyment expressions" (p. 384). It may be that some feelings are universal, and you can take some comfort in this.

VERBAL AFFECT CUES

Although there are many different kinds of feelings, most feelings that are identified by words or nonverbal behaviors fit into one of four mental states: positive/affirming feelings, aggressive/defensive feelings, fear/anxiety feelings, and spiritual/existential feelings (which can range from peaceful to depressed). Many of these feelings can be identified by certain affect word usage. In addition, there are subcategories of affect for each of the major affect categories. In using words to identify affect, it is important to remember that words may occasionally mask more intense feelings, or feelings that are different from the meaning of the words used (e.g., the client who says that she is excited about a new opportunity when she is really terrified). It should also be noted that the language of emotions can vary across cultures. In fact, some cultures may not have a word for a particular emotion, although Ekman (1993) adds that if the language of a culture does not have a word for a specific emotion, it does not mean that the emotion is not present in that culture, but simply connotes the lack of specific terms to represent certain feelings.

Verbal Cues of Positive/Affirming Mental States

Positive expressions reflect good or accepting feelings about oneself and others and indicate positive aspects of interpersonal relationships. Verbal cues in a client's communication are revealed by the presence of words that connote certain feelings. For example, if a client uses the word *wonderful* in describing an event, a location, or a person, that descriptor suggests an accepting, preferred, or desirable mental set toward the referent. Sometimes, the client is more nonspecific about such reactions but nonetheless communicates an affective reaction. Some examples of word cues that connote this positive affect are shown in Table 8.1. Often,

TABLE 8.1 Positive/Affirming Mental State Cues

EMPOWERED	HAPPY	ENJOY	LOVING/LOVED	TRUSTING
Able	Blissful	Beautiful	Adored	Assure(d)
Appreciated	Cheerful	Delight	Appreciated	Believe
Authorized	Creative	Enjoy	Beloved	Certain
Capable	Delighted	Good	Care	Confident
Confident	Elated	Happy	Cherished	Depend
Confirmed	Excited	Indulge	Choose	Expect
Enabled	Extravagant	Nice	Close	Faith
Important	Fascinating	Pleasing	Desired	Hope
Intelligent	Glad	Relish	Esteemed	Rely (Reliance)
Proud	Happy	Satisfy	Friendly	Secure
Respected	Joyful	Terrific	Idolized	Trust
Satisfied	Merry	Tremendous	Like	
Smart	Playful	Zestful	Love	
Supported	Sexy		Needed	
Valuable	Stimulating		Treasured	
Worthwhile	Thrilled		Want	
			Worthy	

nonverbal cues occur simultaneously with these positive affect cues. The most frequent nonverbal mood correlates are facial ones. The corners of the mouth may turn up to produce the hint of a smile, the eyes may widen slightly, and worry wrinkles may disappear. There may be a noticeable absence of body tension. The arms and hands may move in an open-palm gesture of acceptance, or the communicator may reach out as though to touch the object of the affect message. When clients are describing feelings about an object or event, there may be increased animation of the face and hands.

Verbal Cues of Aggressive/Defensive Mental States

Feelings serve functions. Although aggressive or defensive responses sometimes represent an obstruction to be removed, they can also be a signal to protect oneself, or to fight for one's rights or even survival. These are not pleasant feelings to experience, and many clients seek or are referred to counseling with the idea of having them relieved or eliminated. However, attempting to make them go away without looking to see what function they may serve might not be in the client's best interest therapeutically. The feelings may be the result of injustice that the client has suffered, and are therefore a sign of resiliency. At other times such feelings mask a more vulnerable reaction, such as hurt, shame, or inadequacy. Clients may need help in learning how to understand the origins of such mental states, or they may need to learn how to express their feelings in an assertive way rather than in an aggressive/defensive manner. Most people are well acquainted with the words that represent aggression and defensiveness (Table 8.2).

Certain vocal qualities are associated with aggression and defensiveness. Many times, the voice becomes louder, deeper, or more controlled. The pacing of the communication may become more rapid or more deliberate. Usually, communicators make distinct departures from their normal communication when these mental states are present. That said, many communication errors occur because of discrepancies across ethnic groups on such things as volume and animation. What is dangerously excitable for one ethnic group may be just "getting your attention" for another group. Counselors must, therefore, learn to filter communication through a fairly broad lens that is culturally astute.

TABLE 8.2 Aggressive/Defensive Mental State Cues

AGGRESSIVE	GRIM	QUARRELSOME	DEFENSIVE
Angry	Austere	Argumentative	Against
Annihilate	Cruel	Belligerent	Cagey
Argue	Foreboding	Cantankerous	Careful
Attack	Frightful	Combative	Cautious
Criticize	Grave	Contentious	Guarded
Destroy	Grumpy	Disagree	Opposition
Fight	Harsh	Hotheaded	Prepared
Hit	Merciless	Irritable	Protective
Hurt	Ruthless	Litigious	Resent
Offend	Severe	Scrappy	Resistive
Overcome	Solemn	Tempestuous	Withholding

It is possible that a client can experience aggressiveness or defensiveness without immediate awareness of it. Old anger, deep insecurity, or alienation can become so normative that a person accommodates a responsive mental state as though it, too, were normal behavior. Thus, the counselor may find that the client is unaware, at a surface level, of a departure from "wellness." In this case, the counselor's acknowledgment of the condition may be perceived as confrontation by the client. A simple, tentative observation, such as, "You sound as though you may be angry," can bring a defensive reaction. This serves as a signal that deeper and gentler exploration of the client's reactions may be appropriate.

Verbal Cues of Fear/Anxiety Mental States

Fear is a reaction to some kind of danger to be avoided; anxiety is a more latent or generalized response to the same perceived dangers. Either may signal a need to withdraw from a threatening situation, from oneself, or from other people and relationships. The person experiencing fear or anxiety may also feel isolated. The implicit presence of danger signaled by these responses is the likely focal point for counseling. Verbal cues that suggest fear or anxiety in a client's communication may be classified into five categories, as shown in Table 8.3.

As was the case with aggressive/defensive responses, some physical cues are associated with fear and anxiety. The face may express surprise or suspicion, and the body may recoil or appear ready to spring into action. The breathing rate may become more rapid and shallow. As anxiety and tension increase, the number of speech disturbances—such as errors, repetitions, stuttering, and omissions—may also increase. The person may speak at a faster than normal rate, or the voice may take on a more guarded quality.

When the client appears fearful, the counselor may wish to explore the ramifications of that fear. How realistic is the fear? How physically threatening is the feared situation? Is the situation more threatening to one's identity or spiritual self than to one's physical self? How accurate are the client's perceptions of the feared situation?

Verbal Cues of Spiritual/Existential Mental States

Thus far, we have discussed emotional conditions that have direct or concrete connections to a client's physical world (e.g., a fear of speaking to strangers, anger associated with a particular event). However, as you know, some feelings do not seem to be anchored in day-to-day events or

TABLE 8.3 Fear/Anxiety Mental State Cues

FEARFUL	DOUBTING	PAINED	MISTRUSTING	AVOIDING
Anguished	Confused	Angst	Aversive	Copping Out
Anxious	Failure	Dismayed	Dislike	Denying
Concerned	Insecure	Fearful	Doubt	Escaping
Nervous	Stuck	Hurt	Questionable	Fleeing
Scared	Stupid	Struggling	Shady	Neglecting
Worried	Unsure	Suffering	Suspicious	Running

TABLE 8.4 Spiritual/Existential Mental State Cues

PEACEFUL	HOPEFUL	EMPTY	DISILLUSIONED	DESPAIRING
Calm	Anticipate	Abandoned	Cheated	Depressed
Composed	Assurance	Adrift	Cynical	Desperate
Content	Believe	Dejected	Disappointed	Despondent
Loving	Confident	Directionless	Discouraged	Disconsolate
Mellow	Expect	Disconnected	Disheartened	Empty
Pensive	Faith(ful)	Distraught	Dissatisfied	Forlorn
Placid	Inspiring	Downhearted	Failed	Gloomy
Relaxed	Optimistic	Heartsick	Let Down	Hopeless
Satisfied	Providential	Hopeless	Lost	Lost
Serene	Rely	Meaningless	Punished	Morose
Thankful	Trust(ing)	Purposeless	Unattainable	Powerless
Thoughtful	Uplifting	Sad	Unfair	Sullen
Untroubled	Wish(Ful)	Sorrowful	Unworkable	Weary

people. They may have more to do with self-doubt, purpose, or connection to life, and the client's response may be equally vague: a general sense of unwellness or unease, restlessness, sadness, or doom. The feelings themselves can be most unsettling because they don't seem to be associated with causative events.

Spiritual/existential mental states actually form a continuum from wellness to distress (Table 8.4). When a person feels congruent with his or her existential self, a sense of peace and hopefulness is experienced. When a person is out-of-sync with her- or himself, feelings of disillusionment or despair are experienced. Somewhere in between lies a psychic space of neither hope nor despair. It is a feeling of emptiness, which can range from vague discomfort to outright craving for relief. Bishop (1995) observes that "issues such as locus of control, acceptance of responsibility, belief in God, and guilt and shame [often] play a role in problems presented by clients" (p. 64).

Existentialism is, at its core, the study of the human condition. Some might even say that it is a counterdiscipline to theology. *Spirituality,* however, is generally accepted as a term to acknowledge some belief in something bigger than humans as a driving force of life. Spirituality tends to be distinguished from religion or religiosity. *Religion* may be identified as the institutional response to matters of the self and God. Spirituality is the non-institutional response to these same matters. As such, spirituality does not seek to replace the role of religion in one's life but in fact may tide one over in periods of religious alienation. Similarly, religion may be the appropriate approach to addressing a client's spiritual issues, particularly when the client is aware of a personal religious base to life. Richards and Bergin (2005) define *spiritual interventions* as

> those that are more experiential, transcendent, ecumenical, cross-cultural, internal, affective, spontaneous, and personal. Examples include private prayer, spiritual meditation, spiritual imagery with images that are personally meaningful to the client, encouraging forgiveness, and keeping a spiritual journal. (p. 237)

Morgan (2000) addresses these issues as they apply to counseling:

> For counselors today, the task is to understand the particular experiences, communal contexts, and historical-cultural elements that shape a client's spiritual perspective and practice. How does this person experience transcendence, or a higher power, or ultimacy in his or her life? What attitudes and values are important for him or her to live by, in order to feel connected with the spiritual realm? What practices keep the client "on track" in his or her search for meaning? (p. 174)

Powell (1996) describes a case in which a 16-year-old depressed female, whom he diagnosed as experiencing a Major Depressive Disorder, Single Episode, and who was the daughter of missionary parents, received treatment over a period of 18 months. The focus of treatment was on spiritual values clarification, addressing losses that the client had not acknowledged or grieved, and understanding the stresses and pressures her parents were undergoing. Thus, it is appropriate to consider spiritual interventions in one's work as a component of the affective.

If the client appears to be withdrawing from social contact, sleeping poorly, eating poorly or erratically, and focusing extensively on self, then the counselor should perform an assessment of suicide ideation/suicide threat. There are many resources for this process, including many available online, such as the Suicide Risk Assessment Reference prepared by the government to assess such risk for veterans: http://www.mentalhealth.va.gov/docs/Suicide_Risk_Assessment_Reference_Guide.pdf.

HELPING CLIENTS SORT FEELINGS

Some clients enter counseling aware of their emotions but they are overwhelmed by either the complexity or quantity of their unresolved feelings. Such a condition is often triggered by a traumatic life event, such as the death of a parent, spouse, or child; an unexpected divorce; the loss of a career; or the trauma of sexual assault. These traumatic events stimulate feelings associated with the event and, perhaps more significantly, feelings associated with the person's self-worth. Typically, the person is attempting to resolve unanswerable questions, such as, "Why did this happen?" "Why did it have to happen to me?" and "Could I have prevented it from happening?"

One of the counselor's roles in this situation is that of facilitator, guide, and supporter. Counseling interventions include being a sounding board (albeit a skilled sounding board) as the client attempts to uncover a complex series of feelings, helping the client recognize the source of various emotional reactions, and helping the client develop a sense of emotional control. Interventions can range from the experiential to something as simple as giving a client a simple paper-and-pencil exercise to help the client sort out feelings.

Whether the crux of the client's problem is the quantity, complexity, or hiddenness of emotional experience, the process aims to help clients develop some structure or system for understanding and managing those feelings. This process is not as simple as it might sound. The tendency, particularly for the inexperienced counselor, is to offer a logical argument to counter the client's debilitating feelings. Such an argument usually misses the point. Many emotions, especially emotional overloads that lead persons to counseling, are illogical. We say things like, "Your feelings make sense," when they appear to be in line with how we see the world, but arguing against feelings that are not in line with what we think makes sense is not helpful. Rather, as a first step, we must acknowledge feelings as real and legitimate; we can then assist the clients in understanding their internal "logic" that has gotten them to this point. To do so, we rely on cognitive interventions that are described in Chapter 9. But to skip the respectful acknowledgment of a client's affect and move too quickly to cognitive work is to deny the client's experience, and thus is ultimately disrespectful.

Several interventions, exercises, and discussions can help clients sort out feelings. No one intervention is effective with all clients; thus, you must explore and experiment with each new client to find the activities that are acceptable and meaningful for that individual. The interventions range from very simple paper-and-pencil exercises to more complicated and dramatic reenactments of emotional experiences.

Early in counseling, the most appropriate strategy is to use activities that generate expression and classification of feelings. These activities include counselor recognition and reflection of client's expression of feelings, verbal statements, and counselor empathy for the client's emotional description. Chapter 4 contains a full discussion of empathy, affective reflections, and restatements. Other activities include an emotional percentages chart and emotions checklist (which is very effective for the client who says, "I can't describe my feelings") and the emotions balloons chart (which is a helpful aid for children).

It is important to note that not all counselors are comfortable with feelings, especially strong feelings, either the client's or their own. This can be a result of coming from a family of origin that was not affect-friendly, a cultural background that emphasized the cerebral and behavioral over the affective, some personal pain that the client is attempting to deny, and so forth. Teyber and McClure (2011) describe a number of ways in which counselors respond ineffectively when these circumstances prevail, and include becoming overly intellectual with the client, diminishing the moment by assuring the client that everything will be OK, and changing the topic away from the emotionally charged one. Usually, these reactions that also include rescuing behavior are driven by the counselor's need for self-protection. One might wonder if patterns developed in other contexts, such as one's family of origin, come to play at these moments. Teyber and McClure conclude their list of cautions by warning that counselors might make the error of "over-identifying with the client and becoming controlling—pressuring the client to make some decision or take a particular action in order to truncate the therapist's own unwanted feelings" (p. 224). For reasons such as these, best practice requires that beginning counselors receive clinical supervision.

Emotions Inventory

An effective way to introduce adolescents and adults to a discussion of emotions is the emotions inventory (Figure 8.1). This inventory is a checklist of a wide range of emotions that clients frequently report in their counseling sessions. It can be given to the client to fill out prior to or during the first counseling session. The client is asked to identify those feelings that describe his or her life experience in the previous 3 months or in the present moment. In the session(s) that follow, the client's responses may be used as a basis for early discussion and exploration of counseling concerns. As an exercise, look at the emotions inventory in Figure 8.1, and check any feelings that you might have experienced in the past 48 hours.

Emotional Percentages Chart

Some adults have difficulty focusing on feelings. This doesn't mean that they lack feelings; rather, it means that they are probably unaccustomed to talking or thinking about their feelings. Often a

_____	Abandoned	_____	Disoriented	_____	Mad
_____	Adrift	_____	Doubtful	_____	Nervous
_____	Afraid	_____	Empty	_____	Offended
_____	Angry	_____	Fearful	_____	Outraged
_____	Annoyed	_____	Frustrated	_____	Panicked
_____	Anxious	_____	Furious	_____	Pessimistic
_____	Bewildered	_____	Grumpy	_____	Resentful
_____	Confused	_____	Hassled	_____	Sad
_____	Defensive	_____	Heartsick	_____	Scared
_____	Depressed	_____	Hopeless	_____	Skeptical
_____	Desperate	_____	Hurt	_____	Sorrowful
_____	Despondent	_____	Insecure	_____	Tense
_____	Directionless	_____	Irritable	_____	Tired
_____	Discouraged	_____	Irritated	_____	Uneasy
_____	Disillusioned	_____	Lonely	_____	Unsure

FIGURE 8.1   Emotions Inventory

visual aid helps them begin to think or focus. The emotional percentages chart (Figure 8.2) is an exercise that can be quite effective early in counseling. On a sheet of paper, two circles are drawn. One is a pie graph that illustrates a number of different feeling states and how much of the total pie each emotion occupies. The other circle is empty, and the client is asked to draw in his or her emotional percentages. You may want to refer your clients to the emotions inventory if they are having difficulty labeling personal emotions to use in the chart. The emotional percentages chart allows clients to identify the intensity or preoccupation with a particular set of emotions. It also allows the counselor to invite clients to discuss the interrelationships of those identified emotions in the chart. This chart can be used as both a baseline exercise and one that can be returned to later in counseling.

Emotions Balloons Chart

Young children pose a special problem for the counselor. Emotional awareness is a process that develops as the child develops. Very young children may know only happy, sad, and mad. As

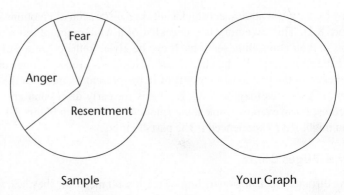

Sample   Your Graph

FIGURE 8.2   Emotional Percentages Chart

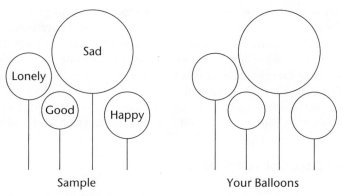

FIGURE 8.3 Emotions Balloons Chart

children grow and their vocabularies increase, they are able to recognize the subtleties that exist within these emotions. Even so, the counselor must relate to the child at the child's level of experience. In part, this means that you use the toys and tools of the child's world to relate to the child's emotions. One example of this is the emotions balloons chart (Figure 8.3).

The child is given the following instructions about this activity:

> Sometimes people have several different feelings at the same time. Some of those feelings are strong and are very hard to forget, while others are important but are sometimes forgotten. Using the chart I am going to give you, write into the large balloons which of your feelings are biggest and hardest to forget. Then write into the small balloons the feelings you do some-times forget. You can use feelings like mad, happy, lonely, scared, upset, proud, or excited to label your balloons.

Another good aid is the happy/sad/angry faces chart, which allows the child to point to the face(s) that best describe his or her feelings. Many such charts are available; school counselors often display one in their offices. There are also websites that display an array of options for counselors to use with the aid of an internet connection.

FOCUSING INTERVENTION

A focusing intervention is used to encourage and facilitate introspection so that problems can be clarified and conceptualized by the client. Focusing as a central aspect of therapy was originally developed by Gendlin (1981) and a full description of the approach is available elsewhere (e.g., Gendlin, 1981; Iberg, 2001). As an intervention, it can be used generically to help clients get in touch with their situations by giving them time to "check in" with their body's inner sensations. An essential assumption of focusing is that the body has a wisdom that is more accurate than what tends to be communicated by our words. Only if we give time to focus on body sensations are we able to access this new awareness.

What is called the *felt sense* is what clients may describe as the pit in their stomach or their sweaty palms, or the ache of emptiness that they have often learned to both live with and ignore. In focusing, the counselor asks the client to sit quietly and describe as fully as possible the felt sense. "Focusing is to enter into a special kind of awareness, different from our every day aware-ness. It is open, turned inward, centered on the present and on your body's inner sensations. When doing Focusing, you silently ask, 'How am I now?'"("What Is Focusing?" n.d., para. 5).

The counselor must take care to give the client adequate time to get in touch with the felt sense and to fully explore and listen to it. Iberg (2001) cautions that interference from the therapist can diminish—if not eradicate—the benefits of focusing. Therefore, early interpretations of what the client is getting in touch with are not advised. By contrast, the focusing intervention should eventually allow the client to have new insights that lead to what Gendlin (1981) refers to as a *felt shift*—that is, new insights develop that can empower the client to see the difficulty in a different and more manageable light. Proponents of focusing argue that when it is used successfully, it can empower the client to confront difficulties anew and with increased creativity.

CASE ILLUSTRATION OF FOCUSING

The Case of Grace

Grace is a 45-year-old woman whose husband died tragically in a car accident five months ago. The person in the other car ran a red light and suffered no serious injury. Grace's friends suggested that she consider counseling because she still seems to be in the throes of extreme grief. In the first session, she reported feeling overwhelmed by emotions and the demands of her two teenage sons. She vacillates among the feelings of sadness, anger, and resentment directed primarily at the other driver, anger at her husband for not being more careful, guilt about her feelings about her late husband and about not attending to her sons, and back to sadness. She has begun to feel truly stuck in this circular process. Grace also shows evidence of being rational, realistic, and in control, except for these "grief bouts," as she calls them, which she admits can last for several days at a time. There is no past history of depression or life-threatening acts by either Grace or any other family member. She does have her good days, although they are few in number. She does not know how to increase these days, and agrees it is time for at least some improvement.

Based on this information, the counselor decided that Grace did not show suicidal tendencies but did ask her to make an appointment with her family physician for a complete physical examination. The counselor also decided that paper-and-pencil exercises were not needed, because the client seemed quite able to verbalize her feelings. The counselor also recognized that a goal of all grief counseling is to assist Grace to cope with her grief in her own unique way, which will most likely include ways to stay in connection with her late husband and the life they had while also reconstructing meaning in her life without her husband (Humphrey, 2009).

After three sessions with Grace, the counselor suggested that they try a focusing exercise that would address one of the feelings she reported as troublesome. Following an explanation of the process and its purpose, they decided together to use the next session as a focusing experiment. Grace arrived at the next session showing some nervousness, but this soon dissipated. The counselor suggested that the session focus on the anger she felt. Once Grace agreed that this was a good place to begin, the counselor suggested that she close her eyes and attempt to get in touch with where her anger resides in her body. The counselor also advised Grace not to attempt to analyze her anger, but simply to follow it. After a period of silence as Grace attempted to achieve a "felt sense" of her anger, she reported that it felt like a heavy weight on her chest. The counselor suggested that she stay with that awareness to see if anything else came to her. Eventually, Grace spoke:

GRACE: You know, it's strange. It feels like an additional weight, but it also feels like my arms are wrapped around it keeping it warm.

COUNSELOR: So you're sort of holding it?

GRACE: More than holding it; it's like I'm protecting it. It's like I'm lying down with the anger on my chest and my arms are around the anger. It's like I'm holding the anger to me and simultaneously suffocating myself!

COUNSELOR: That would feel pretty bad, especially in combination with your sadness.

GRACE: (Quiet for a moment.) You know, when you said "sadness," I felt a real ache in a deeper place. I'm wondering if the anger keeps me occupied so I don't have to feel that ache. The ache is such an awful sinking feeling; it's just so painful. (Tears up.) Can we stop this now?

As Grace and her counselor discussed the experience, Grace wondered aloud if her anger was a way to keep her sadness at bay. She confided that her loneliness scared her, but she also noted that the anger wasn't really helping and it was the emotion that seemed to be upsetting her sons the most. Grace and her counselor acknowledged that there was much more work to do but that the focusing exercise was valuable. The last thing Grace said before leaving was that it helped knowing that the anger may just be a temporary crutch and not necessarily who she had become. Through this statement, Grace is experiencing the beginning of moving forward or the "felt shift."

Hinterkopf (1998) suggests that the focusing method "may be used for the remediation of religious and spiritual problems, the enhancement of already existing spiritual experiences, and the facilitation of new, life-giving connections to spirituality, [all of which] are essential for spiritual wellness" (pp. 2–3). She describes a six-step process by which the focusing method is introduced to clients (pp. 52–55):

1. Clearing a space. Helping the client identify problems or issues, then mentally "setting them aside" as though they were no longer present, and observing the effect of their removal.
2. Getting a felt sense. Asking the client to attend to the whole complexity of the problem(s) and issues and reporting the result.
3. Finding a handle. Identifying words to describe the felt sense of step 2. Such words "help the client hold on to or stay in touch with the vague felt sense or 'pull it back' if awareness of it is lost" (p. 54).
4. Resonating. Examining the words identified in step 3 and seeking better words to identify the felt sense, if appropriate.
5. Asking. Having the client ask him- or herself, "What is it about this issue (problem) that leaves me feeling this way?" (Hinterkopf refers to this as "giving the felt sense a 'friendly hearing'" [p. 55]).
6. Receiving. Helping the client integrate the felt shift that occurs as a result of the focusing process, including those bodily felt changes that the client experiences.

HELPING CLIENTS INTEGRATE OR CHANGE FEELING STATES

In the preceding section, we state that people sometimes cope with emotions by creating a psychological distance from their feelings. This can happen when a person is bombarded by multiple affect reactions stemming from traumatic life situations. It can also happen when a person is confronted by a strong but unacceptable emotional situation. The result of this affect distancing is to postpone the immediate demand to respond to the affect. As the example of Grace depicted, this can occur during the grieving process. However, to postpone an adaptive demand is not a long-term solution. Thus, even the grieving individual must ultimately come to grips with the loss and alter perceptions in whatever way the loss demands.

For our purposes here, we define *dysfunctional affect* as feelings that interfere with day-to-day functioning. Replacement of dysfunctional feelings or establishment of functional feelings is a complicated process; some theorists hold that it requires a cathartic moment in which the client experiences a sudden release of bad feelings followed by a flood of emotional relief, whereas other theorists believe it occurs only when dysfunctional feelings are replaced by more functional feelings through conscious and rigorous efforts to identify and replace. Still other theorists believe dysfunctional feelings are present but unrecognized by the client, and only when the client becomes fully aware of these hidden feelings can they be addressed and dealt with by the client. Through this process, the counselor is an active participant, either in leading the client or in responding empathically to the client so that the dysfunctional feelings can be recognized and addressed. A case illustration helps demonstrate this integration of new feelings.

CASE ILLUSTRATION OF INTEGRATING FEELINGS

The Case of Alice

Alice is a 41-year-old woman who lives alone in a house that she inherited from her parents. She was six weeks away from finishing her teaching degree when she dropped out because of debilitating doubt and fear that resulted in her being unable to complete the prep work for her practice teaching classes. After this incident, she spent several days in bed. Alice reports that she was too depressed to do anything during this time. Since this happened, Alice has gotten a job tending bar. Alice had worked in a bank for fifteen years prior to going back to school to receive teacher training. She always wanted to be a teacher, and her instructors told her that she would be a good one. When she dropped out of school, her advisor suggested that she get counseling about the matter. After a year of feeling that her life was "going nowhere," she

decided to do so. Although she spends many of her days off "basically doing nothing," she reports no incidents of depression as severe as the one following dropping out of teacher training.

After a couple of sessions, Alice's counselor addressed her self-doubt. After completing a focusing exercise, Alice reported that although her working-class parents were "good to her," they never thought of her as having a career and were surprised when she worked her way through college. In addition, Alice was overweight as a child and never felt popular; as a teen and young adult, she never felt desirable to males. As Alice and her counselor processed all of this, she became more aware that much of her self-doubt about her current situation had roots in bad childhood experiences as well as long held fear that she could not be successful as a professional.

Alice's situation illustrates how emotional undercurrents can intrude into a person's consciousness and disrupt emotional commitments to current goals. It also illustrates the interrelatedness of feeling, thought, and behavior, as well as the need to come to some resolution about incompatible emotional states (loving the act of teaching yet fearing failure as a teacher). The counselor will work to help Alice accept some of the latent feelings as reflecting a past she no longer needs to let control her. She must "grow" the part of her that feels confident about her abilities, especially in light of the positive feedback she has received from her instructors. It is likely that Alice will continue to feel insecure in moments, but this will be less debilitating if she recognizes its origins and can allow her insecurity to live alongside her emerging positive feelings.

A number of counseling interventions are derived from person-centered, gestalt, and existential counseling to aid the client with such problems. In this section, we examine role reversal, the alter-ego exercise, and the empty chair (or two-chair) exercise, all of which may be used in working with Alice.

ROLE REVERSAL

Although role-play is primarily a behavioral intervention that we discuss in Chapter 11, *role reversal* is presented here because it offers an avenue for the client to deconstruct affect-driven circumstances—that is, role reversal is a useful exercise when a client is emotionally reactive to a situation or another person and is unable to look beyond his or her reaction to reflect on the situation. Therefore, the purpose of role reversal is to allow clients to project themselves into an alternative view of a situation in order to achieve more clarity about their feelings and to reflect on those feelings and the situation in general. This exercise may meet initial resistance, because it asks the client to challenge safe (albeit dysfunctional) roles or attitudes; however, if the client is encouraged to try playing devil's advocate to a position where the client has been stuck, the exercise can be quite effective.

The counselor becomes an active participant in the role-reversal enactment. He or she must be able to empathize with how the client has been "stuck" and portray this accurately in the role-play. In the following case, Vincent came to counseling because of a problem he was having at work. The counselor soon realized that the issue was Vincent's affective reaction to his boss, and so decided to set up a role reversal to help Vincent explore the conflict from a different angle. The counselor reversed Vincent's role by having him enact an encounter as his boss. The counselor also participated in the enactment in the role of Vincent.

CASE ILLUSTRATION OF ROLE REVERSAL

The Case of Vincent

Vincent entered counseling for the purpose of solving "career problems." As counseling progressed, the problem became more clearly defined as an interpersonal conflict between Vincent and his boss as well as Vincent's strong feelings about this. Vincent found it easy to explore his feelings toward his boss even though he liked his job. However, these explorations always seemed to lead up blind alleys when the counselor raised the topic of setting goals directed toward change. Vincent would become flustered and would jump to the conclusion that the only solution was to change jobs. After this pattern repeated itself for two sessions, the counselor suggested that they try the role-reversal exercise. Vincent responded somewhat suspiciously, but after some discussion of what the exercise involved, he agreed to participate. The next session began as follows:

VINCENT: I don't know how this exercise will improve anything. My boss is insensitive and completely unconcerned about my situation. He'll never change, and working for him is loaded with stress for me. I still think the only solution is for me to look for another job, which makes me crazy, because I really like the job except for him.

COUNSELOR: Before we reach that conclusion, let's try the role-reversal exercise we discussed last week. It may not change anything, but at least we can say we looked at the problem every way we could imagine. Are you still game?

VINCENT: Sure. I'll do it with you.

COUNSELOR: Good. I'd like you to play devil's advocate with your problem for a few minutes. I'd like you to imagine that you are your boss, and I'll be you, and we'll talk about the problem. Try to be as accurate as possible in your boss's role. Try to get into his head. That way, I'll have a much better idea what your boss is like. And I'll try to be as accurate as possible in my role as you. If I tend to respond inaccurately, stop the exercise and give me coaching on how I should respond. Are you ready?

VINCENT: I'm ready. I know I can imitate him. I know him like the back of my hand.

COUNSELOR: Great. You begin as your boss.

VINCENT: Vincent, I see you missed another deadline for the production report. What the hell's going on?

COUNSELOR: I couldn't get the information I needed. You were in a meeting so I couldn't ask you for the stuff I needed.

VINCENT: What the hell do you mean, "You were in a meeting"? If you have to bother me to get the report done, then bother me. But don't miss another deadline. Do you understand?

COUNSELOR: Okay, okay, I hear you. But I knew you would have lost it if I interrupted you yesterday.

VINCENT: So what? Yeah, you're right. I probably would have been annoyed because you've had all week to get this stuff. I know you avoid me. But none of that is an excuse for missing deadlines. And when you do miss a deadline, what do you expect from me? I'm ultimately responsible that these things get done. You've got to stop avoiding me!

COUNSELOR: Well, Vincent, what do you think of that scene?

VINCENT: OK. I get why we're doing this. His anger does really get to me, but I haven't been thinking about the part I play when I avoid him even when I shouldn't.

COUNSELOR: Do you think it might help to work on how you react to his anger?

As you can see in this illustration, Vincent acknowledges his avoidance in a safe enactment of a confrontation with his boss. This acknowledgment does not mean that Vincent will return to his job with new methods for coping. It may be that counseling will move on to an exploration of how Vincent can develop new approaches to working with his boss—or maybe he will end up changing jobs. For the moment, however, Vincent has been able to reflect on his reactivity to his boss rather than being controlled by it.

ALTER EGO

The alter ego exercise is similar to role reversal, but with a novel twist. Merriam-Webster's (2015) online dictionary defines *alter ego* as "a second self, a different version of yourself." The notion is that each individual has another dimension of his or her personality that is more aware, more honest, more perceptive of personal motives, values, and hidden agendas. People's alter egos nag them when they neglect their duties or avoid their responsibilities. Thus, the alter ego knows and is a more honest reporter of one's inner life.

In this exercise, the client is asked to become his or her alter ego, and the counselor assumes the client's public self. Because the counselor must produce an accurate portrayal of the client's public self and because the client must feel safe enough with the counselor to allow the alter ego to emerge, this exercise should not be used early in the counseling relationship. When the alter-ego exercise is effective, it allows clients to confront themselves more honestly. This kind of self-confrontation can be far more effective than confrontations by the counselor. The result is that the client can introduce issues, refute self-rationalizations and the feelings that both motivate and result from them, or question self-motives in a therapeutic encounter with the self. The following case illustrates the use of the alter-ego exercise in a counseling setting.

CASE ILLUSTRATION OF THE ALTER EGO

The Case of Wanda

Wanda is a 35-year-old waitress married to Matt, a 50-year-old auto mechanic. She has an 11-year-old son, Tim, by a previous marriage. Wanda entered counseling because she was concerned about Tim's emotional and academic development. Tim had been identified as having above average intelligence by the school he attends; however, his grades have gotten increasingly worse in the past year, and this has become a source of family concern. As Wanda discussed her concerns for Tim with her counselor, she shifted from her personal issues to how she felt that Matt did not recognize Tim's needs. When this occurred, she became angry toward Matt, and then Tim's issues would become lost.

The counselor asked Wanda to involve Matt and Tim in counseling, but Wanda said that Matt refused and that Tim's school schedule would not permit his participation. The counselor wondered about these explanations, but she accepted Wanda's judgment. Because Wanda was a bright and introspective client, the counselor decided that she was a good candidate for the alter-ego exercise, which, she believed, would help Wanda better understand her own emotional reactions. Wanda, who liked counseling, readily agreed to the counselor's suggestion.

COUNSELOR: In this exercise, I am going to be you, as I have come to know you. I'll try to represent you honestly and accurately. I want you to be the private Wanda, the person I don't really know yet. I want you to be as honest as you are willing to be with yourself. We are going to talk to each other, the public you (my role) and the private you (your role). We might even have an argument, but that's okay. Do you understand?

WANDA: I think so. I'll try.

COUNSELOR: Good, I'll go first. [As Wanda] I just don't know what to do with Tim. He is so bright, but he is wasting his ability.

WANDA: [As alter ego] You always think you ought to know what to do and you don't.

COUNSELOR: Yeah, and that's why I think Matt ought to be helping. He disappears when I need him most.

WANDA: You think Matt knows more about Tim than you do? You just don't want to be responsible for Tim.

COUNSELOR: It's not that I don't *want* to do it alone, it's that I don't think I *can* do it alone. And besides, I want Matt and Tim to have a parent–child relationship, and that isn't happening.

WANDA: It's not happening because you won't let Matt do the important parenting jobs, like discipline.

COUNSELOR: What do you mean, "I won't let Matt be a parent"?

WANDA: I think you're afraid to let Matt be a real parent because Tim

might decide he likes Matt better than he likes you. So, you keep Matt away.

COUNSELOR: That's not true. Matt really doesn't love Tim enough to worry about him.

WANDA: That's not true, Wanda, and you know it. Matt loves Tim a lot. He worries about Tim. But he worries more about you and your relationship to Tim, and that's why he doesn't get involved.

COUNSELOR: I hate it when you say these things.

WANDA: I know it hurts, but you better wake up, Wanda, or you're going to lose both of them someday.

The counselor and Wanda ended the exercise at this point. Wanda had said some very self-confrontational things and was beginning to show some discomfort with her revelations. The counselor sensed that Wanda was beginning to reach a saturation level, so she decided to allow her some time to integrate the ideas and feelings that had been brought up. After stopping the exercise, they took time to discuss the confrontation. During this discussion, Wanda began to relax and look more comfortable with herself. It was a very significant session, and proved to be a turning point in Wanda's counseling, when she acknowledged to herself for the first time that she believed that her husband was conflicted between his love and concern for Tim and his concern for her relationship with Tim.

THE EMPTY CHAIR

The *empty chair* is a dialoging exercise made popular by gestalt therapists but used increasingly by counselors from a wide range of orientations. It is used to help clients explore and develop awareness of subtle feelings that are not surfacing but are affecting client functioning. The exercise may be used with interpersonal issues (in which case the enactment is between the client and the other relevant person) or with intrapersonal issues (in which case the enactment is between the client and the client's other self).

The counselor begins by explaining that this is a dialog or imaginary conversation either with oneself or with a specific person who is also involved in the client's problem. The counselor explains that his or her role is to observe, choreograph the conversation, and at times interrupt to ask questions or share observations. If the client agrees, the next step is to define who the two principals in the conversation will be—that is, with whom the client will converse. This might be the "embarrassed self" or the "intimidated self," or it might be the client's parent, spouse, or any other person with whom the client is struggling.

The counselor must be able to recognize the splits in awareness or the potential conflicts in order to define the elements of the dialog. The next step is to explain to the client how the process works.

> In this exercise, you will be both the Caring You and the Angry You, and the two "yous" will talk it over and explore both points of view, both sides. Let's start by having the Caring You tell the Angry You why you don't want to talk to your parents about their decision. Then I'd like the Angry You to react to the Caring You. Is it clear what you will do? Remember, I'll be right here, coaching when you need help.

CASE ILLUSTRATION OF THE EMPTY CHAIR

Paula and the Empty Chair

Paula, a young woman in her mid-twenties, has just landed a good job. In addition to this, she is currently involved in a most fulfilling intimate relationship with Sue, who is in medical school and will be starting her residency next year. Sue has an opportunity to stay at the local hospital, but she is also exploring several opportunities to do specified residencies in other states. Paula has mixed feelings about this. On the one hand, being in love with Sue, she wants what is best for her, even if that means Sue has to leave town to get the best training. On the other hand, Paula has her own career to think about. Paula especially wants Sue's support as she begins her new job.

Paula wanted to explore these conflicting feelings, and so the counselor suggested the empty chair intervention as a way to do this. When Paula agreed, the counselor described the exercise and then asked Paula to begin in one chair by explaining to the empty chair across from her those feelings associated with Sue's possible departure.

PAULA 1 [WHO WANTS SUE TO STAY] TO PAULA 2: I just don't want her to go. We have such a good thing going. I don't understand why she has to leave when she could do her residency here. I really need her support right now.

[Counselor directs Paula to move to the other chair and be the other Paula]

PAULA 2 [WHO WANTS SUE TO DO WHAT IS BEST FOR SUE]: Well, you know the answer to that. Staying here probably isn't the best thing for her—she'll get better training somewhere else. She's so talented, she needs to get the best training she can.
[Counselor moves Paula back to Chair 1]

PAULA 1: But if she really loved me, she'd stay . . .
[Moving to Chair 2]

PAULA 2: And if you really loved her, you'd feel freer to let her go . . .
[Paula starts to cry]

COUNSELOR: Let's stop a minute. What are you aware of right now, Paula?

PAULA: I feel sad, really sad.

COUNSELOR: Okay, stay with that feeling and see where it takes you.

PAULA: You mean from this chair?

COUNSELOR: Yes.

PAULA 2 [STILL WEEPING]: The sadness feels deep. It feels like I really do want to let her go—I wouldn't want her to stay just because of me— but letting go is hard for me and

I do feel sad [weeps now more easily].

COUNSELOR: Try to accept how you are feeling and allow it to exist for a little while. [Silence]

After a few minutes, Paula began to talk again. Although she didn't feel wonderful, she felt much clearer about her feelings and her position on this issue.

Note that the counselor directed Paula's awareness to her feelings and then encouraged her to be accepting of the feelings that were aroused.

There are two distinct advantages to be derived from the empty chair intervention: (a) Paula's defenses that characterize the conflicting elements tend to diminish as she enacts the dialog, thus permitting her to see elements of the relationship that she could not easily let herself see; and (b) Paula is able to accept two seemingly incompatible feelings and say to herself, "Both of these feelings are me."

CLIENT REACTIONS TO AFFECTIVE INTERVENTIONS

The point was made at the beginning of this chapter that many clients lack the introspective and interpersonal skills to express their feelings accurately and adequately. This does not mean that they do not experience feelings, nor does it mean that they do not need to express their feelings. The inability to express what one is feeling is often experienced as a pressure-cooker effect, in which bottled-up emotions accumulate and add to a person's tensions and anxiety. Eventually, the emotions find an outlet, possibly through psychosomatic illness, substance abuse, physical violence, bursts of anger, or some other socially or personally destructive expression.

Given this kind of condition and its very limited alternatives, most clients experience relief at the expression of feeling states. Some also feel a kind of embarrassment, as though they have broken some unwritten rule about their behavior. The counselor can soften this effect by *normalizing* the feeling—pointing out that this reaction is normal and will pass. Occasionally, a client will continue, almost without limits, to talk about current or old feelings. It is as though an emotional dam has finally been broken.

Culture is an additional consideration in determining client reactions to affective interventions. Clients of non-Western cultural backgrounds may be less inclined to express or even work on feelings—indeed, it may go against a client's cultural values to express feelings openly or even to view the alteration of feelings as the solution to personal problems. In such cases, it is far better for the counselor to use other interventions described in Chapters 9 through 11 with these clients unless they articulate a willingness and desire to focus on their affect.

APPLYING INTERVENTIONS TO DIALECTICAL BEHAVIOR THERAPY AND MOTIVATIONAL INTERVIEWING

It is important for students of counseling to understand how interventions are applied by practicing counselors. Therefore, in this chapter we begin a discussion of how interventions apply to two currently popular therapy approaches, Dialectical Behavior Therapy (DBT) and Motivational

Interviewing (MI), the latter being an intervention itself, albeit a sophisticated intervention that draws from more than one orientation. We end Chapters 9, 10, and 11 with a similar discussion. Because this is the first, we offer a very brief explanation and stated purpose of each of these approaches. Obviously, our intention is not to attempt to do justice to either DBT or MI; we encourage the reader to consult the references included in the following section to begin their study of either of these approaches.

Dialectical Behavior Therapy

Dialectical Behavior Therapy (Linehan, 1981; Linehan, 1993) began as a therapy to work with chronically suicidal adolescents as well as those meeting the criteria for borderline personality disorder. Since its inception, the therapy has grown to be used broadly across populations and has received empirical support. In a nutshell, DBT begins by acknowledging that we are wired to react when threatened. For clients with emotional dysregulation (an inability to handle emotions that comes from a predisposition that makes them vulnerable to emotional dysregulation or a series of life stressors or both), their reactions have become part or the majority of their difficulty (e.g., Cohn, Jakupcak, Seibert, Hildebrant, & Zeichner, 2010; Selby & Joiner, 2009). Koerner (2012) describes a process where attention "tightens" (constricts) when under stress—that is, when we feel threatened, we narrow our focus and our options for how we will react. This might happen to most of us if an intruder were to enter our home. For a client with emotional dysregulation, the trigger for such a narrowing of responses may be a comment from someone that reminds him or her of comments in an environment that was emotionally abusive in their past. The ultimate goal of DBT is to assist the client in learning new strategies when presented with such triggers.

First, the therapist must offer support for the client and validate the client's affective experience. Once *support and validation* has been established, the therapist engages the client in a *cognitive analysis* of the various triggers for the client's pain and the client's (often-dysfunctional) reactions to that pain. Through a process of analysis, looking for options that are more productive, and skills training, the client moves toward behaviors that interfere with the dysfunctional patterns. Once dysfunctional patterns are altered, it is hoped that what follows is an alleviation of the most debilitating negative emotions. Simultaneously, the client also learns to acknowledge and accept that which is unlikely to ever be eliminated totally, including painful memories from the past and difficult situations in the present.

One further important philosophical tenet of DBT is that of the *dialectic*—that is, it is a premise of DBT that each position contains within it the antithesis of the position (Koerner & Dimeff, 2007). As many therapists have learned, a client statement of "I want to die," also includes the statement "I want to live." One may be more true at any one time, but both may be true simultaneously. Another example is the emotional dilemma of the woman in a domestic violence situation who may simultaneously want to leave her partner and yet want to stay. Many therapeutic errors are made because the therapist does not appreciate the dialectic of what is being expressed by the client. Helping clients accept and synthesize both sides of their dialectics and moving toward the more positive side of the dialectic is foundational to DBT.

AFFECTIVE INTERVENTIONS USED IN DBT.   Despite the name of this therapy, DBT therapists rely on affective interventions as part of their work with clients. Proponents of DBT (e.g., Dimeff & Koerner, 2007; Miller, Ratthus, & Linehan, 2007) make clear the importance of empathic understanding and support for the client. In fact, it is a premise of DBT that it is impossible to understand dysfunctional behavior if the therapist does not understand the pain that has given rise to it. Helping the client share their emotional pain in therapy is key to being able to validate the client's reaction to their pain. For example, a client may suffer from the trauma of child sexual abuse and uses drugs to cope with the pain. An essential part of forming a working alliance with such a client is for the therapist to find it "understandable" (even if unfortunate) that the client has used this method to cope with her pain. Only if the client believes that the therapist understands at such an essential level will the client be open to allowing the counselor to influence her in moving toward a less destructive method of coping.

Therefore, affective interventions are necessary to achieve the therapist's process goals within DBT. Clients often do not have a well-developed emotional vocabulary. Therefore, the interventions described early in this chapter that assist in identifying and expanding verbal cues will be most helpful. The affect-focusing intervention is especially compatible with the goals of DBT. Using it, the therapist can assist the client to experience and reflect on their affective life and its consequences. This intervention is similar to some mindfulness exercises that are often included in the practice of DBT. Finally, either the alter-ego intervention or the empty-chair intervention could be used to assist the client in examining the dialectic.

Motivational Interviewing

Unlike DBT, Motivational Interviewing (MI) has not been described as a full therapy by its originator (Miller, 1983), but rather as a specific approach to address the common issue of resistance to counseling. MI began as a method for assisting clients who abused substances to engage in treatment. As this population is known for high levels of resistance, the importance of MI was recognized quickly. It has also been supported empirically, alone and in conjunction with particular therapies, such as cognitive–behavioral therapy (Kertes, Westra, Angus, & Marcus, 2011), as well as with other clinical populations.

Those who adhere to MI do not consider resistance to be a "problem" in therapy but a reality to understand and an opportunity to intervene. Although resistance may be to treatment itself, it is equally likely (and perhaps more likely) to be an expression of the client's *ambivalence* about change (Westra & Aviram, 2013). Those counselors who use MI learn to *roll with the resistance* (Miller & Rollnick, 1991), and view it as ambivalence that should call on the counselor's empathy, not judgment. Beyond empathizing with the client's ambivalence, the counselor trained in MI listens carefully for what is referred to as *change talk*. This, of course, is the part of the client's internal dialog that points toward a desire to move away from being stuck in the present. It is, in MI nomenclature, the kernel of a *discrepancy* between what is and what might be if change were to occur. The MI counselor carefully looks for opportunities to "create and amplify the client's discrepancy in order to enhance motivation for change" (Miller & Rollnick, 1991, p. 55). Finally, it is important to state that MI is not argumentative or overly instructive in nature—that is, it is not up to the MI counselor to argue for the "change" voice, but to use skilled reflective listening skills to allow the client to appreciate the extent to which a lack of change is not what he or she wants. This awareness on the part of the client is key for motivation to be authentic and self-directed. It is also in keeping with the theoretical underpinning of MI which is fundamentally humanistic (Miller & Rollnick, 2009).

AFFECTIVE INTERVENTIONS USED IN MI. Miller perceives MI to be an evolution of Carl Rogers' person-centered therapy (Miller & Rollnick, 2009); therefore, deep empathic listening is essential to the success of MI for those clients who experience ambivalence toward change. Such empathy involves not only caring about the person's current dilemma, but also listening carefully for affect connected to the present and any alteration of affect when the change voice emerges. Therefore, the MI counselor must expertly identify affect cues as described in this chapter. The section entitled "Helping Clients Sort Out Feelings" may also offer critical assistance for this task.

Second, once a discrepancy has been introduced between the present and where the client would like to be, the counselor must not abandon the affective and move to a solely cognitive stance. Instead, the counselor must find ways to continue to empathize with the client on both sides of the equation. Role reversal, alter-ego, or empty-chair interventions could all be used by the counselor to encourage the client's change voice. It is important that the counselor maintain a sensitive and non-demanding demeanor while simultaneously opening a "space" for the change voice to emerge.

Summary

In this chapter, we examined what for some is the baffling subject of human emotions and their expression. You may think of affective interventions as efforts to aid clients in the expression of their innermost fears, hopes, hurts, resentments, and frustrations. Such expression often involves teaching clients how to express their feelings and helping them give themselves permission to express emotions. At another level, you may work with clients who are able to express emotions but who are unable to sort out or conceptualize what they feel. Finally, at the most complex level, you may become involved in helping clients either to accept or integrate affect states or to change affect states.

Whatever your involvement might be, it is vitally important to recognize that human emotions are central to human functioning. Consequently, when therapists work with emotions, they are working near the core of most human beings' reality. Thus, counselors are creating and walking through what amounts to a highly vulnerable passage for clients. Respect for this condition and appreciation that clients invite professional helpers into their inner world is both appropriate and essential.

Exercises

I. Understanding Feelings

Choose a partner. One of you will be the Speaker; the other will be the Listener. The Speaker should select one of the four emotions identified (positive affect, anger, fear, and emotional pain) and communicate that feeling state to the other person. The Listener should record on paper all verbal and nonverbal cues observed but should not respond to the Speaker. After 2 to 3 minutes, the exercise should be concluded, and the Listener should identify the Speaker's feeling state and the cues that support that choice. Check with the Speaker to verify your choice.

II. Identifying Feelings

This is an exercise in verbal affect identification. Identify the feeling state(s) in each of the following four client communications, which have been taken from actual counseling interviews. If more than one feeling state is present in the client response, place an asterisk (*) next to the one that you believe has the greatest bearing on the client's concern. After identifying the feeling states, discuss your choices with other class members.

A. "Well, uh, I'm happy just being with people and having them know me."
B. "And, and, uh, you know, they always say that, you know, some people don't like to be called by a number; well, I don't either."
C. "In speech, I'm, uh, well, in speech, I'm not doing good because I'm afraid to talk in front of a bunch of people."
D. "It seems to me like working in that lab is really harmful; I mean, I enjoy my work, and the people, but that lab, that worries me."

III. Practicing the Process

This exercise is to be done in triads. One of you is the First Respondent, another one is the Listener, and the third is the Observer/Recorder. Rotate all roles twice so each person is in each of the three roles.

Listed next are some incomplete sentences. The Observer's role is to feed each sentence to the Respondent and to record the Respondent's response. The Respondent's task is to respond as quickly as possible without thinking. (If, as the Respondent, you can't come up with a response, just say, "Blah, blah, blah.") The Listener's job is simply to face the Respondent directly—watch, listen, and receive. After you have completed each round, give the Respondent time to process his or her affective states.

Incomplete sentences:

_____ 1. Something I want you to know about me is. . . .

_____ 2. Something I don't want you to know about me is. . . .

_____ 3. Being angry for me is. . . .

_____ 4. When I'm angry, I just want to. . . .

_____ 5. Being sad for me is. . . .

_____ 6. When I'm sad, I just want to. . . .

_____ 7. Right now I'm feeling. . . .

Discussion Questions

1. Does any part of working with clients' affective states worry you? How?
2. Two goals of affective interventions are (a) to help the client express feeling states and (b) to help the client identify and discriminate between feeling states. This implies that clients may be able to express feelings but still not be able to identify or sort out those feelings. Do you think this is possible? Isn't it likely that the expression of a feeling carries with it the awareness of what it is? Discuss this with other classmates or colleagues.
3. Which nonverbal cues communicate anger? Do these same cues communicate some other emotion? If yes, what emotion? How would you know which emotion is being communicated?
4. Do you think of your spiritual/existential self as an affective state? If so, what words would you use to explain how it feels to be spiritually "full" or spiritually "empty"?
5. What are the potential therapeutic gains when using role reversal with a client? What kinds of clients might not be able to participate effectively in a role-reversal exercise?
6. Identify a position you hold. Now identify the dialectic within that position. Does doing so offer you any additional insight into the original position? Discuss with your classmates.

MyCounselingLab® Assignment

Go to the Video Library under Video Resources on the MyCounselingLab site for your text and search for the following clips:

The following two videos provide a demonstration of gestalt therapy and an interview with the therapist. The Session video includes the use of the empty-chair intervention.

- **Video Example: Gestalt Session**
- **Video Example: Gestalt Reflection**
- **Video Example: Delving into Multi-Sensory Experiences** This video uses a focusing on sensory data to help the client get in touch with her issue.
- **Video Example: Staying in the Moment, Focus on Sensations** This video also demonstrates the use of physical sensation to enhance the client's understanding of her emotional life. How successful do you think this intervention was with this client?

- **Video Example: Child: Centering Exercise** This video focuses on using clay to help a child express his feelings. As you watch this session, can you imagine yourself finding this intervention useful in your own life? To what extent do you rely on data from your senses to check in on your emotional life?
- **Video Example: Using "Empty-Chair" in CBT** In this use of the empty-chair intervention, the counselor is constrained by limited physical space; therefore, he suggests that the client speak to him as if he was her father. How does this change the dynamics of the intervention? Do you think it's more effective in that the client has a person to address, or less effective because she is addressing someone other than the person responsible for her pain?

Cognitive Interventions

PURPOSE OF THIS CHAPTER

How many times have you gotten yourself in trouble by thinking too much, or by talking to yourself in a way that wasn't helpful, or because you had a "bad attitude"? This chapter examines the ways that clients think themselves into problems and describes interventions that the counselor can use to reverse this situation. These interventions address mistaken beliefs, attitudes, or patterns of thinking and give the client the tools to change to more productive and accurate thoughts. In this chapter, we describe a variety of interventions and the manner in which they are applied in counseling.

Considerations as You Read This Chapter

- Many people apparently find it difficult to differentiate between their thoughts and their feelings. It is fairly common to hear a person say, "I feel like everyone is against me," when the more accurate statement is, "I think everyone is against me." A lot of thinking people have mislabeled their thoughts as feelings. Is this also the case with you?

- Thinking is a very special capability that human beings possess, but it also can be misused. When this happens, people can become depressed, physically ill, and even suicidal. How does one get out of such difficulties? How does one get into these difficulties in the first place?

- What skills must a counselor possess to be able to help people who have thought themselves into trouble?

Anyone who has ever tried to meditate can give testimony to how difficult it is to clear one's mind of thoughts. We may not always know what we are feeling, and there are times that our behavior is outside of our awareness, but there's pretty much always an answer to "A penny for your thoughts," regardless of whether we choose to be honest with the person asking. Many people might say that thoughts or cognitions are the driving force of who they are, what they do, and how they feel. This view holds that errors in thinking, sometimes called *faulty thinking,* are especially likely to produce distressing emotions and/or problematic behavior. For example, suppose we have a woman who expects to fail; she prepares herself mentally for failure, and the result is that she approaches life events from a failure orientation. With this much going against her, the probability is greater that she really will fail. She could be described as having low self-esteem or lack of confidence, but in fact, she is approaching life with a self-defeating mentality (one that might have been taught her by significant others or society at large), an "I don't think I can do it" life view. This type of person may benefit from strategies that focus primarily on changing beliefs, attitudes, and perceptions about self and others.

As noted in Chapter 8, a "fit" between an orientation and a client may or may not appear obvious. Especially when we talk about *affective life* and *cognitive life,* a person's strength may be that same person's downfall. The person who feels easily may feel too much, and may need to be buffered by thinking and behaving differently; similarly, a person who thinks a lot may analyze too much, leading to overanalyzing or ruminating. We make this point again to remind the reader that it is not necessarily the primary orientation of the client that determines what types of interventions will be most helpful, but how the counselor conceptualizes the problem and how the problem may be most efficiently addressed.

The application of cognitive interventions in counseling is extensive. They have been applied as the primary intervention for such problems as anxiety reduction, stress management, anger control, depression, phobic disorders, and sexual dysfunction. Cognitive interventions are also very helpful for less serious issues, such as those that might be described as developmental or situational. In fact, when we think of problem solving as a process, it begins with identifying a problem (and often our feelings help us do this), thinking it through, making some decision, and implementing that decision. Most of us do this without much thought, and it's only when we seem incapable of dealing with a problem (whether one that has nagged us for years or one that feels new to us) that counseling comes into focus as a possibility. Cognitive interventions, then, are designed to magnify the "thinking it through" aspect of problem solving to help clients gain new insights that can lead to new options for tackling their problems.

THEORIES THAT STRESS THE IMPORTANCE OF COGNITIVE PROCESSES

Cognitive approaches to counseling and psychotherapy include theories such as rational emotive behavior therapy (REBT; Dryden & Ellis, 2001; Ellis & Dryden, 1997; Ellis & Wilde, 2002), cognitive therapy (Beck, 1976; Beck, 2011), and transactional analysis (Berne, 1964; Harris, 1967). Some authors also include the constructivist approach in this group of theories, noting the constructivist tenet that individuals continually adapt their thoughts as a way to create meaning for themselves in the world (e.g., Neukrug, 2007). Whether traditional theorist or constructivist, the emphasis on thoughts and thought processes is the common thread of cognitive therapy. Thus, interventions that are designed to alter thought processes are defined as *cognitive interventions.*

Many cognitive therapists prefer the term *cognitive–behavioral therapy* because of the strong linkage between thoughts and behaviors. In other words, because change in thinking is only observed when behavior changes, it makes sense to link the two. That said, a change in behavior does not necessarily require a change in thought. For the purpose of learning how to counsel, we believe it makes sense to separate cognitive from behavioral interventions, a concept addressed in Chapter 10.

GOALS OF COGNITIVE INTERVENTIONS

The overall aim of any cognitive intervention is to reduce emotional distress and corresponding maladaptive behavior patterns by altering or correcting errors in thought, perceptions, and beliefs. Changes in behavior or feelings occur once the client's distorted thinking begins to change and is replaced by alternative and more realistic ways of thinking about self, other persons, or life experiences. Clients are viewed as direct agents of their own changes rather than as helpless victims of external events and forces over which they have little control. This does not mean that some clients have not been victimized by others. It *does* mean that the extent to which this has controlled their self and other perceptions, such cognitions can be a worthwhile target of change. With cognitive interventions, control always remains with the client. Change can happen only when the client chooses to change the way he or she is thinking about something. This even includes choosing to participate in a cognitive intervention as part of the counseling strategy.

ASSESSMENT OF COGNITIVE PROBLEMS

Cognitive strategies rely heavily on a particular manner of problem assessment. We begin with the assumption that people construct their reality based on their childhood experiences, their personal and cultural beliefs, and their resultant attitudes. Some of that construction is distorted if a person's perceptions of self or others are distorted. Why would anyone distort perceptions? People learn these distortions from their parents, their peer groups, their teachers, and/or society in general. They then apply these distortions, along with their more accurate perceptions, to their view of reality. Cognitive distortion assessment requires that the counselor and client together analyze these perceptions looking for the flaws, errors, or inaccuracies that underlie one's conclusions. Only at that point can cognitive interventions be applied to change errors in thinking, repair cognitive flaws, or correct inaccuracies.

Deconstructing flawed beliefs and assumptions can be a complex task. Judith Beck (2011) provides specific constructs to help us do so. The first is the *core belief,* which is deeply engrained and pervasive. Core beliefs can include such sweeping ideas as "I'm a loser," "I'm not loveable," or "I'm not a good person." Core beliefs can also be about lesser characteristics, such as "I can't do math," or "I'm not good with people." If someone is put in a *situation* relevant to a core belief, what follow are *intermediate beliefs,* including attitudes, rules, and assumptions, that solidify the core belief. Therefore, if my core belief is that I'm not good in social situations and I'm invited to a social event, the invitation (situation) is likely to be followed by such intermediate beliefs as, "It's embarrassing to be at a loss with others" (attitude); "It's best to avoid social situations" (rule); "If I try to interact with others at a get-together, I'll make a fool of myself" (assumption).

Following this barrage of beliefs (often outside of the person's awareness) is what Beck refers to as an *automatic thought.* In this case, the thought is something like, "I'll just skip the get-together; certainly, no one will miss me." The final step in the process as described by Beck is the *reaction,* which includes emotions, behaviors, and physiological states. Regarding the decision to avoid a social situation, I might feel relieved that I won't be put in a place where I would (as a result of a core belief) undoubtedly be uncomfortable; my behavior to avoid social events would be reinforced; finally, I might be further reinforced by a physical state of calm rather than what might have been a momentary sense of jitteriness before my automatic thought kicked in. This, then, is how entrenched beliefs can control our thoughts and behaviors. However, it's also possible that along with relief is a feeling of disappointment in myself, and even some sadness at what I miss out on because of this belief. To the extent that such feelings become bothersome is the extent to which a cognitive approach to counseling may be embraced.

Helping Clients Express Cognition

The cognitive approaches to counseling involve a set of counselor skills and strategies that are designed to recognize and help clients recognize thought patterns, to assess the relationships between client thinking and client problems, to help clients confront unproductive thinking and replace it with productive or positive thoughts, and to provide clients with strategies for maintaining and strengthening productive thinking. The basic assumption that the counselor begins with is that clients acquire faulty thinking habits or patterns without recognizing the effects of those thought patterns. As a result, they are unable to correct life problems without changing the thought patterns that support those problems.

The counselor's challenge lies in recognizing faulty thinking as the client presents it and helping the client recognize the patterns as faulty, too. However, awareness of faulty thinking doesn't lead to change; rather, the counselor then must help the client implement strategies that will effect change. This is done through various assignments and exercises that are designed to stop faulty thinking and replace it with productive thoughts.

Cognitive Intervention Skills

A-B-C-D Analysis

A (activating event), B (belief system), C (consequence), D (disruption). Helping the client analyze his or her thought patterns

Cognitive Disputation

Challenging the client's thought and behavior processes by confronting assumptions and practices

Decibels and Countering Interventions

Identifying and replacing or disputing thoughts that are linked to disturbing feelings

Redecision Work

Examining injunctions the client received as a child (e.g., "Don't be a child") and making a conscious decision whether to continue following those injunctions as an adult

Cognitive Restructuring

Helping the client identify and replace negative self-statements

Thought Stopping

Helping the client develop ways of halting destructive or unproductive thoughts about self and others

Positive Self-Talk

Showing the client ways to replace his or her negative self-talk with positive (confidence-building) self-talk

Anchoring

Helping the client replace unsupportive reactions to situations with positive or supportive responses to those situations

Reframing

Helping the client recognize more constructive or realistic interpretations to events that he or she formerly interpreted negatively

Resisting Therapeutic Change

Suggesting to the client that change may not happen readily or may not be lasting as a way to counter irrational fears about the effectiveness of counseling

Positioning

Agreeing with a client's irrational view in order to "double-bind" the client

Meaning Making

Attending to the unique meaning(s) a client ascribes to events and situations, including those that are spiritual and existential

ELICITING THOUGHTS

Before a counselor knows if cognitive interventions are appropriate, the basic skill set for eliciting the thoughts of the client must be exercised. More than following the story line of what the client has to say, the counselor must understand how clients determine meaning in their lives. From a constructivist perspective, this includes how one interprets life events, circumstances, and interactions. It is human nature to try to make sense of life, but the sense that is made may be close to reality or it may have a tenuous relationship to reality; it may open up opportunities for growth and development or it may be self-defeating. Therefore, a first and essential task for the counselor is to follow the client's logic, to assess outcomes of the client's logic, and—to the extent possible—to determine the client's faithfulness to detail and observation (i.e., to determine the extent to which the client does any reality testing).

Consequently, it is important to draw out the client's thoughts, interpretations, and conclusions about life events in order to examine them. Eliciting client thoughts is really no different from eliciting client feelings. The basic skills described in Chapter 2—reflecting, paraphrasing, and summarizing—are used to understand the client's cognitive processes. Similarly, the affective intervention skills of Chapter 8 are adaptable to cognitive exploration—that is, identifying thought patterns, sorting out thoughts, and helping the client focus on logical conclusions. The professional literature on cognitive interventions is rich with possibilities. There are entire texts on this topic alone (e.g., Beck 2011; Gregory, 2010). Our goal here is to present the reader with examples of such interventions to serve as a primer of sorts that the counselor can expand with additional resources and experience.

COGNITIVE INTERVENTIONS

Several different strategies for change have come from cognitive and clinical psychology. Most of them are exercises that help the client modify existing thought patterns, remind the client to avoid undesirable thoughts, or even help the client assess events more constructively. These strategies derive primarily from the work of Albert Ellis and Aaron Beck, pioneers in the cognitive therapy movement.

A-B-C-D Analysis

The A-B-C-D analysis is a cognitive strategy associated with rational–emotive therapy (Ellis, 1994), created in the 1950s by Albert Ellis, who developed a formula for counselors to follow as they analyze the client's patterns of thought. In this analysis, A represents the *activating* event that begins the faulty thinking pattern; B is the client's *belief* system through which all life experiences are filtered; C represents the *consequence,* emotional or cognitive, produced by the interaction of A and B. These three steps represent the analysis portion of the formula. Once the cognitive errors have been detected, the counselor moves on to the intervention, which involves *disputation* (D) of the irrational beliefs or thought patterns.

Differentiating between rational and irrational beliefs is primarily the responsibility of the counselor. Rational beliefs are those that are truly consistent with reality—in the sense that they can be supported with data, facts, and/or evidence and would be substantiated by a group of objective observers. Rational beliefs may result in moderate levels of consequence (Cs), or emotional consequences, and are useful in helping people attain their goals. Irrational beliefs, however, are those that are not supported by reality through data, facts, and/or evidence and would not be substantiated by a group of objective observers.

Most irrational beliefs are reflected in one or more of Ellis's well-known and often revised 11 irrational beliefs (Figure 9.1). The irrational beliefs are purposely overstated so as to underscore their irrationality. However, many clients' thoughts can be deconstructed to contain some element of irrationality and can be fit into one of the 11. According to Ellis, people both create and maintain unnecessary emotional distress by continually reindoctrinating themselves with their irrational beliefs. Self-indoctrination is analogous to playing a recording in one's head

1. I believe I must be loved or approved of by virtually everyone with whom I come in contact.
2. I believe I should be perfectly competent in everything that comes my way to be considered worthwhile.
3. Some people are bad, wicked, or villainous, and therefore should be blamed and punished.
4. It is a terrible catastrophe when things are not as I would want them to be.
5. Unhappiness is caused by circumstances that are out of my control.
6. Dangerous or risky things are sources of great concern, and I should worry about them constantly.
7. It is easier to avoid certain difficulties and responsibilities than it is to face them.
8. I should be dependent on other persons and should have some person on whom I can rely to take care of me.
9. Past experiences and events are what determine my present behavior; the influence of the past cannot ever be erased.
10. I should be quite upset over other people's problems and disturbances.
11. There is always a right or perfect solution to every problem, and it must be found or the results will be catastrophic.

FIGURE 9.1   Ellis's 11 Irrational Beliefs about Life

repeatedly until the recording's contents are the only reality the person knows. In the A-B-C-D analysis, the client learns to recognize activating events (A), corresponding beliefs about the event (B) that are in one's head, and the emotional–behavioral consequences (C) of interpreting the activating event by using the irrational belief(s). The counselor then teaches the client a variety of ways to dispute (D) the emotional beliefs that are leading to the consequence, and to replace these irrational beliefs with more accurate and rational beliefs.

GETTING TO THE A.   The activating event is usually some noxious or unfortunate situation or person in the client's life, and often the presence of this situation or person is part of what prompts the client to come for counseling. A client may say, "I've lost my competitive edge in the marketing world," or "Potential employers do not see me as competitive with younger applicants," or "My family will never be normal." In helping clients identify the A, it is important for them to understand that this external situation or event does not cause their feelings (which are their reactions to how the external situation makes them feel).

It is also important to discriminate between activating events that can be changed and those that cannot. For those that can be changed, clients can use good problem-solving skills to bring about change. For those situations that are outside the client's control, it is important to focus on reactions to the event rather than the event itself.

GETTING TO THE C.   The emotional consequences of the activating event are often what propel the client into counseling. People cannot tolerate bad or uncomfortable feelings too long, and if such feelings persist, they may be motivated to seek outside assistance. Examples of emotional consequences that lead clients into counseling include guilt, long-term anger, fear, depression, and anxiety.

To identify the C accurately, the counselor must be alert to the presence of affect words that the client uses and the supporting body language or nonverbal cues indicative of emotion. The counselor then proceeds to ask the client what he or she is saying to him- or herself about the activating event. Often, this question must be asked several times before the client begins to realize what the message is. In particular, clients often fail to realize the self-evaluative component of the message (e.g., "My failure to find a job with the same status of the one I lost is a huge discouragement to me, and, therefore, I will be unhappy as long as I work in a place with lesser status").

GETTING TO THE B.   Identifying the B, or the client's belief system, is a major focus of this particular therapeutic intervention. The client's beliefs about a specific activating event may be exhibited in one of two forms—rational beliefs (RBs) or irrational beliefs (IBs). Both RBs and IBs represent a client's evaluations of reality and self.

Rational beliefs are truly consistent with a person's reality in the sense that they can be supported with data, facts, and/or other evidence and would be substantiated by a group of objective observers. Rational beliefs result in moderate levels of consequences and tend not to be destructive. It is irrational beliefs that cause people problems. As a person accumulates more IBs, that person becomes more troubled, not realizing that it is his or her belief system that is the source of the problem.

DISRUPTING (D) IRRATIONAL BELIEFS.   Generally, clients must be convinced that their belief systems are at the root of their problems. This is done by questioning and challenging the conclusions they have drawn regarding a particular event. Even when challenged, deeply committed irrational thinking must be addressed repeatedly until it transforms from "I feel defeated by my job status" to "I choose to feel defeated by my job status." At the point of recognizing choice, the client gains control of the situation and is free to choose a different reaction. The goals of disputation are twofold:

1. To eliminate the irrational beliefs
2. To acquire and internalize a new and more rational belief system

To achieve these goals, disputation occurs in two stages: First, a sentence-by-sentence examination and challenge of any irrational beliefs must take place; second, the irrational belief system must be replaced by a more rational and self-constructive belief system. Disputation can be cognitive (i.e., based on one's thoughts) or imaginal (i.e., drawing on one's fantasies of how life is).

Before we move on to an example of A-B-C-D analysis in action, we encourage the reader to observe the similarity between this process and Beck's (2011) strategy for working from a cognitive frame. Although somewhat different in emphases, both approaches consider similar causes for, and consequences of, faulty beliefs.

The following case about James illustrates how A-B-C-D analysis can be used with a case that extends over a period of time. The client was seen weekly for approximately 15 sessions.

CASE ILLUSTRATION OF A-B-C-D ANALYSIS

The Case of James

James is a 30-year-old Ph.D. student who hopes to complete his degree in the next year and find a position as a college professor, preferably in a southern state. He came to the United States with his Vietnamese family when he was 8 years old. James has a younger brother and two younger sisters. As the oldest male in the family, James always had a privileged position in the family, and with that felt a heavy responsibility to be, in his words, "the perfect son."

James was an excellent student during his early school years, and his parents sent him to private school for high school, an expense that strained the family budget. He received a full scholarship to attend a highly regarded private college, but he performed poorly and lost the scholarship his junior year. After that time, James was riddled with shame that was reinforced by his parents' extreme disappointment in him. That was when the headaches began, and through the remainder of James's college education, they intensified and were ultimately diagnosed as migraine.

When James finally sought counseling on the advice of his neurologist, he found it to be an oppressive experience and almost terminated after two sessions. His counselor finally convinced him to continue, indicating that the referral from his neurologist indicated that the migraines would not get significantly better with medication alone. At that point, James committed to a serious effort with counseling. He reported that, in addition to the headaches, he experienced frequent bouts of depression. At this point, the counselor suspected James's issues were caused by what he was doing cognitively, and proposed that they use a tool called the A-B-C-D analysis to track James's thought patterns.

The counselor began with an assignment that had James identify any situations that he believed might be contributing to his emotional distress. James immediately said, "If I hadn't screwed up in undergraduate school, I'd still have my parents'

respect." At this point, the counselor helped James explore that statement and determine whether he had the power to change. He said that was why he continued with his doctoral studies, but when he returned home for holidays, he believed that his parents were still waiting for him to fall on his face again. This always led to intense migraines that lasted the whole visit. Thus, it was "out of his power" to change if his parents didn't change first. The counselor confronted James at this point: "But you're doing well in a very challenging doctoral program, aren't you?" to which he had to agree. The counselor pointed out to James that he was carrying two contradictory visions— James the failure and James the scholar. Using the A-B-C-D method, the counselor began to help James recognize when his thoughts sabotaged him, and how his mind took on a pattern that inevitably led to his expectation of failure, depression, and migraine attack. The counselor also spent some time talking to James about the year he did poorly, and learned that it was a year of several unique and stressful situations that certainly contributed to James's poor performance. Thus, the assumption that this event would repeat itself could be validly labeled as irrational. James eventually concurred.

At this point, the counselor and James are ready to spend some time working with his beliefs, thoughts, or internal self-talk. The counselor reiterates that some beliefs can cause unnecessary levels of emotional distress, particularly those beliefs that are self-defeating or that cannot be supported by external evidence. The counselor gives some examples of James's irrational beliefs and then contrasts them with more rational or self-enhancing beliefs. When faced with a new academic challenge, James immediately returned to the loss of his scholarship during his undergrad years (the Activating Event). Such thoughts as "I'm a failure" and "It's my fault my parents no longer have faith in me" (his Belief System) are presented to James as self-defeating and inaccurate. They lead James to stress levels that bring on his migraines (Consequence). Such thoughts as "I screwed up in college, but that doesn't mean the future has failed" and "I lost a full scholarship, but I graduated and am still intact" are more consistent with external evidence and thus more rational (Disputation). The counselor also has James practice saying to himself, "Just because my performance in college wasn't steller does not mean I have to feel terribly upset and depressed."

As James grew increasingly able to dispute his irrational beliefs without the counselor's interventions and to make a shift to different feelings and responses in his imagination, the counselor introduced systematic homework assignments designed to help James think and behave in new ways in his real-life environment. Through these homework assignments and his continued discussions with the counselor, James became increasingly skilled at recognizing the vulnerable trouble spots in his belief system and was able to replace them with more rational self-statements that led to more positive feelings. As this process unfolded, he also realized that, although his contacts with his parents had only improved slightly, they didn't upset him like they used to and he was more optimistic about the future. He was more comfortable and in greater self-control now that he could see some of his thoughts as irrational and not "buy into" them as he had in the past. Counseling was terminated when James decided he was able to advance his progress on his own.

Cognitive Disputation

Cognitive disputation makes use of persuasion, direct questions, and logical reasoning to help clients dispute their irrational beliefs. This is one of the few times in counseling where "Why?" questions are useful. Cognitive disputation is driven by specific types of questioning, such as:

Is that good logic?

Is that true? Why not?

Can you prove it?

Why is that so?

Could you be overgeneralizing?

What do you mean by that term?

If a friend held that (self-defeating) idea, would you accept it?

In what way?

Is that very good proof?

Explain to me why . . . (e.g., "you're so stupid"; "you don't belong in college").

What behaviors can you marshal as proof?

Why does it have to be so?

Where is that written?

Can you see the inconsistency in your beliefs?

What would that mean about you as a person?

Does that follow logically?

What's wrong with the notion that you're special?

How would you be destroyed if you don't . . . ?

Why must you?

Let's assume the worst. You're doing very bad things. Why must you not do them?

Where's the evidence?

What would happen if . . . ?

Can you stand it?

As long as you believe that, how will you feel?

Let's be scientists. What do the data show?

Counselors who use cognitive disputation must recognize that this method can lead to client defensiveness and must be sensitive to resulting client responses, particularly to their non-verbal cues. It is important to realize that clients may have difficulty with the disputation process because they are unable to discriminate between irrational and rational beliefs. When this occurs, persistence is called for, often supplemented by counselor modeling of the difference between an irrational and a rational belief.

Humphrey (2009) suggests a technique for disputation that encourages the client to have a dialog with the irrational belief. Therefore, rather than the counselor serving as the alter ego, the client does this him- or herself. This can be an excellent second step in the cognitive disputation process, after the counselor has first modeled how to challenge one's self-defeating thinking.

IMAGINAL DISPUTATION. Imaginal disputation relies on client imagery, and particularly on a technique known as *rational–emotive imagery (REI)*. This intervention is based on the assumption that the emotional consequences of imagery stimuli are similar to those produced by real stimuli. There are two ways this intervention can be applied: First, clients imagine themselves in the problem situation (the A) and then try to experience their usual emotional turmoil (the C). Clients are instructed to signal to the counselor (usually with a raised index finger) when this occurs. As soon as they signal, the counselor asks them to focus on the internal sentences they are saying to themselves—sentences that are usually irrational. Next, the counselor instructs them to change their thoughts from extreme to moderate and to notice the resultant feelings. The counselor points out that, in doing this, they are making the cognitive shift they must make in real life.

In the second application of REI, clients are asked to imagine themselves in the problematic situation, and then to imagine themselves feeling or behaving differently in this situation. As soon as they get an image of different feelings and behavior, they are instructed to signal to the counselor. The counselor then asks them to notice what they were saying or thinking to themselves in order to produce different feelings and responses. The counselor points out that these are the kinds of sentences or beliefs they must use in real-life situations to produce different effects.

REI is an excellent therapeutic technique for taking rational ideas and mental pictures that initially "feel wrong" and making them quickly start to feel right. Experts recommend that, for maximum results, clients use REI several times daily for at least a week or two for it to take hold.

Counselors who use REI may do well to forewarn clients not to expect instant success and to remember to be patient with themselves, even to the point of expecting the new feelings and responses generated during the imagery to feel a little strange at first. Some clients may report that distracting thoughts intrude during REI. In these instances, it is usually helpful to encourage clients to let these thoughts pass and ignore them, but not force the distracting thoughts out of their awareness. Other clients may report difficulty doing REI work because they cannot generate clear and vivid images during the imagery process. The production of strong images is not crucial to the success of the technique, as long as clients continue to focus on rational self-talk and on expected new feelings and behaviors as intensely as possible during their daily practice sessions.

Desibels Intervention

The *desibels intervention* (desibels stands for "DESensitizing Irrational BELiefS") is used to help clients become aware of disturbances in thinking, which simultaneously eliminates consequent distressing feelings. The intervention is usually introduced during the counseling session and then assigned as daily homework. Clients are asked to spend 10 minutes each day asking themselves the following five questions and to either write their responses on paper or record them:

1. What irrational belief do I want to desensitize and reduce?

2. What evidence exists for the falseness of this belief?

3. What evidence exists for the truth of this belief?

4. What are the worst things that could actually happen to me if I don't get what I think I must (or if I do get what I think I must not)?

5. What good things could I make happen if I don't get what I think I must (or if I get what I think I must not)?

The desibels intervention may be more effective if daily compliance is followed by some form of client self-reinforcement, such as engaging in an enjoyable activity.

Countering Intervention

The *countering intervention* involves a process similar to desibels. Clients are asked to identify, both verbally and in writing, counterarguments for each of their significant irrational or problematic beliefs, using the following six "rules."

1. Counters must directly contradict the false belief. For example, if the irrational belief is, "I'm a failure if my wife leaves me," a contradicting counter would be, "My wife's behavior is independent of my own success and accomplishments."

2. Counters are believable statements of reality. For example, a reasonable or believable statement of reality is, "I don't have to get straight As in high school in order to get a reasonably good job," whereas "I don't have to go to high school to get a reasonably good job" is not.

3. Develop as many counters as possible in order to counteract the effects that the irrational beliefs have produced over time.

4. Counters are created and owned by the client. The counselor's role in developing counters is limited to coaching. This rule is important, because clients are likely to be more invested in counters that they themselves generate. Also, effective counters are often highly idiosyncratic to specific clients.

5. Counters must be concise. Lengthy, long-winded counters are easily forgotten. The most effective counters can be summarized in a few words.

6. Counters must be stated with assertive and emotional intensity. It has been suggested that if the client attempts a counter but is unconvincing, the counselor should have the client first repeat the counter nasally; then mechanically (without feeling); and then with vigor, filling her or his lungs with air and vehemently stating the new belief. This helps make an indelible memory for the client.

After counters are developed, clients practice them in counseling and at home until they convince themselves of the wisdom of the counter. When this has occurred, their thinking pattern has changed from an irrational and dysfunctional thought to a rational and functional thought.

Injunctions and Redecision Work

Of the many interesting aspects of *transactional analysis (TA;* Berne, 1964), one is the *injunction* from parents that often becomes part of a person's life script. Some injunctions are benign ("Always to the best you can do"). Others, however, carry damaging consequences that can lead to dysfunction, such as the following:

Don't be close.
Don't feel.

Don't be successful.
Don't fail.
Don't be the center of attention.
Don't play.
Don't grow up.
Don't be who you are.
Don't be healthy.

According to TA, children make early decisions based on the kinds of injunctions they have been taught about life. Many injunctions were unconsciously "taught" to children and may reflect on the insecurities of the adults who were forming the injunctions. *Redecision work* is meant to help clients become aware of the specific injunctions they accepted as children, to reexamine the effect of the injunction(s) for them in their present life, and then to decide whether they want to continue living according to the injunction(s) or to make a new decision. In the application of this technique, specific attention is given to thoughts or beliefs that accompany the long-ago learned injunction that may no longer be true or valid. These are then replaced by new or different beliefs and thoughts that are needed to support a new decision.

Redecision work may be particularly useful with clients whose current behavior is inappropriate in many situations and appears to be based on one or two parental-type messages they still hear or "play" as tapes in their heads.

CASE ILLUSTRATION OF INJUNCTIONS AND REDECISION WORK

The Case of Kelly

Kelly is a 40-year-old woman who is married, has two teenage children, is employed as an attorney, and cannot understand why she is so fatigued, defeated, and generally burned out. In the past year, she has developed a stomach ulcer. Kelly reports that she started being really unhappy about 18 months ago and kept waiting to feel better. That hasn't happened. Kelly discloses that she has attempted "to do it all and do it all perfectly," and has never really considered asking for help from family or friends, nor has she expressed her growing irritation and resentment over their lack of help and support.

In the second session, the counselor asked Kelly to close her eyes and recall what it was like as a child growing up in her house. Next, the counselor asked Kelly to recall anything she remembered Mom telling or showing her not to do when Kelly was a child, or anything Mom said that sounded negative. Kelly revealed that her mother always told her to do things "right the first time," preferably without any help. Kelly recalled that her mother was a perfectionist, an independent woman who never seemed to have any needs of her own and was always doing things for others.

When the counselor asked Kelly to recall what she remembered Dad saying or doing, she stated that Dad always said, "Hold your tongue. Don't get upset or angry with other people even if they really make you mad." Kelly described her father as a very calm person outwardly, who never showed much feeling. He died of heart disease at the age of 50.

The counselor helped Kelly identify the typical injunctions she heard as a child that she still hears or follows in her present life. Kelly identified three:

Don't ask for help or show needs or weaknesses.

Do everything right the first time.

Don't get angry.

Kelly also revealed that she had decided to "work as hard and as independently as possible," and "keep all negative feelings to myself."

The counselor helped Kelly explore how these decisions may have been useful as a child. For example, Kelly learned to please her Mom and get approval from her by doing things without error and by not "bugging" her for help. Similarly, she learned to please her Dad and obtain recognition from him by being "just like Dad—a chip off the old block—able to handle anything without getting upset."

From a feminist perspective, the counselor has a responsibility to help Kelly develop awareness of how growing up in a patriarchal culture produces and reinforces these sorts of injunctions, especially for women. So part of Kelly's redecision work was to develop consciousness about ideas she learned from her family and culture as a way to "keep her in her place" or to be a "nice girl." Part of becoming a woman is reevaluating those societal injunctions that prevent Kelly from reaching her full potential as a person.

The counselor and Kelly considered whether these two decisions were useful or were interfering in her present life. Kelly concluded that her decisions to work independently and contain her feelings had resulted not only in severe stress for her, but had also kept her family and friends at a distance. When she expressed a desire to change these decisions, the counselor helped her identify what new decisions would be helpful and realistic.

Over the next few sessions, Kelly decided she would like to continue to be a hard worker but to ask for help and to express negative feelings whenever her stress approached a certain level. The counselor helped her develop a plan to supplement the new decisions with specific attention to the thoughts or cognitions that could impede or support the plan. Kelly identified the following thoughts that could interfere with the plan:

I don't have the right to ask for help.

I should be able to do it all by myself.

I shouldn't burden anyone else with my feelings or needs.

Together, Kelly and the counselor developed some alternative thoughts to support the plan:

I am a person who is worthy of asking for and getting help from others.

It is unrealistic for me to do everything alone.

I want my family and friends to be more involved in my life.

During the remaining sessions, the counselor continued to encourage Kelly while she tried to implement her plan based on the new decisions she had made for herself. Gradually, Kelly realized that she, rather than other people, presented the main obstacles to making the plan a success. She continued to work on ways in which she would support and carry out her new decisions.

Cognitive Restructuring

Cognitive restructuring (CR), also called *cognitive replacement*, similarly involves identifying and altering irrational or negative self-statements of clients (usually considered to be automatic thoughts because they are so habitual) and helping the client replace them with neutral or positive self-statements. This intervention is more likely to be used when there is a singular issue that brings out unhelpful thoughts; therefore, it has been used to help athletes modify high-performance anxiety, change unrealistic expectations of couples in marital therapy, and alter cognitions around food for clients with eating disorders. Cognitive restructuring has also been used successfully in treating depression in children, adolescents, and older adults; influencing career indecision; treating phobias and panic disorders; and enhancing self-esteem.

Cognitive restructuring begins with an exploration of the client's typical thoughts when in a troublesome situation. These thoughts may include both self-enhancing thoughts and self-defeating thoughts. The counselor uses closed questions to help the client identify specific thoughts that occur before, during, and after the problematic situation. If the client has trouble recalling specific thoughts, the counselor may want to ask the client to start by monitoring what goes through his or her head when problems arise and keep a written record of those thoughts.

Another way to help clients identify their thoughts in problematic situations is to visualize a situation in which the client typically has difficulties and then have the client describe the inner dialog that takes place. For example, "Imagine yourself boarding a commercial airplane. Listen to your internal dialog as you look for your seat, find it, sit down, and strap yourself in. What kinds of statements are you making to yourself during this sequence of events?"

Clients need some preparation or structure to use cognitive restructuring. Without structure, the client cannot be a productive contributor, and the process will be ineffective. By way of introduction, the counselor should explain what automatic thoughts are and give examples, then explain the process by which those thoughts are replaced with more productive or rational thoughts. Following is a sample of how the counselor can introduce the cognitive restructuring intervention.

Introducing Cognitive Restructuring

One of the things we all do involves *automatic thoughts*. When I have automatic thoughts, I am repeating a habitual thought rather than a rational thought. For example, if I trip while walking across the room, I might say, subconsciously, "You are such a klutz!" A more rational thought might be, "Slow down. When you get in a hurry, you often get clumsy." The first thing you must do is to become aware of these silent forces. Let's start by looking at what you typically say when facing (the client's particular issue), making a list of negative self-statements. Then we identify rational (more accurate) statements to counter them. Eventually, we want to replace the negative statements with neutral or positive statements. Once the replacement statements have become typical, we will have achieved our objective and you won't be attacking yourself, and your real strengths will have a better chance to emerge.

Cognitive restructuring can be a potent tool with a client whose self-talk is destructive or erodes confidence. Negative self-talk does not cause these problems; rather, it is the negative self-talk that maintains the issues, keeping them from receding or dissipating (Beck, 2011).

INTRODUCTION AND USE OF COPING THOUGHTS.   After the client has identified typical negative self-statements or thoughts surrounding a particular situation, the learning process begins for substituting a variety of coping self-statements or thoughts (also referred to as *countering thoughts*). These are similar in both content and function to the assertive thoughts used in the thought-stopping procedure (described later in this chapter). The use of coping thoughts is crucial to the overall success of the CR intervention. Awareness of negative or irrational self-statements is necessary but not usually sufficient to result in enduring change unless the client learns to produce incompatible self-instructions and behaviors.

When introducing coping thoughts, the counselor emphasizes their importance and their role in affecting the client's resulting feelings and behaviors. To help the client understand the difference between coping and noncoping thoughts, the counselor may give examples of each. Often, it is helpful to teach clients a variety of coping thoughts. For example, the client may find it helpful to use a particular type of coping before a problematic situation occurs. During the situation, the client may need to use coping thoughts that help confront a challenge or that help cope with a difficult moment. After the situation, clients can learn coping thoughts to encourage themselves or to reflect on what they learned before, during, and after the problem situation occurred.

Example of a Coping Thought

Self-defeating statement: I am afraid of this airplane.

Coping statement: This airplane has just been inspected by a specialist in aviation safety.

SHIFTING FROM SELF-DEFEATING TO COPING THOUGHTS.   After identifying coping thoughts, the client must still learn how to shift from well-practiced self-defeating thoughts to the new coping thoughts. This is not an easy or natural process. It must be practiced once the client has learned to recognize the intrusion of the self-defeating thought. Sometimes it helps for the counselor to model this process for the client first. For example, a counselor could model the shift for a client who is waiting for an important job interview:

> *Okay, I'm sitting here waiting for them to call my name for this interview. Wish I didn't have to wait so darn long. I'm getting really nervous. What if I blow it? [Self-defeating thought] Now, wait a minute—that doesn't help. [Cue to cope]. It'll probably be only a short wait. Besides, it gives me a chance to sit down, relax, pull myself together, take some deep breaths, and review not only what I want to emphasize but also what I want to find out about this employer. I'm going to be sizing up this person, too. It's not a one-way street. [Coping thought established before the situation in the form of planning].*

> *Okay, now they're calling my name. I guess it's really my turn now. Wow, my knees are really shaking. What if I don't make a good impression? [Self-defeating thought and cue to cope] Hey, I'm just going to do my best and see what I can learn from this, too. [Coping thought].*

Thought Stopping

Thought stopping is perhaps the first line of response when working with clients who tend toward negative self-talk or self-defeating thinking. *Thought stopping* is the process of interrupting a particular thought or line of thinking by commanding oneself to stop that thought. It is as though the client creates in his or her imagination a "little commander" who orders the thought to cease.

Positive Self-Talk

Self-talk, when we are having a conversation with ourselves, is a common human activity. Typically when we self-talk, we are not consciously focused on that inner monolog. When the monolog drifts toward negative descriptions of oneself and one's motives and actions, it becomes a drag on the psyche. Often, clients simply do not know how to break out of these negative self-talk patterns. If you think of the last time you felt sorry for yourself, you probably were engaged in an inner monolog that fed you ample reasons for your negative feelings.

Positive self-talk involves the client's recognition of the existing negative patterns, paired with some type of internal alarm that negativity is in control of his or her mental processes. Only then can the client attempt to replace this negativity with positive (and true) self-talk. Thus, this intervention involves an assessment process and a replacement process. Perhaps the best example of negative self-talk comes from the person one would describe as having trust issues. When faced with a challenge, the self-talk may sound like, "I can't trust him to have my back," or, "This won't go well because no one around here cares about me." Such a judgment can be far from accurate. In fact, the person may have ample contradictory evidence from other similar situations. With the counselor's assistance, this realization must be brought to the surface and acknowledged by the client.

Once this acknowledgment has happened, the counselor assists the client in appreciating that the habitual response is more often in error than not, and must be replaced with a response that is more grounded in experience. Because internal self-talk is strongly entrenched, the counselor must be prepared to remind the client of this fact numerous times before the client can start taking over the process.

Anchoring

One of the problems in helping clients change entrenched cognitive patterns is that the patterns have become like autonomic responses. They are not consciously driven. This makes the recognition or even the anticipation of such responses difficult for clients to manage. *Anchors* are signals that the counselor and client have agreed on that alert the client to an impending undesirable response, such as a negative self-assessment. The anchor that alerts can be external (e.g., visual, behavioral, auditory) or internal (e.g., a feeling). When the anchor is recognized, the client is alerted and can respond with the new learned response. For example, the person with a weak self-image experiences much anxiety or impending doom. This feeling can become the anchor alert. So the counselor coaches the client, "When you first become anxious, quickly ask yourself, 'What am I saying to myself? What am I thinking right now?' Then, instead of following your typical thought pattern, replace it with the phrase we have agreed on." Anchors may also be physical. For example, the adolescent who admits to having negative feelings toward one of his teachers can use a physical object in that teacher's room to remind him to check in with his thoughts, and challenge the irrational negative thoughts and replace them with more neutral thoughts. This anchor-based replacement must be rehearsed in the counseling session. The drill might involve the counselor making the client's negative statement, and the client responding with the replacement (e.g., "No, Mr. Smith was fair to me when I had to make up a quiz").

Reframing

Reframing is the gentle art of viewing or thinking about a situation differently. Within a counseling context, it is much more than a Pollyanna view of life. In fact, reframing (also called *reformulation*) is the counselor's attempt to take the definition of the problem and redefine it so that it opens the door to viable solutions. It has been favored by an interesting variety of theorists, ranging from existentialists to strategic family therapists. Sometimes, reframing amounts to redefining an unsolvable problem as solvable, or viewing the problem as not a problem at all. Other times, the reframe cuts through unfounded assumptions about either the person or the problem and provides a fresh and uncomplicated approach to the issue at hand. In its simplest form, reframing takes a relatively simple thought or opinion that is subject to interpretation and offers a differing interpretation to that which is held.

Therapeutic reframing can be effective when it redefines an offensive motive or behavior as inept but well intended, thus making the behavior more personally or socially acceptable. It may be used equally well with the individual client who is dealing with intrapersonal issues or with the person who is reacting to interpersonal issues. The critical test for an effective reframe is that the alternative meaning is credible and often addresses motives more directly. Thus, a mother's overbearing behavior may also be viewed as her inability to communicate her love, or a child's compulsive behavior may be viewed as his attempt to lighten his mother's parenting responsibilities. Only when this credibility criterion has been met is the client likely to accept the new meaning and discard the dysfunctional older meaning. Once this has happened, more appropriate ways to accomplish the positive goal are considered.

A major of advantage of engaging in reframing is that it cannot be arrived at without counselor empathy—that is, only if the counselor is able to appreciate the acceptable motives behind unacceptable behavior can the counselor arrive at a therapeutic reframe of the situation. We are familiar with some of these—for example, the school counselor who understands that Craig's disruptive behavior is an ill-conceived strategy to receive recognition. Other reframes include reinterpreting anger as fear that one's life is out of control, or remarking that a client's high expectations of others is a way to distance them and thus remain emotionally safe from involvement and hurt and/or disappointment. It is important that the counselor believe that his or her reframe is "closer to the truth" than the client's current conceptualization of things, or it should not be attempted. Reframing is not guessing at the client's expense!

Finally, a distinction between reframing and interpretation is warranted. *Interpretation* looks at a series of events or statements and offers or asks the client to offer some conclusion about them. ("How do you make sense of the fact that things seem to go down the tube right after you've had a good contact with your ex?" or "I'm wondering if you get scared when you've had a good contact with you ex, maybe that she'll ask more of you regarding the kids than you're willing to give.") In other words, an interpretation gives the client a way to think about things when the client has not yet formulated a conclusion. By contrast, *reframing* takes the client's current conceptualization and attempts to introduce one that often not only alters it, but alters it dramatically. ("You know, you keep calling yourself a loser because you haven't gotten any further in the company. But I see someone who does some pretty wonderful things there, like offering to take an extra shift so someone can be home for his kid's birthday. I know that you'd like a bigger paycheck, but what you call losing, I'd call valuing other things, maybe more important other things.")

SECOND-ORDER INTERVENTIONS

Most of what we have discussed thus far borrows from fairly accessible logic. That is, it's most likely the case that a client who tells herself that she is worthless and no one will ever love her is in fact worthy of love. Another group of cognitive interventions appear to turn logic on its head. They are what originally were called *second-order change* (Watzlawick, Weakland, & Fisch, 1974) interventions. For example, it is quite logical that if one is not achieving one's goal that one should try harder. However, trying harder may indeed have become part of the problem if, for example, in working harder than anyone else, you have become judgmental of others, humorless, and so focused on your goal that you are missing many parts of the puzzle. Therefore, "Try softer" may be an appropriate strategy to resolve your dilemma. Only when this paradoxical idea has been embraced as being more logical than the former one of "Try harder" are desired outcomes achieved. In other words, it is the challenge of counseling to work with the client to deconstruct first-order thinking (Try harder) that is not working and construct productive second-order thinking (Try softer).

It perhaps comes as no surprise that not everything we think is rational, even if it appears to be logical. Unless questioned or challenged, most of us choose to think of our cognitive processes as rational. How, then, does one challenge a client's irrationality and stimulate a second-order resolution? We introduce a couple of second-order interventions here. Others that address behavioral or systemic change are presented in Chapters 10 and 11.

Resisting Therapeutic Progress

Resisting therapeutic progress is a second-order intervention that can come in the form of cautioning clients against change or warning them that they are improving too quickly. When used in this manner, the intervention is called *restraining*. It offers a preventive prescription to client resistance to change and can be used alone or as part of a more complex intervention. There are many cases in which the counselor can outline what must be done to improve a situation, but can then add a caution to the considered change. Clients can be warned that they are improving too rapidly and should slow down the process of change. If, indeed, the counselor has concerns about change versus what might be pseudo-change, such caution may be wise. If the client then has a setback, he or she is less concerned because the counselor cautioned that this might happen and advised the client not to be concerned about it. If the client does not have a setback, all the better! In fact, this particular second-order intervention often leads to more efficient therapeutic progress than not, because it creates a cognitive double-bind for the client who may be prone to resistance.

Positioning

Most of us have encountered persons who elicit positive statements or sympathy from others by being overly negative about themselves, such as the office worker who volunteers that she is poorly organized so that she draws praise from others regarding her good organization, or the person who claims that everyone hates him when it is clear that this is not the case. When this occurs in the counseling session, counselors may choose to "agree" with the negative self-assessment. Second-order theorists predict that if clients have been positioning in order to manipulate (which is often outside of their awareness), the counselor's agreement will jolt them into either accepting that this is indeed what they believe or taking a fresh look at what they believe and defending themselves from the "unfair" assessments of the counselor. Either way, this "double-bind" moves counseling forward in a positive direction and a more authentic interaction with the counselor. Some authors have even suggested that the counselor can enhance the power of the intervention by exaggerating the negative statement, often eliciting a response such as "I'm not that bad!" from the client (Dowd & Milne, 1986).

Example of a Positioning Response

CLIENT: I'm just a bad mother. I keep screwing up. No matter how hard I try, I just keep making moves that push them away.

COUNSELOR'S POSITIONING RESPONSE: So it sounds like you've come to a decision that being a better mother is beyond you. Maybe it's time to see what other resources are available to your kids so they can get their needs met elsewhere.

In closing this section on second-order interventions we want to underscore the difference between them and those that came before. Interventions such as cognitive disputation and reframing are more immediately transparent to the client. The counselor challenges the thoughts of the client, but in a way that is quite obvious to the client. Second-order interventions are far more subtle and are more often in three steps: first is the counselor's intervention, which may not make much sense to the client; second is the resultant cognitive shift that is desirable in order to achieve counseling goals; and the third step can be a time for counselor and client to process the intervention and how it brought the client to a more logical and productive place than the client's prior logic about his or her issue.

MEANING-MAKING INTERVENTIONS

In reviewing the core counseling skills, we covered the importance of asking clients to share the meaning of something. Understanding the meaning ascribed to an event, a condition, and so forth goes a long way in understanding the client. This, then, is the basic level of assisting a client in meaning making.

Beyond this core technique, we introduce here an emphasis on meaning making that includes the existential or spiritual dilemmas an issue may pose for a client. The counselor's reluctance to address these may prolong the suffering of their clients and might culminate in help that is not so very helpful. Some authors discuss meaning making in a spiritual sense as a central tenet of therapy (e.g., Aten, McMinn, & Worthington, 2011; Richards & Bergin, 2005). Whether one's counseling practice centers on the existential/spiritual or not, there are clients or situations that call for meaning-making interventions.

Meaning Making for the Spiritual Client

For many clients, there is not a clear demarcation between the psychological and the spiritual. For those clients who have belief in a Deity (or, as Alcoholics Anonymous prefers, a Higher Power), the spiritual realm may be a necessary and fruitful area for healing but only if the counselor has both comfort and skill in addressing spiritual matters. Aten, McMinn, and Worthington's (2011) edited text discusses seven major spiritually oriented interventions: prayer, promoting forgiveness, meditation, mindfulness, yoga, sacred writings, and spiritual journaling. Furthermore, each intervention is discussed from both Eastern and Western spiritual traditions. We encourage the reader to consult this kind of comprehensive text for a full understanding of spiritual interventions, not all of which are cognitive in their focus.

SACRED WRITINGS. One example of a cognitive approach to a spiritual crisis is to ask the client to share any sacred writing that the client has found meaningful as they struggle with their problem. What is it about a particular writing that gives them perspective or hope? If they are pulling from a religious tradition that is unfamiliar to the counselor, it is important that the counselor listen carefully and not jump to spiritual conclusions that are informed by the counselor's spiritual context. Furthermore, such a cognitive exercise should be given ample time for layers of meaning to surface. The counselor must ask follow-up questions and then carefully link the message that the client receives from the spiritual writing to a psychotherapy-based intervention. For example, a part of a favorite passage may be used as the alternate thought that the client says to him- or herself when negative thoughts begin to attack the spirit. Such a simple acknowledgment of the client's spiritual life can enhance counseling significantly.

Meaning Making for the Nonspiritual Client

Not all clients have an active or even tangential spiritual life; still, this does not preclude the client's quest for meaning. Particularly for clients who have experienced loss or trauma, meaning-making interventions have been found to be invaluable (e.g., Currier, Holland, & Neimeyer, 2008; Haugen, Splaun, Weiss, & Evces, 2013). Wong (2010) states that it is a common experience that "[T]he future seems more chaotic and uncertain than ever" (p. 85). Haugen et al. (2013) explain that all individuals have what they refer to as "global meanings"—that is, what they can expect of the world, of others, and of themselves. When a situation conflicts with their global meaning, they attempt to work themselves back to a place of stability. If their efforts do not alleviate their stress, symptoms of PTSD can eventually occur. Counselors, then, must be attuned to layers of meaning of an event or series of events for clients. Haugen et al. (2013) suggest that the counselor focus attention on what exactly was distressing about an event, even if it might seem obvious. This kind of deconstruction of the meaning of what life has presented allows the client to appreciate how much their personal global meaning has been assaulted, and along with adequate affective work, can assist clients to construct new and viable meanings for themselves.

Metaphor and Meaning Making

The use of metaphor is particularly familiar to those with a religious background, in part because it is commonly used in the writings of many world religions. The use of metaphor is also compatible with the philosophical position that all change comes from within rather than outside the individual. Whether inspired by the sacred or the secular, whether a sacred writing or poetry, metaphor presents a contextually different scenario that may be close enough to allow the client to draw conclusions and gain insights about the problem. Pearce (1996) observes that "metaphor functions in the affective realm despite the fact that it is delivered and apprehended by the cognitive, intellectual realm" (p. 3). He explains the therapeutic value of metaphor:

> Precisely because metaphor straddles the worlds of cognition and affect, it expedites thought process in the world of feeling. Metaphor can, from its position in the unconscious realm, initiate behavior change. [It] enables clients to transform a painful or unresolved experience by enabling them to transfer the meaning of such events beyond the critical junctures, resulting in an improved destiny or frame of reference. (p. 3)

Most uses of metaphor present an opportunity for the client to gain insight and meaning or to view a situation or condition in a different and more meaningful way. For example, the counselor who is trying to help a quarrelling couple get beyond their combative positions might offer the Buddhist story of two monks arguing:

> Two Monks were arguing about a flag. "The flag is flapping," said one. "No," said the other, "the wind is flapping." The argument went back and forth. The Master happened to be passing by. He told them: "Not the wind, not the flag; your minds are flapping." (Reps, 1981, p. 114)

This story is delivered without explanation. Instead, the counselor allows the couple to find their own meaning in the story—for example, "Are we each distracted by our need to be right?"

Metaphors also come from folk and fairy tales. Pearce (1996) reminds us that Freud turned to folklore, fairy tales, and other forms of imaginative literature to label and categorize symptoms. Bettelheim (1976) extended this use of fairy tales in his book *The Uses of Enchantment: The Meaning and Importance of Fairy Tales,* where he proposes that fairy tales allow children to work through life's great mysteries in socially acceptable ways. However, adults can also gain insight into their beliefs, values, and blind spots through the revisiting of fairy tales. The meaning gained must be provided by the client, however; if a client can see no meaning or relevance in a metaphor or story, then the only thing for the counselor to do is to move on to something else.

CASE ILLUSTRATION OF MEANING MAKING

The Case of Tasha

Tasha, a 26-year-old woman who worked in retail, came to counseling in a depressed state. The onset of her depression occurred when her father suddenly died of a heart attack two months prior. Tasha reports that she "fell apart" after that and eventually lost her job. She lives at home with her mother, who she says is "doing OK" since her father's death. Her mother insisted that Tasha go to their doctor, who has prescribed antidepressant medication, but also recommended counseling.

After the intake process and in the second session, Tasha made the comment, "It's not fair that some people get away with murder and I get punished." Later in the session, Jack, Tasha's counselor, returned to this comment and asked if she could explain a bit more. Tasha hedged and just repeated the sentiment. In the next session, Jack revisited the sudden death of Tasha's father and gently asked her to tell him what she can remember thinking at that time. Among her thoughts, Tasha shared, "It's all my fault." Jack attempted to follow up on this but, again, Tasha resisted sharing any more. Because her comment was a reference to guilt, and because Tasha had noted during the intake that she was Catholic, Jack asked if she considered herself devout. Tasha responded that she was practicing, but hadn't felt devout in several years. Jack asked if she would be willing to bring a Bible verse that she liked into the next session, and she agreed to do this.

Tasha chose the story of Jesus meeting the woman at the well, a woman who was known to be an adulteress. In the story, Jesus forgives the woman and tells her to sin no more. Jack waited and Tasha uncomfortably acknowledged that it wasn't any accident that this was her chosen passage. Tasha shared that in her senior year of high school, a boy she was dating "took advantage of me. We only had sex once and I got pregnant. I didn't know what to do. My parents would have died if I told them. So I got an abortion. That's murder! And now God has taken away my father."

Tasha and Jack had a lot of work in front of them. It was clear that not only had Tasha suffered an assault and a significant loss, but also that the meaning she had made of these events is integral to the effects on her. It was also clear that using a Bible verse was an easier way for Tasha to tell her counselor about a devastating event than to address it in answer to Jack's direct questions. Jack will attempt to help Tasha to rediscover other dormant meanings, especially the meaning of forgiveness in Tasha's belief system. He will rely on aspects of cognitive disputation, but within the realm of spiritual and religious meaning making.

CLIENT REACTIONS TO COGNITIVE INTERVENTIONS

Clients are likely to either respond beautifully to cognitive interventions or find them totally meaningless. When clients respond positively to these approaches, they are likely to be people who are fairly intelligent, can appreciate irony, present less-debilitating symptoms, can generate pictures or internal dialog easily, and value the power of logical thinking. Clients who are unable to engage in cognitive approaches may be in crisis or have more severe problems, want or need a great deal of emotional support from the counseling relationship, process information kinesthetically, and react to issues and make decisions emotionally. It is difficult to use cognitive interventions successfully with clients who are resistant to them. Other types of interventions may be more useful with these individuals.

In addition to these various reactions, other typical reactions are likely to occur soon after introducing cognitive interventions. By anticipating these reactions, you are better able to handle them when and if they occur. One reaction has to do with the language or labels used by some counselors when using cognitive interventions. When the counselor describes the client's thoughts or beliefs as *irrational, mistaken,* or *illogical,* clients sometimes perceive that they themselves, as well as their ideas, are being attacked. This may be especially true for some types of clients (e.g., rebellious teenagers, insecure adults). Clients are also likely to have negative reactions if the counselor's labels are given in the context of a highly directive, active, and confrontational therapeutic style, particularly if the counselor has not established an adequate working relationship with the client.

You can circumvent this reaction from clients in several ways. One is to avoid the use of clinical terms. For example, it may be more advisable to tell a teenage client that his thinking is "messed up" than to state that it's irrational. Another way to avoid this potential pitfall is to remove yourself from the position of determining which of the client's beliefs are rational or irrational. Instead, this procedure can be performed by the client (if he or she is capable), thus eliminating the possibility of a power struggle or misunderstandings between you and the client.

A second fairly typical client reaction is initial disbelief at the counselor's proclamation that the client's thoughts, rather than external events or other persons, are the source of their problems. A client may say, "I told you I wouldn't feel this way if it weren't for her" (or "for it," meaning "for an outside event"). In fact, in initial interviews with clients, many of them believe that everything except their thinking is causing the problem. In their eyes, the problem is a parent or a spouse, their family of origin, how they were raised as children, unconscious material, and so on.

How can you deal with a client's disbelief in a sensitive and yet informative manner? One way is to spend an adequate amount of time describing the rationale on which cognitive interventions are based, thus providing an adequate conceptualization of these strategies to the client. It is important for counselors to do this with clinical sensitivity in a way that avoids blaming or repudiating the client's ideas. Meichenbaum (1977) observes:

> The purpose of providing a framework is not to convince the client—perhaps against his will—that any particular explanation of his problem is valid but rather to encourage him to view his problem from a particular perspective and thus accept and collaborate in the therapy that will follow. (pp. 150–151)

For cognitive interventions to work, it is important in your rationale to refute the "situation/ people cause problems/feelings" theory and subsequently to explain how thoughts create undesired feelings and behaviors. This explanation usually is more helpful if realistic examples and analogies are used. For example, McMullin and Giles (1981) use the following examples with clients:

> When my daughter was three, she used to watch monster shows on TV and get scared. When she was five, she watched the same shows and laughed like crazy. The situations were the same, but the consequences were different. Why do you think this was so?
>
> A New Yorker went to Texas to visit his friend. As they were driving in the desert, the New Yorker spotted what he thought was a boulder in the road, and frantically tried to grab the wheel. The Texan, however, said, "Relax. It's just a mesquite bush." Do you see that it was what the New Yorker thought about the bush that caused his panic?
>
> Two men over-ate one night and woke up the next morning feeling sick. One went to the doctor in a panic, and the other simply took it easy until he felt better. The first man was saying something pretty scary to himself. What do you think that might have been? (p. 34)

Clients can also be asked to describe examples from their lives in which beliefs affect feelings. Another technique involves asking clients to describe a myth, fairy tale, or superstition they believed as a young child but no longer believe as an older child, teenager, or adult.

Finally, there is always the possibility that cognitive interventions do not produce desired changes in particular clients' feelings and behaviors. If, after repeated use of a cognitive procedure, the client's level of distress does not diminish, the counselor's original assessment of the client's problem may have to be reexamined.

APPLYING INTERVENTIONS TO DIALECTICAL BEHAVIOR THERAPY AND MOTIVATIONAL INTERVIEWING

Cognitive Interventions Used in Dialectical Behavior Therapy

Dialectical Behavior Therapy (DBT) is described as a cognitive–behavior therapy. Therefore, it is easily apparent that cognitive interventions are used by DBT therapists. As described in Chapter 8, once the therapist and client have arrived at an awareness of how the client experiences their emotional pain (or dysregulation), an extended analysis of the triggers (i.e., events and thoughts) that cause negative feelings and of the habitual reactions (thoughts and behaviors) to these feelings follows. In their description of assisting clients to understand their own dialectics, Koerner and Dimeff (2007) state that "there is a special emphasis on cognitive modification through conversation that create the experience of the contradictions inherent in one's own positions" (p. 10). In other words, what another theorist might refer to as "irrational thinking," the DBT therapist sees as the dialectic embedded in virtually all of life's problems.

Because the fit is a hand-in-glove one, most of the cognitive interventions described in this chapter could be used at one time or another by the DBT therapist. Exceptions are second-order interventions such as resisting therapeutic change; and positioning responses, because they are theoretically at odds with assumptions of the DBT therapy contract, which is collaborative and based on transparency between the therapist and client.

Cognitive Interventions used in Motivational Interviewing

As noted in Chapter 8, although Motivational Interviewing (MI) is a time-limited intervention and not a complete therapy, it is more complex than the foundational interventions we present in these chapters. We believe that MI combines a significant use of affective interventions with a selected subset of cognitive interventions. Furthermore, MI is not as nondirective as the therapies that claim to be exclusively humanistic; rather, counselors using MI offer feedback and advice when this is called for (Miller & Rollnick, 1991); such interventions fall in the cognitive camp.

Of those cognitive interventions described in this chapter, we steer the reader toward eliciting thoughts, disputing irrational thoughts, and working with injunctions. Although MI does not address irrational thoughts as would Albert Ellis, most resistance contains an element of irrationality (e.g., An overcontrolling mother of two teenage children states, "I want my children to trust themselves, but I must be sure they do the right things."). It's also the case that many clients who are ambivalent about change are controlled by old injunctions. Thus, helping the client recognize injunctions for what they are may be part of strengthening the discrepancy between these injunctions and the change voice.

Finally, many counselors who use MI include the intervention of reframing. It is often through the ability to reframe what is heard, especially if the reframe attends to a deeper truth and is done with empathy that a client can begin to move toward change with less ambivalence. It is also important to note that although MI addresses client resistance, it does not encourage counselors to do so using second-order interventions.

Summary

This chapter describes those empirically supported counseling interventions that help clients recognize how they think themselves into difficulties, and how those thoughts can be challenged and altered in a more constructive direction.

Critical to this type of counseling is the assessment process. Identifying illogical thinking patterns involves the counselor's communication skills, whereas altering those illogical patterns requires specific counseling interventions. The important point is that most illogical thinking patterns are so habitual that clients rarely recognize them as self-defeating. Thus, finding ways to help clients recognize these dysfunctional patterns is a major part of the counselor's role.

Interventions that have demonstrated effectiveness include real and imaginal disputation. These strategies draw heavily on rational–emotive behavior therapy (REBT) and cognitive–behavior therapy (CBT) for their rationale and application. Changing dysfunctional thought patterns requires that the counselor actively use cognitive restructuring interventions, such as introduction of coping thoughts, thought-stopping, positive self-talk exercises, and anchoring.

Altering dysfunctional thought patterns may require more subtle interventions that utilize creative and sometimes paradoxical thinking and cognitive double-binds. These were described by Watzlawick, Weakland, and Fisch (1974) as falling under the category of second-order interventions.

Finally, an important aspect of working within a cognitive orientation is to help clients understand and occasionally deconstruct the meaning of their situations. Depending on the client, this can include addressing the existential or spiritual implications of their thoughts and finding additional or alternative meaning within these contexts.

Exercises

I. **Conduct A-B-C-D Analysis for a Problem You Experience Personally**

A. Identify an external event (person or problem situation) that consistently evokes strong and unpleasant feelings for you. Identify and list in writing typical thoughts you have about this situation. Examine them. Do your usual thoughts indicate that you believe this situation is what causes your distressed feelings? If so, try to write examples of different or new thoughts about the situation in which you take responsibility for your feelings. For example, you might try using an "I message": "I feel _____" rather than "This situation or person makes me feel _____."

B. Identify the specific emotions or feelings that are distressing or uncomfortable. List them. Next, rate the usual intensity of such feelings on a scale of 1 to 10 (1 = not intense; 10 = very intense).

C. For each emotion or feeling you listed in step B, identify any thoughts or self-talk that goes on before and during the occurrence of these feelings. If this is difficult for you, ask yourself such questions as, "What goes through my mind when I feel this way?" or "What am I thinking about before and during these feelings?"

List these thoughts in writing for each emotion. Examine your list, and categorize your thoughts as either rational and true beliefs (RB) or irrational and false beliefs (IB). Remember that if the belief can be supported by data, facts, or evidence and can be substantiated by an objective observer, it is an RB. If it cannot be supported, it is an IB.

You may need to continue step C during actual situations. As these distressing feelings actually present themselves, become aware of your thoughts surrounding these feelings.

D. Examine and challenge each IB you listed in step C on a sentence-by-sentence basis. Use questions such as the following to challenge each of these beliefs: "What makes it so?" "Where is the proof? Let's be scientists—find the supporting data. Where is the evidence for that?"

Next, for each IB on your list, develop at least two counters for that belief. Recall that a *counter* is a statement that is directly opposite to the false belief, yet is a believable statement of reality. Make each counter as concise as possible. After developing these counters, repeat them aloud—first, mechanically, next with as much vigor and emotional intensity as possible. Finally, practice countering your

IBs by whispering or thinking the counter to yourself. During the next 2 weeks, use the counters with actual situations. Each time you become aware that you are starting to think an IB, whisper or think to yourself the counters you have developed to challenge that IB.

E. Become aware of any new effects of using this process over the next few weeks. Identify and list any behavioral effects—new or altered responses—as well as any emotional effects—new or altered feelings. Discover what has happened to the frequency and intensity of the feelings you listed in step B.

II. Transactual Analysis Redecision Work

Using the list of injunctions described in this chapter, identify any injunctions you received as you grew up. Your injunction may not be on the list, or it may be an adaptation of one on the list. Assess how useful this injunction is to you now. Is there a part of the injunction that causes negative consequences (even mildly negative)? List these negative consequences. With these in mind, how might you reauthor your injunction to be more helpful to you in your current life?

III. Cognitive Restructuring

This activity can be done either for yourself or for another person.

A. Identify a situation in which your performance or behavior is altered or inhibited because of unproductive thought patterns. It may be something such as making a presentation in front of a group, a job interview, encountering a difficult person, or taking a test.

B. During the next two weeks, keep a log of the kinds of thoughts that occur before, during, and after this situation, whenever the situation (or thoughts and anticipation of it) occurs. Identify which of these thoughts are negative or self-defeating.

C. For each negative or self-defeating thought from your list in step B, develop an incompatible thought or a coping thought. Try to develop coping thoughts that help you before, during, and after the problematic situation. Make sure the coping thoughts are suitable for you. Try them out and see how they sound. Practice saying them aloud, in the sequence in which you would actually use them. Use an appropriate level of emotion and intensity as you engage in such practice.

D. Practice making a deliberate shift from the negative or self-defeating thoughts to the coping thoughts. Learn to recognize and use the self-defeating

thoughts as a signal to use the coping thoughts. First, talk yourself through the situation; later, practice making this shift subvocally. Use role-play, if necessary, to help you accomplish this. Try to engage in this process whenever the trouble situation occurs in vivo.

IV. Application of Cognitive Intervention Strategies

In this exercise, you are given six client descriptions. Based on the information we give you, decide whether cognitive strategies would be appropriate or inappropriate treatments for each client. Explain your decision. An example is given.

Example: The client is a second-grade boy who is acting out in school and, because of limited intellectual ability, is having difficulty working up to grade level.

Cognitive interventions are not suitable for this client. Because of his developmental age and possible ability limitation, it would be too difficult for him to systematically apply logical reasoning to faulty thinking.

A. The client is a young male adult who is a college senior. He feels depressed over the recent deterioration of his grades and its effect on his graduate school plans for next year.

B. The client is a 6-year-old boy who is an only child. According to his teachers, he is having trouble interacting with the other children in his class and spends much of the time alone. His parents confirm that previous opportunities for interactions with other children have been very limited and have occurred on a sporadic basis.

C. The client is a middle-age man referred to you by his family. From talking with him, you observe flat affect coupled with "loose" or incoherent talk. Occasionally, the client refers to acting on instructions he has been given by a saint.

D. The client is a middle-age woman employed as an elementary school teacher. She was recently elected to a community taskforce, and reports feeling terrified by the prospect of having to get up and speak in front of a potentially unfriendly audience. She explains that she is constantly worried about making a mistake, forgetting her speech, or in some way embarrassing herself.

E. The client is a 12-year-old seventh-grader who comes in to talk to the school counselor because she doesn't think she's as pretty or as smart as the other girls in her class and, as a result, feels sad.

F. The client is a 72-year-old retired woman who complains about her retired husband's chronic dependency on her. According to the client, her husband seems unable to get tasks accomplished without her help. The client is well-defended; seems unable to identify any feelings she is having about this issue in her life; and appears to have strongly held beliefs, which are expressed in a rather dogmatic and rigid fashion.

Discussion Questions

1. A basic assumption of any cognitive intervention is that thoughts cause feelings and behaviors. What is your reaction to this assumption? What effect might your reaction have on your application of cognitive interventions with clients?
2. Discuss the characteristics of people you think would be very suitable for cognitive strategies. For what kinds of clients or problems might cognitive interventions not be appropriate?
3. In what ways might some clients resist working with a cognitive strategy? What might this resistant behavior mean? How could you handle it?
4. What is your reaction to second-order cognitive interventions? Under what conditions might you use them? Under what conditions might you refrain from using them?
5. To what extent do you think of the psychological and the spiritual as separate domains? Discuss this with your peers.

MyCounselingLab® Assignment

Go to the Video Library under Video Resources on the MyCounselingLab site for your text and search for the following clips. The following two videos provide a demonstration of cognitive therapy and an interview with the therapist. Notice how the counselor relies on specific incidents in the Session video to track how the client thinks.

- **Video Example: Cognitive Session**
- **Video Example: Cognitive Reflection**
- **Video Example: Brainstorming** In this video, the counselor asks the client to allow a variety of thoughts

for action to emerge, even knowing that some are far more likely to be helpful than others. This intervention is predicated on the assumption that we often judge and reject thoughts before giving them ample consideration. As a result, our options for problem resolution are limited, even foreclosed.

- **Video Example: Countering** In this example, the counselor assists the client in identifying her irrational thoughts and finding competing thoughts that are not only more rational, but that also allow her to cope better.

Behavioral Interventions

PURPOSE OF THIS CHAPTER

Most of our behavior is not *new* behavior. In fact, most of our behavior patterns, whether they are how we put on our shoes, eat our meals, walk the dog, or pay our bills, have such a history that we probably can't remember why we started doing them the way we do. These behavior patterns have power in our lives—power to make our lives less complicated, and a competing power to make us more resistant to change. In this chapter, we examine how persons change patterns of behavior that have become dysfunctional, less effective, or even unnecessary. Some patterns relate to behaviors that interfere with a client's goals, hopes, or needs; others are behaviors that might be missing from a client's patterns of interaction, leading to a failure to achieve desired goals, hopes, or needs. Perhaps the most important aspect of this chapter is the emphasis on a client's responsibility in this process of change, and how the client and counselor work together to accomplish the client's objectives. A variety of symptoms can be treated using the behavioral interventions described in this chapter, including affective symptoms such as phobic responses, cognitive symptoms such as compulsive thought patterns, and behavioral/systemic patterns.

Considerations as You Read This Chapter

- Behavior is the part of human existence that communicates to others how a person feels, what a person thinks, and who a person is. Because it is available to others through their observations, behavior becomes the communication channel that connects an individual to other people.

- Behavior is the tool or means by which people accomplish, perform, or in other ways achieve the goals that they set.

- Behavior can be the cause of a person's failures, mistakes, or disappointments.

- Because behavior is the outward manifestation of a person's inner self, it may sometimes seem to be unconnected to him or her. Many client problems involve some manifestation of behavior; often, the best approach to working with client problems is by addressing behavioral changes.

Thus far, we have examined how feelings and thinking are implicated in human problems, and how affective and cognitive interventions can alleviate problems. In this chapter, we address problems that are established in behavior patterns—the things people do, or fail to do. Behavioral interventions are intended to help clients change their habits when they interfere with achievement of their goals, ambitions, or values, or when they contribute to negative outcomes. Behavioral interventions are based on learning theory. Because of this, behavioral interventions are often thought of as skill development and to draw upon the teaching aspect of counseling.

Clients present with a vast range of skill deficits, from some that are mild and not terribly debilitating to those that are serious and far-reaching. One example of such a contrast is the middle-age man who wishes he could stand up to his father. He does not "suffer" from their relationship except when he is with his father, which only occurs when he travels to his parents' home for holidays. He is quite satisfied, by contrast, with his relationship to his wife and children. On the other end of the spectrum, Pinto, Rahman, and Williams (2014) describe a program to teach recently incarcerated women advocacy skills, such as learning new interpersonal behaviors as well as some fundamental skills of leadership, as an important means by which they can be empowered to succeed after incarceration. Based on the life situations clients present and the counselor's willingness to engage in behavioral interventions, the life skills to be mastered may be life-enhancing or life-changing.

Although a large number of interventions can be classified as behavioral in nature and focus, perhaps the most common ones include imitation learning (social modeling), skills training (including behavioral rehearsal or role-playing), relaxation training, systematic desensitization, and self-management exercises.

BEHAVIORIAL INTERVENTIONS AND THEORY

Most behavioral interventions can be traced back to three originating schools of behavioral thought: Pavlov's original conceptualizations, called *classical conditioning;* B. F. Skinner's later modifications of Pavlov's work, known as *operant conditioning;* and Albert Bandura's additions to these approaches, referred to as *social modeling.*

The classical conditioning model was based on Pavlov's animal experiments in which he sought to understand how learning occurs. It assumed that behavior changes when new conditions in the environment emerge. When his dogs learned to associate the ringing of the bell at the gate to their kennels with feeding, they began to anticipate the feeding time whenever the bell rang. In human terms, the theory holds that when the smell of pie in the oven typically means the arrival of favorite relatives (and enjoying a delicious pie), just the aroma can change one's mood. This model for learning tended to address very basic human physiological responses.

B. F. Skinner used the research laboratory to explain more-complicated learning patterns typical of human behavior. Again, by using animals to study patterns of learning, he looked at how a behavior or skill is acquired. He found that newly acquired skills could be refined, enhanced, and shaped by the manner in which rewards were given. This approach, called *shaping,* is based on the following axiom:

The likelihood of occurrence of any future event is directly related to the consequences of past similar events.

Most parents have learned that a bedtime story when a child is agreeable about bedtime is an incentive for the child to be agreeable the next evening. The child has learned that agreeable behavior is followed by something pleasant—that is, a reward. Skinner called this *operant conditioning.* As the child grows, and especially when parenting challenges occur, it is important to reward behavior that leans toward the desired goal, whether that is cleaning one's room or doing one's homework. In other words, rewards are not only paired with a completed task, but with positive steps toward the completed task as well. Because many behaviors are unlikely to be changed all at once, this aspect of operant conditioning is an important one.

Bandura (1969) viewed both Skinner's and Pavlov's models as basic but not complete explanations for how most human learning occurs. He reasoned that most people learn in a "safe" way—by observing other people learning and then imitating their behavior. Most children have learned that this really works—that is, copying the behavior of others who seem to gain the approval of adults. Bandura called this approach *social learning.* It has also been referred to as *observational learning, vicarious learning,* and *imitation learning.* It is based on the use of a model—someone or something—to observe carefully and then imitate. The more influential the model, the more quickly learning occurs. Therefore, children tend to follow other children they deem as attractive models; adults are influenced by advertisements that include favorite athletes or popular entertainment personalities.

All three of these approaches are based on experimental study of human learning. People use all three of these patterns when they learn something new; therefore, it makes some sense that these learning approaches might also be viable when behavior change is called for. This is the rationale for introducing behavioral interventions into the counseling process.

Behavioral interventions share certain common assumptions and elements:

- Maladaptive behavior (behavior that produces undesirable personal or social consequences) is often the result of learning.
- Maladaptive behavior can be weakened or eliminated, and adaptive behavior can be strengthened or increased through the use of learning principles.
- Behavior (adaptive or maladaptive) occurs in specific situations and is functionally related to specific events that both precede and follow these situations. For example, a client may be aggressive in some situations without being aggressive in most situations. Thus, behavioral practitioners attempt to avoid labeling clients using such arbitrary descriptors as *aggressive.* Instead, emphasis is placed on what a client does or does not do that is aggressive, and what situational events cue or precipitate the aggressive response, as well as events that strengthen or weaken the aggressive response.
- Clearly defined outline or treatment goals are important for the overall efficiency of these interventions and are defined individually for each client.
- Behavioral interventions focus on the present rather than the past or future and are selected and tailored to each client's set of problems and concerns.

Characteristics of clients who seem to have the most success with behavioral interventions include

- A strong goal orientation—people who are motivated by achieving goals or getting results
- An action orientation—people who have a need to be active, goal-focused, and participating in the helping process
- An interest in changing a discrete and limited (two to three) number of behaviors

Behavioral interventions have also been used extensively and found to be very suitable in schools, mental health agencies, or situations with time-limited counseling.

GOALS OF BEHAVIORAL INTERVENTIONS

Although the definition of the term *behavior* has expanded in recent years to include covert or private events such as thoughts, beliefs, and feelings (when they can be specified clearly), as well as overt events or behaviors that are observable by others, this chapter is focused primarily on overt behaviors. The goal of behavioral interventions is to increase what could be called *adaptive behavior*—that is, those behaviors that assist the client in meeting stated goals. In addition to developing new behaviors, a goal of behavioral interventions may also involve weakening or eliminating behaviors that work against the desired outcome (e.g., eating unhealthy snacks when you wish to lose weight).

Behavioral interventions have been used in many different settings (such as schools, agencies, business and industry, and correctional institutions), with a great variety of human problems (including learning and academic problems, motivational and performance problems, marital and sexual dysfunction, skills deficits, and anxiety), and with maladaptive habits (such as over-eating, smoking, substance abuse, and procrastination). In this chapter, we focus primarily on the behavioral interventions that seem to be most useful for working with people in the general population (as opposed to those in institutional settings). These include social modeling, behavioral rehearsal and skills-training approaches, relaxation training, systematic desensitization, and self-management interventions.

Behavioral Intervention Skills

Behavioral Skills

Describing Behaviors

Helping the client understand the complexity of behavioral tasks; breaking tasks down into sequential behaviors

Modifying Behaviors

Helping the client change behavior patterns when it is deemed appropriate

Contracting

Helping the client establish commitments, timelines, and recordkeeping for change

Supporting and Reinforcing

Helping the client assess and recognize levels of progress toward goals

Behavioral Interventions

Social Modeling

Using examples from other sources to teach the client how and what to change; included in this cluster of interventions are overt modeling, symbolic modeling, and covert modeling

Role-Play and Rehearsal

Using simulations to examine and rehearse new behaviors, verbal interactions, and so on; relies on practice and feedback

Anxiety Reduction Methods

Helping client assume control over muscular or kinesthetic processes as a method to counter learned anxiety responses to certain stimuli

Symptom Prescription

Helping clients regain control over their behavior by instructing them to engage the symptom rather than attempt to avoid it

Self-Management

Helping the client learn how to observe and manage behavior patterns over time; includes self-monitoring (observing and recording one's behavior), self-contracting (making a commitment to oneself to work on changing behaviors outside of counseling), and self-reward (learning ways to reward oneself when behavioral goals are achieved)

BASIC BEHAVIORAL SKILLS

Counselors working on behavioral change use a number of basic skills in their work that involve ways of conceptualizing behavior and behavior change. The starting point is the task of describing behavior.

Describing Behaviors

Describing or deconstructing one's behavior is not as easy as it might appear. Athletes and their coaches have become adept at behavior description because they must break behavioral processes down (e.g., a successful free throw in basketball) into the many sub-behaviors that are part of the behavior. Thus, their description for a free throw includes how the athlete's feet are positioned, the rhythm of the throw, the arc that is created as the ball approaches the net, and so on.

However, if you are on a basketball team and not successfully converting many free throws, one of the first things a coach may do is analyze your present actions and then reconstruct them toward the "model" free throw. Counselors helping clients make behavioral changes do much the same thing. Consequently, counselors must understand how to do behavioral analysis and how to restructure behavior patterns so they can coach their clients in this change process.

Modifying Behaviors

As already noted, many people simply do not think behaviorally. Before the counselor can gain a commitment from clients to enter into behavioral change processes, the client must recognize the relationship between certain target behaviors and their consequences. Thus, you might find yourself saying, "It seems like every time you do this, then that happens. Do you agree? Because you don't like it when that happens, perhaps we could start thinking about ways of breaking the pattern." Saying this does not resolve the issue, however. The point is that you will find it necessary to help clients understand the process of behavior change as well as giving them strategies to implement change.

Contracting

Several times we have mentioned the importance of gaining client commitment with counseling goals. One demonstrated way to do this is the counseling contract. It seems to be a human quality to feel more committed to a task if a contract is involved. The contract is developed between the counselor and client. The interesting part about contracting is that a contract tends to be more effective when the client actually signs his or her name to it (e.g., Smith, 1994). There is nothing legal about this act, but psychologically it does seem to make a difference for clients. Regardless of whether the client signs the contract, writing down the conditions of the contract together is quite important.

Supporting and Reinforcing

As clients begin the challenging process of changing behaviors that have long been part of their repertoire, and thus are familiar, they often need support and reinforcement. This can be as simple as telling the client, "You can do it," or "That was a good effort." Not to give the client this kind of feedback may be interpreted by some that they are not doing it right or that they are failing. It is also possible to overdo these supporting words. If that happens, the comments begin to lose their effect, or you may be viewed as having lower standards than the client has.

USING BEHAVIORAL INTERVENTIONS

Social Modeling

Much of the work associated with social modeling has been initiated or stimulated by Bandura (1977). Three approaches, or models, have emerged: the overt model, the symbolic model, and the covert model. Each of these approaches can be used in working with clients.

The *overt social modeling* approach uses one or more persons as a model to illustrate the behavior to be learned or refined. The overt model may be live (also called *in vivo*) or recorded for viewing at a later time. It is overt because it is apparent that this model is someone to be observed and imitated.

The *symbolic social modeling* approach might include animated cartoon or fantasy characters, schematics, narratives, or slides. A good example is the training videos produced to help a person learn how to use new computer software. The process takes the learner through a step-by-step process, with the ultimate goal that the learner can repeat the process later without the help of the training video.

The *covert modeling approach* uses imagination in the learning process. We noted earlier that this mental process makes covert interventions cognitive rather than behavioral. However, because so many behavioral counselors refer to this process, we break our own rule to include it here as well. The covert model—whether a person, cartoon character, or schematic diagram—is imagined rather than shown. Covert models may be the client (called *self-modeling*) or someone else enacting the behavior with increasing deftness. Various cues (e.g., specifying sensory images or inner reactions) can be supplied to support the imagined scenario.

LIVE (OVERT) MODELING.   With live modeling, the desired behavioral response is performed in the presence of the client. Live models can include the counselor, a teacher in a developmental guidance class, or a client's peers in a counseling group. Usually, the counselor provides a modeled demonstration via a role-play activity in which he or she takes the part of the client and demonstrates a different way that the client might respond or behave.

Live modeling can be a most versatile tool for the school counselor, the rehabilitation counselor, or the family counselor, to name only a few. Scenarios can vary from helping youth understand how to manage conflict (by observing a videotape of other youth doing so after an altercation), to helping long-term unemployed adults whose lives are complicated by a mental disability learn stronger self-presentation skills (by having successful persons from the same program agree to present to these clients), to helping family members see a new way to communicate. The counselor's role can vary from being an actor in the modeling exercise to being the choreographer or being the narrator. What follows is a modeling session in which the counselor served as narrator. The scene is a group guidance session involving 12 seventh-graders. The counselor has been working with 6 of the students on a project, "Using the Library to Learn about Careers." The second 6 students are new to the group and are just beginning the project.

Live modeling is particularly useful in instances in which the client is assessed as truly lacking a skill set. The modeled demonstration provides cues that the client can use to acquire

Using Live Modeling with Middle-School Students

COUNSELOR: Today, we have some new faces in our group. I think all of you already know each other. For convenience, I'm going to call you the "Old-Timers" and you the "New Bunch." The Old-Timers have been working on a project to learn about jobs. I'm going to ask them to demonstrate some of the things they have been doing. We'll use something called a *fishbowl.* What that means is that the Old-Timers sit in a small circle. The rest of us sit outside the circle and observe the Old-Timers as they talk about their project. We do this for about 15 minutes and then we trade places. The New Bunch will come into the inner circle and the Old-Timers will sit around the outside. Any questions? [Nervous noises, chairs moving, people getting settled. The Old-Timers are familiar with this exercise. They were introduced to it when they were in the role of the New Bunch a few weeks earlier.] Now, if everyone is ready, Old-Timers, I would like for you to talk to each other about the topic: "Fifty ways to choose a career—all in the library."

OLD-TIMERS: [A discussion begins, slowly at first, about how to use the library to find out about careers. Different members of the group talk about how they got started, who in the library helped them find the right books, which books were most helpful, how they preferred the computer career software for some of the research, funny things they discovered about some careers, and so on. There is a lot of joking. It doesn't look like a great learning experience, but the point is made that learning about jobs can be fun and that the library is a neat place to get career information. They also learned the process of approaching the right librarian and knowing what to ask for. After about 15 minutes, the counselor interrupts, summarizes what was said, and asks the two groups to trade places. Some groans, teasing, playful putdowns follow as students change seats.]

COUNSELOR: Now, New Bunch, it's your turn. I'd like you to show the Old-Timers what you can do. This time, the topic will be, "Things I am going to do in the library to learn about jobs."

NEW BUNCH: [More groans, jokes, moving of chairs. Talk begins slowly. Someone makes a joke. All laugh. Finally, someone gets into the spirit and says she would like to find out about becoming an astronaut. Everyone laughs. Counselor intervenes, commends student for her question, challenges group to come up with a plan for using the library to help her find out about becoming an astronaut. The group begins, more or less in earnest, and the information that characterized the first group's discussion comes out again, this time focusing on the topic of finding out about becoming an astronaut.]

those new responses to replace those that blocked learning the desired skill. For example, a client who wishes to be more assertive may benefit from seeing the counselor or a peer demonstrate such behaviors in role-played situations. The following exchange between the counselor (model) and the client (wishing to be more assertive) illustrates how such a session might go.

Modeling Assertive Responses

COUNSELOR: Today, Nancy, I thought we might do a role-play—that's where you and I enact someone other than ourselves, and our "play" is a scenario in which you are returning some unusable merchandise to a local store.

NANCY: That sounds awful. I don't like to have to return things to the store.

COUNSELOR: I know. But you said you wished you could do that sort of thing without getting turned inside out. Don't worry. I'm going to play you and you are going to play the part of the store employee. Okay?

NANCY: [smiling] Well, that's a little better. Okay.

COUNSELOR: You begin first, by asking me if I need some help.

NANCY: Hello, can I help you?
[AS EMPLOYEE]

COUNSELOR: Yes. I purchased this baptismal
[AS NANCY] gown for my daughter's baby, but after the baby was born, my daughter realized it was too small. I'd like to exchange it if I may.

NANCY: How long ago did you purchase it?
[AS EMPLOYEE]

COUNSELOR: Two months ago, I'm afraid. I
[AS NANCY] know your return policy is 30 days, but I hope you will accept it in exchange.

NANCY: Well, since you only want to
[AS EMPLOYEE] exchange it, I think we can do that.

Following the role-play, the counselor and Nancy discussed the interaction, and then they conducted a second role-play, this time with Nancy as herself and the counselor as the store employee. Then they evaluated Nancy's performance and identified some ways she could improve. This was followed by a third role-play in which Nancy again was herself. Her performance in the third role-play was much improved and she felt successful. Live modeling in which the client is a participant is limited by the client's willingness to participate in an imagined situation as an actor, unless you and the client can take an impending real situation that both of you can rehearse. If your client is particularly withdrawn, you may wish to use other persons as the modeling participants.

SYMBOLIC MODELING. Although live models have much impact on the client, they are sometimes difficult to use because the counselor cannot control the accuracy of the demonstration of the behavior being modeled. To correct for this, many counselors use symbolic models through video recordings, audio recordings, or films in which a desired behavior is introduced and presented. For example, symbolic models could be used with clients who want to improve their study habits. Reading about effective study habits of successful people and their scholastic efforts is a first step to help clients identify desired behaviors. Next, clients can listen to a recording or watch a video illustrating persons who are studying appropriately. Once effective symbolic models are developed, they can be stored easily and retrieved for future use by the same or different clients.

COVERT MODELING. *Covert modeling,* also called *imaging,* is a process in which the client imagines a scene in which the desired behavior is displayed. The imagined model can be either the client or someone else. The first step is to work out a script that depicts the situation(s) and desired responses. For example, if an avoidant client desires to learn to communicate more successfully with a partner, scenes could be developed in which the client is having a successful discussion. One scene might be as follows:

It's Friday night. You would like to go to a movie, but your partner is very tired. You acknowledge your partner's tiredness, but suggest that a movie might prove relaxing as well as entertaining. Your partner thinks about it for a moment, and then agrees.

Imaging serves two purposes: It brings the appropriate behaviors into focus, and it serves to construct a success image into the person's mind. Both are desired outcomes. This is often used in coaching athletes. However, the same intervention can be used to coach persons who must learn to be calmer under stress, to avoid taking that first drink, to bypass a sarcastic comment to one's partner, and so forth.

CHARACTERISTICS OF THE MODELED PRESENTATION. The way in which a presentation is modeled can affect the client's ability to pay attention to and remember the demonstration. It is important that the model be presented in a way that engages the client. The first part of the modeled presentation should include instructions and cues about the features of the modeled behavior or activity. A rationale for the use of modeling should also be given to the client prior to the demonstration.

Behaviors to be modeled should minimize the amount of stress that the client might experience in the presentation. Distressing and anxiety-provoking stimuli may interfere with the client's observation powers, processing, or remembering. For this reason, the counselor should be checking in with the client frequently regarding the client's reaction to the model.

Complex patterns of behavior should be broken down and presented in smaller and more easily understood sequences. If too many behaviors or an overly complex model is presented to the client at one time, the likelihood of learning is greatly diminished. You can seek the client's input about the presentation of modeled behaviors to ensure that the ingredients and pace of the modeled demonstration are presented in a facilitative manner and to be sure that the client noticed the key ingredients of the modeled behavior(s).

It is advisable to process the modeled behavior after it has been completed, or even during the demonstration. If the counselor models taking initiative, for example, he or she could stop the demonstration and make a point about what he or she did that is different from being passive in a situation.

Practicing the goal behavior or activity also increases the effectiveness of the modeling procedure. In addition to practice in the counseling session, the counselor might assign homework to the client for practice outside the session. Self-directed practice can enhance the generalization of the target behavior from within the session to real-life situations. If a client experiences difficulty in performing a particular activity or behavior, instructional aids, props, or counselor coaching can facilitate successful performance.

MODELING AND SELF-EFFICACY. *Self-efficacy* refers to the perception a client has about his or her ability and confidence to handle a situation or to engage in a task successfully. It has been found to be a major variable that affects the usefulness of modeling interventions (Bandura, 1988). It is not sufficient to assume that clients will simply observe a model—live, symbolic, or covert—and acquire the skills to achieve desirable results. Clients "must also gain enough self-efficacy [confidence] that they can perform the needed acts despite stress, changes, moments of doubt, and can persevere in the face of setbacks" (Rosenthal & Steffek, 1991, p. 75). Thus, modeling interventions must be designed that emphasize not only outcomes but also attitudes and beliefs about oneself. Self-efficacy is not a global concept—that is, it does not reflect self-confidence in general—but rather it refers to the confidence in oneself to achieve a particular goal. For example, Ozer and Bandura (1990) developed a modeling program to teach women self-defense skills. The program not only included modeling various self-defense skills, but also modeled ways in which the women could acquire trust in their self-defense skills, particularly in the face of adverse situations.

DESIRABLE CHARACTERISTICS OF MODELS.   Clients are more likely to learn from someone whom they perceive as similar to themselves. Cultural characteristics such as cohort, gender, social class, ethnic background, and attitudes should be considered when selecting potential models. When a "match" is not possible, we have some evidence (e.g., Atkinson, Casas, & Abreu, 1992) that a sensitivity and respect for the client's culture can bridge the dissimilarity divide. In other words, the feminist male counselor can successfully counsel the feminist female client; the middle-class African American counselor who is sensitive to her privilege can counsel the economically disadvantaged African American client, and so forth. This being said, achieving a connection across major cultural identities is a multistep process. Therefore, counselors must be vigilant in determining if they continue to be credible models for their clients.

In an early contribution to the literature on modeling, Meichenbaum (1971) suggests that a coping model might be more helpful to clients than a mastery model—that is, a client may be able to identify more strongly with a model who shows some fear or some struggle in performing than the model who comes across perfectly. Clients can also learn more from modeling when exposed to more than one model. Warmth and nurturance by the model also facilitates modeling effects.

When modeling fails to contribute to desired client changes, the counselor should reassess the characteristics of the selected model(s) and the format of the modeled presentation. In many cases, modeling can provide sufficient cues for the client to learn new responses or to extinguish fears. In other instances, modeling may have more impact when accompanied by practice of the target behavior. This practice can occur through role-play and rehearsal in the counseling session or as assigned homework.

Role-Play and Behavior Rehearsal

Role-play and behavior rehearsal interventions promote behavior change through simulated or *in vivo* enactment of desired responses. Common elements in the application of role-play and rehearsal interventions include the following:

1. A reenactment of oneself, another person, an event, or a set of responses by the client
2. The use of the present, or the here and now, to carry out the reenactment
3. A gradual shaping process in which less difficult scenes are enacted first and more difficult scenes are reserved for later
4. Feedback to the client by the counselor and/or other persons

Depending on the therapeutic goal, role-playing procedures can be used to uncover affect or to achieve catharsis. It can also be a stimulus for the client to increase awareness. We next discuss role-play as a way to facilitate behavior changes.

ROLE-PLAY AS A METHOD OF BEHAVIOR CHANGE.   Behavior rehearsal uses role-play and practice attempts to help people acquire new skills and to help them perform more effectively under threatening or anxiety-producing circumstances. Behavior rehearsal is used primarily in three situations:

1. The client does not have but must learn the necessary skills to handle a situation (skill acquisition).
2. The client must learn to discriminate between inappropriate and appropriate times and places to use the skills (skill facilitation).
3. The client's anxiety about the situation must be reduced sufficiently to allow the client to use skills already learned, even though the skills are currently inhibited by anxiety (skill disinhibition).

Suppose you have a client who wants to be more self-disclosing with others but doesn't know where to start learning how. In this case, the client might have a *deficit repertoire* (lack of skills and knowledge) in self-disclosure and must learn some new communication skills. Or the client may have the necessary communication skills but needs clarification or discrimination training to learn when and how to use those skills to self-disclose. Many clients have the skills but use them inappropriately. A person may self-disclose too much to disinterested persons and then withhold from persons who are interested in them. In another case, the client's anxiety can inhibit the use of these skills. Behavior rehearsal can then be used to help the client gain control over the anxiety reaction.

In addition to the practice effects gained from behavior rehearsal, the intervention can often provide important demonstrations about how the client actually behaves in real-life situations. For example, it isn't unusual for clients to describe a behavior or interaction one way, and then portray the interaction in a different way. Such contradictions can then be resolved in the session. Experts believe that the role-played behavior is far more likely to be accurate than the interaction as described by the client. This makes role-playing an important part of the assessment process, too.

The procedure for behavior rehearsal using role-play consist of a series of graduated practice attempts in which the client rehearses the desired behaviors, starting with a situation that is manageable and is not likely to backfire. Behaviorists call this process *successive approximation*— that is, learning easier parts of a complex skill, then moving to the next more difficult part, and so on. The rehearsal attempts may be arranged in a hierarchy according to level of difficulty or gradations of stress. Adequate practice of one situation is required before moving on to a scene that requires more advanced skills. The practice of each scene should be very similar to the situations that occur in the client's environment. To simulate these situations realistically, you may wish to use props and portray the other person involved with the client as accurately as possible. This portrayal should include acting out the probable response of this person to the client's new or different behavior.

Behavior rehearsal can be either overt or *covert* (imagined). Both seem to be quite effective. It's probable that a client could benefit from engaging in both of these approaches. Initially, the client might practice by imagining and then move on to acting out the scenario with the counselor. Covert rehearsal can also be assigned as a homework intervention. The client is asked to rehearse more challenging situations once he or she reports some command over those skills, building up to a more challenging situation, and the counselor's in-session observations are in line with the client's report.

Feedback is an important part of role-play and behavioral rehearsal interventions and is a way for the client to recognize both the problems and successes encountered in the practice attempts. Feedback also should be constructive, specific, and directed toward behaviors the client can potentially change; it should also include positive comments about skills that are adequately demonstrated. Feedback may be supplied by video- and audio-recorded playback of the client's practices. These recorded playbacks are often more useful objective assessments of the client's behavior than verbal descriptions alone. You may find that your assessment of the client is more important early in the feedback process, but eventually, it is desirable for the client to begin using accurate self-assessments in the feedback process.

Skill Training

Skill training is an intervention composed of several other interventions that we have already discussed: modeling, behavioral rehearsal, successive approximation, and feedback. It may target a variety of issues, including problem-solving skills, decision-making skills, communication skills, social skills, assertion skills, and various coping skills. To develop a skill-training program, you must first identify the components of the skill to be learned; then you arrange components in a learning sequence that reflects a continuum from less difficult to more difficult or less stressful to more stressful. Training then proceeds by modeling each skill component, having the client imitate the modeled behaviors, providing feedback, and repeating the sequence, if appropriate. Skill-training protocols exist for most skills that might be taught in the counseling setting and may be found in the professional counseling literature or online. To illustrate how a training protocol might be developed, let's examine an assertion-training protocol.

Assertion training is a tool for overcoming social anxiety that inhibits a person's interactions with others. Many persons who need assertiveness training describe an early history in which they have been taught that the rights of others supersede their own rights. Typical assertion skills involve the ability to make requests; to refuse requests; to express opinions; to express positive and negative feelings; and to initiate, continue, and terminate social interactions. In assertion training, you begin by having the client identify one situation in which he or she wants to be more assertive, and then identify what assertive behaviors are involved and what the client would like to say or to do. The situation is modeled and role-played consistently in the session until the client can be assertive without experiencing any anxiety. Then the learned skill is transferred to situations outside the counseling setting through homework assignments. Once the client is able to exhibit the desired skills independent of counseling, the process is deemed successful. Success at assertiveness will generalize to other situations, as well—that is, it becomes easier for clients to be assertive on their own without assistance and feedback.

As an illustration, suppose you are working with a young woman who expresses unease about her relationship with the young man she is dating. She reports that he physically "comes on too strong" for her on occasion, but she doesn't want to offend him because she really likes him. In light of the epidemic of date rape in our society, this is an opportunity for this young woman to learn some protective skills that will reduce the likelihood that she will be a victim of sexual assault, either with this present boyfriend or in her future. In such an instance, you must first help your client identify the very first cues that her consciousness gives her that she is uncomfortable, probably using some visualization work with this client. Some cognitive work may also be necessary to address some irrational beliefs that interfere with the behavior she would like to execute. For example, she may be reluctant to make her boyfriend angry because he may break up with her, and this is perceived by her as a loss. Only after these issues have been addressed are you ready to move to skill development. This is an important point: Often clients have fears and thoughts that undercut their ability to act. Counselors must address these first, or behavioral interventions will fail because they are premature. Once it is appropriate to proceed, you work with your client to imagine the kind of situation where she has difficulty being assertive, model more assertive responses, have your client practice new behaviors, offer feedback, and so on. Finally, with this and many other behaviors, it is desirable for the client to practice her new skills in less personally vulnerable situations than those posed by her boyfriend. For example, she may say no to a friend who wants her to see a movie that she has already seen and didn't particularly like, something she wouldn't do in the past. Practice in the real world, noting reactions (and perhaps recording them in a journal), and discussing progress with you as her counselor are important steps that assist her in reaching her ultimate goal.

CASE ILLUSTRATION OF SKILL TRAINING

The Case of Andrew

Andrew is a 27-year-old Caucasian male who lives in a group home for persons with intellectual challenges. The home supervisor, Phil, has suggested to Andrew that he might want to talk to the counselor about improving some social skills. Phil reports that Andrew is very timid in the home, and this leads others to take advantage of him. When Andrew lived at home, his parents were overly protective of him, made all decisions for him, and took care of all interactions with the outside world. After Andrew's father had a heart attack, his parents decided that Andrew needed to be prepared to live separately from them, and applied for him to enter this residence. Andrew has been here for four months. He says that he's happy enough, likes the other residents, and doesn't mind that they tease him. Phil, however, suggests that he might not always like his apartment mates in the future and that he might want to learn additional ways of interacting. Andrew agrees that this would be okay with him.

Fred, the counselor who is assigned to the residence, first explained the process of skill training, noting that it involves a good bit of role-playing. Andrew thought that sounded like fun. Fred also asked if he could involve Phil in a session or two, and Andrew liked that idea a lot. With Phil's help, Fred and Andrew came up with a list of incidences in the residence where Andrew might have been at a disadvantage because of a lack of skills. Some of these involved assertiveness; others were more about Andrew's inexperience in social situations that added to his reputation as an outsider.

Eventually, Andrew and Fred identified several "moments" (again, with some help from Phil) that had occurred in the past few weeks where social skills were lacking. Once they had their list, Fred worked with Andrew to put them in order from easier to most difficult. At this point, Andrew was ready to start working with the first situation on the list. Fred proceeded to do role-plays with Andrew for the easiest situation. Fred played Andrew in these role-plays to model new skills. Andrew then practiced the skill, and reported that this was more fun than he expected. Fred followed each practice session with pointers. They then identified a situation that was likely to occur within the next day where Andrew could practice his new skill. With Andrew's permission, Phil was recruited to monitor Andrew's progress and would spend a few minutes in each subsequent counseling session to inform Fred how Andrew was doing. According to Phil at the third such briefing, Andrew had made a new friend in the residence and things were going quite well. Andrew's smile indicated that he agreed.

There is a tendency during skill training for counselors to terminate role-playing with too few trials, possibly because the counselor assumes clients are more comfortable with the new skills than they really are. The counselor may also want to discuss how the client can handle unexpected or varied responses from the other party who is involved in the scenario. For example, in Andrew's situation, Andrew had little experience to draw on to predict others' responses. Therefore, Fred had to role-play multiple responses to each of Andrew's emerging skills in order to enhance the likelihood that things would go well when Andrew tried them out with other residents.

Anxiety Reduction Methods

Many clients who seek help do so because of strong negative emotions labeled as fear or anxiety. Researchers have identified several types of anxiety, including *somatic anxiety*, which may manifest itself in body sensations such as stomach butterflies, sweaty palms, and rapid pulse rate; *cognitive anxiety*, which may be apparent in an inability to concentrate or in intrusive, repetitive, panicky, or catastrophic thoughts; and *performance* or *behavioral anxiety*, typically manifested by avoidance of the anxiety-arousing situation.

Some anxiety is believed to be helpful and can actually lead to successful performance; however, when it reaches an intolerable or uncomfortable level, a person should seek help for it. Various strategies are used for anxiety reduction. In this chapter, we describe two of the more common behavioral interventions: relaxation training and systematic desensitization.

RELAXATION TRAINING. The most common form of relaxation training used by behavioral counselors is called *progressive relaxation* or *muscle relaxation* (Jacobson, 1939). Muscle relaxation has long been used to treat, or complement other treatments for, a wide variety of problems, including generalized anxiety and stress, headaches and psychosomatic pain, insomnia, and chronic illnesses such as hypertension and diabetes. Relaxation training is often used as an adjunct to short-term counseling. Relaxation can be an effective way of establishing rapport and a sense of trust in the counselor's competence. Muscle relaxation is also a major component of systematic desensitization, which we discuss in the next section.

The basic premise of using muscle relaxation to treat anxiety is that muscle tension exacerbates or adds to anxiety and stress; in addition, relaxation and anxiety are not compatible states. Consequently, an individual can experience a reduction in felt anxiety by causing relaxation to occur in muscle groups on cue or by using self-instructions. The procedure involves training clients to contract and then relax various muscle groups, to recognize differences between sensations of muscle contraction and relaxation, and to induce greater relaxation through the release of muscle tension and suggestion. Suggestion is enhanced by counselor comments throughout the procedure, directing the client's attention to pleasant (relaxed) sensations, heavy or warm sensations, and so on. After going through the procedure several times with the counselor's assistance, clients are encouraged to practice it on their own, daily if possible, and often with the use of recorded instructions as a guide. (Commercially prepared relaxation CDs and DVDs are available, as are models on the Web, or you can suggest that the client record the session in which you are teaching the client how to relax muscle groups on their smart phone or another device so they have it at home to use for practice.)

Relaxation training should occur in a quiet environment free of distracting light, noise, and interruptions. If possible, the client should lie on a couch, a reclining chair, or a pad on the floor. (This latter option is most practical when working with a relaxation training group.) The counselor uses a quiet, modulated tone of voice when delivering the relaxation instructions. Each step in the process (tensing and relaxing a specific muscle) takes about 10 seconds, with a 10-second pause between each step. The entire procedure takes 20 to 30 minutes, and it is important not to rush. The process is illustrated next.

Tension Release through Muscle Relaxation

First, let your body relax. Close your eyes and visualize your body letting go. [Pause] Now we are going to the muscles of your face. First, smile as broadly as you can. Tighter. Relax. [Pause] Good. Now again, smile. Smile. [Pause] Relax. Now your eyes and forehead. Scrunch them as tightly as you can. Like a prune. Tighter. [Pause] Relax. Good. Note the difference between the tension and relaxation. Feel the warmth flow into the muscles as you relax. Now, again, make a prune face. Tighter. [Pause] Relax. Relax.

Let all of the muscles in your face relax. Around your eyes, your brow, around your mouth. Feel your face becoming smoother as you let go. [Pause] Feel your face become more and more relaxed.

Now, focus on your hands. Clench them into fists and make the fists tight . . . tighter. Study the tension in your hands as you tighten them. [Pause] Now release them. Relax your hands and let them rest. [Pause] Note the difference between the tension and the relaxation. [Pause] Now, tighten your hands into fists again. Tighter . . . tighter. Relax. Let them go. Feel the tension drain out of your hands as they release. [Pause]

Now bend both hands back at the wrists so the muscles in your lower arms tighten. Tighter . . . Relax. Again, feel the tension flow out of your arms and hands. As the tension releases, a warmth enters your muscles to replace the tension. Try to recognize the warmth flowing in. [Pause] Bend both hands back and tense your lower arms again. Tighter. Relax. Feel the warmth replacing the tension. Relax further. Deeper. Good.

Now we will move to your upper arms. Tighten your biceps by pulling your bended arms to your chest. Tighter. Tighter. [Pause] Relax. Let your arms drop. Let the tension flow out. Let the warmth flow in. Relax. Deeper. Try to reach an even deeper level of relaxation of your arms.

And now your shoulders. Shrug your shoulders and try to touch them to your ears. Feel and hold the tension. Tighter. [Pause] Now relax. Relax. Let go. Feel the tension leave. Deeper. Good. Tighten your shoulders again. [Pause] Relax. [Pause] Relax. Feel all of

the muscles in your hands, arms, shoulders, face. Feel them letting go. Deeper into relaxation. Deeper.

As these muscles relax, direct your attention to your chest muscles. Tense them. Tighter. [Pause] Relax. Again. Pull your chest muscles tighter and tighter. Tighter. [Pause] Relax, relax. [Pause] Now your stomach muscles. Tighten your stomach. Harder. Tighter. [Pause] Relax. Feel the tension flow out of those muscles. Feel them grow softer. Relax. Feel the warmth. Relax. [Pause] Now tense the stomach muscles again. Good. Tighter. Relax, relax. Feel the difference. Good.

Focus now on your buttocks. Tense your buttocks by holding them in or contracting them. Feel the tension. Tighter. Relax. [Pause] Now tighten them again. Tighter. [Pause] Relax. Let your whole body go. Feel the tension flow out of your body. Feel the warmth flow into your body. Feel the warmth pushing the tension out. Let go. Relax. [Pause]

Now locate your legs. Tighten your calf muscles now by pointing your toes toward your head. Tighten them. Relax. Let your feet drop. Feel the muscles letting go. Again now. Tighten your calf muscles. Point your toes toward your head. Tighter. [Pause] Relax. Good. Feel the muscles go soft, smooth, warm.

Stretch both legs out from you. Reach as far as you can with your legs. Extend them. Extend them. [Pause] Relax. Let them drop. Feel the difference in your muscles. Feel the leg muscles relax. Concentrate on the feeling. Now stretch your legs again. Point your toes. Extend, extend. [Pause] Relax. Drop your feet. Relax. Deeper. Feel the warmth rush in. Let the tension go. Let your legs relax even deeper. Let them relax deeper still. Feel your whole body letting go. Feel it. Remember the feeling. Relax.

Now I am going to go over all of the muscle groups again. As I name each group, try to notice whether there is any tension left in the muscle. If there is, let it go. Let the muscle go completely soft. Think of draining all of the tension out. Focus on your face. Explore your face for tension. If you feel any, drain it out. Let the face soften, become smooth. Your hands. Let the tension drip from your fingertips. Visualize it dripping out, draining from your hands, your arms. [Pause] Your shoulders. Is there any tightness, tension there? If so, let it loose. Open the gates and let it flow outward, filling the space with warmth. Now your chest. Let your mind explore for any tension. Your stomach. Let the tightness go. Softer. Your buttocks. [Pause] If you find any tension in your buttocks, let it flow out. Down through your legs, your calves, your feet to your toes. Let all of the tension go. Sit quietly for a moment. Experience the relaxation, the tension is gone. Your body feels heavy, soft, relaxed. [Pause] With your eyes still closed, record this memory in your mind. What it feels like to be so relaxed. [Pause]

Now, before you open your eyes, think about how relaxed you are. Think of a scale from 0 to 5, where 0 is complete relaxation, no tension. A 5 is extreme tension, no relaxation. Tell me where you place yourself on that scale right now.

SYSTEMATIC DESENSITIZATION. *Systematic desensitization* is an anxiety-reduction intervention developed by Wolpe (1958, 1990) and based on the learning principles of classical conditioning. This type of learning involves the *pairing* (occurring close together) of a neutral event or stimulus with a stimulus that already elicits or causes a reflexive response, such as fear. Desensitization uses *counterconditioning*—the use of learning to substitute one type of response for another—to desensitize clients to higher levels of fear or anxiety. In desensitization, a counteracting stimulus such as relaxation is used to replace anxiety on a step-by-step basis. Wolpe (1982) explains this process:

> After a physiological state inhibiting anxiety has been induced in the [client] by means of muscle relaxation, [the client] is exposed to a weak anxiety-arousing stimulus for a few seconds. If the exposure is repeated, the stimulus progressively loses its ability to evoke anxiety. Successively stronger stimuli are then similarly treated. (p. 150)

Desensitization is often the treatment of choice for phobias (experienced fear in a situation in which there is no obvious external danger) or any other disorders arising from specific external events. It is particularly useful in instances in which the client has sufficient skills to cope with the situation or perform a desired response, but avoids doing so or performs below par because of interfering anxiety and accompanying arousal.

However, desensitization is inappropriate when the target situation is inherently dangerous (such as mountain climbing) or when the person lacks appropriate skills to handle the target situation. In the latter case, modeling, rehearsal, and skill-training approaches are more desirable. Counselors can determine whether a particular client's anxiety is irrational or is the result of a truly dangerous situation or a skills deficit by engaging in a careful assessment of the presenting problem. Effective desensitization usually also requires that a client be able to relax and to engage in imagery, although occasionally responses other than relaxation or imagery are used in the intervention.

The intervention involves three basic steps and takes about 10 to 30 sessions, on average, to complete, depending on the client, the problem, and the intensity of the anxiety:

1. Training in deep muscle relaxation
2. Construction of a hierarchy representing emotion-provoking situations
3. Graduated pairing through imagery of the items on the hierarchy with the relaxed state of the client

In addition to these three, a fourth step is often added, which is to test out one's progress *in vivo*—that is, with the actual feared circumstance. For example, a client who has developed a fear of driving after an accident may begin by turning on her car and backing up to the end of her driveway as a first step. If this is too stressful, she may begin with her husband in the car with her at first. Each successive step is discussed with the counselor to review any level of anxiety that occurs. If necessary, imagery work is repeated until such time that the client reports virtually no anxiety.

Training in deep muscle relaxation follows the procedure discussed earlier. If the client is unable to engage in muscle relaxation, some other form of relaxation training, such as that associated with yoga or meditation, may be used.

HIERARCHY CONSTRUCTION. *Hierarchy construction* involves identification of various situations that evoke the conditioned emotion to be desensitized, such as anxiety or fear. It may also involve something extrinsic to the client, such as snakes or airplanes, as well as something intrinsic, such as feelings of losing control. The counselor and client can discuss these situations in the counseling sessions, and the client can also keep track of them as they occur *in vivo* by using notes. As each situation is identified, it is listed separately on a small index card.

Three possible types of hierarchies can be used in desensitization, depending on the parameters and nature of the client's problem: spatio-temporal, thematic, or personal. The *spatio-temporal hierarchy* consists of items that relate to physical or spatial dimensions, such as distance from a feared object, or time dimensions, such as time remaining before a feared or avoided situation (e.g., taking a test). Spatio-temporal hierarchies are particularly useful in reducing client anxiety about a particular stimulus object, event, or person.

Thematic hierarchies consist of items representing different parameters surrounding the emotion-provoking situation. For example, a client's fear of heights may be greater or less depending on the contextual cues surrounding the height situation (e.g., a cliff with no guardrail) and not just one's distance from the ground; or a client's social anxiety may vary with the type and nature of various interpersonal situations.

Personal hierarchies consist of items representing memories or uncomfortable ruminations about a specific person or situation with which the client has some personal history. Personal hierarchies can be quite useful in desensitizing a client to conditioned emotions produced either by a loss-related situation (e.g., loss of one's job) or dissolution of a relationship (e.g., by death, divorce, separation). Personal hierarchies can also be used to countercondition a client's avoidance behavior to, for example, a particular person who has become aversive to the client. A typical personal hierarchy might begin with an item that has almost no effect on the client's anxiety, and then move up a scale of anxiety stimuli to the point where the client typically reacts with high anxiety. Possible sources of client anxiety include sensitivity to criticism, fear of losing a personal relationship, and fear of looking stupid.

Regardless of which type of hierarchy is used, each usually consists of 10 to 20 different items. After each item is listed on a separate index card, the index cards are arranged by the client in order from the lowest or least anxiety-provoking to the highest or most anxiety-provoking. The ordering process is also facilitated by a particular scaling and spacing method. Although there are several possible scaling methods, the most commonly used is the *Subjective Units of Disturbance Scale (SUDS;* Wolpe & Lazarus, 1966). The scale ranges from 0 to 100: 0 represents absolute calm or no emotion; 100 represents panic or extreme emotion. The client is asked to specify a number between 0 and 100 that best represents the intensity of his or her reaction for each item. Effective hierarchies usually consist of items at all levels of the SUDS. If there are more than 10 points between any two items, probably another item should be inserted.

After the hierarchy has been constructed and you have trained the client in muscle relaxation or some variation thereof, you are ready to begin the pairing process. This aspect of systematic desensitization can be summarized in the following steps adapted from Wolpe (1990):

1. You and your client discuss and agree on a signaling process that the client can use to let you know if and when anxiety begins to be felt. A common signaling system is to have the client raise an index finger if any anxiety (or other conditioned emotion) is experienced.

2. You then use the exercise to induce a state of relaxation for the client.

3. When your client is deeply relaxed, you describe the first (least emotion-provoking) item on the hierarchy to the client and ask him or her to imagine that item. The first time, you present the item only briefly, for about 10 seconds, provided the client does not signal anxiety first. If the client remains relaxed, you instruct him or her to stop visualizing the scene and either to relax or to imagine a pleasant (or comforting) scene (e.g., a sandy beach in summer). Stay with this scene for about 30 seconds.

4. Return to the first anxiety hierarchy item, describe it again, and remain with it for about 30 seconds. This second presentation should include as much detailed description as you gave the first time.

5. If the client again indicates no anxiety, you have the option of repeating steps 3 and 4, or moving to the second item in the hierarchy. Typically, an item may require from 3 to 10 repetitions before achieving a SUDS of 0. Scenes that have been desensitized in a prior session may need to be presented again in a subsequent session.

6. When your client signals anxiety present (by lifting an index finger), you immediately return to the relaxation process (step 2) until the client is fully relaxed again. Then you return to the anxiety hierarchy at a lower level (one where the client experienced no anxiety) and begin the process again. Gradually, you work back to the hierarchy level where anxiety was experienced. If anxiety is experienced again, repeat this process. Usually within two to three repetitions, the client is able to move through this level of the hierarchy without experiencing anxiety. If a client continues to experience anxiety in a given item, Cormier and Nurius (2003, p. 561) note there are at least three things a counselor can do to eliminate continued anxiety resulting from presentation of the same item: add a new, less anxiety-provoking item to the hierarchy; present the same or the previous item to the client again for a shorter time period; or assess if the client is revising or drifting from the scene during the imagery process.

There is one note of caution regarding the manner in which the counselor responds to a client who is indicating no anxiety. The tendency is to respond to the client's relaxed state by saying "Good," or some similar remark. The counselor's intent is to communicate to the client, "You are doing just what you should be doing." However, early on, Rimm and Masters (1979) note that this could have just the opposite effect, reinforcing the client's not signaling anxiety, and thus disrupting the process. For this reason, it is better if the counselor gives no response as long as the client is not indicating the presence of anxiety.

Each new desensitization session begins with the last item successfully completed during the previous session and ends with a no-anxiety item. The pairing process is usually terminated in each session after successful completion of three to five hierarchy items, or after a duration of 20 to 30 minutes (10 to 15 minutes for children). Occasionally, however, a client may be able to concentrate for a longer period and complete more than five items successfully.

Because systematic desensitization may continue over several weeks, it is important that you keep accurate written notations about what you did and your client's success each session.

Notes should include what item on the hierarchy has been achieved, how many times the item was presented, the length of time in seconds for the presentation of the last two items, and the SUDS scores for each presentation. As items are successfully completed without anxiety within the counseling session, you may assume that your client will be able to confront them in real-life settings also without experiencing undue anxiety or discomfort. However, you should caution your client not to attempt to encounter the hierarchy situations *in vivo* until 75 to 80 percent of the hierarchy desensitization process has been completed successfully.

CASE ILLUSTRATION OF ANXIETY REDUCTION

The Case of Carole

Carole was mugged on her way home from a neighborhood bar and restaurant two months ago. After trying to put it behind her, she has sought counseling because her fears have interfered with her way of life. Carole is a healthy woman in her mid-thirties. She enjoys walking and running and reports that she lives in a "relatively safe" neighborhood. The person who mugged her had mugged another person the same night and was apprehended. Carole has never been afraid before, but now reports looking over her shoulder whenever she goes for a run or a walk, even during daylight, but especially after dark. Carole has a small dog and wants to be able to walk her dog in the evenings without concern. She understands that the mugging has affected her more deeply than she thought, has tried to rationalize her way out of it, but has not been successful. She is open to any other method the counselor can suggest.

Carole's counselor suggested systematic desensitization and explained the process. They began by creating a hierarchy of stimuli that appear to make Carole apprehensive. Once completed, the counselor used the relaxation method and subsequently began to introduce items at the bottom of Carole's hierarchy. Carole had a difficult time maintaining a relaxed state even at the bottom of her hierarchy. Upon further discussion with the counselor, it became evident that Carole had not really started at the beginning—that is, Carole started her hierarchy when she approached the door to leave her apartment. The fact was that Carole's anxiety would actually begin at least 30 minutes

prior to this, when she realized that the evening news was beginning and once it was over, it would be time to walk her dog.

Over several sessions, Carole worked hard to tackle her fears. She began visualizing daytime walks or runs outside and eventually moved to evening walks. When asked about an image that would help her return to a relaxed state when she felt anxious, she chose interacting with her dog, who always makes her smile. Therefore, when Carole would reach a new step on her hierarchy, felt some anxiety, and raised her index finger to cue her counselor, the counselor would direct her to think of Violet, her dog.

Carole's situation was complicated by the fact that she couldn't totally avoid walking outside during the initial stages of desensitization because of her dog. Therefore, at the counselor's suggestion, she asked a neighbor who also owned a dog if they could walk together, telling the neighbor about her situation and that she was in counseling to become more comfortable. This request was received well, and only when Carole felt ready for *in vivo* work did she start to take walks alone, first in daytime only, and eventually at twilight. She also talked about the mugging event with her neighbor, and they had good conversations about what is safe and what is not. Carole decided that she had been a bit foolhardy walking home alone later in the evening the night she was mugged. Therefore, while engaged in systematic desensitization, Carole was also letting in other opinions about her behaviors and altering them somewhat.

For example, she decided that if she had to walk her dog after twilight, she would only walk up and down her street. Counseling ended when Carole reported that she felt reasonably improved in terms of anxiety. She was pleased to report that she had encountered a man walking toward her recently as she was walking her dog and, although she was aware of him, her anxiety was relatively low. She felt especially pleased that she did not feel any need to look behind her after he passed.

Symptom Prescription: A Second-Order Behavioral Intervention

Symptom prescription is an intervention under the general category of *paradoxical interventions* that are used by some therapists. Worden (1994) notes that within the context of family therapy, removing a client's symptom may threaten the family's *homeostasis*—that is, the patterns and relationships that have become familiar to family members. We posit that this can also be true for individuals—that is, changing one behavior may throw clients off their game, so to speak. Therefore, as hard as they try to change that behavior, something appears to sabotage their efforts. Introducing a paradoxical intervention may be of help in this case, even if it seems illogical at first (as most second-order interventions do).

Telling a person to "be spontaneous" is a good example of a paradox. By definition, you can't *make* yourself be spontaneous. Sometimes, one way to assist a client is to "assign" the problem that, paradoxically, helps the client break through whatever is interfering with their ability to do so on their own efforts. For example, if an anxious client follows an instruction to deliberately become more anxious at a time that is convenient to the client (i.e., a time when it won't interfere with daily activity), the client's compliance with the instruction actually brings the anxiety under the control of the client, something that has eluded the client until that point. Discovering that the anxiety is controllable in this manner is a first and necessary step toward symptom control.

Types of problems that lend themselves to symptom prescription are those in which the client feels no sense of control, such as compulsive worrying. For example, let's say you have a client who suffers from insomnia and reports a long list of solutions that have been tried but found lacking. Insomnia tends to be accompanied by excessive or even compulsive rumination. The typical complaint is, "I just can't seem to turn my mind off when I go to bed."

Given this complaint, you might wish to prescribe the symptom, which would be for the client not to try to go to sleep even if it requires doing some other task. The point of this intervention is that one can be trapped into fighting oneself when trying to control a spontaneous process (falling asleep). Trying to control its opposite (staying awake) somehow manipulates the person's internal processes such that he or she can then let go. Yet another example, one that is used frequently and with considerable success, is to warn the client not to expect to get over a crisis too quickly. By prescribing the symptom—in this case, the client's fear that the crisis will not recede—the counselor may actually help the client recover more quickly. Such is the paradoxical nature of the psyche.

Symptom prescription is potentially a fruitful intervention. We hope it goes without saying, however, that any symptom that is overtly harmful to the client should never be prescribed. One would never prescribe that a parent shame a child or drink alcohol if one is addicted or any other such dangerous activity.

Self-Management

Self-management interventions are based on a participant model of counseling that emphasizes client responsibility and are specifically designed to strengthen client investment in the helping process. Self-management may eventually eliminate the counselor as a middle person and ensure greater chances of success because the client invests so directly in the change process.

Self-management interventions are among the easiest and most effective tools to use with clients. However, it is the counselor's responsibility to introduce and structure the interventions so that the client fully understands the assignment and the payoff. Self-monitoring, self-reward, and self-contracting are among the more frequently used interventions.

SELF-MONITORING.   Self-monitoring involves two processes: self-observation and self-recording. In *self-observation*, the client notices or discriminates aspects of his or her behavior. *Self-recording* involves using very specific procedures to keep a record of what the client is doing. Taken together, *self-monitoring* involves having your client count and/or regulate a target behavior—for example, an undesirable habit or a self-defeating thought or feeling. The process of self-monitoring seems to interfere with the target by breaking the stimulus–response association and drawing the behavior into consciousness or awareness, where a choice or decision to enact the behavior can occur. Most weight-reduction systems use self-monitoring as part of their weight-reduction plan.

The initial step in setting up a self-monitoring intervention with a client is selection of the behavior to be monitored or changed. Usually, clients achieve better results if they start by counting only one behavior. Self-monitoring seems to increase the frequency of positive or desirable behaviors and to decrease the frequency of negative or undesirable behaviors, an effect called *reactivity*. Self-monitoring of neutral (neither positive nor negative) behaviors results in inconsistent behavior change. For this reason, it is important to have clients monitor behaviors they value or care most about changing.

Deciding how to monitor the behavior depends on the circumstances of the client's environmental context and the nature of the behavior to be monitored. Generally, clients are asked to count either how often a behavior occurs or how long a particular condition lasts. If the counselor is interested in focusing on how often a behavior occurs, frequency counts are obviously appropriate. However, if the counselor simply wants to reduce the amount of time dedicated to a particular behavior pattern, then recording the length of time spent talking on the telephone, studying, playing a computer game, or participating in any other activity is appropriate. Occasionally, clients may wish to record both the time and frequency of a behavior.

Where the observed behavior is qualitative (e.g., better or worse, warmer or colder, happier or sadder), a response scale may be used in which 0 and 7 represent the extremes. The client is asked to rate the quality of his or her behavior somewhere between 0 and 7 at each interval. For example, the therapist might say to the client, "On a scale of 0 to 7, rate how confident you are feeling right now?"

The timing of self-monitoring can influence any change that is produced by this intervention. If the client wishes to decrease the frequency or duration of a monitored behavior (e.g., reduce the number of cigarettes smoked), it is more effective to record the event prior to lighting the cigarette. If the objective is to increase the frequency or duration of a monitored behavior (e.g., a positive self-statement), then the intervention is more effective if the client records the event after its occurrence.

Counting behaviors is the initial step in self-monitoring. The second and equally important step is charting or plotting the behavior counts over a period of time. This permits your client to see progress that might not otherwise be apparent. It also permits your client to set daily goals that are more attainable than the overall goal (successive approximation). Clients can take weekly cumulative counts of self-monitored behaviors and chart them on a simple line graph. After initial recording efforts are successful in initiating change, it is useful for clients to continue recording in order to maintain change. Often, clients' motivation to continue self-monitoring is enhanced if they reward their efforts for self-monitoring.

SELF-REWARD.   *Self-reward* involves intentionally giving oneself a reward following the occurrence of a desired response or behavior. Self-rewards seem to function in the same way as rewards that are external reinforcements.

There are three major factors to consider when teaching clients how to use the self-reward intervention: (a) choosing the right reward, (b) knowing how to give the reward, and (c) knowing when to give the reward. Rewards can be objects; contact with other persons, activities, images, and ideas; and positive self-talk.

Self-reward is a normal human behavior. You go shopping and see a new pair of exercise shoes and say to yourself, "I'm going to buy those and start exercising." The only problem is that the self-reward was not predetermined, and it was given before the desired behavior. We have already noted that if you wish to increase a particular behavior, you should reward yourself after the behavior occurs. Thus, the better approach is, "I'm going to start exercising four times a week. If I complete the first two weeks, I'll buy myself a new pair of shoes."

Self-rewards do not have to be objects—rather, they can be a favorite walk with the purpose of thinking about one's success. It can be watching a movie or TV show recorded on DVR. In short, whatever the client views as pleasant can be used as a reinforcement, as long as it doesn't undercut the desired change (e.g., it's not a good idea to smoke a cigarette as a reward for not smoking for two weeks!).

Clients can be asked to create a so-called reward menu that varies from small to quite large rewards that they value and would like to receive. These rewards can be further defined as *current reinforcers* (something enjoyable that occurs on a daily basis, such as eating or reading) and *potential reinforcers* (something that could occur in the future and would be satisfying and enjoyable, such as going out to dinner with friends or taking a trip).

The rewards clients select should be potent, but not so valuable that the clients would not give them up in the event that the target behavior was not achieved—in other words, the reinforcer should be strong enough to make working for it worthwhile and, at the same time, not so indispensable that the client refuses to make it something that must be earned.

If clients select material rewards that aren't portable enough to be carried around for immediate reinforcement, they might consider the following intermediate options as immediate rewards:

1. Tell a significant other about their behavior to elicit their encouragement. Social reinforcement can be very powerful in helping clients to find extra opportunities to be reinforced, and also to ward off urges and temptations.

2. Assign points to each occurrence of the desired behavior; after accumulating a specified number of points, trade it in for a larger reinforcer. Points (sometimes called *tokens*) are useful because they make it possible to use a variety of reinforcers and also make it easy to increase a behavior gradually.

SELF-CONTRACTING.   Clients who are able to identify and be responsible for their behaviors often acknowledge that their current actions are resulting in some undesirable consequences. They can see how they would like the consequences to be different. They may or may not realize that in order to change those consequences, they must first modify the behaviors producing them. Behavior change of any kind can be slow. Therefore, getting clients to make behavior changes is not easy. You must first obtain the client's commitment to change.

The behavioral contract is a useful intervention for gaining a client's cooperation and commitment. Behavioral contracting is used by a growing number of theoretical approaches but has been popularized by behavioral and reality therapists. The contract specifies what actions the client agrees to take in order to reach the desired goal. Contracts provide important structure for clients. In addition to giving the client a "map" to follow and steps that are within the client's ability, contracts also extract a level of commitment from the client. The contract contains a description of the conditions surrounding the action steps: where the client will undertake such actions, how (in what manner) the client will carry out the actions, and when (by what time) the tasks will be completed. Because these contract terms are specified in writing and signed by the client, we refer to this intervention as *self-contracting*. The most effective contracts have terms that are completely acceptable to the client, are very specific, and reflect short-range goals that are feasible. Self-contracts often are more successful when they are paired with self-reward.

In some cases, a self-contract may also include sanctions that the client administers for failure to meet the contract terms. However, the rewards and sanctions should be balanced, and a self-contract that emphasizes positive terms is probably more effective.

Self-contracts are very useful in working with children and adolescents because the conditions are so concrete. When contracts are used with children, several additional guidelines are applicable, including the following:

1. The required behavior should be easy for the child to identify.

2. The total task should be divided into subtasks, and initial contracts should reward completion of each component or subtask. Other steps can be added later, after each successive target behavior is well established.

3. Smaller, more frequent rewards are more effective in maintaining the child's or adolescent's interest in working for change than larger, less frequently administered rewards.

4. In the case of a self-contract, rewards controlled by the child or teenager are generally more effective than those dispensed by adults. For example, a child who completes his workbook pages at school by lunchtime may dispense a variety of accessible rewards to and for himself, such as free time, visiting the library, and drawing. This helps the child feel in control of his or her work.

5. Rewards follow rather than precede performance of the target behavior to be increased. The client must agree to complete the specified activity first before engaging in any part of the reward.

6. The client must view the contract as a fair one that, in an equitable way, balances the degree of work and energy expended and the resulting payoffs or consequences.

CLIENT COMMITMENT TO SELF-MANAGEMENT. A critical problem in the effective use of any self-management intervention is having the client use the intervention regularly and consistently. Clients are more likely to carry out self-management programs if certain conditions exist, including the following:

1. The use of the self-management program provides enough advantages or positive consequences to be worth the cost to the client in terms of time and effort.

2. Clients believe in their capacity to change. Because beliefs create one's reality, the belief that change is possible helps clients try harder when they get stuck or are faced with an unforeseen difficulty in their change plans.

3. Clients' use of self-management processes reflects their own standards of performance, not the standards of the counselor or of significant others. (One note of caution: Counselors sometimes suggest a goal, or society often seems to suggest a goal. Such borrowed goals work against self-management efforts if clients are merely learning how to behave in accordance with standards that are foreign to them.)

4. Clients use personal reminders about their goals when tempted to stray from the intervention plan. A written list of self-reminders that clients can carry at all times may prove helpful in this respect.

5. If the client secretly harbors an escape plan (e.g., "I'll study every day except when my friend drops over" or "I'll diet except on Sundays"), this should be made explicit. Concealed escape plans are likely to wreak havoc on the best-conceived self-management programs.

6. The self-management program is directed toward maintenance as well as initial acquisition of target behaviors. For this to occur, you must take into account the client's lifestyle.

7. The client's use of the program may be strengthened by enlisting the support and assistance of other persons—so long as their roles are positive, not punishing. Peers or friends can aid the client in achieving goals through reinforcement of the client's regular use of the self-management strategies and reminders to resist temptations.

8. The counselor maintains some minimal contact with the client during the time the self-management program is being implemented. Counselor reinforcement is quite important in successful implementation of self-management efforts.

You can provide reinforcement easily through verbal approval or by acknowledging progress. Have the client contact you regularly during the course of the self-management program. This enables you to provide immediate encouragement and, if necessary, to modify the program if it is flawed.

CASE ILLUSTRATION OF SELF-MANAGEMENT

The Case of Kareem

Kareem is a 14-year-old boy who has scored very high on ability tests but has performed consistently below his ability level in school. He admits that his poor grades are the result, for the most part, of what he describes as "not really trying." When asked by the counselor to define and give examples of this, Kareem notes that he rarely takes homework home, or if he does, he doesn't complete it. He also says that he rarely opens a book, and often had not studied for tests. As a direct result of a series of events that occurred in his neighborhood, Kareem sought out the counselor for help in changing his behavior. He has decided that he wants to go to college and was starting to realize that his bad grades would adversely affect this possibility unless he pulled them up. He is concerned because he doesn't know how to change what he refers to as "bad study habits."

The counselor supports Kareem's newly found goals and explains some of the rationale and process of a strategy called *self-management*. She points out that Kareem, rather than she, would be in charge of setting specific goals for his performance and monitoring his progress. She assures him that she will be there to help him start the process and to assist whenever he needs help. This appeals to Kareem, who states that he is tired of having so many other people on his back about doing better in school.

Because Kareem's present base rate for studying is almost zero, the counselor initially discusses some realistic goals that he might want to set for himself as part of a self-contract. She helps him build in a self-monitoring system and a self-reward process. Kareem decides to set the following goals and action steps for his contract:

Goal: To improve my rate of homework assignment completion during the next nine-week grading period from 20 to 85 percent.

Action Steps: To keep a daily record of assigned homework and to establish a time and place at home where I will work on homework every day. On Fridays, I will do Monday's homework. On Saturdays, I will be free from schoolwork, but on Sundays, I will review my assignments and organize my books for the next school day.

In addition, he completes a reinforcement survey and selects eight potential rewards that he could use to reinforce his action steps. Kareem includes a bonus clause in his self-contract, which specifies an additional reward any week he exceeded the 85-percent level of homework completion. His self-contract is illustrated in Figure 10.1.

Name of Contractor: _____ *Kareem L.* _____

Date of Contract: _____ *2/5/15* _____

This I Will Do:

Goals of Contract: To improve my grades by improving my homework assignment completions from 0 percent to 85 percent.

Action Steps:

1 a. I will keep a homework assignment book and will write down each homework assignment before leaving my desk after each class period.

1 b. I will transfer my homework assignments from my book to my record poster before I become involved in any other activity at home.

2 a. I will clear space in my room and move the old desk from the basement into the room as a working place.

2 b. I will start my homework assignment no later than 4:00 P.M. each day, and will not stop until it is completed (unless dinner interrupts my plans, in which case I will return to homework until it is finished).

3 a. I will indicate on my record poster which assignments I completed, and I will record the percentage at the end of the week.

3 b. I will bring my record poster to Miss Bancroft on Mondays at 7:45 A.M. and will review my progress before classes begin.

Rewards:

1. Watch the sports channel news at 10:00 P.M.

2. Listen to my music between the end of school and 4:00 P.M.

3. Play pool with the guys on Friday night.

4. Go to the mall and take in a movie on Saturday night.

5. Hang out with Kaleb.

6. Order a pizza.

Date contract will be reviewed: _____ *2/12/15* _____

Signatures: _____ *Kareem L. (client)* _____

_____ *Miss Bancroft (counselor)* _____

FIGURE 10.1 Behavioral Self-Contract

The counselor explains a self-monitoring system that Kareem could use to track his progress. She suggests that he use a daily log to record completion of each homework assignment (a large poster board with each school day of the month and a thermometer-like graph to show the percentage of his homework that he completes). She also asks Kareem if he wants to use any outside source to verify completion of assignments, but he indicates that he doesn't need that. Finally, she and Kareem agree to meet each Monday morning, and he is to show her his monitoring chart (which he could roll up and store in his locker easily). Kareem's log for the first week is shown in Figure 10.2.

Scoreboard

Name: _____ Kareem L. _____

Behavior Record: 1. _____ Management of homework assignments _____

2. _____ Completion of homework assignments _____

Week of: February 5

Day	Assignments	Done	Reward
Monday	English (read)		
	Math (problems)	X	
	Biology (lab report)	X	Listen to music
	History (read)		
Tuesday	English (nothing—read Monday's)	X	
	Math (problems)		
	Biology (read)	X	Listen to music
	History (questions)	X	Watch sports news
Wednesday	English (read)	X	Listen to music
	Math (nothing)		
	Biology (questions)	X	Watch sports news
	History (read)	X	Hang out with Kaleb
Thursday	English (study for quiz)	X	
	Math (problems)	X	Listen to music
	Biology (read)	X	Watch sports news
	History (questions)	X	
Friday	English (theme)		
	Math (study for test)	X	Listen to music
	Biology (read)	X	Watch sports news
	History (study for quiz)	X	Order pizza

Amount completed: 15 out of 19 assignments

FIGURE 10.2 Assignment Record

Kareem found the self-management strategy to work. Several conditions contributed to this outcome: He was highly motivated; he did not want others to be monitoring him; he chose a reasonable goal and action steps; he liked the counselor; the counselor liked him and was clearly supportive of his goal, his motivation, and his plan; and the counselor followed up religiously on the Monday morning commitments.

CLIENT REACTIONS TO BEHAVIORAL INTERVENTIONS

Behavioral interventions are often very appealing to clients, particularly in the initial stages of counseling, when clients are highly motivated and want something to be done about their situations. The specificity, concreteness, and emphasis on action that these interventions offer help clients feel as if something important is being done on their behalf.

As the helping process continues, some of the clients' initial enchantment with the procedures may wear thin as they discover the difficult and sometimes painful work of changing fixed and established behavior patterns. Successful use of behavioral interventions requires a significant investment of time, energy, and persistence from clients—daily practice, homework assignments, accurate record keeping, and so on.

To counteract any potential pitfalls or letdowns, counselors who rely heavily on behavioral interventions during the helping process must also generate involvement with the client through a positive relationship and commitment to action. When counselors use behavioral approaches, they must find ways to strengthen the client's compliance with the demands of the intervention. Compliance can be enhanced in a number of ways, including creating positive expectations, providing detailed instructions about the use and benefits of an intervention, having the client rehearse the intervention, and having the client visualize and explore beneficial aspects of change.

APPLYING INTERVENTIONS TO DIALECTICAL BEHAVIOR THERAPY

Behavioral Interventions Used in Dialectical Behavior Therapy

Dialectical Behavior Therapy (DBT) uses affective and cognitive interventions, but not because emotional catharsis or insight is the goal; rather, DBT is founded on the premise that once the client trusts the therapist adequately and feels validated and understood by the therapist, the real goal of developing life skills that will offer new and healthier options for the client becomes evident. Thus, behavioral change is the crux of DBT, and the word *skills* is used throughout the DBT literature to describe the desired outcome of the therapy (Dimeff & Koerner, 2007; Miller, Rathus, & Linehan, 2007).

For programs that have invested in DBT as their primary delivery method, group work is often the context for skill development. Therefore, the portions of this chapter that discuss role-play, behavioral rehearsal, and the receiving of feedback are descriptive of the interventions used by DBT therapists in their work. Of course, counselors who align themselves with DBT tenets can use these same behavioral interventions within individual counseling. In group work or individual counseling, once the stage of skill development has been reached in DBT, all of the interventions described in this chapter could conceivably be used. Each DBT therapist develops his or her preferred interventions for behavioral change, and the DBT literature describes the use of a host of such interventions across different clinical populations. The content of this chapter can serve as a primer for developing one's own repertoire.

Summary

In this chapter, we explore a variety of counseling interventions based on action-oriented helping approaches. These approaches focus on direct modification of a client's behavior and rely heavily on principles of learning to facilitate behavior change.

The modeling and rehearsal interventions we describe are major components of skill training programs such as assertiveness training, job interview skills training, and social skills training. These interventions are most useful when clients have skill deficits or lack effective skills for selected situations.

Anxiety-reduction strategies such as systematic desensitization are useful for dealing with the behavioral excess of fear, worry, and anxiety. Muscle relaxation is used as either a single strategy or as part of systematic desensitization. Prescribing the symptom can be another intervention to consider when the client appears stuck and unable to break through habits that are experienced as undesirable and the symptom itself is not in any way dangerous.

Self-management intervention programs are growing in popularity and success. Clients are put in charge of their change program and the counselor acts as a facilitator of that process. Common components of a self-management program include self-monitoring, self-reward, and self-contracting.

Behavioral interventions are very appealing to many clients because they offer specificity, concreteness, and something that can be done by the client. A major problem with continued use is management of the appropriate level of client commitment to ensure success.

Exercises

I. Modeling

Think of a commercial you have seen on TV, your tablet, or your phone that uses a well-known personality to sell a product or convey a message. What is it about this person that you think makes him or her an attractive model? What characteristics do you think the advertisers were considering when this person was chosen? Consider both individual and cultural characteristics of your choice. Discuss your choice with others who have also completed this exercise.

II. Behavior Rehearsal

With a partner, try the process of behavior rehearsal. One of you should take the client's role, and the other can assume the role of helper. Have the client present a problem in which the desired behavior change is to acquire a skill or to extinguish a fear. The counselor should try the behavior rehearsal intervention to help the client meet this goal. The tasks to remember are

A. Specify the target behavior(s).
B. Determine the situations in which the skills must be used or the fear must be reduced.
C. Arrange these situations on a hierarchy, starting with the least difficult or least anxiety-producing situations and gradually moving up to situations of greater difficulty, complexity, or threat.
D. Beginning with the first situation on the hierarchy, have the client engage in covert rehearsal of the target response(s). Following this practice attempt, ask the client to analyze it.
E. Using the same situation, have the client engage in a role-play (overt) rehearsal. Give the client feedback about the strengths and limitations of this practice. Supplement your feedback with an audio or video recording analysis, as feasible.
F. Determine when the client has demonstrated the target skills or reduced anxiety within the interview rehearsals satisfactorily. Assign homework consisting of *in vivo* rehearsal of this one situation.
G. Repeat steps D through F for the other situations on the hierarchy.

III. Relaxation

Using triads or small groups, practice providing muscle relaxation training for someone in the group. You can follow the instructions found in this chapter. After the procedure, obtain feedback both from your role-play "client" and from observers. Some of the items you may wish to solicit feedback about are the following:

A. Your voice—pitch, tempo, volume
B. The pacing or speed with which you took the person through the procedure
C. The clarity of your instructions

After you have practiced with this intervention and received feedback from another person, you may want to record yourself giving instructions and critique yourself.

IV. Systematic Desensitization

Pick one of the client descriptions from the following list and develop a corresponding hypothetical hierarchy for the client. Consult with a colleague or instructor after your hierarchy is completed.

Client Descriptions
1. The client is very stressed after the recent dissolution of a 5-year relationship.
2. The client becomes increasingly anxious about a speech as the time of the speech draws near.

3. The client becomes anxious in situations that involve other people.
4. The client becomes more anxious as she gets farther away from her house.

V. Self-Management

This exercise is designed to help you modify some aspect of your helping behavior with the use of a self-management program.

A. Select and define a behavior you wish to increase or decrease that, when changed, will make you a better counselor. The behavior may be an overt one, such as asking open questions instead of closed questions, or the behavior may be covert, such as reducing the number of apprehensive thoughts about seeing clients or increasing some self-enhancing thoughts about your helping potential.

B. Record the occurrence of the behavior for a week or two to obtain a baseline measure; the baseline gives you the present level of the behavior before applying any self-management interventions.

C. After obtaining some baseline data, deliberately try to increase or decrease the behavior (depending on your goal) using self-monitoring. Remember, employ prebehavior monitoring to decrease a response and postbehavior monitoring to increase a response. Do this for about 2 weeks. Does the behavior change in the desired direction over time? If so, you may want to continue with self-monitoring for a few more weeks. Charting and posting the data will help you see visible progress.

D. Work out a self-reward plan, or write a self-contract related to the behavior change you are seeking.

E. Continue to self-record the occurrence of the behavior during step D, then compare these data with the data you gathered during baseline (step B). What change occurs?

Discussion Questions

1. Behavioral approaches assume that much maladaptive behavior is acquired through learning. What is your reaction to this assumption?
2. In what ways does learning occur through counseling?
3. In using behavioral approaches with clients, to what extent do you think that you are treating real problems or merely symptoms?
4. In what counseling settings do you think behavioral interventions would be most useful?

MyCounselingLab® Assignment

Go to the Video Library under Video Resources on the MyCounselingLab site for your text and search for the following clips:

• **Video Example: Connecting Feeling and Behaviors** In this short video, the counselor skillfully emphasizes that if feelings are not expressed, they are likely to fester. How would you continue with this client to help him move from this point to being able to communicate more accurately in the moment.

• **Video Example: Challenging Clients' Thoughts and Behaviors** You saw this video at the end of Chapter 7. View again, and focus on the behaviors that must be altered in this family for things to change. Who would be the primary target of your intervention? What would be the next step?

• **Video Example: Helping Clients Become More Assertive** This video depicts a role-play between the counselor and the client. The counselor has conceptualized the issue as a lack of assertiveness in his client. Are there other ways you might conceptualize the issue? Could you conduct this role-play? Are there ways you might alter the intervention?

• **Video Example: Encouraging Client to Use the "As If" Principle** There are times that clients resist engaging in new behaviors because they don't feel authentic to them. In this session, the counselor introduces the helpful suggestion that feelings do not always come before behaviors; occasionally, behaviors must change first in order for feelings to change.

• **Video Example: Barbara: Parenting—Task Setting** This video demonstrates the use of a second-order intervention. Rather than punish a child for lack of responsibility, the counselor suggests giving him what he wants, but with clear parameters controlled by the parent. Do you see the "logic" of this approach? Is the approach attractive to you as a counselor?

Systemic Interventions

PURPOSE OF THIS CHAPTER

Chapters 8 through 10 discuss counseling interventions that have an impact on feelings, thoughts, and actions and might seem to imply that the problem lies within the individual client. Although this perception may be correct, it is not entirely complete. The systems within which we exist can be powerful enough to have a life of their own, so to speak. As systemic interventions are most commonly associated with family counseling, we use the family as our example. How is it that the mid-30s son always surprises his wife at how "immature" and even petulant he can become when in his parents' and siblings' presence for more than a few hours? Systemic theorists would say that it is because the roles and rules established long ago within his family of origin pull him back into habitual behavior. Although families are usually the strongest of the systems to which we belong, other places where relationships are patterned (e.g., the workplace, the social club, a place of worship) can all produce issues for individuals for which systemic interventions might have some promise. Often, this is because the roles we learned to play in our families of origin are available in these other settings. Although it is easiest to implement systemic interventions within family counseling, it is also possible (although more challenging) to work systemically with individuals. We attempt to demonstrate both in this chapter. It is also important to note that conducting family counseling does not rely on systemic interventions solely. Much of what was covered in Chapters 8 through 10 are used by family and couples counselors. System interventions, then, are those that are used when a change between or among members of the system is the desired outcome.

Systemic interventions draw from different assumptions than those described as affective, cognitive, or behavioral. Specifically, this chapter examines a variety of counseling interventions that assume (a) human problems are not based in the individual, but rather in the system in which the individual functions; (b) change in any part of the system affects all parts of the system, and thus affects the individual who is experiencing the problem as well as others in the system; and (c) systemic interventions must take into account not only the immediate social system but also larger cultural contexts, because they interface and often dictate the system's characteristics and values.

Considerations as You Read This Chapter

- Central to systemic thinking is the notion that behavior, including problem behavior, is rooted in systems. One criticism of this is that it removes responsibility from the individual for his or her problems. Do you agree? How might this affect the individual's participation in counseling?

▪ Also note that the systemic counselor seems to be quite active and emphasizes change rather than insight. What advantages could you predict from this approach? What problems could you foresee?

▪ To what problems in social units other than the family might these interventions be applied? How do you think the process would be different from that in which the family is the focus?

In systemic thinking, families and other social systems have inherent structure, dictated by rules, roles, boundaries, and patterns of behavior. These structural qualities inform individual members on how they are to participate in the family. Often, individuals look for parallel systemic properties outside of the family (although this is typically outside of the individual's awareness). Other strong interpersonal systems affect individuals as well; some may even be stronger than the family, especially if the family is itself a weak or disconnected (disengaged) system. What follows are some of the properties of systems.

SYSTEM PROPERTIES

1. *Cohesive Interpersonal Systems Develop a Self-Sustaining Quality.* The integral parts (members) of the system collectively seek to maintain the system, even when the system may be failing to meet the needs of an individual member; thus, the system's preservation (homeostasis) becomes the dominant motive for functioning. Healthy systems are flexible enough to adjust to individual needs. This is observed regularly as families adjust to the independence needs of maturing children. Less-healthy systems are more rigid and lack flexibility. A good example of this is the neighborhood gang that does not allow its members to act autonomously.

2. *The Internal Organization of the Cohesive System Is Defined by Systemic "Rules."* The term *systemic rule* is a euphemism for interactions between individual members that are so predictable that one might think a rule exists to govern the behavior. For example, the manner in which the father reenters the family system each evening (no one is to disturb him until he has had time to answer his email or drink a beer), or the manner in which a particular child is disciplined (only the mother may discipline Sal). Such rules contribute to the family's drive to sustain the system. When rules are broken, the violator may be dealt with by the entire system or by a designated enforcer. For example, if the father is a habitual grouch, family rules will evolve that attempt to control those stimuli that will trigger a bad mood. Strong pressure is exerted on maverick family members to keep them from breaking the rules that might lead to the father's bad temper.

3. *Most Individuals Function within a Network of Systems Embedded within Systems.* As you begin to conceptualize how and perhaps why the individual functions as he or she does, you must realize that more is involved than just the sociological family unit. Clearly, families also function within other systems. One of those systems is the family's cultural heritage, whether it is visibly obvious or apparent only through the family's ceremonial patterns. When viewed inclusively to include not only ethnicity and race but socioeconomic status, religion, ability, and so forth as well, it is clear that larger and interconnected systems influence the rules and roles within each family.

   Another way that individuals function within a network of systems is to focus on the different subsystems within the system. In families, for example, siblings have different rules with each other than they have with either parent. Parents have one set of rules as parents; another set as a married couple. This is true for other systems as well. We are different with our favorite coworker than we are with other coworkers. We establish patterns that are different when interacting with clients than with supervisors. Such systemic rules are necessary, or our worlds would be too random and devoid of purpose. That said, it's important that systems work for individuals, and not the other way around.

4. *Dysfunctional Systems Tend to Develop Rigid Boundaries.* The psychological boundaries that define the system (e.g., separate the family system from other social units, such as neighbors) identify and sustain the system. Because dysfunctional systems experience greater vulnerability, the systemic tendency is to become more rigid and resistant to change. Thus, the dysfunctional family finds change to be more difficult to accomplish than the family with more flexible boundaries. This can be particularly problematic when the dysfunctional system involves a cultural dimension in which family identity and solidarity are emphasized (e.g., the Italian American family), thus possibly magnifying the intensity of the problem. As noted in our reference to the community gang earlier, other systems can also be rigid. It can be argued that some systems are rigid by design—for example, the military, because much is at stake if persons resist system rules. It is testimony to the power of systems that so many former military personnel have a difficult time readjusting to civilian life.

In this chapter, we examine the use of systemic interventions, including the use of such outside of the family unit and with individuals. When counseling is sought, you must make an assessment whether the issue(s) presented by the client(s) is primarily systemic in nature. If possible, it may be necessary to include all relevant family members (often, this means the entire nuclear family). In doing so, you are viewing the family system (rather than individual family members) as the client. When treating the system, your conceptual approach must reflect an awareness of governing rules, structure, systems within systems, and other ecological factors.

When the issue appears to be systemic but you are working with an individual, it may be necessary to create a virtual system in the counseling room in order to work systemically. This is much more challenging (and some might say unlikely to succeed) than working with the system in its entirety. Still, with a committed client, systemic principles may still be of assistance to the client.

THERAPIES THAT STRESS THE IMPORTANCE OF SYSTEMS

The roots of family systemic theory date to the 1950s, when Gregory Bateson was first studying the relationship between schizophrenia and interpersonal functioning within the family. Stimulated by Bateson's early thinking, the next 20 years saw an explosion of new concepts on the functioning of family systems. These concepts began to crystallize into recognizable schools of family therapy: the object relations school, which includes writers such as Framo (1982) and Zuk (1975); experiential family therapy, represented by Satir (1972), who stressed communication within families, and Whitaker (Whitaker & Bumberry, 1988), who looked for opportunities for family members to explore their covert worlds in therapy; intergenerational family therapy, represented by Bowen (1978); the structural family therapy school, identified in the writings of Minuchin and Fishman (1981); and the strategic intervention school, which embraces a wide-ranging group of theorists and therapists. Strategic intervention gained recognition as a result of the work and writings of therapists associated with the Mental Research Institute (MRI) of Palo Alto. These therapists included Jackson (1961); Haley (1963, 1973, 1976, 1980); and Weakland, Fisch, Watzlawick, and Bodin (1974). Haley later established his own Family Therapy Institute in Washington, DC, where he and Cloe Madanes developed their particular variations of systemic thinking. More recently, systems theory has been expanded to include social constructivist models (Anderson, 1997; deShazer, 1991) and narrative approaches (White, 1995).

As noted earlier, families are the delivery mechanism for culture for most individuals. Therefore, it is impossible to consider any systemic intervention without attending to the ecology within which a family exists. As observed by Rigazio-DiGilio (1993), "ethnicity is a filter through which families and individuals understand and interpret their symptoms, their attitude toward helpers, and their preferred treatment methods" (p. 338). Therefore, it is important to recognize that the structure and social organization of families are strongly influenced by cultural and ethnic factors, thus producing wide-ranging variations among families in U.S. culture (McGoldrick, Giordano, & Garcia-Preto, 2005). What White, middle-class U.S. families find acceptable as therapeutic interventions may alienate or completely miss the mark with many other U.S. families. For example, Berg and Jaya (1993) note that systemic therapists often assume a middle-class standard of young adults fighting their way out of the family in order to emancipate or individuate themselves. By contrast, these authors argue that Asian American families view being excluded from the family as something to be avoided ardently; therefore, emancipation and individuation are much weaker concepts in these families.

SYSTEMIC SKILLS AND INTERVENTIONS

Relationship Building and Assessment

Joining with the Family

The process by which the counselor connects with each member of the family while also establishing neutrality across the system.

Structuring

Establishing ground rules within which the family functions while in counseling.

Circular Questioning

A method of gaining information by asking one member of a family to predict what another member's answer would be to a given question.

Generating and Observing Interactions

A method of choreographing interactions among family members in order to study the system and each member's contributions to the system.

Assessing Family Structure

Based on the results of observing interactions and so forth, determining the extent to which coalitions, triangulation, and scapegoating are operating within the family. Family genograms can also be used to arrive at these conclusions.

Assessing Family Functions

Using data collected to determine the various functions within the family, including how roles operate, how emotions are expressed, and how power is wielded.

SYSTEM INTERVENTIONS
Communication
Increasing Awareness

As an intervention to increase communication within a family, an intervention to assist individuals to understand the internal process by which they filter their reactions to others in the family.

Shared Meaning

Teaching the process of active listening between and among family members.

Role-Play

Asking the clients to engage in a typical conversation around a challenging issue for the purpose of deconstructing their communication patterns.

Negotiation and Conflict Management

For known issues of contention, counselors teach how to negotiate with another that leads to resolution rather than continued discontent.

Family Structure
Altering Hierarchy and Boundary Making

An intervention aimed at interrupting habitual and dysfunctional sequences and patterns so that the family must create new and healthier patterns.

Enactment

This intervention encourages family members to play out a chronic dysfunctional sequence so the counselor can then intervene with suggestions for improvement.

Prescribing the Symptom

A second-order intervention that places family in a double-bind by prescribing that they do that over which they have claimed to have no control. In addition, prescribing the symptom can help reestablish a functional hierarchy.

ESTABLISHING A THERAPEUTIC RELATIONSHIP AND ASSESSING SYSTEM ISSUES

The skills covered in Chapters 4 through 5 on therapeutic relationships and assessment are relevant to working with family and members of other systemic units. In addition, there are special skills that pertain specifically to systems that we cover now. In order to make our writing less cumbersome, we refer to the family most often as the *system unit*. We encourage you to consider application of skills and interventions to other units, including work units, social units, and residential units.

Joining with the Family

Joining is the process by which you "enter" the system. Paramount at this early juncture is for you to make contact with each member of the system and to communicate a posture of neutrality. The process can be as simple as a personal exchange with each family member, either verbal or in the form of a handshake or some such gesture. The goal of these exchanges is that each member has a sense of personal recognition by you. Everyone—even the youngest member of the family—matters, and each person's voice will be heard. Joining does not carry with it the conditions associated with an empathic relationship, but it is essential for a working relationship with the family. It is important that joining occur before you begin assessment.

In a statement about joining, Nichols and Schwartz (1994) note

> It is particularly important to join powerful family members as well as angry ones. Special pains must be taken to accept the point of view of the father who thinks therapy is hooey, or of the angry teenager who feels likes a hunted criminal. It's also important to reconnect with such people at frequent intervals, particularly as things begin to heat up. (p. 229)

Joining does not mean that you are catering to any particular family member; rather, it means that you acknowledge all family members, all of the time, even when a particular member's effect may be negative or overpowering.

Structuring

Earlier in this text, we discussed the importance of orienting the client to counseling. This is equally, if not more, important to do with a family or other systemic unit. Early in family therapy, Napier and Whitaker (1978) emphasize the importance of therapists winning the "battle for structure" with clients. In a way, this was an acknowledgment on their part of the strength of systems and the importance of establishing ground rules early on regarding both process and content. By how you demonstrate respect for each member of the family, what kinds of topics you introduce and encourage, and so forth, structuring is occurring. Furthermore, you must establish important process rules, such as the importance of attending each session, when sessions will begin and end, and what kinds of interactions are acceptable. For example, it is important for you to demonstrate in words and actions that bullying will not be tolerated and that escalating arguments will be stopped. As Patterson, Williams, Edwards, Chamow, and Grauf-Grounds (2009) emphasize, "an umbrella of safety" must be characteristic of the therapeutic environment. They also suggest that structure may be extended beyond counseling itself—that is, they advocate when needed that clients be advised to limit the discussion of certain topics to counseling sessions, at least until better communication skills have been developed within the family.

Circular Questioning

Circular questioning is an assessment and therapy tool that can assist you in recognizing patterns within a family. When using this technique, you ask one member to describe the behavior of another member around the problem. For example, you might ask Dad how Mom reacts when Petrina digs in her heels about the use of her cell phone. Then Mom could describe how Petrina engages Dad around the issue. Not only does this technique provide you with invaluable information about how each person keeps the problem alive by playing his or her part, it can give members of the system insight into how interconnected they have become around a particular concern. Patterson et al. (2009) stress the importance that thinking and feeling around problem events are captured as well as behavior when using circular questioning. Therefore, in our example, Mom might be asked how she reacts emotionally when Petrina resists her and then engages her father for support. It may be new information to Dad that Mom feels undercut by him or that she feels like a failure as a parent. Petrina may also become more aware of the effect her behavior has on her mother. Mom may appreciate more fully that her issues are more with Dad than with Petrina.

To make our point about the utility of systemic interventions in working with individuals, you could ask an individual client to report behaviors of others in the system as an issue is being played out. Of course, you cannot ask the client to report on motive, nor can change in others be expected, but by tracking of an issue covertly through the client's memory, at least his or her role in the system may become clearer and may lead to an intervention to address change. The client may also become more aware that changing his or her role might have the power of altering system dynamics in a positive direction. In summary, circular questions can give insight into what is called the *circular causality of the problem,* thus leading to a more accurate assessment.

Generating and Observing Interactions

Bringing a group together, whether a family or another system, allows you an opportunity to observe interactions between and among members, thereby adding significantly to your understanding of how the system functions. However, merely gathering the members together does not ensure that all members become participants. For that to happen, you must generate or choreograph interactions among members. The most obvious example is having each member react to a particular response by another member. For instance, because families tend to have a spokesperson who assumes responsibility for interpreting the family, you might ask each family member to add to what the spokesperson has described, or you might describe a family scenario and ask each member to describe his or her role in that scenario. Consider the following example of this dynamic.

A family was in counseling because an adolescent daughter had become unmanageable. The parents reported an incident when the daughter refused to go with the family for a holiday dinner. The counselor asked the family to go back in time and recall the event, comment by comment, as the crisis played itself out. Because of the safety of counseling and because of the ground rules, this was done more as an exploration than a true enactment—that is, the counselor stopped often and asked each person what he or she was thinking at that moment. One of the more insightful members of the family was the girl's slightly younger brother, who reported what seemed like an innocuous exchange between his sister and their mother as the beginning of the crisis. Once he said this, his surprised family agreed that he was right, although no one saw it coming at the time besides him. This kind of systemic untangling is extremely helpful during the assessment phase of counseling and can lead to meaningful goal setting down the road.

Assessing Family Structure

As noted earlier, systems are dynamic interactions of persons who have developed (and seemingly been given) roles and rules that make the system predictable. Prior to using a systemic intervention, you must make some assessment of the family structure and the rules that dictate interactions within the family. We discuss a few of these next.

USE OF SPACE. Prior to each session, counselors arrange a sufficient number of chairs in the counseling room so that each person has a seat. As family members enter the room, they are encouraged to sit wherever they wish. The counselor observes closely who chooses to sit by whom, what kind of negotiation occurs when two members want the same chair, or who moves chairs (increasing or decreasing distance). This early expression of family dynamics is seen as a metaphor for the family's system, including elements of dysfunction within the system.

As the session progresses and subsystems become more apparent through interactions, the counselor may ask specific family members to exchange chairs, thus physically altering a boundary by separating subsystems. Alternatively, if the counselor senses that the family has excluded a member, he or she may physically move to sit beside that excluded member, again realigning the dynamics of the counseling scene. As counseling progresses in later sessions, family members become aware of this realignment activity and begin to realize that such alterations do change the dynamics of the family interaction. In the assessment phase, however, the counselor is simply attempting to assess where natural alliances appear to operate, and where boundaries are drawn between family members.

RECOGNIZING COALITIONS. A mention of boundaries leads us naturally to the topic of *coalitions*, which are alliances between two members of a group. They can be very apparent, as illustrated by two persons who actively agree with or support one another, or they can be subtle, recognized only by occasional eye contact or a nonverbal gesture. Generally, coalitions are formed and directed against a third family member (e.g., mother and child against father, two children against third child). Coalitions serve a function for family members. A coalition may provide support to someone who seems powerless, or it may serve to isolate a person.

Some coalitions are both necessary and appropriate; for example, the coalition that parents form with each other to provide healthy parenting practices for children. Coalitions define boundaries and as such have powerful effects on family dynamics. It is important that group boundaries are recognized, acknowledged, and understood for their impacts. Thus, it is important that you watch for and recognize the coalitions and boundary making that occur in systems and determine which boundaries are functional and which boundaries have negative effects.

TRIANGULATION AND SCAPEGOATING. Both triangulation and scapegoating are attempts to involve others to diffuse stress in the family. *Triangulation* involves pulling in a third person when there is stress within a dyad. This is a common human activity that can be seen in the workplace every day (e.g., when two coworkers disagree, one seeks out the opinion of another) (Worden, 1994). This dynamic becomes a problem when it leads to coalitions (e.g., coworkers joining forces against another coworker). At the very least, triangulation always points to an inability of a dyad to work out their differences. When generational boundaries are crossed in family triangulation, it is virtually always dysfunctional. One common occurrence is the triangulation of a child in a divorce situation, in which each parent attempts to form a coalition with a child against the other parent. Such a dynamic is fairly easy to uncover during the assessment stage.

Another indicator that triangulation is normative in a particular system is if someone attempts to triangulate the counselor—that is, an overt or covert attempt is made for the counselor to agree with one perspective on the problem or, more likely, one perspective on *who* is the problem. Again, this is useful information for the counselor during the assessment phase and underscores the importance of counselor neutrality.

Scapegoating is a variation of the theme of triangulation (Worden, 1994) and is defined as blaming one member of the family for all the family's woes. This destructive dynamic directs all the anger and frustration toward one member of the family, with the message that things would be fine if it weren't for this person's behavior (or even existence!). Sadly, scapegoats often absorb this message and become increasingly disruptive, giving the system even more ammunition to blame him or her. Again, we want to make the point that this systemic dynamic occurs in other systems as well as in families. In all cases, scapegoats distract members of the system from dealing with real issues they have with other members of the system. Scapegoating is even more apparent during assessment than is triangulation. In fact, it is the scapegoat (also referred to as the *identified patient,* or IP) who is often the reason that a family seeks counseling. Usually, triangulation or scapegoating call for boundary renegotiation and, at times, a second-order intervention, both of which are described later in this chapter.

USING THE GENOGRAM FOR SYSTEM ASSESSMENT. We discuss the use of the genogram in Chapter 5 as a helpful assessment tool in working with individuals because family history is often so interconnected with present issues. When used as part of assessment with a family, it offers the family a unique experience to review their shared heritage. The genogram maps out the family's personal and private history of relationships (e.g., cut-off, divorce, teen pregnancies, abuse, depression) and helps the counselor identify those distortions that families tend to make regarding how one functions in systems (McGoldrick, Gerson, and Petry, 2008). It can also be used to locate resources in the system (e.g., strong role models, successful job histories, good parenting skills, resiliency). Estrada and Haney (1998) underscore the use of genograms to address cultural dimensions of the family, and particularly stress the use of genograms with immigrant families.

In addition to the information that can be gleaned by conducting a genogram with a family, the astute counselor also gathers information about how information is shared within a family; whose opinion of extended family members is considered most authoritative; what role secrets, scapegoats, and coalitions have played in the extended family; and so on. In short, conducting a genogram with a family is a rich assessment experience, and one that may prove to be uniquely eye opening for family members as well.

Assessing Functions of the System

Finally, Brock and Barnard (1999) stress the importance of assessing what functions are being performed well (even optimally) in families despite their troubles. They identify six areas of functioning that should be reviewed: (a) roles (including roles that complement each other, new roles adopted by individuals, and shared roles), (b) emotional expression (including the emotional tone of the family, how family members share emotion with each other, and sensitivity to each other), (c) interdependence/individuation (i.e., the extent to which autonomy is supported vs. connection to each other), (d) power (including how each family member has influence over other members), (e) communication (i.e., the methods of delivery and reception of the enormous amount of verbal and nonverbal information generated within families, and (f) functioning subsystems (i.e., those smaller units within the family that offer emotional and functional support to its members).

A challenge when assessing how a system functions is to resist being drawn in by statements of system *dys*function. Even the most dysfunctional system meets some of its goals some of the time. Making this part of assessment is both part of counselor neutrality and a strategic move, in that it provides the counselor with information that can be drawn on in later stages of counseling.

One final note about system assessment: The reason that families are most often the recipients of systemic counseling is that change of a system is difficult and requires a commitment on the part of members within the system. Families usually (although, sadly, not always) have high motivation to work things out and improve their functioning as a family, especially if the problem is serious. Other systems are only as strong as the commitment of individuals to them. Some work environments where it is unlikely that anyone will leave in the short term may have a high enough commitment to the system for such interventions to work. Systems made up of relatively healthy persons but with some negative interpersonal dynamics can especially benefit from systems work. However, an unhealthy system in which individuals feel little authority and to which they do not experience loyalty is a system that is unlikely to be a candidate for systemic intervention.

GOAL SETTING

Similar to the comment we made about assessment, we stress here that the information in Chapter 6 on goal setting is relevant to working from a systemic orientation. However, there are additional points to be made that are specific to working with a systemic unit.

Precursors to Goal Setting

Although each family member sees the problem from his or her own perspective, usually there is some agreement about the behavioral manifestation of the problem. For example, a father might see his teenage son's behavior as disrespectful, whereas the son experiences his father as overbearing. With the counselor's help, however, they might both be able to agree that they can define the problem as "the number of times they get into explosive arguments." Thus, the problem becomes the frequency of their arguments rather than each person's bad attitude. If the arguments tend to gravitate toward a specific theme—for example, the son getting home too late with the family car—then the problem could be defined as getting home too late. It is important not to rush this phase of counseling, and to be willing to negotiate and renegotiate until one problem (or at least one at a time) is identified as the goal of counseling and that the problem is not one individual but the results of interaction between or among individuals. In other words, the transition between assessment and goal setting is for the counselor to help individuals reframe the problem(s) as a system issue, not an individual issue.

It is also imperative that the counselor collect information regarding attempted solutions that have failed. There are several reasons for doing this. First, a great amount can be learned about the family system by hearing the members describe their attempts to solve their problems. This information is essential when attempting to identify an appropriate intervention for the family. Second, this discussion of failed solutions establishes the fact that the family does, indeed, have a problem that it has been unable to solve. Because most families continue to deny their problem even in counseling, this admission is important. Third, the process establishes that the counselor respects the efforts put forth by the family thus far. The counselor is saying, "I know you take your problem seriously and that you have already invested considerable energy in trying to solve it. I won't frustrate you by asking you to do what you have already tried without success." This part of the counseling process also gives the counselor another opportunity to watch the family operate and to determine the distribution of power in the family through such mechanisms as alliances within the family.

Setting Realistic Goals

It is not enough for the family and counselor to reframe the problem systemically; the family must also agree on what degree of improvement will be considered a therapeutic success. The description of *success* must be as concrete and well defined as the description of the problem. Using our previous example of father and teenage son, it is not appropriate to switch from "too many arguments" as the problem to "having a better relationship" as the measure of success (relationship quality not being of the same category as frequency). Rather, the goal might be "going from daily arguments to weekly arguments." Once the arguments are under control, it might be appropriate to work toward a positive goal, such as "spending more leisure time together." The consequence of reducing the number of arguments added to spending more enjoyable time together might result in having a better relationship, but this cannot be measured, and therefore is not considered an appropriate counseling goal. We encourage you to review Chapter 6 for more information about setting goals and subgoals.

CASE ILLUSTRATION OF REFRAMING FOR GOAL SETTING

The Case of Melanie and Chuck

Chuck was attracted to Melanie because she was his opposite socially—he is an introvert, so he admired Melanie's ability to socialize. Melanie found Chuck attractive because he was "the strong, silent type." She also liked his gentleness, which made him different from many of the men she had dated. After a year of dating, they were married. Both were optimistic about the future because each brought something to the marriage personality characteristics that the other did not.

After a year of marriage, Melanie found herself critical of Chuck when they went out with family or friends. Although he didn't think he was any different from before, Melanie described him as "distant." After some time, Melanie felt the same was true at home, and she believed that they weren't as close as they could be as a result. Chuck wasn't as forthcoming as Melanie wanted him to be. According to Melanie, he didn't share little things that had happened during the day, moments that she believed most couples shared with each other. In an attempt to open him up, she would ask questions—and then more questions. Chuck felt interrogated. He started to wish that Melanie and he were more alike. He also believed that Melanie viewed him as the person at fault in their relationship. This made him try harder at times, but also made him angry.

Ten years later, Melanie is openly harsh about her husband's patterns. "You never tell me anything! What do you think it's like to live with a stranger?" Chuck has become increasingly distant. Melanie's role is to nag. Chuck's role is to hide.

By the time Melanie and Chuck come to counseling, they believe that their differences are irreconcilable. They spend their time talking about their personalities and how different they are. They even see the same differences in their two small children, one being far more outgoing and social than the other. Although they are devoted to their children, they report that they have come to a conclusion that they each married the wrong person. Only after careful joining and assessment does the counselor begin to reframe the issues as systemic rather than *intra*personal—that is, she helps them unravel the patterns they have developed over time until they have become caricatures of their former selves. Melanie and Chuck are highly motivated to change these patterns and keep the marriage going for the sake of their children. They are enthusiastic with the alternative to the "blame game" they have been locked into for years. They decide that the first goal is to change how they interact with each other when they both return from work. Chuck suggests that he could call Melanie during their mutual lunch breaks and share something from the morning, and that they could pick up on this conversation, at least for a few minutes, when they both get home from work. Melanie approves of this plan wholeheartedly. Their counselor suggests that they do this for three of the five workdays in the next week and report how it goes.

Chuck and Melanie's difficulties are most certainly a product of personal qualities each brought into the marriage—that being said, they have been complicated and intensified by the couple's lack of awareness of the systemic properties of their issues. In other words, it is not Chuck's introversion or Melanie's extroversion *per se* that is the problem, but the predictable pattern of distancing and pursuing, along with the negative reactions to the other's role, that has led to the couple's unhappiness. Taking the problem away from blaming their personalities to blaming how they interact with each other gives each hope that they can change enough to have a satisfying marriage.

EXTERNALIZATION. Another way to reframe a problem is what narrative therapists refer to as *externalization* (Goldenberg & Goldenberg, 2008). What may appear to be a simple reframe can have a profound effect on families. The problem is described as existing outside of the family rather than inside the family as dysfunction or inside an individual in the family as pathology. The family then organizes around the goal of beating this external threat rather than turning on each other. For example, Goldberg and Goldberg offer the case where depression is reframed as attempting to control a family member's life.

The depression is described as both external to the family and is also personified so it can be "attacked" as an unwelcome intruder that the family wants to conquer. "By viewing the problem as outside themselves, the family is better able to collaborate in altering their way of thinking and developing new options for dealing with the problem, rather than merely being mired in it" (p. 424).

In conclusion, we offer reframing in our section on goal setting as it is central to helping family (and other) systems understand that systems have a life of their own, and individuals play their parts in keeping the system going as is. Once system members understand this, goals for system change lead to systemic interventions. That being said, we also remind you that reframing is introduced in Chapter 9 as a cognitive intervention, and as such, it can be used with system members as well, helping individuals "see" things differently, leading at times to profound and welcome change.

SYSTEMIC INTERVENTIONS

The remainder of this chapter discusses a variety of systemic interventions. The first cluster is the largest and focuses on the important tasks of communication within systems. Beyond that, we look at ways to alter the structure of a system in a variety of ways. Finally, we consider one important second-order systemic intervention.

Altering Communication Patterns

Family or group dysfunctions may be approached from a variety of directions. Sometimes the underlying issue appears to be a fundamental misunderstanding among members. This misunderstanding may relate to members' expectations, roles in the system, or responsibilities. When communication either appears to have broken down or fails as a result of lack of communication skills, the counselor may use a variety of interventions to teach or develop insight and skills for family or system members to use. When communication is the focus, most of the interventions consist of teaching methods of clear communication, analyzing and interpreting communication patterns, and manipulating interactions to allow for better communication.

COMMUNICATION SKILL BUILDING

Often, building communication skills begins with an introduction to basic rules of communication. These "rules" are really guidelines to sending and receiving clear and concise messages. Gestalt therapy, reality therapy, transactional analysis, and rational emotive therapy all emphasize these rules. In addition, programs such as the Minnesota Couples Communication Program (Miller, Wackman, Nunnally, & Miller, 1989) have contributed to communication rules training. Effective communications rules are fairly simple. They include (a) speaking in the first person singular, (b) speaking for self (i.e., limiting your communication to your own experience), and (c) speaking directly to the person for whom the communication is intended.

These simple guidelines often prove to be rather difficult to master, particularly when they run counter to the individual's habitual or even cultural patterns of communication. Consequently, the acquisition of a new pattern may require instruction, rehearsal, evaluation, and continued practice (as discussed in Chapter 10). For example, some people develop a communication style in which the personal pronoun "I" is almost never used. In its place, the impersonal second person ("you") or the collective ("we" or "people") is used. This is illustrated by a brief dialog between George and his wife, Beth.

BETH: George, are you going to going to take the kids to see your mother tomorrow?

GEORGE: You know the kids don't like going there.

BETH: Well, actually, I don't know that. I just know that your mother hasn't seen the kids in over a month.

GEORGE: We'll see.

The counselor might point out to George that when he uses such referents as "the kids," he doesn't speak for himself and own his own thoughts and reactions. He is speaking in terms that Miller et al. (1989) refer to as *underresponsible*. This notion of responsible communication is the same as the gestaltist notion of *claiming ownership*. In other words, if George says, "I want to talk to the kids about the importance of visiting their grandmother, even though I think the last visit didn't go as well as they hoped," he is taking responsibility for his position rather than using his kids as the rationale for what should be an adult decision.

Underresponsible communication is a style. It does not necessarily reflect an intention to avoid responsibility, although it can. The counselor might work with George and Beth to increase George's awareness of both his style and the consequences of his style.

COUNSELOR: George, when you said, "You know the kids don't like it there," were you speaking for the kids, or sharing your own thoughts?

GEORGE: My own thoughts, I guess. Last time we were there, Jackie complained the whole ride home.

COUNSELOR: Did you share that with Beth?

GEORGE: No, I don't think I did; I forgot about it until Beth brought up bringing the kids over there again.

COUNSELOR: Could you think of a more direct way to handle the situation?

GEORGE: Yeah, I guess I should have talked to Beth about it, and then maybe to Jackie too.

COUNSELOR: I tend to agree. You might also want to ask yourself if Jackie's reaction was a good excuse for you to avoid bringing the kids over to your mother's regularly.

GEORGE: Ouch. You may be right.

COUNSELOR: Beth, is it different when you know what George is thinking?

BETH: Well, I definitely like it better when George tells me what he's thinking. And I *do* think it's more his issue than Jackie's. She loves her grandmother, and I think she'd feel bad if she learned that George was avoiding bringing her over because she was in a bad mood the last time. And what about Zach? Why shouldn't he get to see his grandmother? I think George isn't really thinking of the kids.

The other type of communication style is the indirect message. Beth adds an indirect message at the end of her comment to the counselor when she says, "I think George isn't really thinking of the kids." By tacking this opinion onto her answer, she is actually communicating to George through the counselor. Speaking directly to the person for whom the communication is intended is responsible communication. When the message is made through another person (children, friends, coworkers), the communicator is, once again, using an underresponsible style. In this case, the counselor might turn to Beth and say:

COUNSELOR: Beth, you answered my question, and then you said something to me that George needed to hear.	BETH: He already knows now. [Beth resists being responsible.]
BETH: What do you mean?	COUNSELOR: I know, but this is just for practice.
COUNSELOR: You told me your opinion that George's reluctance for bringing the kids to see his mother is more about him and not as much about the kids. I think you really wanted George to hear your opinion. Is that right?	BETH: (To George) I've thought for a while that you just don't want to deal with your mother. You were a real bear the last time you took the kids to see her. I think the kids are picking up on your mood. I've wanted to talk to you about all of this, but I guess I've been avoiding it. I'm sorry about that part.
BETH: Well, yes, I guess so.	
COUNSELOR: Then turn to George and tell him.	

At this point, the counselor reviews what is happening in the two communication styles and how underresponsible styles lead to ambiguity, confusion, and frustration. This is the teaching time, and is as important as the rehearsal. During this time, the counselor can appraise each person's style, the consequences of that style, and its apparent effect on the other person.

Awareness: A Precursor to Clear Communication

Miller et al. (1989) offer an intervention that can form the basis of good communication, either with one's partner or anyone else. They introduce the Awareness Wheel, which helps an individual track his or her own reactions to another or to a situation. Their premise is that it's impossible to communicate clearly with another if one isn't clear about what it is that makes up one's own awareness. Although it's rare for us to be fully aware, by breaking down our levels of awareness, we can often identify the crux of our reaction, thus becoming more fully aware and in a better position to communicate with another. Awareness begins with *sensing* or receiving data into awareness (e.g., hearing what another says or seeing an expression on another's face). Next is *thinking* about that data (interpreting what one has received through one's senses). As already noted elsewhere, thinking is followed by *feeling.* Faced with thoughts and feelings, a person has some idea of what he or she wants; thus, this fourth level of awareness is called *intending.* Finally, the last level of awareness is *doing,* even if the action is doing nothing. For example, the following could be one person's awareness, a person we will call Peg:

Sensing: I see an unpleasant (irritated) look on your face.

Thinking: This makes me wonder if I did something to make you mad.

Feeling: I'm nervous and uncomfortable with that thought.

Intending: I'd like for you to be friendly and warm toward me.

Acting: I'll ask you if I did something to upset you. If I did, I'll apologize. If I didn't, I'll ask what I could do to make your day more pleasant.

Let us suppose, however, that the other person in the dyad responded thusly:

Sensing: Just as I was opening the door to the house, my cell phone rang and it was Joyce from the office.

Thinking: I was thinking that she calls me for the least little thing, and I decided to ignore the call.

Feeling: I was feeling resentful because I put in enough hours at work; I want some time just for me and my family.

Intending: I intended to put this behind me as soon as I could, but also to talk to Joyce about what justifies calling me off hours.

Acting: I approached Peg, but she looked anxious (sensing, thus beginning another cycle of awareness).

This description of a moment in a couple's life will probably be quickly and easily put to rest *if* they share their separate realities. If they do not, they can easily find themselves adding layer upon layer of miscommunication. The Awareness Wheel, then, becomes an excellent intervention to help persons unravel miscommunication. Although the application for persons in intimate relationships is obvious, it can be used in any setting in which persons report feeling misunderstood.

Before we move on, we must add that most of us favor parts of our awareness and are less tuned in to other parts. Some of us are highly sensitive to our affective life, but have a difficult time stating what it is we want (intending); others are action-oriented and quickly become aware of what they want to do, seemingly skipping over adequate thinking or feeling. In using this intervention, then, you can help individuals become more aware of the weaker parts of their awareness and shore them up both for themselves and for those with whom they wish to communicate.

A final point to make about awareness is that it is not always "neat"—that is, we can have more than one thing going on at the same time. This causes mixed feelings. For example, Peter just got a new job that requires him to relocate to Denver. He's really excited about the opportunity and loves the idea of living in Colorado. However, Peter had been dating Gerry for three months and they were really getting along well. Gerry has a career in New York and doesn't want to move. They decided to end their relationship, and Peter is mourning the loss of a potential partner. Therefore, depending on what is occurring in Peter's day, he may be in touch with the part of him that is happy about his new situation, or missing Gerry and what they had. Sorting out these conflicting internal states is important so his communications are not confusing to his new coworkers.

Shared Meaning

Accurate and responsible communication is only half the goal of good communication patterns. If a message is sent clearly and responsibly, but the receiver does not comprehend, then communication has failed. This may happen if the message is too threatening, or if the receiver is preoccupied or otherwise blocked from perceiving the intent of the message. The person trying to communicate the message cannot know this without some feedback from the receiver. In other words, the communicator must know if the receiver (a) hears and (b) hears accurately what is being said. This leads us to our second intervention from Miller et al. (1989): *shared meaning.* The shared-meaning intervention is a conversation in slow motion. The communicator (encoder) is asked to phrase a communication (restricting it to not more than two or three parts). After stating the message, the communicator asks, "What did you hear me saying?" The receiver (decoder) tries to repeat the elements of the communication in his or her own words and ends with, "Is that what you meant to say?" If the message was perceived accurately, the communicator can move on to the next phase of the communication. If the message was perceived inaccurately or incompletely, then the communicator corrects the misperception and the receiver tries again to state what he or she heard, again using words that are different from what were used by the communicator. It is essential that the counselor monitor the process carefully so that the encoder does not acquiesce until the message has been decoded accurately. For persons who have a lot of history and do not communicate well, it may take more than a couple of rounds for the decoder to get it right. Although seemingly quite simple, shared meaning can stimulate systemic changes by challenging communication assumptions that often lead to *mis*communication. Once persons in a relationship are communicating more accurately and feeling heard by the other, positive feelings can infiltrate other layers of their relationship.

This intervention can be used in individual counseling between you and the client. Many clients are unaware how obtuse their communication is until someone engages in such an exercise with them. If successful, this can encourage clients to bring the elements of the intervention into their personal lives. At the very least, they can become open to asking what others heard them saying, thus showing an openness that can have positive systemic consequences.

As already noted, communication is often complicated by history; therefore, even innocuous communications have the potential of kicking in systemic issues, making it difficult for those within the system to make things better without the help of a professional. For example, as a result of her past frustrations, Suzette may have come to the conclusion that her partner Barry does not care to communicate. This may cause Suzette to assume a defensive stance when she needs to communicate with Barry. Regardless of whether her perception is accurate, by communicating defensively, she elicits a certain kind of response from Barry. This response, which is in part the result of Suzette's approach, may give her further reason to think she is right. Such a sequence of events is obviously systemic. The counselor must recognize when poor communication is a systemic problem and develop an intervention that addresses the systemic issue rather than the quality of the communication *per se*. This can be done by observing how the couple (or parent and child, or any other dyad with history) interacts, identifying patterns, and intervening in the pattern development. However, if the problem is unique to one particular environment, the best means for observation is to ask clients to enact a typical encounter by role-playing.

Role-Playing

Role-play, or role enactment, has already been discussed in Chapters 8 and 10 as a useful intervention in individual counseling. It is also used in working with families or other systems so that communication patterns can be observed and altered. Thus, you may decide to ask a family member to role-play a problematic encounter, or to play the role of another family member in order to see how each communicates his or her position. The purpose here is to teach communication skills. Thus, role-plays can be used as a precursor to increasing awareness of teaching shared meaning. Clients are often surprised to learn that they are able to listen to a family member within the structure of counseling when they have had great difficulty doing so at home.

Role-plays are also used to divulge systemic structure (e.g., where functional boundaries exist, where there is enmeshment). These types of role-plays are typically referred to as *enactments* and are discussed later in this chapter.

Negotiation and Conflict Management

Many people find negotiation and decision making to be a time when communication is most likely to break down. In family counseling, negotiation is an ongoing process that involves both process issues and family issues. Consequently, the counseling setting provides an ideal opportunity for you to observe family negotiation skills and to provide strategies the family can use to improve communication and negotiation. It's important for you to enquire about ways each person learned to negotiate and handle conflict from his or her family of origin, thus opening up a discussion of familial and cultural differences that may be operating.

Marital conflict has been shown to correlate with poorer physical health (Gottman, 1993). Gottman (1991) also conducted a series of studies (with Levenson) that examine the specific role of marital conflict in predicting marital dissatisfaction, separation, and divorce. His findings suggest that there are a series of events based around conflict that unfold in predictable ways. For example: Conflict begins, and the husband becomes physically uncomfortable and stonewalls his wife by withdrawing as a listener and subsequently by withdrawing emotionally. The husband's stonewalling is aversive to the wife, and she responds by trying to reengage the husband. Failing to do so, she becomes critical and contemptuous and also withdraws, increasing her husband's fear. Gottman notes, "The husband's withdrawal from tense marital interaction is an early precursor of the wife's complementary withdrawal. When both partners withdraw and are defensive, the marriage is on its way toward separation and divorce" (p. 5).

Gottman (1991) found, however, that if tense marital conflict is offset by positive expressions of communication, such as "affection, humor, positive problem-solving, agreement, assent, empathy, and active non-defensive listening" (p. 5), arousal is reduced and the conflict is handled with better contact rather than withdrawal. Clearly, couples need substantial help in learning effective negotiation and conflict management skills (Gottman & Silver, 2011); however, there remains a need for a third party (the counselor) who acts as a mediator.

Family Meeting Activity.   Gottman, Notarius, Gonso, and Markman (1976) developed an intervention that helps build negotiation skills. Despite its name, the *family meeting activity* can be used with a variety of systems or groups in addition to families. The exercise is divided into three parts: (a) gripe time, (b) agenda building, and (c) problem solving. The counselor should preface the exercise by explaining that all family members can have gripes and resentments and that these gripes are viewpoints rather than truths. They are the way the individual views the moment, the situation, or the relationship. They can change and, if ignored, they can get worse. It is important that each person's viewpoint be respected and aired. The counselor can help ensure each person's cooperation by introducing rules for griping (Figure 11.1).

After all members have been allowed time to express their gripes (and this may require some encouragement from the counselor), the group moves into the second stage: agenda building. The purpose of agenda building is to evaluate the relative importance of gripes that have

Do state clearly and specifically the gripes you have about other family members.	**Don't** try to define yourself by showing that the other person is wrong.
Do be honest and constructive when you gripe.	**Don't** sulk and withdraw.
Do listen and accept gripes as legitimate feelings.	**Don't** respond to gripes with a gripe of your own.
	Don't assume you know what the other person means; make sure you know.

FIGURE 11.1 Dos and Don'ts

been expressed and select one or more that members believe should be remedied. The counselor is an active arbitrator during this process and thus helps members define specific dimensions of a particular gripe.

Having identified and defined a particular gripe, the group moves into the problem-solving stage. This is characterized by identification of positive behaviors that address the complaint(s) and the writing of a contract that (a) specifies behaviors each member will change and (b) specifies incentives designed to increase the frequency of desired behaviors.

In summary, this—as well as other interventions discussed in this section for conflict management—has the potential of changing the relationship dynamics (systems) of those involved. They also all refer to clients changing specific behaviors as part of the intervention. Therefore, as is often the case, interventions are a blending of orientations (systemic and behavioral) rather than representing one orientation exclusively.

ALTERING SYSTEM PROPERTIES

Thus far, we have focused on building interpersonal communication skills that have the power to change the system. These skills enhance the interpersonal repertoire of each person in the system and are transferable across systems—that is, if we learn to communicate better with family members through the use of shared meaning, we are empowered to communicate better in the workplace, in our other social groups, and so on. Therefore, these "systemic" interventions also have real benefits for the individuals who learn them as well. We next look at interventions that are more contained in their effects—altering the properties of one particular system.

Altering Hierarchy and Boundary Making

System structure refers to the patterns of interaction, the rules and roles that emerge to support these patterns, and the alliances that result from these rules and roles. All structure begins with family or group transactions that, when repeated, become patterns of behavior. As interaction patterns become well established, they begin to dictate how, when, and with whom family members interact. For example, a young child falls, skins his knee, and runs to his mother for comfort. As this scene repeats itself again and again, a nurturing alliance forms between mother and child. Thus, the mother assumes a nurturant (role) posture, and the child learns to seek his mother when hurt (rule). The alliance between mother and child defines a subsystem within the family.

All families have subsystems determined by interaction patterns, rules, roles, and alliances. The spousal subsystem is the obvious beginning point. When the first child is born, two things happen: The spousal subsystem accommodates a new parental subsystem, and the mother–child and father–child subsystems emerge. Subsystems become differentiated from one another by boundaries. Additional children, grandparents, and other family relatives develop alliances within the larger family structure to the point that many subsystems emerge, with individuals occupying significant roles within more than one subsystem. There is a random as well as systematic dimension to the development of family structure. Consequently, families are often at a loss to explain how certain rules or subsystems become so powerful or how they could be changed.

One important aspect of system structure is the *hierarchy* that has been created. Even in families who prefer to think of themselves as egalitarian, it is important that someone be in charge. During assessment, the counselor might realize that the children in the family appear to have power equal to that of the parents (flat hierarchy) or, in the case of what is often referred to as the *parentification of a child,* the children may have seemingly more power than the parents (incongruous hierarchy; Patterson et al., 2009). These situations typically occur when parents default on their responsibility to guide their children, are incapable of doing so for any number of reasons, or are misguided in their understanding of the capacity of children to bring themselves into adulthood. If the counselor determines that the hierarchy is flat or incongruous, the first chore is to determine if the adults are capable of making changes to empower themselves to carry responsibility for family functioning. For example, if parents are abusing drugs and this has caused them to default on parenting, are they committed to ceasing this destructive behavior prior to working to alter the systemic structure of the family? Once it is determined that there is commitment for change, reconfiguring the hierarchy virtually always requires boundary making.

Boundary making is an intervention where the counselor works either to make a boundary more permeable between people or subsystems or to make a boundary clearer. This can be done in a counseling session. Usually, homework follows to reinforce boundary readjustment. For example, it may be the case that an only child who is 9 years old has too much "say" in her after-school activities, whether to do her homework, when to go to bed, and so forth. The counselor may have noticed that she sits between her parents and often interrupts them when they are speaking either to the counselor or to each other. As a first step in boundary making, the counselor can assign seats so that the child is no longer sitting between her parents. The counselor can also establish a "rule" that the child not interrupt her parents during the session and facilitate the keeping of this rule. This, of course, is only the beginning. Boundaries are made in a natural setting, and this is where the real work occurs. The parents are asked to choose a behavior they want changed (e.g., bedtime for their child) and need assistance in how to make this happen, thus altering the systemic properties that have been operating until now. In effect, the counselor is helping the parents build a boundary around the parental subsystem, one that has disintegrated as their child has grown from infancy to the present.

The counselor can use space to accentuate boundary making. For example, if the counselor believes parents are failing to respect the sibling subsystem by interfering or invading the system, the counselor might invite the invading parents to join the counselor in an "adult observer" group in the corner of the room because children "think differently these days than in our time and may have solutions [that] we couldn't even imagine" (Minuchin & Fishman, 1981, p. 149). By creating an adult observer group, the counselor has pulled the parents away from the sibling subsystem and assigned them the role of observer. Because one cannot be an effective observer and participant at the same time, the counselor has created a new boundary by separating parents from siblings.

The counselor has other ways as well to manipulate the spatial relationships that reflect boundaries between subsystems. It was noted earlier that the counselor might use the seating arrangements in the counseling room as a means of observing how subsystems operate. By moving family members to other chairs, thus altering the spatial arrangements, the counselor also alters the spatial expression of boundaries. Imagine a counseling scene in which the clients are a stepfamily composed of a mother, teenage son, and stepfather. The stepfamily has existed for about 12 months. During this time, the mother has created an obvious boundary between herself and her son on the one side, and the stepfather on the other. By moving the stepfather's chair in such a way that he now sits beside the stepson, the counselor has made a symbolic intervention into the family system. This intervention can be extended by asking the mother to become an observer of stepfather/stepson interactions, thus encouraging the stepfather and stepson interaction to happen, and removing the mother from active involvement.

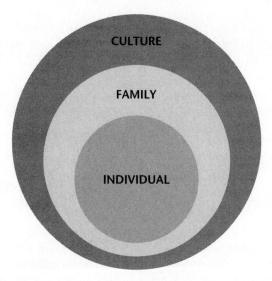

FIGURE 11.2   The Individual in Context

By altering family structure, the objective is to interrupt habitual and dysfunctional sequences and patterns so that the family must create new patterns. With the counselor's help, these new patterns can be more functional and constructive for family relationships as well as individual needs.

Szapocznik and Kurtines (1993) observe that in structural family work, not only must an individual client be understood in the context of one's family, but the family must also be understood in the context of its culture. All three of these contexts overlap, as shown in Figure 11.2. In these authors' studies of Hispanic families, they found that understanding of the family dynamics was enhanced when the families were viewed not just from a Hispanic context, but also from a culturally pluralistic or diverse context. For example, they found that the conflict in these families resulted often from parents who had strong generational Hispanic cultural alliances, while the youth in the families rapidly had become acculturated into a broader bicultural identity. The elders struggled for greater connectedness; the youth fought for greater freedom. Such a dynamic is a familiar one to many immigrant families from a wide range of ethnicities.

CASE ILLUSTRATION OF ALTERING HIERARCHY AND BOUNDARY MAKING

The Case of the Gloria and Bradford Brooks

Gloria and Bradford are recently married. It is a second marriage for Gloria who has an 11-year-old daughter, Denise, from her first marriage. This is the first marriage for Bradford. Gloria has been divorced for five years; her ex-husband sees Denise every other weekend. Gloria describes him as an "OK" father. Gloria and Denise are very close, and enjoy doing what Gloria refers to as "girl things" together. Bradford has been very supportive of their relationship, even though he admits that he sometimes feels like an outsider, especially when one of their "girls'" TV shows is on. Bradford states that he is trying to learn to be a good husband and a good stepfather all at once. Denise is polite to Bradford and reports that she likes him enough. Gloria says that it's hard on Denise because they had so much time together during Gloria's single days between her divorce and meeting Bradford. She is sensitive to how her remarriage must be hard on Denise.

Recently, Bradford came home after a particularly hard day at work. He was eager be with Gloria. When he got home, he found Gloria and Denise in the kitchen giggling over something that had happened to Denise at school. When he tried to enquire about what was so funny, he was at first ignored and then told by Denise that it was a secret.

Bradford stormed out of the house. When he came back an hour later, Gloria asked, "What was that all about?" Bradford told her that he was really trying, but the "Girls have their secrets" thing was getting old. He also shared with her that he had swallowed his pride when Gloria and Denise made the decision about where they would go for vacation next summer without his input, as well as other smaller decisions where he felt his opinion was not valued. Because Gloria really loves Bradford and knows how quickly things in a marriage can turn sour, she suggested they see a counselor.

In this case, the family system is still struggling to admit Bradford; furthermore, his entry thus far is in a position that is less powerful than his stepdaughter. Although it is understandable how all of this evolved, it is not a healthy situation for Gloria's and Bradford's marriage if he does not feel that he is part of the leadership of the family unit. Therefore, a boundary must be strengthened around the couple system so that family decisions are made primarily in this subsystem. This does not mean that Gloria and Denise will not have their own special space in the family. It is important that the boundary around them as mother and daughter remain. However, a goal should be that this boundary becomes more permeable than it is to date, and it certainly should be more permeable than the boundary around Gloria and Bradford. The counselor will work on helping Gloria and Bradford establish some new patterns that reinforce their special relationship as spouses and their responsibility as mother and stepfather of Denise. As a small change—but one that Bradford really appreciated—they decided on a Netflix series that they wanted to watch together and planned a schedule for doing so. They also agreed that any decisions that would affect Bradford would be made by him and Gloria, with Denise's input as appropriate.

Enactment

In the section on assessment, we address the importance of generating interactions among family members to see how the system functions. As an intervention, *enactment* allows the counselor to see the system in action and to intervene rather than letting destructive interactions continue. Further, once a negative interaction is interrupted, then the counselor can direct the interaction toward a more positive outcome (Butler, Davis, & Seedall, 2008). For example, perhaps the father in a family becomes angry and intimidating whenever challenged by his son, and this is followed by the mother attempting to silence her son and appease her husband. Having seen this pattern repeated, the next time it occurs, the counselor should intervene prior to mother entering the discussion, and attempt to have the father hear the son and respond without intimidation. Assuming this can be done, it allows mother to see that her role as peacemaker and silencer is not needed at this time. This allows the counselor to ask mother what role she would rather have in the family with both her husband and her son.

In the following family therapy case of Calvin and Jeannette, the counselor uses enactment as a means to generate awareness of each spouse's perceptions of their problem. The situation selected for enactment was the end-of-day scene, in which father and mother each arrive home from work.

CASE ILLUSTRATION OF ENACTMENT

The Case of Calvin and Jeannette

COUNSELOR: Calvin, I'd like you to produce the scene at home when you and Jeannette arrive from work. We'll assume the kids are also home. Place each person in whatever is the typical activity they would be doing. Do this without discussion. Merely place them in a particular space, and tell them what they should be doing. Do you understand what I want you to do?

CALVIN: I'm not sure. Do I just say, "Jeannette, you yell at the kids," or something like that?

COUNSELOR: If that is what Jeannette typically does, yes. And then go on to tell the kids what they should be doing.

CALVIN: Okay. Jeannette, you are sitting in the living room with a martini. Beau [7 years old], you are downstairs watching cartoons with Karen [9 years old]. Then Beau, you and Karen come to the living room when I arrive home. [Calvin acts as though he is coming in the front door of their house; both children rush up.] Now, I sit down with Mommy, and you start talking and demanding attention. Mommy and I are trying to talk to each other while you try to talk to both of us. [Both children somewhat sheepishly begin talking about something. Calvin and Jeannette try to begin a conversation, but children won't let them complete the conversation.]

COUNSELOR: Okay. Now, what happens?

CALVIN: Well, if Jeannette and I try to ignore the kids, they end up in a fight. If we stop trying to talk to each other, I end up mad.

COUNSELOR: Okay, everyone. Act out that scene that Calvin just described.

The family members begin to act out their parts. Just as Calvin sits down and begins to talk to Jeannette, Beau comes in to ask Mommy a question. Calvin waits until Jeannette answers, at which time Beau asks another question. Enter Karen, who proceeds to tell Mommy that Beau ate all the potato chips. Jeannette responds, and it becomes obvious that the focal unit is Jeannette and the children. Calvin, trying to look patient, asks the children to return to their activities so he and Mommy can talk. The children leave, and Jeannette turns to Calvin and tells him that the children need some parent time also after being away from them all day. Calvin responds impatiently that he needs some spouse time and accuses her of not noticing that.

In the discussion that followed this scene, Jeannette and Calvin discuss their reactions. Jeannette is somewhat surprised that Calvin wants relationship time with her but is unable to have it because the kids keep interrupting. She indicates that such interruptions didn't bother her as much as they apparently bother Calvin. Instead, she presumed that his reactions to her (this scene was a common one in their home) were merely reflecting a bad day at work. Calvin, however, says that he thinks Jeannette understands his relationship needs but opts to take care of the children instead. He assumes that her choice is in reaction to feeling guilty that she has been away from the kids all day. As they discuss their individual perceptions, each becomes aware of the other's needs, motivations, and misperceptions.

Throughout this type of interaction, the counselor also observes and looks for ways the couple might sabotage their negotiations. This process involves the recognition of dysfunctional sequences and the behaviors that maintain the sequences. It also includes recognition of boundaries and how they are creating or sustaining problematic behavior sequences. Diagnosing family interactions does not involve specific therapeutic interventions. However, you may want to point out the family boundaries and how they are operating in a particular interaction.

MODIFYING BOUNDARIES USING ENACTMENT IN THE COUNSELING SESSION. Having determined what sequences appear to be maintaining the dysfunctional interactions, the counselor proceeds to bring the family's attention to the sequence. In the following example, the parents attempt to deal with a 3-year-old child who is having a tantrum. The counselor observes and eventually intervenes.

> MOTHER: Wendy, settle down! [Said with emphasis. Wendy wails louder.]
>
> FATHER: Wendy, you heard what your mother said. [Mother places Wendy on her lap and begins to soothe her. Wendy continues to wail and starts hitting her mother. Father turns to the counselor and shrugs.]
>
> COUNSELOR: Aren't you going to do anything? Are you just going to let her continue to disrupt us?
>
> MOTHER: Well, do something.
>
> FATHER: [To mother] Let me have her.
> [Mother hands Wendy over to father.]
>
> FATHER: Wendy, stop now or you'll have to go to the other room. [Wendy doesn't stop.]
>
> COUNSELOR: [To mother] Does he really mean that he'll send her away until she stops?
>
> MOTHER: I don't know.
> [Father carries Wendy to waiting room and returns. Wendy wails for 5 minutes.]
>
> MOTHER: Don't you think we should go check on her?
>
> FATHER: I don't know.
>
> COUNSELOR: She can't hurt herself out there. And I'm sure our receptionist is keeping an eye on her.
>
> FATHER: Right. She's just mad.

In this interaction, the counselor is forcing the parents to confront the issue. Mother attempts to intervene, and Father withdraws. The counselor turns to Father and challenges him to stay involved. Father becomes involved by threatening the child with removal, but neither follows through. At that point, the counselor increases the tension by asking Mother if Father intends to do what he threatened. This confronts Father, and he follows through. The parents then begin to waver as Wendy turns up the intensity from the other room. The counselor assures them that their daughter is really all right, and they regain their resolve to win this battle of wills.

FAMILY SCULPTURE. *Family sculpture* is another form of enactment. The exercise calls for the family to physically portray a dynamic in the family. Zimmerman (1998) describes one such sculpture in which a man is caught between his wife and his family of origin. In the depiction, his wife pulls on one arm while the family of origin pulls on the other arm. The dilemma this causes to the man in question is seemingly more obvious by such a physical depiction. Many family (or other system) dynamics can be depicted physically and can lead to powerful insights and serious discussions about what must change structurally for the system to become more functional.

SECOND-ORDER INTERVENTIONS

Prescribing the Symptom

Second-order interventions that are systemic are primarily identified with strategic family therapy. They are framed as directives that are often paradoxical in nature and place the family members in a therapeutic double-bind by *prescribing the symptom.* As introduced in Chapter 9, the rationale behind the paradoxical directive is that many problems do not follow the laws of logic. Consequently, a solution that follows the typical laws of logic completely misses the point and simply will not work. For example, let's say that an adolescent breaks curfew and is grounded for a weekend. The problem is presumed to have been addressed. However, what if he breaks curfew again? The linear solution might be to punish him similarly for an entire week. In this illustration, can it be said that the punishment had the desired effect? Punishment was intended to produce good behavior in the future, a linear solution, but clearly, it did not. These types of solutions are called *more-of-the-same solutions,* and occasionally do not work, especially if the real problem is systemic and the individual's behavior is simply a manifestation of a system in trouble. You might wonder if allowing a teenager to continue to violate curfew might be a dangerous intervention, and it certainly could be; but depending on the individual involved (and this is where assessment is crucially important), there may be little desire on the adolescent's part to engage in risky behavior after hours. It could be, instead, that the adolescent is chafing against parents who are overprotective. It could also be that the parents do not agree on his curfew, and his breaking it is an unconscious way to alert the parent subsystem that it's not working. Therefore, prescribing that this adolescent determine his own curfew for a two-week period and give it to his parents ahead of time might be far more functional than what has transpired thus far. Furthermore, it might expose the issues between his parents, and this too would be a positive outcome systemically.

CASE ILLUSTRATION OF PRESCRIBING THE SYMPTOM

The Case of the Marla

Marla is the 10-year-old daughter of Ed and Dawn. Although Ed and Dawn divorced 2 years ago, Ed remained close to Marla with frequent contact. Two months ago, things changed, however, as Ed was promoted and transferred in his company to a location 100 miles away. Although he continues to visit when he can and tries to call Marla at least three times a week, his new job is demanding, and there have been times when Marla expected a call and didn't hear from him.

Marla has been a good student and considered a "pleasure" by her teachers. However, since her father moved, she often doesn't do in-class work when the students are instructed to work independently. When the teacher recently asked

Marla what she was thinking about when she was obviously daydreaming, Marla said that she was worried about her father, who is alone in a new city. The teacher reported this to Dawn, who then shared it with Ed. As a result, he increased his contacts and tried to reassure Marla. This pattern has continued for a month, with Marla basically remaining distracted in school and Ed calling frequently to reassure her and encourage her to do better. Marla says that she will try, but things do not seem to be improving.

During Ed's next visit, he and Dawn decide to seek the input of a counselor. Upon hearing the situation, the counselor asked if they would be willing to try something novel to see if they can break the pattern. The counselor also notes that the teacher must be involved in the plan. This is what was proposed: First, when Marla is caught not doing her schoolwork, her teacher should comment that this is OK, because worrying about her father was more important than her schoolwork, even if it meant failing the school year. In other words, the teacher should indicate full respect for Marla's "choice" of how to use her time and demonstrate no concern. In addition, Ed is instructed to do his very best to call Marla on a regular schedule. Equally important, he is not to check in on Marla's school behavior when they speak. If Marla brings it up, he is to change the topic. Both Dawn and Ed saw the paradoxical wisdom of this strategy; luckily, Marla's teacher also agrees to play her role, if this is what the parents wanted.

As you might suspect, by the end of the second week of using this strategy, Marla's schoolwork improved, and soon she was back to the model student she had been prior to Ed's relocation. In short, whereas the system was organizing around her failure and concern about her, it eventually reverted to its prior organization around solid parent–child relationships. Prescribing the symptom of "worrying" made the act of worrying lose its power to get Marla what she wanted—a link to her father. Once Ed demonstrated that he would be there despite the move, the symptom was unnecessary.

In another example, an individual was in counseling complaining of a systemic issue. Even when only one person is the client, a paradoxical directive may have the power to alter the system. Charity was a graduate student attempting to redefine her life as separate from overinvolved parents. Charity was still somewhat dependent on her parents for financial support (loans), but felt that they were attempting to micromanage her life, calling almost daily to see "how she was doing." These daily phone calls had the effect of undermining her self-confidence and keeping her parents in control of her life. Her primary counseling goal was to get some emotional distance from her parents and to begin to build her own life as a responsible adult. The counselor suggested the following paradoxical prescription:

> I'd like you to try an experiment with me. It'll feel strange and risky to do. I want you to become overly dependent on your parents for a while. Instead of waiting for them to call each day, I want you to call first with questions about how to deal with your life. Call more than once a day even. When your parents do call to give unsolicited advice, tell them how much you need their help; keep them on the phone and ask all of the detailed little questions you can think of. Try this for a month, and I think you'll find some dramatic changes taking place in your relationship with them.

Charity was reluctant at first to accept this prescription. It seemed to take her life in exactly the wrong direction, but she finally agreed to try it. After a week, she reported that she had followed the prescription to the letter, but the only change was that her parents called her less because she was calling them more. After 2 weeks, Charity reported that her parents seemed to be backing off a little when she would call. They seemed more worried about her, however. After 3 weeks, she came to the session in a very positive frame of mind. Her parents had visited over the weekend and had explained that they were very concerned about her inability to assume adult responsibility. They asserted that Charity must not keep relying on them for the kinds of decisions she should be making for herself, and they were proposing that she enter counseling for help with this matter. For their part, they would pay for the counseling sessions, but they would not be available to help her make the mundane decisions of life and she must resist calling and asking for help. Their only request was that, for the time being, she call on Saturday mornings "just to catch up on the week." Charity ended by saying to the counselor, "Mission accomplished!"

CLIENT REACTIONS TO SYSTEMIC INTERVENTIONS

As stated earlier, most people see problems as situated in individuals, either themselves or those with whom they live, work, or play. For this reason, systemic interventions are received either as a great relief or with resistance. Despite these initial reactions, systemic interventions bring home the fact that we create and participate in complex human networks and that these, once established, are likely to continue as is without the benefit of an intervention. However, it is freeing and sometimes exhilarating for clients to see others change in response to their new behaviors. People they considered too stubborn, too authoritarian, or too weak to be different in their relationships with them become less stubborn, authoritarian, or weak in their responses.

Another familiar response of clients to systemic interventions is to be surprised that the systems to which they belong follow "rules" of interactions. It is like a whole new dimension of reality has been opened to them, often one that they find quite intriguing. Similarly, clients may be surprised to learn that ethnic families tend to have similar patterns (McGoldrick, Giordano, & Garcia-Preto, 2005). They are taken aback to learn that cutting-off members of the extended family, for example, is not uncommon in their ethnic group, whereas it is quite unusual for another ethnic group. These insights help clients to "make sense" of their background, the assumptions they made about families and other close groups of people, and allow them new freedom to consider different behaviors.

Systemic Interventions Used in Dialectical Behavior Therapy

Dialectical Behavior Therapy (DBT) was developed for work with individuals; however, it is clear even in relatively early writings that some of the skills that clients developed were designed to change family systems. When adolescents were encouraged, for example, to learn new ways to interact with their parents in order to draw out different responses, this definitely falls in the systemic realm. Several DBT authors focus specifically on the use of DBT for work with families (Fruzzetti, Santisteban, & Hoffman, 2007; Hoffman, Fruzzetti, & Swenson, 1999; Miller, Glinski, Woodberry, Mitchell, & Indik, 2002; Woodberry, Miller, Glinski, Indik, & Mitchell, 2002). For these authors, applying DBT to family "groups" is a natural extension of the group work done in traditional DBT. Because much of family work is indeed helping families change their interactions with each other (i.e., learn new skills), this assertion is well founded.

That being said, although DBT therapists who work systemically use several systemic interventions described in this chapter, it is important to realize that some systemic interventions are not compatible with DBT. For example, Fruzzetti et al. (2007) note that interventions embedded in structural family therapy are compatible with DBT, whereas those embedded in strategic family therapy are not because of the paradoxical nature of many strategic interventions. Therefore, the interventions described in this chapter that stress altering communication patterns within families and that attend to altering system structure are compatible with DBT; however, those described as second-order interventions are not DBT friendly.

Summary

As noted earlier, systemic interventions do not originate in the traditional theories of counseling or personality; instead, they derive from an ecological epistemology that many trained counselors find both unique and effective. The systemic orientation begins with a set of assumptions about human behavior that include (a) a self-sustaining quality known as *system homeostasis,* (b) the tendency of dysfunctional systems to develop rigid boundaries, and (c) an internal system organization determined by systemic "rules" as defined by repeated behavioral interaction patterns.

Like all orientations, emphasis is placed on assessment as well as intervention. A frequent admonition of the systemic counselor is that the problem cannot be treated until it has been identified accurately. Systems thinking has particular relevance in working with couples and families. Indeed, many family interventions make no sense unless you think of the family as an ecosystem that is self-reinforcing and self-sustaining. Therefore, we recommend that you become well informed in family systems approaches if you plan to work with families or use family interventions.

Finally, we must underscore that none of this is to imply that there is no such thing as individual pathology, or that we are responsible for each other's behaviors. Certainly, Alcoholics Anonymous has taught us that each person must make a personal choice to be healthy or not, to abuse others or not, and so forth. Rather, systemic interventions address *only* those issues that are embedded in our relationships with others. It is not an "either/or" situation, but a "both/and" situation. We all operate as individuals *and* as members of systems. The interventions in this chapter attend primarily to the latter.

Exercises

I. Consider your family of origin. On a sheet of paper, write the names of your parents first. Then, as you add the names of siblings, place the names nearest that parent with whom you think there was a primary identification. Draw lines connecting the subsystems you believe were operating in your family.

II. (This is a two-part exercise.) With a group of three to four class members, define yourselves as a family. Each person should assume a family member role: father, mother, oldest sibling, and so on. Given this "system," the family should discuss and make plans for a weeklong vacation at the beach. After the plan has been finalized, step out of your roles and analyze the process and the system.

In the second part of the exercise, the family is to repeat the exercise, assuming the same roles. However, one family member in this second exercise is to be a dysfunctional member (exhibiting a marginal level of functioning). Given this condition, repeat the planning of the vacation. Once the plan has been finalized, step out of your roles once again and analyze the process and the system. How did a dysfunctional family member alter the system? How did the individual family member roles accommodate this change?

III. In the case of Melanie and Chuck, the problem was identified as the product of personal qualities each brought into the marriage. Identify two or three individual goals for both Melanie and Chuck that would have a positive effect on their relationship.

Discussion Questions

1. In a small group of class members, discuss what you think would be the most difficult type of family problem on which to work. As you discuss the problem(s), consider whether you would choose to work with individuals or the total family in addressing the problem(s).

2. In this chapter, we compare the family's system to an ecological system. In what ways are the two similar? How is this illustrated by the so-called empty-nest syndrome?

3. In a group of employees who have worked together in the same office area for 10 years, what kinds of systemic

rules are likely to be developed? How easy would it be to alter those rules?

4. Less attention is given in this chapter to soliciting input from clients themselves regarding goal setting.

Why is there less emphasis on asking members of the system to help identify counseling goals than there is in individual counseling?

MyCounselingLab® Assignment

Go to the Video Library under Video Resources on the MyCounselingLab site for your text and search for the following clips:

- **Video Example: Challenging Repetitive Transactions**
  In this clip, the counselor patiently tracks one interaction between mother and daughter. Although the topic is "pancakes," it demonstrates how family roles are structured. By taking this specific situation and deconstructing it, the counselor is able to introduce the idea of new behaviors that could generalize to other interactions. This is an example of how systems are altered.
- **Video Example: Couple Assertiveness and Self-Actualization in the Here and Now Part II**   This video portrays a couple who fall into the classic distancer/pursuer roles. Yet, we are seeing this couple at a point where this pattern has become destructive to their marriage. The therapist in this video is very directive in his style. He realizes early on that he has to model for the husband how to "stand up" to his wife. It may appear that the therapist is "taking sides" at one point in the session. By the end of the session, however, the therapist is moving toward helping the husband to understand that behavior that was adaptive for him as a child is undermining intimacy in his marriage.

- **Video Example: Couple: Paradoxical Intervention**
  This is a demonstration of prescribing the symptom. How do you think the couple reacts to their assignment? Remember that the point of doing this is to take behavior that is considered "out of one's control" and putting it under one's control. What do you think of this kind of intervention?

The following two videos depict the use of reframing in the form of externalization. As we discussed earlier in the chapter, this intervention places the problem "out there" and allows the client, the family, and the counselor to work together to beat the problem. These videos show a counselor working with a mother and son.

- **Video Example: Using Externalizing Questions—Part 1**
- **Video Example: Using Externalizing Questions—Part 2**

Finally, many feminist therapists identify as systemic. The following session and reflection clearly is systemic in its focus. Although the therapist is working with an individual, she is looking at the client's behaviors, thoughts, and feelings that are dictated by the systems within which she operates. In the session video, you will see opportunities for the counselor to move toward one of the other three orientations. Would you do so? What do you think of this counselor's approach? Is it what you expected feminist therapy to look like?

- **Video Example: Feminist Session**
- **Video Example: Feminist Reflections**

CHAPTER 12

Termination and Evaluation

PURPOSE OF THIS CHAPTER

Termination, the fourth and final stage of counseling, is the transition by the client from assisted functioning to counseling-free functioning. In this chapter, we discuss the dynamics that affect this transition, the counselor's role and responsibilities in seeing that this transition occurs, and the occasional necessity to make client referrals to other mental health professionals. It is important to keep in mind through each of the counseling stages that the ultimate goals of any counseling relationship are success and termination. How this is accomplished is a key focus of this chapter.

Beyond assisting the client through this transition, the counselor should use this opportunity to evaluate his or her work. Without some form of evaluation, counselors will most likely repeat strategies and methods, regardless of whether they are the most efficient or most beneficial for the clients they serve.

Considerations as You Read This Chapter

- Beginnings and endings often prove problematic to people, particularly to sensitive people. Sensitive individuals are more aware of the importance of good beginnings, and they are particularly aware of the implications of ending relationships that have been productive, rewarding, and meaningful.

- Where do you fit in this picture? What have the beginnings and endings of relationships been like for you? Has it been your tendency to think of endings as a positive experience?

- Can you, as a counselor, put yourself in the client's world? How might termination be seen?

- What is the most constructive way for a client to view termination? How might you as a counselor enhance the client's ability to see termination in that constructive way?

- Evaluation is often viewed as judgment. Do you tend to seek feedback from others, or do you shy away from it? How do you tend to handle feedback that is disappointing? How do you tend to handle feedback that is positive?

In Chapter 3, we described *termination* as one of the four stages of counseling. This suggests that it functions as part of the therapeutic process and is not simply a significant moment in the counseling relationship. The dynamics of a termination are some indication of just how important the treatment of this stage can be. It has been described by writers as a "loss experience";

an "index of success"; a "recapitulation of the multiple preceding goodbyes in life"; a mixture of sadness and pleasure, pride and accomplishment; and a "transformative growth experience." Teyber and McClure (2011) describe it as possibly "the first positive ending of a relationship (clients) have ever experienced" (p. 440). However one wishes to describe termination, the emotional dynamics of letting go, trusting gains, and facing future potential with only partially tested new skills translate to a pivotal moment for clients.

The counselor also experiences pride and regret when a successful counseling relationship ends. Alternatively, if the relationship has been somewhat less than successful, the counselor probably feels unfinished or even unsure of the manner in which the counseling was conducted. In this chapter, we consider termination to be a therapeutic stage and address such issues as who determines when termination should occur, problems in the termination process, and characteristics of successful termination.

THE TERMINATION STAGE

Termination is not so much an ending as it is a transition from one set of conditions to another. Pate (1982) caught the spirit of this perspective, saying,

> When counseling is viewed as a process in which an essentially competent person is helped by another to solve problems of living, solving the problem leads to termination, not as a trauma, but as another step forward in client growth. (p. 188)

At some level, both the counselor and client know from the beginning of the counseling relationship that it will eventually end. However, the knowledge that counseling ultimately will end provides no guidelines for making the decision. This raises the question, "What are the determinants for when counseling should terminate?" The answer to this question is based on both theoretical orientations and counselor–client interactions.

Determinants of Termination

Counselors begin counseling with some idea of appropriate parameters for termination. Counselors with a phenomenological theoretical orientation and in private practice may view the process as highly tailored to each client—that is, especially if insurance is not limiting the length of counseling unduly, counseling goals can be short term or longer term, depending on the readiness of the client to address major psychological barriers to their well-being.

Other counselors are constrained by third-party payors or workplace expectations that counseling will be relatively short in its duration. At the very least, counselors in these situations must be prepared to defend continuing with a particular client based on progress toward specified goals.

Finally, some counselors work from a brief therapy orientation by choice and are focused on symptom removal as the primary function of their counseling. They tend to believe that short-term counseling, even if clients return to counseling on occasion, is more realistic and allows clients more immediate opportunity to apply new skills in their naturalistic world.

In each of these examples, the question of when termination should occur is answered by the counselor's theoretical stance or workplace constraints. There are, however, other variables that play a role in determining termination, including client input and the counselor's judgment.

Determinants of Termination: Client and Counselor Input

In practical terms, counseling ends when the client, the counselor, or the process indicates that termination is appropriate. Teyber and McClure (2011) offer what is probably the most pragmatic answer to the question of when counseling should end:

> Therapists know that clients are ready to terminate when they have converging reports of client change from three different sources: (1) when clients report that they consistently feel better, can respond in more adaptive ways to old conflict situations, and find themselves capable of new responses that were not available to them before; (2) when clients can consistently respond to the therapist in new, more direct, egalitarian, and reality-based ways that do not enact their old interpersonal coping styles or maladaptive relational patterns; and (3) when clients' significant others give them feedback that they are different or make comments such as, "You never used to do that before." (p. 441)

Such a convergence is not only pragmatic, but is also optimal. We might argue that termination is not usually quite so clear-cut.

WHEN CLIENTS INITIATE TEMINATION. Clients may elect to terminate for a number of reasons. They may believe that their goals have been accomplished. They may believe that the relationship (or the counselor) is not being helpful, or may even be harmful. They may lack the financial means to continue, or the third-party coverage for counseling has ended. They may move to a new community or, if they are students, finish the school year. Whatever the client's reason for terminating, it should be emphasized that the counselor's legal and ethical responsibilities do not end with the client's decision. Ethical standards are quite clear on this, including the requirement that pre-termination counseling is offered when other services are recommended following counseling (American Counseling Association [ACA], 2014, *Code of Ethics,* Section A.11).

WHEN THE COUNSELOR TERMINATES. Often, the counselor is the first person to introduce the notion that counseling is approaching termination. This decision may be based on the client's progress toward identified counseling goals, or the counselor may determine that his or her expertise does not match the client's needs.

When counseling has been predicated on a behavioral or other form of contract, progress toward the goals or conditions of the contract present a clear picture of when counseling should end. Although clients may be in the best position to experience counseling-based change, they are not always in the objective position necessary to recognize change. Thus, the counselor may need to say to the client, "Do you realize that you have accomplished everything you set out to accomplish?" Ordinarily, the counselor can see this event approaching several sessions before it occurs. It is appropriate to introduce the notion of termination at that time, thereby allowing the client an opportunity to adjust to the transition. A fairly simple observation, such as, "I think we probably have about three or perhaps four more sessions and we'll have finished our work," is enough to say. It provides an early warning, opens the door for discussion of progress and goal assessment, and focuses the client's attention on what life may be like after counseling.

Occasionally, as a case unfolds, the counselor may become aware that the demands of the client's problem call for skills or qualities the counselor does not possess. For example, after a few sessions, a client may reveal that she is manifesting symptoms of an eating disorder. If the counselor is unacquainted with the treatment procedures for such a condition, the client should be referred to a professional who is recognized as competent with this problem. Another, and often preferred, alternative to termination is for the counselor to receive additional supervision specific to the client's diagnosis.

One reason that is not acceptable for termination is when clients pose a value dilemma for the counselor. The *ACA Code of Ethics* is quite clear that in such cases, it is expected that counselors will seek additional training and supervision so that their values do not hamper their client's progress toward their goals. To do otherwise is discriminatory in nature and an ethical violation (ACA, 2014, *Code of Ethics,* A.11.b)

PREMATURE TERMINATION.   Among the more demoralizing occurrences for inexperienced and seasoned counselors alike is premature termination. Very often, termination occurs almost before a working alliance can be formed. This can be a function of many different conditions. One important reason is client readiness. Smith, Subich, and Kalodner (1995) report that clients who are in a "precontemplation stage" or a stage with low potential for change are far more likely to terminate after only one session than those who initiate counseling at a contemplation stage. Other reasons for early or premature termination may be related to matching of gender, ethnic, or other cultural factors (Kim, Lee, Chu, & Cho, 1989; Lin, 1994; Tata & Leong, 1994).

Sometimes counselors suggest that counseling terminate before an appropriate point has been reached. Because many clients rely heavily on the counselor to be the best judge of such matters, clients may go along with the counselor's recommendation, and the relationship may end prematurely. It has already been suggested that there are some legitimate reasons why the counselor may decide to terminate counseling and refer the client to another professional. Aside from these situations, three precipitating conditions can lead the counselor to initiate inappropriate premature termination:

1. The counselor experiences interpersonal discomfort.
2. The counselor fails to recognize and conceptualize the problem accurately.
3. The counselor accurately conceptualizes the problem, but becomes overwhelmed by it.

Personal discomfort may result from the counselor's fear of intimacy or inexperience with intense counseling relationships. With good supervision, this situation remedies itself through continued counseling exposure and awareness. If the counselor's conceptual skills are weak or if the counselor's approach to all problems is to minimize the situation, then the result may be premature termination because of a failure to understand the client. This situation obviously calls for a careful reassessment of the counselor's decision to become a mental health professional and whether additional training and supervision can remedy the situation. The third reason for premature termination is that the counselor accurately conceptualizes the client's problem, but becomes overwhelmed by its complexity. When this happens, it is most likely that the counselor is not receiving adequate supervision. The assumption of the mental health professions is that supervision is endemic to becoming competent (Bernard & Goodyear, 2014). Too often, supervision is ended when counselors reach a minimal level of competence; therefore, they do not continue to advance in their ability over time. The outcome affects all stages of the counseling process when more challenging clients appear, including that of termination.

The special case of the counselor-in-training or the counselor who relocates should be acknowledged. In most cases, counselor trainees provide services in a practicum or internship setting that conforms to university semester or quarter schedules. When counselor trainees know that their practicum will end at a certain date and the client will either be terminated or referred to another counselor, ethical practice dictates that the client be informed in the first session that a terminal date already exists. This allows the client a choice to enter into what might be brief counseling or potential longer-term counseling with the condition of referral, or to seek another counselor who does not impose this terminal limitation on the counseling relationship.

The Termination Report

Whether counseling is brief or long term, a summary report of the process is appropriate, desirable, and often mandated for several reasons. Assuming that the client may have a need for future counseling, the termination report provides an accurate summation of the client's responsiveness to counseling and to specific types of interventions. Should the client request the counselor to provide information to other professionals (e.g., social worker, psychiatrist) or the legal system, the report provides a base for the preparation of that information.

The counseling case can usually be summarized in two or three typewritten pages and should include the counselor's name and address, date that counseling began and concluded, number of sessions, presenting problem(s), diagnosis (if one was made), types of counseling interventions used and their effectiveness, client reaction to the counseling relationship over time, client reaction to termination, and the counselor's assessment of the client's success with counseling. The termination report is a confidential document and should not be released without the client's written permission (see Appendix B, Forms B-5 and B-8).

TERMINATION AS A PROCESS

The termination process involves several steps. The first is a careful assessment by the counselor and client of the progress that has been made and the extent to which goals have been achieved. Depending on the results of this assessment, the counselor takes one of two directions: termination or referral. Assuming termination is the appropriate choice, the counselor and client may proceed to discuss in depth the gains that have been made; how those gains might be affected by future situations; making plans for follow-up; and, finally, saying goodbye. Typically, the termination process is characterized by cognitive discussions interspersed with acknowledgment of emotional aspects of the relationship. When termination is appropriate and is done properly, the process has a constructive and positive quality.

Assessing Progress

Quintana (1993) views the role of assessment during termination as

> [a] particularly critical opportunity for clients and therapists to update or transform their relationship to incorporate clients' growth. For this transformation to occur, clients need to acknowledge the steps they have taken toward more mature functioning. Perhaps most important to clients is for therapists to acknowledge and validate their sense of accomplishment. (p. 430)

This notion of transformation from the helping relationship to a more autonomous and normal lifestyle is related to the maintenance after counseling of those therapeutic gains that have been made. If the counseling agreement was based on specific goals identified by the client, or if some form of counseling contract was established early in the process, then the assessment of change may take a rather formal character. Each goal that had been set becomes a topic to discuss, changes related to that goal are identified, perhaps environmental consequences that grow out of those changes are enumerated, and so forth. In this approach, there is a sense of structure as the counselor and client review the outcomes. When counseling has involved couples or families, the assessment becomes even more complex because each member's change is considered, as well as systemic changes in patterns of interaction.

Summarizing Progress

It may seem redundant to suggest that the assessment of progress should be followed by some sort of summary of that progress by the counselor. The rationale for providing a summary is twofold. First, hearing one's progress from another person or perspective is quite different from hearing oneself describe progress. Most clients benefit from the counselor's statement, even though it is not new information. As one client described it, "I knew I had made some gains, but it sure helps to hear you say it, too." Clients' efforts to internalize the counseling relationship are also enhanced when the counselor validates their accomplishments and encourages them to take credit for all of the steps they have taken toward their goals.

The second reason for a summary is that the counselor can inject some cautions if some counseling gains need to be reinforced or monitored by the client. This is related to future client efforts to preserve or generalize the progress that has been achieved.

Generalizing Change

Having identified the changes that have occurred directly or indirectly through counseling, the counselor and client should turn to how those new behaviors, attitudes, or relationships can be generalized to the client's world. This step in the process calls on the client to extend beyond the immediate gains to potential future gains. The counselor might introduce this with such questions as, "In what other situations could you anticipate using these social skills you have acquired?" or "If your husband should develop some new style of troublesome behavior next month, how do you think you might handle it?" The basic goal of the generalizing step is to test the client's willingness and ability to adapt learned skills or new attitudes to situations other than those that provoked the original problem.

Planning for Follow-Up

Follow-up in counseling refers to the nature and amount of professional contact that occurs between the counselor and client after termination has occurred. Some counseling approaches place greater emphasis on follow-up than others. For example, some therapists take the position that an individual or the family therapist is like a family physician. Over the years, the people they serve will encounter new crises and problems and will reenter counseling as these situations demand. This approach acknowledges that some persons enter adulthood with complicated histories that make functional living more challenging for them. Thus, counseling is viewed as a service that can extend, intermittently, over a sizable portion of the client's lifetime. Other approaches, most notably those that emphasize self-actualization, view counseling as a developmental experience, the object of which is to facilitate the client's growth and capability of dealing with new problems more effectively. In this context, future returns to counseling are not expected, although they are certainly not discouraged.

Follow-up also has an ethical aspect. Even when the counselor and client agree that sufficient progress has been made to warrant termination, it is appropriate for the counselor to

(a) make his or her future services available and (b) explain to the client how future contact can be made. In so doing, the counselor has established a link between the client's present state and future needs. This link can also be an effective intervention for those clients who believe termination is appropriate but experience anxiety at the prospect. For such clients, it may help if the counselor suggests a 3- or 6-month "checkup." Depending on the client's response to the suggestion, the counselor can even schedule an appointment or suggest that the client call to make an appointment if needed. This is an effective bridging intervention because it gives the client a sense of security and relationship continuation, even when counseling has terminated. The counselor might also suggest to the client that should the future appointment not seem necessary, a phone call to cancel the appointment would be appreciated. Our experience has been that clients are responsible about either keeping the appointment or canceling it. Even when they call to cancel, the telephone contact provides some follow-up information on how the client is coping.

If counseling outcomes include post-counseling activities that the client has decided to pursue, the counselor might want to follow up on the success of these goals. For example, if a client decides to make a career change that involves future job interviewing, the counselor might ask the client to keep him or her informed of progress, either through written or telephone contact.

In the Absence of Termination

We have already mentioned the frustration of premature termination. There are other settings where termination is not a viable construct. The most obvious of these is the school counseling context, where counseling is interwoven into the overall developmental goals of students. School counselors are either assigned "grades" or cohorts of students whom they follow throughout the students' progress in their school building. For these counselors, promotion to the next grade level or graduation are more normative constructs than termination.

There are exceptions, of course, and these include the student who moves from the area, or the student who has been referred to a mental health professional outside of school, thus terminating within-school counseling. In such instances, we believe that the content of this chapter is relevant.

A danger for counselors when termination is not normative is to default on the good practice of assessing progress in counseling. When a particular problem has been tackled in counseling, the counselor should be careful to process the progress that has been made with the client in as concrete a manner as possible. It should never be assumed that the client understands both progress and generalizability in a way similar to the counselor. Furthermore, longer time frames, such as the summer break, must be planned for in a way that includes many of the conversations that occur during a termination process. In short, *all* counselors should operate with an internal framework that identifies their work as beginning, middle, and ending, even if the ending is not a permanent one.

THE REFERRAL PROCESS

Referrals are of two types: (a) a referral may be *additive*—that is, the counselor may refer the client for services that he or she cannot provide but with no intention of terminating the client; and (b) a referral may be necessitated when the counselor is unable to continue working with a particular client for a number of reasons.

Additive Referrals

There are many reasons for an additive referral. The client may benefit from career counseling or need input from a nutritionist or consult with a psychiatrist regarding medication. Most mental health agencies, for example, have a psychiatrist on their team who consults with clients on a regular basis, while a primary therapist continues to offer counseling. This example brings us to an important matter of coordination and client releases. Although there might be exceptions, in most cases, it is important for counselors to be able to consult with any other professional who is offering services to their clients. Therefore, counselors should have a release of information form readily available for clients to sign as part of an additive referral.

If a release of information has been signed, it can be highly productive for the counselor to contact the second professional to offer a reason for the referral and to establish a professional relationship (if one does not already exist). The counselor can also determine whether the second professional is open to having the client sign releases in their practice as well, thus creating a cycle of information sharing between professionals for the benefit of the client. Although this kind of sharing is the normal routine within organizations (agencies, hospital, schools), it takes more effort to accomplish across organizations.

Referrals That Include Termination

Client referral is a special form of termination. Referral occurs when the counselor is unable to continue working with a particular client for a variety of reasons. For example, as the counselor is continuing the case assessment, it may become apparent that the client's problems are beyond the counselor's capabilities, and referral to a counselor who has the necessary expertise is warranted (*ACA Code of Ethics*, 2014, Section A.11.a). Another fairly common reason to refer is that the counselor is taking an extended leave of absence from employment, moving to another position with another organization, or relocating beyond commuting distance from a current place of employment. Ideally, a referral involves a number of steps: (a) identifying the need to refer, (b) evaluating potential referral sources, (c) coordinating the transfer, and (d) preparing the client for the referral.

THE NEED TO REFER. The most frequent reason for referral is that the client needs some specialized form of counseling. This does not mean that the client is exhibiting serious symptoms, although that can be the case for referral. It is more likely that the client needs a specific form of counseling that the counselor does not offer (e.g., career counseling, gerontological counseling, a specialist in post-traumatic stress disorder). Because clients rarely are informed consumers of the various forms that counseling can take, counselors should be keenly attuned to specialized needs and their own ability to provide quality services.

Clients may also need or prefer special conditions for counseling related to gender, ethnicity, religion, or sexual orientation, to name just a few potential cultural factors. Such specific needs might be apparent early in counseling or might be more evident later in the relationship. Whenever they do emerge, it is the counselor's responsibility to respond to them.

Clients may resist the first suggestions that a referral is appropriate. After all, having risked themselves by sharing their concerns or vulnerabilities, they probably prefer not to have to go through the same process with yet another person. If the counselor provides explanations that are complete, answer the client's questions clearly and thoroughly, and support the client's ambivalence, this resistance will most likely ease.

EVALUATING POTENTIAL SOURCES. It is important that counselors be familiar with potential referral sources in the community. Some communities publish a mental health services directory that lists public agencies and practitioners, services provided, fees, and how referral can be accomplished. Another obvious source is the Internet. By doing a search for the terms *mental health counselor, marriage and family therapist, psychologist,* or *psychiatrist* for your city or county, you can obtain a list of licensed professionals and their areas of practice. Such lists or directories may provide little more than names and possible affiliations. For example, a listing under "Marriage, Family, Child, and Individual" counselors might read:

Psychotherapy/Counseling

Ralph T. Marcus, Ph.D.

Center for Psychotherapy

• Marriage Enrichment

• Divorce Bereavement

• Family Mediation

Conveniently located in the Meridian Center

Call for appointment: 555–5555

Just what can be learned from this listing? Dr. Marcus offers psychotherapy for marriages that may require enrichment, surviving divorce, and resolving family conflict issues. What is not known is (a) the kind of training Dr. Marcus received, (b) whether his doctorate was earned in psychology or a related mental health field or whether he is licensed as a mental health practitioner in his state, (c) his therapeutic orientation (e.g., individual vs. family, theoretical base), or (d) his skill level or success rate with different types of problems. The best way to find answers to such questions is through exposure to different sources. Lacking that, the counselor could call Dr. Marcus and ask him such questions. After obtaining this information, the counselor should ask Dr. Marcus if he is accepting referrals and what referral procedures he prefers to follow. Over time, counselors can build up their own listings of referral sources based on direct experience. Such listings are by far the best resource when the need to refer a client arises.

Making referrals has legal ramifications. Because one can never know with certainty that a referral to a specific mental health provider will prove to be a positive experience for the client, it is probably best to provide the client with choices of referral sources. In that way, the client has the opportunity to choose a professional whose personal characteristics and professional qualities are closest to the client's perceived needs. If the referring counselor provides only one potential referral professional to the client and that proves to be a problematic experience, the referring counselor cannot be said to have met his or her responsibility fully.

COORDINATING THE TRANSFER. Whenever a client is referred to another professional, the counselor hopes that the referral will occur successfully and without undue strain on the client. If the client is highly anxious or if the counselor thinks the client might not accept the referral, special attention should be devoted to the client's concerns. In addition, successful referrals require that the counselor make contact with the receiving professional and provide information that facilitates the referral process.

PREPARING THE CLIENT.   Preparing the client for referral involves both details of the referral and the client's anxieties about any aspect of working with a new professional. It helps if the counselor has discussed the case with the receiving professional and can assure the client that painful details may not have to be repeated. It also helps if the counselor can tell the client some details about the potential new professional(s), including personal characteristics, professional competency, and the person's receptiveness to the referral. Referral details may include helping the client identify what he or she should be looking for in a new counselor or in a professional with the required expertise.

COMMUNICATION WITH THE RECEIVING PROFESSIONAL.   Before any referral recommendation is made, you should establish whether potential receiving professionals are willing or able to accept the referral. Once an acceptable receiving professional has been identified, the transfer of information about the case must be addressed. Usually, a receiving counselor requires a written case summary. The termination report described earlier provides sufficient information to meet this requirement. Before sending any written material, however, you must obtain signed consent from the client to share this information. Most counseling centers and educational settings use a standard consent form. Private practitioners should develop a referral form that gives the counselor power to transfer written information with the signed consent of the client to other specified professionals, agencies, or authorities.

BLOCKS TO TERMINATION

Counseling can be such an intimate and valued personal experience for both the counselor and client that the thought of ending the relationship may be most unappealing. From the counselor's perspective, helping a client who grows, overcomes obstacles, and accomplishes goals is an immensely rewarding experience. In addition, counselor–client relationships often assume a personal as well as a professional dimension. Counselors begin to like clients and appreciate their humanity and idiosyncratic qualities. Thus, there can be some personal investment in maintaining the relationship. Clients often experience counselors in ways they wish could have happened in their family relationships. In this context, termination often means saying goodbye to a very valued person.

However, Quintana (1993) challenges the termination-as-crisis concept, suggesting that it lacks empirical support. In other words, counselors who assume that termination will be a highly charged and difficult transition for their clients may be overestimating their role in their clients' lives and might even be guilty of creating a crisis where one would not otherwise occur. Quintana instead advocates an alternative definition of termination-as-development that views termination as a transformation that encourages growth and development in the client "that is applicable across gender, ethnicity, and race" (p. 429).

Client Resistance to Termination

Much has been written in both the theoretical and experimental literature about the termination experience and its effect on clients. The theoretical notions of its impact appear to be in conflict with the empirical evidence. For example, according to psychoanalytic thinking, "the most desirable state of affairs is for the patient to slowly wean himself away, for him to eventually accept his limitations and be willing to relinquish the desires which cannot be realized" (Lorand, 1982, p. 225). In his review of the theoretical views of termination,

Quintana (1993, p. 427) describes how "clients are expected to react to termination with a plethora of neurotic affective, cognitive, interpersonal, and defensive reactions related to grief reactions [and] clients' reactions are . . . intense enough to overwhelm positive gains made earlier in therapy." However, Quintana describes the research on termination's effect on client reactions:

> The frequency and intensity of clients' reactions to termination do not reflect inherent crisis over loss. Results [of research by Marx & Gelso, 1987; Quintana & Holahan, 1992] suggest that only a small minority of clients experience a psychological crisis over the end of therapy, and the crisis seems to focus on the disappointing level of client outcome rather than specifically on loss. (1993, p. 427)

Whatever may be the more likely reaction, it is appropriate for the counselor to evaluate the client's degree of concern with the prospect of termination and respond therapeutically.

Counselor Resistance to Termination

It may be surprising that counselors often resist terminating with clients even though the client has reached a logical hiatus in the counseling process. Yet most counselor resistance is understandable. The counselor forms real human attachments to clients. In fact, it might be argued that counselor investment in the person of the client is a prerequisite to successful counseling. When this is part of the relationship, letting go has an emotional impact. Goodyear (1981) identifies conditions that can lead to the counselor's experience of loss when termination occurs. In addition to those having to do with a positive working relationship, Goodyear also includes instances when the counselor may feel guilty or anxious that counseling was not more effective, instances when termination may signify the end of a unique learning experience for the counselor, and instances when termination may trigger unresolved farewells in the counselor's personal life.

The counselor trainee may have a supervisor who can point to any apparent resistance, but what does the professional counselor do? Most experienced counselors know, at some level of consciousness, when the relationship with a client has grown quite important. This is a cue to the counselor that peer consultation or supervision would be both appropriate and desirable. The more human counselors tend to be, the more susceptible they are to personal intrusions in their professional practice. Having a colleague who can provide a level of objectivity through discussion and peer supervision is a valuable asset.

CASE ILLUSTRATION OF TERMINATION

The Case of Alex

Alex is a 34-year-old stockbroker who has been unemployed for 14 months as a result of his firm's downsizing. He has tried to see this dilemma as an opportunity to move his career in new directions; however, he has decided to seek counseling at this time for two reasons. Although he had extensive outplacement counseling, he really doesn't know in what direction he would like to go with a new career and, in fact, has growing uncertainties about his potential. Added to this uncertainty, during the past few months Alex has grown increasingly bitter about being let go and how the outplacement was handled by his supervisor, whom he considered a close friend. The case was seen in a private psychotherapy group practice.

First Session

The first session began with the counselor orienting Alex to the conditions he could expect, including confidentiality, the necessity for the sessions to be recorded, and the fact that the counselor belonged to a consortium of mental health professionals who met periodically to provide and receive peer supervision. In addition, the counselor indicated that he practiced "short-term" psychotherapy, which meant that clients contract for 10 sessions. If, at the end of that time, the client had any remaining issues, the contract could be extended for an additional brief period of counseling.

COUNSELOR: Alex, one of the things we will be doing at each session is a review of your progress and how it is reflecting your goals. Because you have already had extensive career assessment, I would like your permission to request those results and they will become part of our weekly focus. So how would you like to begin this ten-week exploration?

ALEX: If you don't mind my saying so, I don't see how you can solve all my problems in ten weeks.

COUNSELOR: You may be right, but of course, it won't be me doing it. It will be the two of us doing it.

ALEX: Still, I don't see how it can be done. I've been sweating this out for more than a year already.

COUNSELOR: Yes, and hopefully we can find some new and more efficient ways to look at your issues. But the first thing we need to address is which concern we should consider first: your future or your anger.

ALEX: Well, it's my future that brings me here.

COUNSELOR: Yes, but do you think your anger and your loss of confidence are having any effect on your ability to make sound decisions about your future?

Fourth Session

As the fourth session was about to end, the topic of termination was initiated by Alex.

ALEX: This was a really tiring session today.

COUNSELOR: Yes, we covered a lot of ground. I do think you are making some good progress.

ALEX: Yeah, I do feel better about things, but that worries me, too.

COUNSELOR: What is it about a good feeling that makes you worry?

ALEX: Oh, it's not the good feeling. I'm just aware that things have been moving awfully fast and we only have six more sessions. I'm not sure I trust this idea of only ten sessions and boom, you're fixed.

COUNSELOR: I don't think I said, "Boom, you're fixed," when we started. And we can renegotiate for a couple more sessions when the time comes. But let's not jump to conclusions too quickly. Most of the time, when clients are feeling good about their progress for several weeks, the feeling can be trusted. I'm glad you raised the issue, because we are almost halfway through our ten-week contract. We don't have to do anything about that except to be aware that we will be terminating one of these days.

The counselor took this opportunity to extend Alex's awareness of the termination process. In effect, this discussion became the starting point for the termination process. The seed of awareness was planted, and the client took that awareness with him at the end of the session. Three sessions later, the awareness had grown and matured.

Seventh Session

Nearing the end of this session, which had been a difficult but significant session, the counselor introduced the termination topic again with Alex.

> COUNSELOR: Well, you've worked hard today, Alex. How are you feeling about your progress?
>
> ALEX: To tell you the truth, I'm exhausted. But I feel pretty good about how things are going. I'm glad I've gotten over that anger I was feeling toward Jim. That was really getting in the way.
>
> COUNSELOR: About a month ago, you mentioned that one of your fears was feeling too optimistic about your improvement. Do you still feel that way?
>
> ALEX: When was that?
>
> COUNSELOR: Oh, I was reviewing the recording of our fourth session and heard you say that you didn't trust that you could get your situation under control in only ten sessions.
>
> ALEX: Well, I still wonder about that. But I do feel like I'm a lot clearer on things now than I was then. I don't feel as shaky.
>
> COUNSELOR: What about terminating soon. Do you feel shaky about that?
>
> ALEX: [Laughing] Well, you still owe me three sessions. I'm not

ready to terminate today. But, unless the bottom falls out, I don't think I will need another 10 sessions.

> COUNSELOR: [Chuckling] No, if you had another ten sessions, you'd probably begin to lose the ground you have gained.
>
> ALEX: What do you mean? Do people lose ground if they stay in counseling too long?
>
> COUNSELOR: I think so. There's a time to leave your parents; a time to leave your training; a time to leave a job; and, in our case, a time to leave counseling. If we don't make that break when it's time, then you could grow dependent on the process and that would be self-defeating.

In this dialog, the counselor is able to present the therapeutic effects of appropriate termination so that it is seen as a normal, developmental process, like growing up. That does not remove all of the client's fears, but it does place termination in a context that is anything but catastrophic. Quintana (1993) suggests that counselors can greatly facilitate the termination process by framing it as outgrowing rather than losing a valued relationship. At the same time, Quintana emphasizes that counselors "should be careful not to imply that clients have outgrown their needs for therapy definitely . . . [because] future therapy should remain an option for clients as a way to support or catalyze their continued development" (p. 430).

Ninth Session

The counselor begins this session by introducing the topic of termination.

> COUNSELOR: Well, Alex, this is our next-to-last session. How shall we use it?

ALEX: We could call it a tie and go into extra innings.

COUNSELOR: You're right, we could say that your weaknesses are still equal to your strengths.

ALEX: Well, I don't believe that and you don't either, I don't think.

COUNSELOR: No, I don't think that at all. In fact, I think your strengths are real and many of your weaknesses were imagined.

ALEX: Yeah, I'm feeling that. But it's good to hear you say it, too. Maybe that's how I'd like to spend today.

COUNSELOR: What do you mean? Talking about your strengths?

ALEX: Yeah. I think I know what I want to do with my life. The graduate school idea seems right and I did have an interview at the university this week.

The counselor intentionally introduced termination at the beginning of the ninth session to allow Alex time to process his feelings about the imminent ending of the relationship. Alex might have dwelt on the insecurity of ending a meaningful relationship, he could have negotiated an extension at this time, or he could try to cement the gains he has realized through discussion and review. In this case, Alex chose the last alternative.

Tenth and Final Session

Alex began this session with the acknowledgment that it was the final session.

ALEX: Well, this is it.

COUNSELOR: Meaning?

ALEX: This is the last time I'll be seeing you, I think.

COUNSELOR: I think so, too.

ALEX: It's been good. When we started, I really wasn't so sure this was going to work. But things are starting to pull together. Oh, by the way, Jim and I went out for a drink last Friday night. It was good to see him again. And I'm filling out application forms for an MBA [masters of business administration] program.

COUNSELOR: That sounds good. Did Jim call you, or did you call him?

ALEX: I called him. And it's neat. I think he's going to be able to help me with some contacts.
[Later in the session]

COUNSELOR: Before we finish today, I want you to know that I would like to hear from you in six months or so. Just a quick call telling me how things have been going would be fine. Would you do that?

ALEX: Sure. What if I need a booster shot between now and then?

COUNSELOR: If that happens, you can call and set up an appointment.

In this final session, the counselor provided a bridge to aid the transition by asking Alex to get back in touch in 6 months with an informal progress report. This is as much for Alex's benefit as it is for the counselor, because it says, "I'm not just dropping you from my appointment book and my consciousness. You will remain my client *in absentia*." In addition, the counselor has provided a termination structure that allows Alex to make contact for future needs, should they arise. This would seem to be assumed, but clients often do not take this privilege for granted or are reluctant about such a move. In fact, an invitation to clients to return seems to result in greater levels of client satisfaction and lower levels of distress.

EVALUATION OF COUNSELING

Thus far in this chapter, we have discussed ways to assist clients at the end of your counseling relationship with them. There is another important opportunity, we might even say duty, at the end of counseling, and that is to do what you can to evaluate your counseling so you have the data you need to know that you have offered the best counseling possible. Unfortunately, evaluation of counseling has not received the same attention in professional research as other topics. Still, there are some methods worth your consideration.

Evidence-Based Practice

Although not evaluation *per se,* one way to have increased confidence in your work is to remain a student of the professional literature. The term *evidence based* has become quite popular, and it means only that some treatments have been studied for their success with certain clinical populations. Although there are critics of some of the emphasis on evidence-based practice (EBP) in certain settings, counselors should still be aware of the research in their field, especially if they work with one particular clinical population. In short, one way to evaluate your work is to evaluate your professional knowledge on an ongoing basis. Training programs give the counseling trainee adequate generic knowledge to begin practice; this knowledge is not adequate, however, for the length of a career. EBP is one place to begin to keep yourself current with which intervention combinations have been found to be successful for particular diagnoses or for particular populations.

Although the EBP literature is a good place to begin, it is not sufficient. Membership in your professional organization(s) connects you to an ongoing literature for your practice. Counseling is a rich profession with a broad array of resources for practice. Counselors who have a desire to excel need not go it alone.

Exit Interviews

An exit interview is a relatively easy way to gain some feedback about the counseling we have provided our clients. As part of a last session, counselors simply devote a bit of time discussing process goals rather than outcome goals. Statements like, "We've been working together over the last few months, and our sessions weren't all alike. Can you recall anything I did that was particularly helpful?" Perhaps even better is for the counselor to list interventions and ask for feedback. "During our work together, I gave you some homework to do regarding your thoughts and feelings between sessions. I also did that empty-chair exercise and followed that with work regarding the thoughts you were having that didn't add up once we took a look at them. As you think back, is there anything that you found particularly helpful as far as reaching your goals?"

Of course, especially if counseling has been relatively successful, the danger is that clients will want to please their counselor at the exit interview and will say that everything was wonderful; therefore, the counselor must frame the request as doing the counselor a favor. "Although I hope that my approach with my clients is productive overall, I'm under no delusion that everything I do is equally helpful. I know that you think our work together was good. I wonder if you could identify what you think was the least helpful thing we did and tell me a little about why that was the case. I would be grateful for that input."

There are two other ways to conduct exit interviews. One is to arrange for another person to conduct it. Again, it is important for it to be framed as a desire for improved service, and not to evaluate the counselor as a professional Finally, a written form could be given to the client with a request for feedback. In order for this to be helpful, the counselor must customize the form for each client so that questions asked relate to particular interventions used with the client. Forms that are too generic do not produce the kind of feedback that is helpful for a counselor's clinical development.

Client Satisfaction Surveys

A rather common feedback tool used by counseling centers is the client satisfaction survey. Although this is unlikely to give specific feedback about interventions, it does provide information about overall tenor of counseling and its helpfulness to the client. Typically, such forms are a list of statements and the clients check from "Strongly agree" to "Strongly disagree." The items most often included are the general atmosphere of the counseling office, the interest in the client communicated by the counselor, respect for the client, confidence in the counselor, helpfulness of counseling, and whether the client would refer others to the counseling center.

Although satisfaction surveys are too broad to offer help with increasing intervention expertise, they are not without value. For example, the surveys can be used to determine if persons who are more culturally different from the counselor respond as favorably as those who are more similar to them. A counselor can also use the surveys to see if using a distinct intervention changes clients' overall satisfaction with his or her work. In other words, even the most generic feedback is more useful than no feedback, and sometimes it can identify patterns that are useful for counselor development.

For those who do not presently use client satisfaction surveys, models used by a variety of counseling centers are easy to access online.

Referral Input

When appropriate and possible, feedback from persons who provided the original referral for counseling can be valuable. Although school counselors often receive informal feedback for their efforts, more formal feedback can be invaluable when counseling positions need to be defended. Forms that stipulate the reasons for a referral and a subsequent form to assess the helpfulness of counseling are included as Appendix B-9 and B-10. These forms were created for use with school counseling interns but have utility for any school counseling professional. We argue that similar forms could be used for any "in-house" or "within-system" referrals.

Follow-Up

We covered follow-up earlier as providing benefit for the client, but it can also be used to provide benefit for the counselor. Some may argue that only after a few months can clients more objectively evaluate the counseling they received. This, then, is yet another opportunity for counselors to receive feedback that may improve their practice. Hearing what was helpful when the experience is no longer fresh adds credibility to the feedback. Furthermore, with some distance from the relationship, clients may be more willing to give feedback about anything that was distinctly not helpful. A follow-up can be done as a phone conversation or as a mailed survey.

Summary

Often, termination is viewed as the moment when counselor and client conclude a successful counseling relationship. We try to dispel this notion and replace it with a broader definition of termination as a stage in the counseling process. As a stage, termination can be seen as the time when positive change is solidified and the transition to self-reliance is accomplished. Viewed in this way, termination can be as critical to successful counseling as are the assessment, goal-setting, and intervention stages.

Many desirable consequences accrue from the discussion of termination. The client becomes increasingly aware of new strengths and skills, the counselor is able to reinforce those gains, future demands and expectations can be considered, and fears and concerns can be considered. The process addresses unfinished business and enhances a sense of completion. In all of this, the counselor has responsibility to see that the client's well-being is protected and preserved. When termination occurs through referral, the counselor has primary responsibility to see that the transfer to the receiving professional is handled smoothly and sensitively.

Successful termination must be seen as part of successful treatment. Without it, even the most impressive counseling gains are tempered in the client's perception, and future needs may be negatively affected.

****

This chapter on termination is also the end of this text. We want to "terminate" our discussion with the reader with an eye to your future. Our text has been devoted to helping you at the beginning of your career. We hope that you have many years of applying the skills and interventions we have presented. As you do so, we share the recent work of Tracey, Wampold, Lichtenberg, and Goodyear (2014), who found that experience alone has not been found to be correlated to expertise among therapists. As a result of their analysis of the available research, they suggested that seeking feedback about your work and adopting a posture of *questioning* your approach rather than attempting to *confirm* it might be more productive for growth as a counselor than acquiring experience only. In other words, seeking supervision, attempting to gather feedback from as many sources as possible, and consistently challenging your assumptions about your clients and your work with them is perhaps the best combination of behaviors and dispositions to help you become a better and better counselor. The review offered by Tracey et al. (2014) reinforces the earlier work of Schön (1987), who found that a career-long habit of reflecting on one's work was central to becoming an expert counselor. We wish you well in this quest.

Exercises

I. **Class members divide into groups of three. Each group member assumes one of the following roles: Counselor, Client, or Observer. The Observer's responsibility is to record both the Counselor's and Client's behaviors during the exercise. Both the Counselor and Client should select a role from the following lists. Do not reveal your role to the other persons.**

Counselor	Client
Resisting termination	Resisting termination
Encouraging termination	Requesting termination
Uncertain about termination	Uncertain about termination

Conduct a 10-minute counseling session simulation using the roles you selected. Following the session, discuss your reactions with one another. The person who observes the participants should provide feedback to each regarding the dynamics he or she observed.

II. **In the following role-play, one person is the Counselor, the second is the Client, and the third is an Observer/Recorder.**

The Client is being referred to a psychologist. The reason for the referral is that the Counselor has realized that the Client's problems are beyond his or her level of training and competence to treat. The Client has seen the counselor for two sessions.

Allow 10 minutes for this role-play. Following the role-play, discuss among yourselves the dynamics of the interaction. What did you learn from this experience about its effect on the Client? On the Counselor? What interpersonal skills were required?

Discussion Questions

1. What are the pros and cons of early discussion about termination?
2. What types of clients are most in need of gradual introduction to the idea of termination? Why?
3. In this chapter, reference is made to premature termination. What are some of the conditions that might lead to premature termination? Can all be controlled by the counselor?
4. Discuss the idea of counselor resistance to termination. Do you possess any characteristics that might cause you to resist terminating a client?

5. Discuss the ways in which referral is similar to termination. How is referral different from termination, in terms of the counselor's responsibilities? What are the interpersonal dynamics of both referral and termination?
6. What conditions might encourage you to seek evaluation of your counseling? What conditions might discourage you from seeking evaluation? What might you do to increase the possibility that conditions remain evaluation-friendly?

APPENDIX A

Integrative Practice Exercises

Learning to counsel is somewhat like learning any other complex task: It involves acquiring a set of skills, mastering a set of subtasks, and—eventually—putting everything together in some integrated fashion. Perhaps you can recall what the process of learning to drive a car was like. At first, the mere thought of being able to drive a car was probably an overwhelming idea. Now you drive and hardly pay any attention to the process because it is so familiar and has become such a part of you. In between the initial overwhelming idea of learning to drive and your current state of driving with relative comfort and ease, you practiced and mastered a variety of skills related to driving. You learned how to steer the car, use the accelerator, perhaps use a clutch, brake the car, and, while doing all of this, watch out for other drivers. Moreover, you learned all of this in a relatively short time period—although certainly not overnight.

Now it is time to try to put some counseling skills and strategies together for yourself—to take what you have learned in a somewhat isolated fashion and integrate it in a meaningful way. The purpose of these exercises is to help you put the parts together in a conceptual framework that allows you to make even greater sense of the helping process for yourself. At the same time, it is important to realize that your ability to synthesize the tools and stages of counseling will necessarily stretch beyond the experience of these exercises, particularly if you are not yet in a field or job experience in which you can apply the tools with actual clients.

Although simulation such as role-playing can be an invaluable way to learn under conditions of reduced threat, it is not a substitute for actual encounters and interactions with persons whose lives are distressed, whose emotions are conflicted, and who are sitting in front of you somewhat expectantly, relieved, and scared, all at the same time. As you accumulate actual counseling experience, your understanding and integration of the tools and stages of helping will continue to grow, just as you will also continue to grow and develop personally and professionally.

In this appendix, we present a variety of exercises designed to help you pull together the skills and strategies we present in this text into some meaningful whole. In addition, we believe that completion of these activities will enable you to understand better the counseling process as it unfolds over an extended period of time with a client.

EXERCISE 1

In this exercise, we present three client cases. After reading each case, respond to the questions following the cases. In your responses, indicate issues that may arise in each of the four stages of the counseling process, as well as your ideas for dealing with these issues effectively. You may wish to jot down your ideas in writing or to use a partner or small group to help you brainstorm with this material.

Case 1. Leah is a 20-year-old woman requesting counseling at a mental health center. Her presenting issue is anxiety that has interfered with her keeping a job in the community. Leah has used cocaine in the past, but reports that she has been drug-free for 1 year. She lives with her mother and her

18-month-old child. She has little contact with her child's father, because he is still using drugs. Leah believes that her anxiety is what is keeping her from improving her life situation. In addition to a desire to work, Leah would like to complete her GED, because she dropped out of school halfway through her junior year.

Case 2. Mr. and Mrs. Yule have been married for two years. Both are in their sixties, and this is their second marriage; their previous spouses had died within the past 10 years. Mr. and Mrs. Yule are concerned that they "rushed into" this second relationship without adequate thought. They report that they argue constantly about everything. They believe they have forgotten how to talk to each other in a "civil" manner. Mrs. Yule states that she realizes her constant nagging upsets Mr. Yule; Mr. Yule discloses that his spending a lot of time with his male buddies irritates Mrs. Yule.

Case 3. Arthur is a fourth grader at Smith Elementary School. He is constantly "getting into trouble" for a number of things. Arthur admits that he starts a lot of fights with the other boys. He says he doesn't know why or how, but suddenly he is punching them. Only after these fights does he realize his anger got out of hand. Arthur realizes his behavior is causing some of the other kids to avoid him, yet he believes he would like their friendship. He is not sure how to handle his temper so that he doesn't lash out at his peers.

Building Relationship and Assessment

1. List specific issues that may arise with this client in terms of establishing rapport and an effective helping relationship.
2. Did you make any assumptions about the cultural backgrounds of any of these clients? Race? Socioeconomic status? How would your assessment be altered if you learned that you are incorrect?
3. How might this particular client respond initially to the counselor? After several sessions?
4. List what seem to be the major problem areas for this client. Consider the affective, behavioral, cognitive, and interpersonal dimensions.
5. What seem to be the client's main strengths, resources, and coping skills?
6. Can you identify any probable payoffs of the client's dysfunctional or problematic behavior?

Goal Setting

7. What might this client seek or expect from counseling?
8. What seem to be the ideal outcomes for this person?
9. How different might your choice of outcomes for this client be from the client's choice of outcomes? If the difference is great, what impact might this have on the helping process?

Intervention Strategies

10. Develop a list of possible intervention strategies that might be most useful in working with this particular client. Provide a rationale for your selection.
11. What theoretical approach underlies each of the intervention strategies on your list?
12. Would you *generally* favor using affective, cognitive, behavioral, or systemic strategies with this person? Why or why not?

Termination and Follow-Up

13. What are some indicators you would look for that suggest this client is ready to terminate counseling?

14. How would you help this client plan for transfer of learning from the counseling situation to the person's actual environment? What potential obstacles in his or her environment must be anticipated?

15. How would you follow up on the progress of this client once the helping process is terminated?

EXERCISE 2

Select one of the three cases described in Exercise 1 to use for the purpose of conducting an extended series of role-play counseling sessions. Enlist the help of a colleague or classmate who can meet with you regularly over the next five weeks. This person's task is to assume the role of the client from one of these cases and to "become" this client in the sessions with you. Your task is to meet with this person for five scheduled sessions during the next five weeks.

The first and second sessions should be directed toward building an effective therapeutic relationship and conducting an assessment with your client(s) using the information found in Chapter 5. In the third session, try to help the client develop outcome goals, using the process and skills described in Chapter 6. In the fourth session, based on the assessed problem areas and defined goals, select one or two interventions from Chapters 8 through 11 and implement these interventions with the client. Also in this session, begin to prepare the client for termination. In the fifth and final session, help the client summarize and evaluate the helping process and plan for changes in his or her environment. Terminate the counseling process, and develop a follow-up plan.

Video record your sessions. After each interview, assess and rate your behavior using the corresponding part of the Counseling Skills Checklist that follows. Your instructor or supervisor may also want to assess your performance. Your "client" can also provide you with informative feedback that you can use as well as your ratings to determine which skills and parts of the helping process you have mastered and which areas need additional improvement and practice.

THE COUNSELING SKILLS CHECKLIST

The Counseling Skills Checklist (CSC) is divided into six parts: (I) The Process of Relating; (II) Assessment; (III) Goal Setting; (IV) Intervention Selection and Implementation; (V) Termination and Evaluation; and (VI) Individual Skills Summary. The CSC can also be used following each type of session to determine the presence or absence of the skills associated with a particular stage of counseling.

Using the Counseling Skills Checklist

Each item in the CSC is scored by circling the most appropriate response—*Yes, No,* or *NA* (Not Applicable). The items are worded such that desirable responses are *Yes,* and that *NA* or *No* is an undesirable response.

After you have observed and rated each interview, sit down and review the ratings. Where noticeable deficiencies exist, you should identify a goal or goals that will remedy the problem. Beyond this, you should list two or three *action steps* that permit you to achieve this goal.

Part I: The Process of Relating

1. The counselor maintained eye contact with the client.
   Yes   No   NA

2. The counselor's facial expressions reflected the mood of the client.
   Yes   No   NA

3. The counselor demonstrated some variation in voice pitch when talking.
   Yes   No   NA

4. The counselor used intermittent one-word vocalizations (e.g., "mm-hmm") to reinforce the client's demonstration of goal-directed topics or behaviors.
   Yes   No   NA

5. The counselor made verbal comments that pursued the topic introduced by the client.
   Yes   No   NA

6. The subject of the counselor's verbal statements usually referred to the client, by either name or the second-person pronoun *you*.
   Yes   No   NA

7. A clear and sensible progression of topics was evident in the counselor's verbal behavior; the counselor avoided rambling.
   Yes   No   NA

8. The counselor made statements that reflected the client's feelings.
   Yes   No   NA

9. The counselor verbally stated his or her desire and intent to understand.
   Yes   No   NA

10. At least one time during the interview, the counselor provided specific feedback to the client.
    Yes   No   NA

11. The counselor expressed reactions about the client's strengths and/or potential.
    Yes   No   NA

12. The counselor made responses that reflected his or her liking and appreciation of the client.
    Yes   No   NA

Part II: Assessment

1. The counselor asked the client to provide basic demographic information about him- or herself.
   Yes   No   NA

2. The counselor asked the client to describe his or her current concerns and to provide some background information about the problems.
   Yes   No   NA

3. The counselor asked the client to list and prioritize problems.
   Yes   No   NA

4. For each identified problem, the counselor and client explored the
   a. Affective dimensions of the problem
      Yes   No   NA

   b. Cognitive dimensions of the problem
      Yes   No   NA

    c. Behavioral dimensions of the problem
       Yes   No   NA

    d. Systemic dimensions of the problem
       Yes   No   NA

    e. Cultural dimensions of the problem
       Yes   No   NA

    f. Intensity of the problem (i.e., frequency, duration, or severity)
       Yes   No   NA

    g. Antecedents of the problem
       Yes   No   NA

    h. Consequences and payoffs of the problem
       Yes   No   NA

5. The counselor and client discussed previous solutions the client had tried to resolve the problem.
Yes   No   NA

6. The counselor asked the client to identify possible strengths, resources, and coping skills the client could use to help resolve the problem.
Yes   No   NA

Part III: Goal Setting

1. The counselor asked the client to state how he or she would like to change his or her behavior (e.g., "How would you like for things to be different?").
Yes   No   NA

2. The counselor and client decided together on counseling goals.
Yes   No   NA

3. The goals set in the interview were specific and observable.
Yes   No   NA

4. The counselor asked the client to state orally a commitment to work for goal achievement.
Yes   No   NA

5. If the client appeared resistant or unconcerned about achieving change, the counselor discussed this with the client.
Yes   No   NA

6. The counselor asked the client to specify at least one action step he or she might take toward his or her goal.
Yes   No   NA

7. The counselor suggested alternatives available to the client.
Yes   No   NA

8. The counselor helped the client develop action steps for goal attainment.
Yes   No   NA

9. Action steps designated by counselor and client were specific and realistic in scope.
Yes   No   NA

10. The counselor provided an opportunity within the interview for the client to practice or rehearse the action step.
Yes   No   NA

11. The counselor provided feedback to the client concerning the execution of the action step.
    Yes   No   NA

12. The counselor encouraged the client to observe and evaluate the progress and outcomes of action steps taken outside the interview.
    Yes   No   NA

Part IV: Intervention Selection and Implementation

1. The counselor suggested some possible interventions to the client based on the client's stated goals.
   Yes   No   NA

2. The counselor provided information about the elements, time, advantages, and disadvantages of each intervention.
   Yes   No   NA

3. The counselor involved the client in the choice of interventions to be used.
   Yes   No   NA

4. The counselor suggested a possible sequence of interventions to be used when more than one intervention was selected.
   Yes   No   NA

5. The counselor provided a rationale about each intervention to the client.
   Yes   No   NA

6. The counselor provided detailed instructions about how to use the selected intervention.
   Yes   No   NA

7. The counselor verified that the client understood how the selected intervention would be implemented.
   Yes   No   NA

8. For less-transparent interventions, the counselor processed the intervention with the client as soon as possible.
   Yes   No   NA

Part V: Termination and Evaluation

1. The counselor and client engaged in some evaluation or assessment of the client's attainment of the desired goals.
   Yes   No   NA

2. The counselor and client summarized the client's progress throughout the helping process.
   Yes   No   NA

3. The counselor identified client indicators and behaviors suggesting termination was appropriate.
   Yes   No   NA

4. The counselor and client discussed ways for the client to apply or transfer the learnings from the helping interviews to the client's environment.
   Yes   No   NA

5. The counselor and client identified possible obstacles or stumbling blocks the client might encounter after termination, and discussed possible ways for the client to handle these obstacles.
   Yes   No   NA

6. The counselor discussed some kind of follow-up plan to the client.
Yes   No   NA

7. The counselor sought feedback about his or her counseling from the client, or engaged in an alternative evaluation plan.
Yes   No   NA

Part VI: Individual Skills Summary

Instructions: Check (✓) any of the skills that were used by the counselor in the observed interview. Use the space under "Comments" to record your qualitative assessment of the use of this skill. For example, how appropriately and effectively was it used?

SKILLS OF COUNSELING	COMMENTS
Nonverbal attending	
Verbal attending	
Paraphrase	
Reflection of content	
Reflection of affect	
Self-disclosure	
Immediacy	
Pacing	
Open-ended questions	
Closed questions	
Clarifying questions	
Confrontation	
Introjection	
Summary	
Ability potential	
Interpretation	
Information giving	
Modeling	
Rehearsal/Practice	
Feedback	
Affective intervention (specify)	
Cognitive intervention (specify)	
Behavioral intervention (specify)	
Systemic intervention (specify)	
Ending counseling	

APPENDIX B

Forms and Guides for Use in Counseling Practice

B-1 Client Intake Form
B-2 Extended Client Intake Form
B-3 Counseling Progress Notes—Continuing Sessions
B-4 Outpatient Treatment Plan (OTP)
B-5 Consent to Release Confidential Information
B-6 Permission to Audio- or Videorecord Counseling Interviews
B-7 Audio or Video Critique Form
B-8 Termination Summary Report
B-9 Referral to the School Counselor
B-10 Evaluation of School Counseling Services
B-11 Evaluation of Counselor Trainee Skills*

Case #: _____

Date: _____

Referred by: _____   Phone: _____

Client Intake Form

Name: _____   SS#: _____

Address: _____   DOB: _____

_____   Sex: M   F

Phone: (H) _____ (W) _____

(C) _____

Employer: _____   Length of employment: _____

Reason for seeking counseling:

_____

_____

_____

_____

Medications:

_____

_____ Date: _____

Previous counseling?   Yes   No   How long? _____

Name of counselor: _____

In case of emergency:

Person to contact: _____   Relation: _____

Address: _____

_____

Phone: (H) _____ (W) _____

(C) _____

To be signed by client:

I give permission for _____ (counselor) to contact the
above person in the event of an emergency.

_____   _____
Client's signature   Date

Appendix B-2

Case #: _____

Date: _____

Referred by: _____ Phone: _____

Extended Client Intake Form
(To be completed by counselor)

Name: _____ SS#: _____

Address: _____ DOB: _____

_____ Sex: M   F

Phone: (H) _____ (C) _____ (W) _____

Employer: _____ Position: _____

How long? _____ Highest educational level: _____

Previous employment history:

_____

_____

Presenting problem(s):

_____

_____

_____

In case of emergency:

Person to contact: _____ Relation: _____

Address: _____

_____

Phone: (H) _____ (C) _____ (W) _____

Allergies? _____

Medical insurance?   Yes   No   Policy #: _____

Name of provider: _____

Family history: Single   Married   Divorced   Remarried   Children? _____

Names/ages of children: _____

Currently on medications?   Yes   No

Med/Dose: _____ How long: _____ Dr.: _____

Med/Dose: _____ How long: _____ Dr.: _____

Med/Dose: _____ How long: _____ Dr.: _____

Appendix B-2

Physical/somatic complaints: Yes   No

Sleeping: _____   Nightmares, sweats: _____

Headache: _____   Stomach: _____

Heart palpitation: _____   Weight: _____

Blood pressure: _____   Panic attacks: _____

Shortness of breath: _____   Appetite: _____

Use of alcohol or drugs to relieve stress?   Yes   No

Frequency: _____

Initial Assessment of Client Stability

	Excellent	Above Average	Average	Below Average	Poor
Attention span	___	___	___	___	___
Self-image	___	___	___	___	___
Physical appearance	___	___	___	___	___
Verbal acuity	___	___	___	___	___
Affective functioning	___	___	___	___	___
Cognitive functioning	___	___	___	___	___
Interpersonal functioning	___	___	___	___	___

Descriptors of Initial Client Presentation

Aggressive ___	Personable ___	Assertive ___	Engaging ___
Dependent ___	Depressed ___	Shy ___	Preoccupied ___
Avoiding ___	Friendly ___	Social ___	Withdrawn ___
Motivated ___	Distracted ___	Impulsive ___	Argumentative ___

Factors that are operating in client's favor:

_____

_____

_____

Factors that are operating to client's disadvantage:

_____

_____

_____

(continued)

Counselor characteristics that would facilitate client progress:

_____

_____

_____

Counselor characteristics that would impede client progress:

_____

_____

_____

Date: _____   Intake counselor: _____

Disposition: _____

Client assigned to: _____   Date: _____

Counseling Progress Notes—Continuing Sessions

Counselor: _____   Date: _____

Supervisor: _____   Client*: _____
                                         *First name only or case number.

What were your objectives (goals) for this session?

Describe the dynamics in the session (your reactions to the client and the interactions between you and the client).

Summarize the key issues discussed during the session. Indicate who (you or client) initiated each issue to be discussed.

Describe relevant cultural or developmental information revealed in the session as it relates to the session content or to the client's history.

To what extent were your objectives (goals) for this session achieved?

Explain changes (or expansion of your conceptualization of the client's problem[s]).

(continued)

Explain changes (or expansions) of your treatment plan for this client.

Explain any changes to your diagnostic impressions (*DSM-5* code).

What are your objectives for the next session?

Question(s) you would like answered by your supervisor:

_____   _____
Counselor's signature   Supervisor's signature

Outpatient Treatment Plan (OTP)

Counselor: _____

Client: _____ Birthdate: _____ Age: _____ Sex: M F

SS#: _____ Phone: (W) _____ (H) _____

(C) _____

A. Initial Assessment: Date: _____

Presenting problem:

_____

_____

Precipitating events:

_____

_____

Relevant medical history:

_____

_____

Presenting mental state evaluation (circle appropriate):

Appearance	*Judgment*	*Stability*	*Intelligence*	*Memory*
Appropriate	Intact	Stable	High	Intact
Inappropriate	Impaired	Variable	Average	Impaired
Not Assessed	Not Assessed	Unstable	Low	Not Assessed

B. Diagnostic Assessment: (*DSM-5*) [Include all relevant diagnoses, including *V* codes.]

_____

_____

_____

_____

_____

Brief summary:

_____

_____

_____

(continued)

C. Treatment Plan

Type of treatment: Insight/Affective   Systemic/Interpersonal   Cognitive/Behavioral

Goal #1: _____

Time frame: _____

Success indicator: _____

Subgoal A: _____

Intervention strategy: _____

Time frame: _____

Alternate intervention/strategy: _____

Subgoal B: _____

Intervention strategy: _____

Time frame: _____

Alternate intervention/strategy: _____

Subgoal C: _____

Intervention strategy: _____

Time frame: _____

Alternate intervention/strategy: _____

Goal #2: _____

Time frame: _____

Success indicator: _____

Subgoal A: _____

Intervention strategy: _____

Time frame: _____

Alternate intervention/strategy: _____

Subgoal B: _____

Intervention strategy: _____

Time frame: _____

Alternate intervention/strategy: _____

Subgoal C: _____

Intervention strategy: _____

Time frame: _____

Alternate intervention/strategy: _____

D. Treatment Update #1   Date: _____

Goals (see above)	Progress	Comments
Goal #1	1 2 3 4 5 (Achieved)	_____
Subgoal A:	1 2 3 4 5	_____
Subgoal B:	1 2 3 4 5	_____
Subgoal C:	1 2 3 4 5	_____
Goal #2	1 2 3 4 5 (Achieved)	_____
Subgoal A:	1 2 3 4 5	_____
Subgoal B:	1 2 3 4 5	_____
Subgoal C:	1 2 3 4 5	_____

E. Treatment Update #2   Date: _____

Goals (see above)	Progress	Comments
Goal #1	1 2 3 4 5 (Achieved)	_____
Subgoal A:	1 2 3 4 5	_____
Subgoal B:	1 2 3 4 5	_____
Subgoal C:	1 2 3 4 5	_____
Goal #2	1 2 3 4 5 (Achieved)	_____
Subgoal A:	1 2 3 4 5	_____
Subgoal B:	1 2 3 4 5	_____
Subgoal C:	1 2 3 4 5	_____

F. Termination Report: Date: _____

Goals (see above)	Success Criterion Met				Termination Reason
	Yes	Partial	No	Comment	___ Goals met
1. _____	___	___	___	_____	___ Client terminated
2. _____	___	___	___	_____	___ Client moved
3. _____	___	___	___	_____	___ Ineffective treatment

Counselor signature: _____   Date: _____

Supervisor signature: _____   Date: _____

Appendix B-5

Consent to Release Confidential Information

I, _____, (_____)
　　　　　　(Client's name)　　　　　　　　　　　　　(Social Security number)

of _____
　　　　　　　　　　　　　　　　(Client's address)

authorize _____
　　　　　　(Name of counselor and agency/organization making the disclosure)

to disclose to _____
　　　　　　(Name of person and agency/organization receiving the disclosure)

the following information:*

_____

_____

_____

_____

*(including counseling/psychotherapy records related to emotional illness, and including diagnoses and interventions used in the treatment of diagnosed illnesses)

for the purpose of:

_____
　　　　　　　　(Purpose of information to be released)

_____

_____

_____

I also understand that I may revoke this consent at any time except to the extent that action has already been taken in reliance on it, and that, in any event, this consent expires automatically as described below:

Specific date upon which this consent expires: _____

Executed this _____ day of _____, 20 _____.

_____
　　　　　　　　　Client's signature

_____
(Parent, guardian, or authorized representative's signature)

Appendix B-6

**Permission to Audio or Videorecord
Counseling Interviews**

I hereby give permission to _____,
(Counselor's name)

representing _____,
(Training institution or agency)

to make audio and/or video recordings of our counseling interviews.
I understand that these recordings will be used only for the purpose of providing
clinical supervision to the counselor-in-training in the above institution/agency.
These recordings may be heard or viewed only by professional training staff of the
above institution/agency, and professional staff from the agency/school from
which I am receiving services. This permission may also include consultation
with other mental health professionals, if that seems professionally appropriate.
If any other use of the recording(s) is desired by the training institution, I must first
be asked for permission and must give that consent separate from this agreement.

_____   _____
(Signature of client)   (Signature of witness)

_____   _____
(Date)   (Date)

If the client is a minor (under 18 years), his or her parent or legal guardian must also
sign this agreement.

_____   _____
(Parent or legal guardian)   (Date)

Audio or Video Critique Form

Counselor: _____   Date: _____

Placement: _____

Client*: _____   Sex: _____   Session #: _____
*First name only or case number.

Counseling format: Individual _____   Group _____   Family _____   Other _____

Please respond to the following questions for each audio or video of counseling session(s). This form is primarily for training purposes and should not be viewed as an assessment.

Client's presenting problem(s):

_____

_____

Your theoretical conceptualization of the problem(s):

_____

_____

Counseling goals/objectives for this session? Explain your rationale for focusing on each.

_____

_____

Identify verbal or behavioral interventions that facilitated the session:

_____

_____

Identify any verbal or behavioral interventions that detracted from the session:

_____

_____

If you could do the session over again, what would you do differently?

_____

_____

Termination Summary Report

Counselor: _____   Date: _____

Supervisor: _____   Client*: _____
                                         *First name only or case number.

Initial reason for seeking counseling:

_____

_____

_____

Number of sessions: _____, beginning on _____ and concluding on
                                                  (date)
_____.
  (date)

Treatment plan called for the following:

_____

_____

_____

The following aspects of the treatment were accomplished:

_____

_____

_____

Counseling was terminated for the following reason(s):

_____

_____

_____

Client's status in the final session:

_____

_____

_____

Referral was made to: _____

_____   _____
     Counselor's signature   Supervisor's signature

Referral to the School Counselor

Student name: _____ Date: _____

Grade: _____ Referred by: _____

Major concern about the student:

___Academic Development
    Quality of work
    Scholastic ability
    Time management
    Task management

___Career Development
    Identification of post-secondary options
    Knowledge of careers
    Post-secondary goals
    Engagement in process to achieve goals

___Personal Development
    Personal awareness/acceptance
    Management of behaviors
    Management of emotions
    Personal safety, health, survival

___Social Development
    Peer relationships
    Adult–student relationships
    Diversity tolerance/acceptance
    Respect for rules and rights

Please check the following observations:

I. Academic Performance Observed

___Declining/poor quality of work
___Declining/poor grades earned
___Work often incomplete
___Work not handed in
___Difficulty staying on task
___Motivation appears low
___Lacks organization skills
___Work is not challenging to student

II. Classroom Conduct Observed

___Talks frequently in class
___Distracts other students
___Dramatic attention getting
___Sleeps in class
___Has been caught cheating
___Frequent visits to the lavatory

III. Other Observed Behavior

___Continual breaking of rules

For example:

___Quarrelsome with peers
___Avoided or shunned by peers
___Seeks constant adult contact
___Frequently withdraws; a loner
___Low frustration tolerance
___Perfectionist
___Depressed (appears sad/cries)
___Neglects personal hygiene
___Negative
___Erratic behavior/mood swings
___Inappropriate sexual behavior/language
___Physically/verbally abusive toward others
___Frequent visits to school nurse
___Frequent physical injuries
___Talks about hurting self
___Has attempted to hurt self

Courses	Teacher	Grades	# Tardy	#Absences	
					____# of discipline referrals
					____# of detentions
					____# of suspensions

Other discipline information: _____

_____

_____

Other relevant data (test scores, etc.): _____

_____

_____

Actions:

___ Data gathering/evaluation   ___ Ind. Counseling   ___ Group work   ___ Advising

___ Consultation with _____   ___ Classroom lesson   ___ Other

Evaluation of School Counseling Services

To be completed by school counselor:

Name: _____ Date: _____

Referral Source: _____

Relationship to student: _____

_____ was referred for counseling services on _____ for the following concerns
(student)

_____

_____

___Academic Development   ___Personal Development
   Quality of work   Personal awareness/acceptance
   Scholastic ability   Management of behaviors
   Time management   Management of emotions
   Task management   Personal safety, health, survival

___Career Development   ___Social Development
   Identification of post-secondary options   Peer relationships
   Knowledge of careers   Adult–student relationships
   Post-secondary goals   Diversity tolerance/acceptance
   Engagement in process to achieve goals   Respect for rules and rights

I have engaged in the following activities with the student:

To be completed by the referring person:
Please indicate the progress of the student on the items below (as taken from the referral form) and comment on observations:

	Concern is worse		No progress		Progress	
_____	1	2	3	4	5	6
_____	1	2	3	4	5	6
_____	1	2	3	4	5	6
_____	1	2	3	4	5	6
_____	1	2	3	4	5	6

Comments:

_____   _____
Signature of Referral Source   Date

Appendix B-11

Evaluation of Counselor Trainee Skills*

Student: _____ Semester: _____

Faculty Supervisor: _____ Individual Supervisor: _____

1 = needs significant improvement   2 = minimally adequate

3 = meeting expectations (average)   4 = strength of student   5 = excels in this area

	Not Observed	Low				High
Relationship/assessment skills						
1. Listens carefully and communicates an understanding of the client.	N	1	2	3	4	5
2. Is genuine and warm with client.	N	1	2	3	4	5
3. Is immediate with the client.	N	1	2	3	4	5
4. Is respectful of, and validates, the client.	N	1	2	3	4	5
5. Is appropriate regarding the cultural context of the client.	N	1	2	3	4	5
6. Is appropriate regarding the developmental context of the client.	N	1	2	3	4	5
7. Uses interpersonal strengths appropriately, including humor and self-disclosure.	N	1	2	3	4	5
8. Is comfortable with a variety of feelings and/or issues shared by the client.	N	1	2	3	4	5
9. Provides support to the client when appropriate.	N	1	2	3	4	5
10. Challenges the client when appropriate.	N	1	2	3	4	5
11. Tracks the main issues presented by the client.	N	1	2	3	4	5
12. Is able to organize session data into meaningful frameworks.	N	1	2	3	4	5
13. Appreciates cultural and/or developmental issues that may affect assessment.	N	1	2	3	4	5
14. Is able to recognize normative from problematic behavior during assessment.	N	1	2	3	4	5
15. Can assist the client in considering different components and sequences that make up and sustain problems.	N	1	2	3	4	5
16. Is able to identify cognitive components of client issues.	N	1	2	3	4	5
17. Is able to identify affective components of client issues.	N	1	2	3	4	5
18. Is able to identify behavioral components of client issues.	N	1	2	3	4	5
19. Is able to identify systemic components of client issues.	N	1	2	3	4	5
Goal-setting skills						
20. Identifies appropriate process goals.	N	1	2	3	4	5
21. Can assist client in translating problems into realistic outcome goals.	N	1	2	3	4	5
22. Can help the client break down goals into subgoals.	N	1	2	3	4	5

Appendix B-11

Intervention skills

23. Maintains an appropriate pace during sessions.	N	1	2	3	4	5
24. Uses questions skillfully.	N	1	2	3	4	5
25. Uses nondirective interventions skillfully.	N	1	2	3	4	5
26. Can direct the session in a meaningful manner.	N	1	2	3	4	5
27. Can deliver appropriate confrontations.	N	1	2	3	4	5
28. Can demonstrate an appropriate use of affective interventions.	N	1	2	3	4	5
29. Can demonstrate an appropriate use of cognitive interventions.	N	1	2	3	4	5
30. Can demonstrate an appropriate use of behavioral interventions.	N	1	2	3	4	5
31. Can demonstrate an appropriate use of systemic interventions.	N	1	2	3	4	5
32. Is able to work effectively with multiple clients.	N	1	2	3	4	5

Professional skills

33. Is aware of personal issues (counter-transference/parallel processes) that might impact counseling.	N	1	2	3	4	5
34. Demonstrates openness to and use of supervision.	N	1	2	3	4	5
35. Appreciates own limits without overreacting to them.	N	1	2	3	4	5
36. Is helpful to peers in the role of observer.	N	1	2	3	4	5
37. Is able to demonstrate empathy for different life situations in the role of client.	N	1	2	3	4	5

Additional aspects of practicum

38. Participation in group supervision.	N	1	2	3	4	5
39. Written work.	N	1	2	3	4	5

Comments relevant to areas of strength:

Comments relevant to areas on which to focus:

Final grade: _____   Ready to begin practicum: Yes _____ No _____

_____   _____   _____
Student   Faculty Supervisor   Date

Developed by Janine M. Bernard (1998); updated 2015.

REFERENCES

Alcott, L. (1988). Cultural feminism versus post-structuralism: The identity crisis in feminist theory. *Signs, 13,* 405–436.

American Counseling Association. (2014). *ACA Code of Ethics.* Alexandria, VA: ACA Press.

The American Heritage Dictionary (5th ed.). (2012). Boston, MA: Houghton Mifflin.

American Psychiatric Association. (2013). *Diagnostic and statistical manual of mental disorders* (5th ed.). Washington, DC: American Psychiatric Press.

Anderson, H. D. (1997). *Conversation, language, and possibilities: A postmodern approach to therapy.* New York, NY: HarperCollins.

Aten, J. D., McMinn, M. R., & Worthington, E. L., Jr. (Eds.). (2011). *Spiritually-oriented interventions for counseling and psychotherapy.* Washington, DC: American Psychological Association.

Atkinson, D. R., Casas, A., & Abreu, J. (1992). Acculturation, ethnicity, and cultural sensitivity. *Journal of Counseling Psychology, 39*(4), 515–520.

Bandura, A. (1969). *Principles of behavior modification.* Englewood Cliffs, NJ: Prentice Hall.

Bandura, A. (1977). *Social learning theory.* Englewood Cliffs, NJ: Prentice Hall.

Bandura, A. (1988). Self-efficacy conception of anxiety. *Anxiety Research, 1,* 77–88.

Barnland, D. C. (1975). Communication styles in two cultures: Japan and the United States. In A. Kendron, R. M. Harris, & M. R. Key (Eds.), *Organization of behavior in face-to-face interaction* (pp. 427–456). The Hague: Mouton.

Beck, A. T. (1976). *Cognitive therapy and the emotional disorders.* New York, NY: International Universities Press.

Beck, J. S. (2011). *Cognitive behavior therapy: Basics and beyond* (2nd ed.). New York, NY: The Guilford Press.

Berg, I., & Jaya, A. (1993). Different and same: Family therapy with Asian-American families. *Journal of Marital and Family Therapy, 19,* 31–38.

Bernard, J. M., & Goodyear, R. K. (2014). *Fundamentals of clinical supervision* (5th ed.). Upper Saddle River, NJ: Pearson.

Berne, E. (1964). *Games people play: The psychology of human relationships.* New York, NY: Grove Press.

Bettelheim, B. (1976). *The uses of enchantment: The meaning and importance of fairy tales.* New York, NY: Knopf.

Birdwhistell, R. (1970). *Kinesics and context: Essays on body motion communications.* Philadelphia, PA: University of Pennsylvania Press.

Bishop, D. R. (1995). Religious values and cross-cultural issues. In M. T. Burke & J. G. Miranti (Eds.), *Counseling: The spiritual dimension* (pp. 59–71). Alexandria, VA: ACA Press.

Bordin, E. S. (1979). The generalizability of the psychodynamic concept of the working alliance. *Psychotherapy: Theory, Research, and Practice, 16,* 252–260.

Bowen, M. (1978). *Family therapy in clinical practice.* New York, NY: Jason Aronson.

Brock, G. W., & Barnard, C. P. (1999). *Procedures in marriage and family therapy* (3rd ed.). Boston, MA: Allyn & Bacon.

Butler, M. H., Davis, S. D., & Seedall, R. B. (2008). Common pitfalls of beginning therapists utilizing enactments. *Journal of Marital and Family Therapy, 34,* 329–352.

Carkhuff, R. R., & Berenson, B. G. (1967). *Beyond counseling and therapy* (2nd ed.). New York, NY: Holt, Rinehart and Winston.

Castonguay, L. G., Constantino, M. J., & Holtforth, M. G. (2006). The working alliance: Where are we and where should we go? *Psychotherapy, 43,* 271–279.

Chung, R. C. Y., & Bemak, F. (2002). The relationship of culture and empathy in cross-cultural counseling. *Journal of Counseling and Development, 80,* 154–159.

Cohn, A. M., Jakupcak, M., Seibert, L. A., Hildebrandt, T. B., & Zeichner, A. (2010). The role of emotional dysregulation in the association between men's restrictive emotionality and use of physical aggression. *Psychology of Men & Masculinity, 11,* 53–64.

Collins, B. G., & Collins, T. M. (2005). *Crisis and trauma: Developmental-ecological intervention.* Boston, MA: Lahaska Press.

Combs, A. (1986). What makes a good helper. *Person-Centered Review, 1*(1), 51–61.

Corey, G. (2011). *Issues and ethics in the helping professions* (8th ed.). Pacific Grove, CA: Brooks/Cole.

Cormier, S., & Hackney, H. (2012). *Counseling strategies and interventions* (8th ed.). Boston, MA: Allyn & Bacon.

Cormier, S., & Nurius, P. S. (2003). *Interviewing and change strategies for helpers* (5th ed.). Pacific Grove, CA: Brooks/Cole.

Cormier, S., Nurius, P. S., & Osborn, C. J. (2013). *Interviewing and change strategies for helpers—fundamental skills and cognitive behavioral interventions* (7th ed.). Belmont, CA: Brooks/Cole.

Currier, J. M., Holland, J. M., & Neimeyer, R. A. (2008). Making sense of loss: A content analysis of end-of-life practitioners' therapeutic approaches. *Omega, 57,* 121–141.

Deffenbacher, J. L. (1985). A cognitive–behavioral response and a modest proposal. *The Counseling Psychologist, 13,* 261–269.

deShazer, S. (1991). *Putting differences to work.* New York, NY: Norton.

Dimeff, L. A., & Koerner, K. (Eds.). (2007). *Dialectical Behavior Therapy in clinical practice: Applications across disorders and settings.* New York, NY: Guilford Press.

Dixon, D. N., & Glover, J. A. (1984). *Counseling: A problem-solving approach.* New York, NY: Wiley.

Donley, R. J., Horan, J. J., & DeShong, R. L. (1990). The effect of several self-disclosure permutations on counseling process and outcome. *Journal of Counseling and Development, 67,* 408–412.

Dowd, E. T., & Milne, C. R. (1986). Paradoxical interventions in counseling psychology. *The Counseling Psychologist, 14,* 237–282.

Drummond, R. J., & Jones, K. D. (2010). *Assessment procedures for counselors and helping professionals* (7th ed.). Upper Saddle River, NJ: Pearson/Prentice Hall.

Dryden, W., & Ellis, A. (2001). Rational emotive behavior therapy. In K. S. Dobson (Ed.), *Handbook of cognitive–behavioral therapies* (2nd ed.; pp. 295–348). New York, NY: Guilford.

Egan, G. (2014). *The skilled helper: A problem-management and opportunity-development approach to helping* (10th ed.). Belmont, CA: Brooks/Cole.

Ekman, P. (1973). Cross-cultural studies of facial expression. In P. Ekman (Ed.), *Darwin and facial expression.* New York, NY: Academic Press.

Ekman, P. (1993). Facial expression and emotion. *American Psychologist, 48,* 384–392.

Ekman, P., & Friesen, W. V. (1967). Head and body cues in the judgment of emotion: A reformulation. *Perceptual and Motor Skills, 24,* 711–724.

Ellis, A. (1994). *Reason and emotion in psychotherapy.* New York, NY: Citadel Press.

Ellis, A., & Wilde, J. (2002). *Case studies in rational emotive behavior therapy with children and adolescents.* Upper Saddle River, NJ: Merrill/Prentice Hall.

Estrada, A. U., & Haney, P. (1998). Genograms in a multicultural perspective. In T. S. Nelson, & T. S. Trepper (Eds.), *101 more interventions in family therapy* (pp. 269–275). New York, NY: Haworth Press.

Framo, J. (1982). *Family interaction: A dialogue between family therapists and family researchers.* New York, NY: Springer.

Fruzzetti, A. E., Santisteban, D. A., & Hoffman, D. A. (2007). Dialectical behaviour therapy with family. In L. A. Dimeff & K. Koerner (Eds.), *Dialectical behaviour therapy in clinical practice: Applications across disorders and settings* (pp. 222–244). New York, NY: Guilford Press.

Gazda, G. M., Asbury, F. S., Balzer, F. J., Childers, W. C., & Walters, R. P. (1984). *Human relations development: A manual for educators* (3rd ed.). Boston, MA: Allyn & Bacon.

Gendlin, E. T. (1981). *Focusing* (rev. ed.). New York, NY: Bantam.

Gladding, S. T. (2012). *Counseling: A comprehensive profession* (7th ed.). Columbus, OH: Merrill.

Gladstein, G. (1983). Understanding empathy: Integrating counseling, development and social psychology perspectives. *Journal of Counseling Psychology, 30,* 467–482.

Goldenberg, I., & Goldenberg, H. (2008). *Family therapy: An overview* (7th ed.). Pacific Grove, CA: Brooks/Cole.

Goodyear, R. K. (1981). Termination as a loss experience for the counselor. *ThePersonnel and Guidance Journal, 59,* 347–350.

Gottman, J. (1991). Predicting the longitudinal course of marriages. *Journal of Marital and Family Therapy, 17,* 3–7.

Gottman, J. (1993). A theory of marital dissolution and stability. *Journal of Family Psychology, 7,* 57–75.

Gottman, J. M., & Levenson, R. W. (1992). Marital processes predicative of later dissolution: Behavior, physiology, and health. *Journal of Personality and Social Psychology, 63*, 221–233.

Gottman, J. M., Notarius, C., Gonso, J., & Markman, H. (1976). *A couple's guide to communication.* Champaign, IL: Research Press.

Gottman, J. M., & Silver, N. (2011). *The seven principles for making marriage work.* New York, NY: Random House.

Gregory, B. (2010). *CBT skills workbook: Practical exercises and worksheets to promote change.* Eau Claire, WI: PECI, LLC.

Hackney, H. (1974). Facial gestures and subject expression of feelings. *Journal of Counseling Psychology, 21*, 173–178.

Hackney, H. (1978). The evolution of empathy. *The Personnel and Guidance Journal, 55*, 35–39.

Halstead, R. W., Brooks, D. K., Goldberg, A., & Fish, L. S. (1990). Counselor and client perceptions of the working alliance. *Journal of Mental Health Counseling, 12*, 208–221.

Halstead, R. W., Pehrsson, D.-E., & Mullen, J. A. (2011). *Counseling children: A core issues approach.* Alexandria, VA: ACA Press.

Hansen, J. T. (2004). Thoughts on knowing: Epistemic implications of counseling practice. *Journal of Counseling and Development, 82*, 131–138.

Harris, T. (1967). *I'm OK, you're OK: A practical guide to Transactional Analysis.* New York, NY: Springer.

Haugen, P. T., Splaun, A. K., Weiss, D. S., & Evces, M. R. (2013). Integrative approach for the treatment of Posttraumatic Stress Disorder in 9/11 first responders: Three core techniques. *Psychotherapy, 50*, 336–340.

Henderson, D. A., & Thompson, C. L. (2011). *Counseling children* (8th ed.). Belmont, CA: Brooks/Cole.

Hill, C. E. (2014). *Helping skills: Facilitating exploration, insight and action* (4th ed.). Washington, DC: APA Press.

Hinterkopf, E. (1998). *Integrating spirituality in counseling.* Alexandria, VA: American Counseling Association.

Hoffman, L. (2006, December). Understanding psychology's diversity in a postmodern perspective: Theoretical orientations, specialties, and the role of dialogue. *Postmodernism & Psychology's Diversity.* Retrieved from www.postmodernpsychology.com /Topics/Postmodernism_Psychologys_Diversity.html

Hoffman, P. D., Fruzzetti, A., & Swenson, M. D. (1999). Dialectical behavior therapy: Family skills training. *Family Process, 38*, 399–414.

Holdstock, T. L., & Rogers, C. R. (1977). Person-centered theory. In R. J. Corsini (Ed.), *Current personality theories* (pp. 125–151). Itasca, IL: F. E. Peacock.

Humphrey, K. M. (2009). *Counseling strategies for loss and grief.* Alexandria, VA: American Counseling Association.

Hutchins, D. E. (1982). Ranking major counseling strategies with the TFA/Matrix system. *The Personnel and Guidance Journal, 60*, 427–431.

Iberg, J. R. (2001). Unconditional positive regard: Constituent activities. *Rogers' therapeutic conditions: Evolution, theory and practice, 3*, 155–171.

Ivey, A. E. (1994). *Intentional interviewing and counseling* (3rd ed.). Pacific Grove, CA: Brooks/Cole.

Ivey, A. E., D'Andrea, M., & Ivey, M. B. (2012). *Theories of counseling and psychotherapy: A multicultural perspective* (7th ed.). Thousand Oaks, CA: Sage.

Ivey, A. E., Ivey, M. B., & Zalaquett, C. P. (2014). *Intentional interviewing and counseling: Facilitating client development in a multicultural society* (8th ed.). Belmont, CA: Brooks/Cole.

Jacobs, E. E., Masson, R. L., Harvill, R. L., & Schimmel, C. J. (2012). *Group counseling: Strategies and skills* (7th ed.). Belmont, CA: Brooks/Cole.

Jacobson, E. (1939). Variation of blood pressure with skeletal muscle tension and relaxation. *Annuals of Internal Medicine, 2*, 152.

James, R. K., & Gilliland, B. E. (2012). *Crisis intervention strategies* (7th ed.). Boston, MA: Cengage Learning.

Jessop, A. L. (1979). *Nurse-patient communication: A skills approach.* North Amherst, MA: Microtraining Associates.

Kanel, K. (2011). *A guide to crisis intervention* (4th ed.). Boston, MA: Cengage Learning.

Kertes, A., Westra, H. A., Angus, L., & Marcus, M. (2011). Client experiences of cognitive behavioral therapy for generalized anxiety disorder: The impact of adding motivational interviewing. *Cognitive and Behavioural Practice, 18*, 55–69.

Kim, S. C., Lee, S. U., Chu, K. H., & Cho, K. J. (1989). Korean-Americans and mental health: Clinical experiences of Korean-American mental health services. *Asian American Psychological Association Journal, 13*, 18–27.

Klopf, D. W., Thompson, C. A., Ishii, S., & Sallinen-Kuparinen, A. (1991). Non-verbal immediacy differences among Japanese, Finnish, and American university students. *Perceptual and Motor Skills, 73,* 209–210.

Knapp, M. (1978). *Nonverbal communication in human interaction* (2nd ed.). New York, NY: Holt, Rinehart and Winston.

Knox, S., Hess, S. A., Petersen, D. A., & Hill, C. A. (1997). A qualitative analysis of client perceptions of the effects of helpful therapist self-disclosure in long-term therapy. *Journal of Counseling Psychology, 44*(3), 274–283.

Koerner, K. (2012). *Doing Dialectical Behavior Therapy: A practical guide.* New York, NY: Guilford Press.

Koerner, K., & Dimeff, L. A. (2007). Overview of Dialectical Behavior Therapy. In L. A. Dimeff & K. Koerner (Eds.) *Dialectical Behavior Therapy in clinical practice: Applications across disorders and settings* (pp. 1–18). New York, NY: Guilford Press.

Kottler, J. A. (1991). *The compleat therapist.* San Francisco, CA: Jossey-Bass.

L'Abate, L. (1981). Classification of counseling and therapy theorists, methods, processes, and goals: The E-R-A Model. *The Personnel and Guidance Journal, 59,* 263–265.

Lazarus, A. A. (1966). Behavioral rehearsal vs. non-directive therapy vs. advice in effecting behavior change. *Behavior Research and Therapy, 4,* 209–212.

"Learn Focusing: What Is Focusing?" (n.d., para. 5). *The Focusing Institute.* Retrieved July 15, 2015, from www.focusing.org/learn_focusing.html#what

Lin, J. C. H. (1994). Americans stay in psychotherapy? *Journal of Counseling Psychology, 41,* 288–291.

Linehan, M. M. (1981). A social–behavioral analysis of suicide and parasuicide: Implications for clinical assessment and treatment. In H. Glaezer & J. F. Clarkin (Eds.), *Depression: Behavioral and directive intervention strategies* (pp. 229–294). New York, NY: Garland.

Linehan, M. M. (1993). Cognitive–behavioral treatment of borderline personality disorder. New York, NY: Guilford Press.

Loganbill, C., Hardy, E., & Delworth, U. (1982). Supervision: A conceptual model. *The Counseling Psychologist, 10,* 3–42.

Lorand, S. (1982). *Techniques of psychoanalytic therapy.* New York, NY: St. Martin's Press.

Lynch, T. R., Chapman, A. L., Rosenthal, M. Z., Kuo, J. R., & Linehan, M. M. (2006). Mechanisms of change in dialectical behavior therapy: Theoretical and empirical observations. *Journal of Clinical Psychology, 62,* 459–480.

Marx, J. A., & Gelso, C. J. (1987). Termination of individual counseling in a university counseling center. *Journal of Counseling Psychology, 34,* 3–9.

McGoldrick, M., Gerson, R., & Petry, S. (2008). *Genograms: Assessment and intervention* (3rd ed.). New York, NY: Norton.

McGoldrick, M., Giordano, J., & Garcia-Preto, N. (Eds.). (2005). *Ethnicity & family therapy* (3rd ed.). New York, NY: The Guilford Press.

McMullin, R. E., & Giles, T. R. (1981). *Cognitive–behavior therapy: A restructuring approach.* New York, NY: Grune & Stratton.

Meador, B. D., & Rogers, C. R. (1984). Person-centered therapy. In R. J. Corsini (Ed.), *Current psychotherapies* (3rd ed., pp. 142–195). Itasca, IL: F. E. Peacock.

Meichenbaum, D. (1971). Examination of model characteristics in reducing avoidance behavior. *Journal of Personality and Social Psychology, 17,* 298–307.

Meichenbaum, D. (1977). *Cognitive-behavior modification: An integrative approach.* New York, NY: Plenum.

Merriam-Webster Online Dictionary. (2015). Retrieved July 20, 2015, from the Merriam-Webster Online Dictionary website: www.merriam-webster.com/dictionary/alter%20ego

Miller, A. L., Glinski, J., Woodberry, K. A., Mitchell, A. G., & Indik, J. (2002). Family therapy and dialectical behavior therapy with adolescents: Part I: Proposing a clinical synthesis. *American Journal of Psychotherapy, 56,* 568–584.

Miller, A. L., Rathus, J. H., & Linehan, M. M. (2007). *Dialectical Behavior Therapy with suicidal adolescents.* New York, NY: The Guilford Press.

Miller, S., Wackman, D. B., Nunnally, E. W., & Miller, P. (1989). *Connecting.* Minneapolis, MN: Interpersonal Communication Programs.

Miller, W. R. (1983). Motivational interviewing with problem drinkers. *Behavioural Psychotherapy, 1,* 147–172.

Miller, W. R., & Rollnick, S. (1991). *Motivational interviewing: Preparing people to change addictive behavior.* New York, NY: The Guilford Press.

Miller, W. R., & Rollnick, S. (2009). Ten things that motivational interviewing is not. *Behavioural and Cognitive Psychotherapy, 37,* 129–140.

Minuchin, S., & Fishman, H. C. (1981). *Family therapy techniques.* Cambridge, MA: Harvard University Press.

Morgan, O. J. (2000). Counseling and spirituality. In H. Hackney, *Practice issues for the beginning counselor.* Boston, MA: Allyn & Bacon.

Moursund, J., & Kenny, M. C. (2002). *The process of counseling and psychotherapy* (4th ed.). Englewood Cliffs, NJ: Prentice Hall.

Myers, J. E., & Sweeney, T. J. (Eds.). (2005). *Counseling for wellness: Theory, research and practice.* Alexandria, VA: American Counseling Association Press.

Napier, A., & Whitaker, C. A. (1978). *The family crucible.* New York, NY: Harper and Row.

Nelson, M. L. (2002). An assessment-based model for counseling strategy selection. *Journal of Counseling and Development, 80,* 416–421.

Neukrug, E. (2007). *The world of the counselor* (3rd ed.). Pacific Grove, CA: Brooks/Cole.

Nichols, M. P., & Schwartz, R. C. (1994). *Family therapy: Concepts and methods* (3rd ed.). Boston, MA: Allyn & Bacon.

Norcross, J. C., & Wampold, B. E. (2011). Evidence-based therapy relationships: Research conclusions and clinical practices. *Psychotherapy, 48,* 98–102.

Okun, B. F. (2015). *Effective helping: Interviewing and counseling techniques* (8th ed.). Stamford, CT: Cengage.

Ozer, E. M., & Bandura, A. (1990). Mechanisms governing empowerment effects: A self-efficacy analysis. *Journal of Personality and Social Psychology, 88,* 472–486.

Pate, R. H. (1982). Termination: End or beginning? In W. H. Van Hoose & M. R. Worth (Eds.), *Counseling adults: A developmental approach.* Pacific Grove, CA: Brooks/Cole.

Patterson, J., William, L., Edwards, T. M., Chamow, L. & Grauf-Grounds, C. (2009). *Essential skills in family therapy* (2nd ed.). New York, NY: Guilford Press.

Pearce, S. S. (1996). *Flash of insight: Metaphor and narrative in therapy.* Boston, MA: Allyn & Bacon.

Pedersen, P. B. (1991). Multiculturalism as a generic approach to counseling. *Journal of Counseling and Development, 70,* 6–12.

Perls, F. (1969/1976). *Gestalt therapy verbatim.* New York, NY: Real Person Press/Bantum.

Pinto, R. M., Rahman, R., & Williams, A. (2014). Policy advocacy and leadership training for formerly incarcerated women: An empowerment evaluation of ReConnect, a program of the Women in Prison Project, Correctional Association of New York. *Evaluation and Program Planning, 47,* 71–81.

Powell, J. (1996). Spiritual values clarification. In F. H. McClure & E. Teyber (Eds.), *Child and adolescent therapy.* Ft. Worth, TX: Harcourt Brace.

Prochaska, J. O., & Norcross, J. C. (2014). *Systems of psychotherapy: A transtheoretical analysis.* Stamford, CT: Cengage.

Quintana, S. M. (1993). Expanded and updated conceptualization of termination: Implications for short-term individual psychotherapy. *Professional Psychology, 24,* 426–432.

Quintana, S. M., & Holahan, W. (1992). Termination in short-term counseling: Comparison of successful and unsuccessful cases. *Journal of Counseling Psychology, 39,* 299–305.

Reps, P. (1981). *Zen flesh, Zen bones.* Garden City, NY: Doubleday.

Richards, P. S., & Bergin, A. E. (2005). *A spiritual strategy for counseling and psychotherapy* (2nd ed.). Washington, DC: American Psychological Association.

Rigazio-DiGilio, S. (1993). Family counseling and therapy. In A. Ivey, M. B. Ivey, & L. Simek-Morgan (Eds.), *Counseling and psychotherapy: A multicultural perspective.* Boston, MA: Allyn & Bacon.

Rimm, D. C., & Masters, J. C. (1979). *Behavior therapy: Techniques and empirical findings* (2nd ed.). New York, NY: Academic Press.

Rogers, C. R. (1957). The necessary and sufficient conditions of therapeutic personality change. *Journal of Consulting Psychology, 21,* 95–103.

Rogers, C. R. (1977). *Carl Rogers on personal power: Inner strength and its revolutionary impact.* New York, NY: Delacorte Press.

Rogers, C. R. (1989). A client-centered/person-centered approach to therapy. In H. Kirschenbaum (Ed.), *The Carl Rogers reader* (pp. 135–152). Boston, MA: Houghton Mifflin.

Rosenthal, T., & Steffek, B. (1991). Modeling methods. In F. H. Kanfer & A. P. Goldstein (Eds.), *Helping people change* (4th ed., pp. 70–121). New York, NY: Pergamon.

Satir, V. (1972). *Peoplemaking.* Palo Alto, CA: Science and Behavior Books.

Schaefer, C. E. (2011). *Foundations of play therapy* (2nd ed.). Hoboken, NJ: John Wiley.

Schön, D. A. (1987). *Educating a reflective practitioner.* San Francisco, CA: Jossey-Bass.

Selby, E. A., & Joiner, T. E., Jr. (2009). Cascades of emotion: The emergence of borderline personality disorder from emotional and behavioral dysregulation. *Review of General Psychology, 13,* 219–229.

Seligman, L. (2004). *Diagnosis and treatment planning in counseling* (3rd ed.). New York, NY: Plenum.

Seligman, L. (2009). *Conceptual skills for mental health professionals.* Upper Saddle River, NJ: Pearson Merrill.

Seligman, L., & Reichenberg, L. W. (2014). *Selecting effective treatments: A comprehensive, systematic guide to treating mental disorders.* Hoboken, NJ: John Wiley.

Sexton, T. L., Whiston, S. C., Bleuer, J. C., & Walz, G. R. (1997). *Integrating outcome research into counseling practice and training.* Alexandria, VA: ACA Press.

Smith, K. L., Subich, L. M., & Kalodner, C. (1995). The transtheoretical model's stages and processes of change and their relation to premature termination. *Journal of Counseling Psychology, 42,* 34–39.

Smith, S. E. (1994). Parent-initiated contracts: An intervention for school-related behaviors. *Elementary School Guidance & Counseling, 28,* 182–187.

Sue, D. W., Gallardo, M. E., & Neville, H. A. (2014). *Case studies in multicultural counseling and therapy.* Hoboken, NJ: John Wiley.

Sue, D. W., & Sue, D. (1990). *Counseling the culturally different: Theory and practice* (2nd ed.). New York, NY: Wiley.

Szapocznik, J., & Kurtines, W. M. (1993). Family psychology and cultural diversity: Opportunities for theory, research and application. *American Psychologist, 48,* 400–407.

Tata, S. P., & Leong, F. T. L. (1994). Individualism–collectivism, social-network orientation, and acculturation as predictors of attitudes toward seeking professional psychological help among Chinese Americans. *Journal of Counseling Psychology, 41,* 280–287.

Taussig, I. M. (1987). Comparative responses of Mexican-Americans and Anglo-Americans to early goal-setting in public mental health clinics. *Journal of Counseling Psychology, 34,* 214–217.

Tepper, D. T., & Haase, R. F. (1978). Verbal and nonverbal communications of facilitative conditions. *Journal of Counseling Psychology, 25,* 35–44.

Teyber, E. & McClure, F. H. (2011). *Interpersonal process in therapy: An integrative model* (6th ed.). Pacific Grove, CA: Brooks/Cole.

Thomas, A. J. (1998). Understanding culture and worldview in family systems: Use of the multicultural genogram. *The Family Journal, 6*(1), 24–32.

Tracey, T. J. G., Wampold, B. E., Lichtenberg, J. W., & Goodyear, R. K. (2014). Expertise in psychotherapy: An elusive goal? *American Psychologist, 69,* 218–229.

Watzlawick, P., Weakland, J., & Fisch, R. (1974). *Change: Principles of problem formation and problem resolution.* New York, NY: Norton.

Welch, I. D., & Gonzalez, D. M. (1999). *The process of counseling and psychotherapy: Matters of skill.* Pacific Grove, CA: Brooks/Cole.

Westra, H. A., & Aviram, A. (2013). Core skills in motivational interviewing. *Psychotherapy, 50,* 273–278.

Whitaker, C. A., & Bumberry, W. M. (1988). *Dancing with a family: A symbolic–experiential approach.* New York, NY: Brunner/Mazel.

White, M. (1995). *Re-authoring lives: Interviews and essays.* Adelaide, South Australia: Dulwich Centre Publications.

White, P. E., & Franzoni, J. B. (1990). A multidimensional analysis of the mental health of graduate counselors in training. *Counselor Education and Supervision, 29,* 258–267.

Wilks, D. (2003). A historical review of counseling theory development in relation to definitions of free will and determinism. *Journal of Counseling and Development, 81,* 278–284.

Wolpe, J. (1958). *Psychotherapy by reciprocal inhibition.* Stanford, CA: Stanford University Press.

Wolpe, J. (1982). *The practice of behavior therapy* (3rd ed.). New York, NY: Pergamon.

Wolpe, J. (1990). *The practice of behavior therapy* (4th ed.). New York, NY: Pergamon.

Wolpe, J., & Lazarus, A. A. (1966). *Behavior therapy techniques.* New York, NY: Pergamon.

Wong, P. T. P. (2010). Meaning therapy: An integrative and positive existential psychotherapy. *Journal of Contemporary Psychotherapy, 40,* 85–93.

Woodberry, K. A., Miller, A. L., Glinski, J., Indik, J., & Mitchell, A. G. (2002). Family therapy and dialectical behavior therapy with adolescents: Part II: A theoretical review. *American Journal of Psychotherapy, 56,* 585–602.

Worden, X. X. (1994). *Family therapy basics*. Pacific Grove, CA: Brooks/Cole.

Wrenn, C. G. (1962). The culturally encapsulated counselor. *Harvard Educational Review, 32,* 444–449.

Wright, H. N. (2011). *The complete guide to crisis & trauma counseling: What to do and say when it matters most!* Ada, MI: Bethany House Publishers.

Young, M. E. (2012). *Learning the art of helping* (5th ed.). Upper Saddle River, NJ: Merrill.

Zimmer, J. M., & Anderson, S. (1968). Dimensions of positive regard and empathy. *Journal of Counseling Psychology, 15,* 417–426.

Zimmer, J. M., & Park, P. (1967). Factor analysis of counselor communications. *Journal of Counseling Psychology, 14,* 198–203.

Zimmer, J. M., Wightman, L., & McArthur, D. I. (1970). *Categories of counselor behavior as defined from cross-validated factorial descriptions.* Final Report, Project No. 9-A-003. Washington, DC: U.S. Department of Health, Education, and Welfare, Office of Education, Bureau of Research.

Zimmerman, T. S. (1998). Sculpting stepfamily structure. In T. S. Nelson, & T. S. Trepper (Eds.), *101 more interventions in family therapy* (pp. 33–35). New York, NY: Haworth Press.

Zuk, G. (1975). *Process and practice in family therapy.* Haverford, PA: Psychiatry and Behavioral Science Books.

INDEX

A

A-B-C-D analysis, 160, 161–165
  case illustration of, 163–164
Acceptance, and positive regard, 68
Active listening, 41
Adaptive behavior, 186
Additive referrals, 247
Adjunctive data, 81
Adlerian counseling, 68
Advanced empathy, 56
Affective development, 107
Affective interventions, 123, 124,
    127, 131–155
  alter ego, 133, 148–150, 155
  children and, 134, 142–143
  client reactions to, 152
  conditions for, 134–135
  dialectical behavior therapy and,
    152–155
  empty chair, 133, 150–151, 155
  focusing, 133, 143–144
  goals of, 134
  integrating feeling, 145–146
  motivational interviewing and,
    154–155
  nonverbal affect cues, 135
  role reversal, 133, 147–148, 155
  skills associated with, 133
  sorting out feelings, 140–143
  theories underlying, 132–133
  verbal affect cues, 136–140
Affective life, 159
Affective reflection, 63
Affirming/positive mental states,
    136–137
Aggressive/defensive mental states,
    137–138
Alter ego exercise, 133, 148–149, 155
  case illustration of, 149–150
Ambiguity, tolerance for, 14
Ambivalence, to change, 154
American Counseling Association, 2
  Ethical Standards, 16
Americans with Disabilities Act, 81
Anchoring, 160, 172
Anxiety
  reduction methods, 196–202
  types of, 196
Anxiety/fear mental states, 138
Anxiety reduction methods, 186,
    196–202
  assertion training, 194

case illustration of, 201–202
hierarchy construction, 199–201
relaxation training, 196–197
systematic desensitization, 198–199
Asian Americans, and family
    therapy, 215
Assertion training, 194
Assessment, 39–41, 75–95
  approaches to, 75
  boundaries and, 42
  case conceptualization and, 121
  checklist, 262–263
  of children, 81–83
  client's experience in, 48–49
  in cognitive interventions, 159–160
  of couples/families, 83–85
  crisis, 94–95
  dimensions of, 77–81
  effects, on clients, 90–94
  exercises, 260
  information gathering, 40
  initiating a working relationship
    during, 41–42
  inquiry, 41
  observation, 40
  problem definition, 80–81
  progress assessment, 50
  purposes of, 76–77
  skills associated with, 85–90
  using information from, 85
Attending behavior, 41
Attentiveness
  nonverbal, 60–61
  verbal, 61–62
Audio/Video Critique Form, 278
Automatic thought, 159, 169–170
Awareness, communication and,
    225–226
Awareness Wheel, 225–226

B

Bandura, Albert, 184, 185, 188
Bateson, Gregory, 214
Beck, Judith, 159
Behavioral anxiety, 196
Behavioral interventions, 124, 183–209
  anxiety reduction methods, 196–202
  client reactions to, 209
  counselor skills in, 186–188
  dialectical behavior therapy and, 209
  goals of, 186
  operant conditioning, 184–185

role-play and behavior rehearsal,
    192–194
self-management, 202–208
skill training, 194–196
social modeling, 188–192
symptom prescription, 202
theory underlying, 184–185
Behaviors
  contracting, 186, 187
  describing, 186, 187
  modifying, 186, 187
  supporting and reinforcing, 186,
    187–188
Body language, 22, 135
Boundaries, 14–15, 42
  coalitions, 218–219
  dysfunctional systems and, 214
  modifying, 234
Boundary making, 230

C

Carkhuff, Robert, 57
Carkhuff Scale, 57
Case conceptualization, 116–122
  components of, 116
  diagnosis and, 121
  presenting problems and, 119–121
  theory and, 117–118
  time orientation and, 117, 121–122
  worldview and, 117, 118–119
Change
  ambivalence to, 154
  assessment of, 244–245
  behavioral (See Behavioral
    interventions)
  facilitating desirable, 44–45
  as function of counseling, 3
  generalizing, 245
Change talk, 154
Children. See also Families
  affective interventions with, 134,
    142–143
  assessment of, 81–83
  communication and, 72
  counseling and, 71–72
  genuineness and, 72
  goal setting with, 107–108
  injunctions and, 167–168
  intake interview, 82
  intervention strategies for, 128
  self-contracts and, 205
  social learning, 185

Circular causality of the problem, 217
Circular questioning, 217
Claiming ownership, 224
Clarification (verbal communication),
  26, 32
Clarifying questions, 87–88
Classical conditioning, 184
Client-centered counseling (example),
  86–87
Client Intake Form, 267
Client intake interviews. *See* Intake
  interviews
Clients
  ambivalence of, 154
  assessment of, 39–41, 90–94
  building rapport with, 37–39
  characteristics and context, 117
  commitment to counseling (client
    buy-in), 6
  confronting or challenging,
    29–30, 33
  context of, 3–4
  culture of (*See* Multiculturalism)
  effects of goal setting on, 107
  effects of therapeutic relationships
    on, 69–70
  individuals vs. groups, 2
  manipulative, 14
  messages, restating/paraphrasing,
    62–63
  motivation of, 99
  nonspiritual, 175–176
  outcomes for, 8–11
  spiritual, 175
Client satisfaction surveys, 255
Closed questions, 25, 32, 88, 89
Cognition, expressing, 159–160
Cognitive analysis, 153
Cognitive anxiety, 196
Cognitive-behavioral theory, 5, 45
Cognitive-behavior therapy, 159, 180
Cognitive development, 107
Cognitive disputation, 160, 165–166
Cognitive interventions, 123, 124,
  157–180
  A-B-C-D analysis, 160, 161–165
  anchoring, 160, 172
  assessment in, 159–160, 180
  client reactions to, 177–179
  cognitive disputation, 160, 165–166
  cognitive restructuring, 160, 169–171
  counselor skills in, 159–160
  desibels intervention, 160, 166
  dialectical behavior therapy and, 179
  eliciting thoughts, 160–161
  goals of, 158–159

imaginal disputation, 166
injunctions and redecision work,
  160, 167
meaning-making interventions, 160,
  175–177
positive self-talk, 160, 171–172
reframing, 160, 172–173
second-order interventions,
  173–174
theories underlying, 158
thought stopping, 160, 171
Cognitive life, 158
Cognitive reflection, 64
Cognitive restructuring (cognitive
  replacement), 160, 169–171
  coping thoughts, 170–171
Cognitive therapy, 158
Communication, 7, 20–33. *See also*
  Listening skills
  altering patterns of, 223
  awareness and, 225–226
  children and, 72
  cultural factors in, 23
  in effective counselor-client
    relationship, 55
  of empathy, 59–60
  families and, 223–229
  nonverbal (*See* Nonverbal
    communication)
  open-mindedness and, 14
  systemic interventions and,
    223–229
  verbal (*See* Verbal communication)
  verbal affect cues, 136–140
Competence, 15
Conceptual foreclosure, 76
Confidentiality, consent form, 276
Confirmatory statements, 88, 89–90
Conflict management, 228–229
Confrontation, 29, 33
  goal setting and, 103–104
Confusion, in developmental
  process, 17
Congruence, 58, 65
Consent to Release Confidential
  Information, 276
Constructivist approach, 158
Content, reflection of, 28
Contextual conditions, of client
  problem, 81
Coping thoughts, 170–171
Core belief, 159
Counseling. *See also* Multiculturalism
  children and, 71–72
  client's experience in, 48–51
  conditions, 55

content of, 2
context of, 1
culture and, 7–8
defined, 2–3
enhancement counseling, 3
evaluation of, 254–255
forms and guides, 266–283
functions of, 3
goal setting, 42–44
need for, 3
parameters of, 3–8
philosophies underlying, 4–5
possible outcomes, 8–11
process of, 37–48
resistance to, 154
skills checklist, 261–265
specialties, 2–3
strategies, defining, 126–128
theories (*See* Theories, of
  counseling)
Counselors
  ambiguity, tolerance for, 14
  boundaries and, 14–15
  characteristics of, 12–16
  competence of, 15
  cultural awareness of, 13–14
  education/training of (*See*
    Education/training,
    of counselors)
  ethical behavior and, 16
  interpersonal attractiveness, 16
  open-mindedness, 14
  psychological health and, 13
  self-awareness and, 12–13
  self-disclosure and, 7
  theoretical approaches, 5–7
  trustworthiness of, 15–16
Counterconditioning, 198
Countering thoughts, 170
Countertransference, 12, 15, 39
Couples
  assessment of, 83–85
  negotiation and conflict
    management, 228
  termination with, 245
Covert modeling, 188, 190–191
Crisis, and goal setting, 108
Crisis assessment, 94–95
Cultural context, 4
Cultural empathy, 57
Cultural encapsulation, 7–8
Culture, counseling and. *See*
  Multiculturalism
Culture-general perspective, 119
Culture-specific orientations, 118
Current reinforcers, 204

D

Defensive/aggressive mental states,
   137–138
Deficit repertoire, 193
Desensitization, systematic, 198–201
Desibels intervention, 160, 166–167
Diagnosis. *See* Assessment
*Diagnostic and Statistical Manual
   (DSM-5),* 81, 83, 121
Dialectical behavior therapy
   (DBT), 237
   applying interventions to, 152–154
   behavioral interventions and, 209
   cognitive interventions in, 179
Directive responses, 31, 33
Discrimination, systemic, 10
Distorted perceptions, 159
Dysfunctional affect, 145–146
Dysfunctional systems, 214

E

Eclectic approach, 6
Educational function, of goal
   setting, 99
Education/training, of counselors,
   16–17
Ellis, Albert, 161
Emotional bond, 37
Emotional dysregulation, 153
Emotional percentages chart, 141–142
Emotions. *See* Affective interventions
Emotions balloons chart, 142–143
Emotions inventory, 141, 142
Empathy, 14, 56–58, 141
   Carkhuff Scale, 57
   communicating, 59–60
   cultural, 57
   empathetic understanding of the
      client, 55
   language of, 56
   Rogers on, 56
   as two-stage condition, 56
Empty chair exercise, 133,
   150–151, 155
   case illustration of, 152–153
Enactment, 232–234
Encouraging response, 29, 33, 104
Enhancement counseling, 3
Enhancing responses, and positive
   regard, 68
Entry behavior, 55–56
Environment
   as source of client problem, 81, 128
   spatial relationships and, 230
Essentialism, 4
Ethical codes/behavior, 6, 16

Evaluation, of counseling, 254–255
   client satisfaction surveys, 255
   evidence-based practice, 254
   exit interviews, 254–255
   follow-up, 255
   referral input, 255
Evaluation of Counselor Trainee
   Skills, 283
Evaluation of School Counseling
   Services form, 281
Evaluative function, of goals, 99
Evidence-based practice, 254
Existentialism, 5, 139
Existential/spiritual mental states,
   138–140
Exit interviews, 254–255
Experiential family therapy, 214
Expertness. *See* Competence
Extended Client Intake Form,
   268–270
Externalization, 222–223

F

Facilitative condition, 58
Families. *See also* Children
   assessment of, 83–85
   coalitions within, 218–219
   communication skills of, 223–229
   dysfunctions, 214, 219, 234
   family meeting activity, 228–229
   genogram, 84–85, 219–220
   goal setting by, 220–223
   interaction among, 217–218
   joining with the family, 215, 216
   multiculturalism and, 215
   negotiation and conflict
      management, 228–229
   role play with, 227
   structure of, 218–220
   subsystems within, 229
   systemic interventions and (*See*
      Systemic interventions)
   triangulation and scapegoating, 219
Family sculpture, 234
Family Therapy Institute, 214
Faulty thinking, 157
Fear/anxiety mental states, 138
Feedback, 193–194
Feeling, reflection of, 27–28
Felt sense, 143–145
Felt shift, 144, 145
Focusing, and empathy, 59
Focusing intervention, 133, 143–144
   case illustration of, 144–145
Folk tales, 176
Follow-up

   counseling evaluation, 255
   ethical issues in, 245–246
   planning for, 245–246
Foreclosure, 76
Forms and Guides, 266–283
   Audio/Video Critique, 278
   Client Intake Form, 267
   Consent to Release Confidential
      Information, 276
   Evaluation of Counselor Trainee
      Skills, 283
   Evaluation of School Counseling
      Services, 281
   Extended Client Intake Form,
      268–270
   Outpatient Treatment Plan (OTP),
      273–275
   Permission to Record Counseling
      Interviews, 277
   Referral to School Counselor, 280
   Termination Summary Report, 279
Freud, Sigmund, 176
Functional behavior, 4

G

Genogram
   family, 84–85, 219–220
   multicultural, 85
Genuineness, 58
   with children, 72
   conditions conveying, 65–67
Gestalt therapy, 150, 223
Goal setting, 42–44, 98–114, 117
   assessing, 111
   case illustrations of, 111–114,
      221–222
   checklist, 263–264
   with children, 107–108
   client participation in, 109–110
   client's experience with, 49–50
   crises and, 108
   culture and, 108–109
   effects, on clients, 107
   exercises, 260
   families and, 220–221
   functions of, 99–100
   interventions and, 122–123
   map, 105
   obstacles to, 102
   outcome goals, 100–101
   parameters of, 100–101
   precursors to, 220–221
   process goals, 100
   realistic goals, 221
   resistance to, 110–111
   skills involved in, 43, 102–106

Goal setting (*continued*)
structuring skills, 103, 104–106
systemic interventions and, 220–223
timeline, 106
working relationship during, 43–44
Grieving process, 145

H

Haley, Jay, 214
Hierarchy, altering, 229–230
Hierarchy construction, 199–201
Hispanic Americans, and family
therapy, 231
Holistic approach, 133
Homeostasis, 202, 213, 238
Humanistic theory, 5, 45, 55

I

Image management, 55
Imagery, 111, 198
Imaginal disputation, 166
Imaging, 190–191
Imitation learning, 185
Immediacy, 30, 33, 67
Incongruence, 55
Indirect message, 224–225
Individualistic orientation, 118–119
Individual skills summary
checklist, 265
Individuation, 108–109
Information, providing, 31, 33
Injunctions, 160, 167
case illustration of, 168–169
Inquiry, assessment and, 41
Intake interviews
case illustration, 91–92
children and adolescents, 82
formal, 77–78
forms and the written intake, 78–80
integration of material from, 92–93
problem-definition analysis, 93–94
Integrating feeling, 145–146
case illustration of, 146
Integration, in developmental
process, 17
Integrative approach, 6
Integrative practice exercises,
259–261
Interactions, generating and
observing, 217–218
Intergenerational family therapy, 214
Interjecting (verbal communication),
26, 32
Intermediate beliefs, 159
Internal concerns, 2
Interpersonal attractiveness, 16

Interpersonal concerns, 2, 7–8
Interpretation response, 28–29, 32
Interpretation vs. reframing, 173
Interventions, 44–46
affective (*See* Affective interventions)
behavioral (*See* Behavioral
interventions)
case conceptualization and, 116–122
case illustration of, 125, 126
categories of, 123–125
children and, 128
client reactions to, 45–46, 50
client's experience with, 50–51
cognitive (*See* Cognitive
interventions)
defining a counseling strategy,
126–128
diagnosis and, 121
goal setting and, 122–123
interactional, 124
presenting problems and, 119–121
second-order, 235–237
selecting, 127
selection and implementation
checklist, 264
skills related to initiation of, 45
strategy exercises, 260
systemic (*See* Systemic
interventions)
theory and, 117–118
time orientation and, 117, 121–122
worldview and, 117, 118–119
Intrapersonal concerns, 2
Involvement, 68
Irrational beliefs, 161, 163, 165

J

Joining, 215, 216

L

Language of empathy, 56
Legal issues, in referrals, 248
Life enhancement, 3
Linking statements, 88, 89
Listening skills, 41
Live (overt) modeling, 188–190

M

Madanes, Cloe, 214
Meaning-making interventions, 160,
175–177
case illustration of, 177
metaphors and, 176
for nonspiritual clients, 175–176
sacred writings, 175
for spiritual clients, 175

Mental Research Institute, 214
Mental states
aggressive/defensive, 136, 137–138
fear/anxiety, 136, 138
positive/affirming, 136, 137
spiritual/existential, 136, 138–140
Metaphors, and meaning making, 176
Minimal responses, 24, 32
Minnesota Couples Communication
Program, 223
Modeling. *See* Social modeling
Mode of treatment, 122
Moral development, 107
Motivation, of clients, 99
Motivational interviewing (MI),
154–155
cognitive interventions in, 179
Multicultural genogram, 85
Multiculturalism, 6, 7–8
affective interventions and, 136, 137
communication and, 23
family therapy and, 215
genograms, 85
goal setting and, 108–109
sensitivity to and understanding of,
13–14
social modeling and, 192
Muscle relaxation, 196–198

N

Narrative therapy, 214, 222
National Board for Certified
Counselors, 16
Negotiation, 228–229
Nonverbal affect cues, 135
Nonverbal attentiveness, 60–61
Nonverbal communication, 21–23, 135
body language, 22
cultural factors, 23
physical conditions, 21–22
silence, 22–23
vocal cues (paralanguage), 21
Normalcy vs. functionalism, of
clients, 3–4
Normalizing a feeling, 152

O

Object relations school, 214
Observation, assessment and, 40
Observational learning, 185
Open-ended questions, 25, 32, 88–89
Openness, 65–67
Operant conditioning, 184–185
Outcome goals, 100–101, 112–114
Outpatient Treatment Plan (OTP),
273–275

Overt social modeling, 188–190
"Owning" a problem, 10

P

Paradoxical interventions, 202
Parallelism, 66–67
Paraphrasing (verbal communication), 24, 32
  client messages, 62
Parentification of a child, 230
Pavlov, Ivan, 184
Performance anxiety, 196
Perls, Fritz, 30
Personal constructs, psychology of, 133
Personal hierarchies, 199
Personality theory, 5
Person-centered therapy, 132
Phenomenological therapies, 132
Philosophies, underlying counseling, 4–5
Phobias, 198
Play therapy, 72
Plot-centered counseling, 76, 86
Positionality, 13–14
Positioning, 160, 174
Positive/affirming mental states, 136–137
Positive regard, 58–59
  acceptance and enhancing responses, 68
  conditions conveying, 67–68
  nonverbal behaviors and, 67–68
Positive self-talk, 160, 171–172
Postmodernism, 5
Potential reinforcers, 204
Prescribing the symptom, 235–237
Prevention, as function of counseling, 3
Primary empathy, 56
Probes. *See* Questions (verbal communication)
Problem definition, 80–81. *See also* Assessment
  children and, 82
Process goals, 100
Process Scale, 132
Progress assessment, 50
Progressive relaxation, 196
Progressivism, 4
Projection, 12
Psychodiagnostic assessment method, 75
Psychodynamic theory, 5
Psychological contact, 55
Psychometric assessment method, 75

Q

Questions, 25, 32
  circular questioning, 217
  clarifying, 87–88
  closed, 88
  inquiry, assessment and, 41
  open-ended, 88

R

Rapport, 37, 38
Rational beliefs, 161, 163, 165
Rational-emotive behavior therapy (REBT), 158, 161, 180, 223
Rational-emotive imagery (REI), 166
Reaction, 159
Reactive process, 107
Reactivity, 203
Reality Therapy, 68, 223
Redecision work, 160, 167–168
  case illustration of, 168–169
Referrals, 246–249
  additive referrals, 247
  communication with receiving professional, 249
  coordinating transfers, 248
  evaluating potential sources, 248
  legal issues, 248
  preparing the client, 249
  reasons for, 247
  referral input, 255
  termination and, 247
Referral to School Counselor form, 280
Reflections, 27–28
  advanced level of, 64
  of content, 28, 32
  of feeling, 27–28, 32
  reflecting client thoughts/feelings, 63–65
Reformulation, 172
Reframing, 160, 172–173, 179
Relating
  empathy and, 60
  process checklist, 262
Relational concerns, 2
Relationship-building skills, 60–65
  case illustration of, 70–71
  exercises, 260
  nonverbal attentiveness, 60–61
  paraphrasing client messages, 62–63
  reflecting client thoughts/feelings, 63–65
  restating client messages, 62
  verbal attentiveness, 61–62
Relationship paradox, 47–48

Relationships, in counseling setting, 38
Relaxation training, 196–197
Religion. *See* Spirituality/religion
Resisting therapeutic progress, 160, 173–174
Responsible communication, 224
Restatement (verbal communication), 24, 32
  client messages, 62
Restraining, 174
Rogers, Carl, 14, 27, 55, 58
  on empathy, 56
  person-centered therapy, 132, 154
Role-play, 111, 186, 227
  behavior rehearsal and, 192–194
Role reversal, 133, 147–148, 155
  case illustration of, 147–148
Roll with the resistance, 154

S

Sacred writings, 175
Scapegoating, 219
Second-order interventions, 235
  positioning, 160, 174
  resisting therapeutic progress, 160, 173–174
Selective attending, 62
Self-contracting, 205
Self-defeating statements, 170–171
Self-disclosure, 66, 193
Self-efficacy, 191–192
Self-indoctrination, 161–162
Self-management, 186, 202–208
  case illustration of, 206–208
  client commitment to, 205–206
  self-contracting, 204–205
  self-monitoring, 203
  self-reward, 204
Self-monitoring, 203
Self-observation, 203
Self-recording, 203
Self-reward, 204
Self-talk, 160, 171–172
Shaping, 184
Shared goals, 100
Shared meaning, 226–227
"Significance of the story," 56
Silence, as nonverbal communication, 22–23
Skill training, 194–196
  case illustration of, 195
Skinner, B. F., 184
Social constructivist models, 214
Social influence model, 15
Social learning, 185

Social modeling, 184, 186, 188–192
 characteristics of, 191
 covert, 190–191
 desirable characteristics of, 192
 live (overt), 188–190
 self-efficacy and, 191–192
 symbolic, 190
Somatic anxiety, 196
Spatio-temporal hierarchy, 199
Spiritual/existential mental states,
  138–140
Spiritual interventions, 139–140
Spirituality/religion, 139
 meaning making and, 175
Spontaneity, 58
Stagnation, in developmental
  process, 17
Structural family therapy, 214
Structuring, 216–217
Structuring skills, 103, 104–106
*Subjective Units of Disturbance Scale
 (SUDS)*, 199
Successive approximation, 106, 193
Successive approximations, 101, 106
Suicide ideation/suicide threat, 140
Summary statement, 27, 32
Symbolic modeling, 188, 190
Symptom prescription, 186, 202
Systematic desensitization, 198–199
System homeostasis, 213, 238
Systemic interventions, 124, 212–238
 altering system properties, 229–231
 case illustrations of, 221–223, 231–237
 with children, 128
 client reactions to, 237
 communication in, 223–229
 in Dialectical Behavior Therapy, 237
 goal setting, 220–221
 relationship building and
   assessment, 215–220
 second-order, 235–237
 system properties, 213–214
 therapies, 214–215
Systemic rule, 213
Systemic theory, 5
System structure, 229
System unit, 216. *See also* Families

T

Tension release, through muscle
  relaxation, 197–198
Termination, 240–256
 in absence of, 246
 assessment for, 244–245

blocks to, 249–250
 case illustration of, 250–253
 by client, 242
 client's experience with, 51
 by counselor, 242–243
 determinants of, 241–242
 ethical issues in, 242–244
 evaluation (checklist), 264–265
 evaluation of counseling, 254–255
 follow-up, 245–246, 255, 261
 maintaining positive relationship
   during, 47–48
 planning, 46–48
 premature, 243–244
 as process, 244–246
 referral process, 246–249
 "relationship review" and, 48
 report, 244
Termination by degree, 46
Termination Summary Report, 279
Thematic hierarchies, 199
Theories, of counseling, 5–7
 classification of client conditions, 40
 interventions and, 44–46
 philosophical positions, 4–5
Theory, defined, 5
Therapeutic relationship, 37–39
 characteristics of, 55–59
 children and, 71–72
 effects of, on clients, 69–70
 functions of, 68–69
Thought stopping, 160, 171
Timeline, in goal setting, 106
Time orientation, case conceptualiza-
  tion and, 117, 121–122
Transactional analysis, 158, 223
Transference, 39
Transparency. *See* Openness
Treatment assessment function, of
  goals, 100
Treatment planning. *See* Interventions
Triangulation, 219
Trustworthiness, 15–16

U

Unconditional positive regard, 55,
  58–59
Underresponsible communication,
  224–225
*The Uses of Enchantment: The
 Meaning and Importance of Fairy
 Tales* (Bettelheim), 176

V

Validation, 153
Verbal affect cues, 136–140
 of aggressive/defensive mental
   states, 137–138
 of fear/anxiety mental states, 138
 of positive/affirming mental states,
   136–137
 of spiritual/existential mental states,
   138–140
Verbal attentiveness, 61–62
Verbal communication, 23–33. *See
  also* Communication
 advanced skills, 26–31
 basic skills, 23–26
 clarification, 26, 32
 confrontation or challenge, 29–30, 33
 directive responses, 31, 33
 encouraging response, 29, 33
 immediacy, 30, 33
 information, providing, 31, 33
 interjecting, 26, 32
 interpretation response, 28–29, 32
 minimal responses, 24, 32
 paraphrase, 24–25, 32
 questions, 25, 32
 reflections, 27–28, 32
 restatement, 24, 32
 summary statement, 27, 32
Verbal goal-setting skills, 102–103
Verbal linking, 66–67
Vicarious learning, 185
Visualizing, 103, 111
Vocal qualities, 137
Vulnerability, 76

W

Wellness models, 133
Working alliance, establishing, 37–39
Working relationship, positive
 assessment and, 39–42
 development of, 54–72
 initiating interventions and, 44–46
 setting goals in, 42–44
 termination and, 44–48
Worldview. *See also* Multiculturalism
 case conceptualization and, 116,
   117–119
 of clients, 7, 40, 59, 69, 85, 116
 of counselors, 3, 7, 13, 116
 race/ethnicity and, 118